DATE DUE

			PRINTED IN U.S.A.

SOMETHING ABOUT THE AUTHOR

ISSN 0276-816X

something ABOUT THE AUTHOR

Facts and Pictures about Authors
and Illustrators of Books for Young People

EDITED BY
ANNE COMMIRE

VOLUME 42

GALE RESEARCH COMPANY
BOOK TOWER
DETROIT, MICHIGAN
48226

Editor: Anne Commire

Associate Editors: Agnes Garrett, Helga P. McCue

Senior Assistant Editor: Joyce Nakamura

Assistant Editors: Dianne H. Anderson, Linda Shedd, Cynthia J. Walker

Sketchwriters: Rachel Koenig, Eunice L. Petrini

Researchers: Kathleen Betsko, Catherine Ruello

Editorial Assistants: Lisa Bryon, Carolyn Kline, Elisa Ann Ferraro

Permissions Assistant: Susan Pfanner

Production Director: Carol Blanchard

External Senior Production Associate: Mary Beth Trimper

External Production Associate: Dorothy Kalleberg

Internal Production Associate: Louise Gagné

Internal Senior Production Assistant: Sandy Rock

Layout Artist: Elizabeth Lewis Patryjak

Art Director: Arthur Chartow

Special acknowledgment is due to the members of the *Contemporary Authors* staff
who assisted in the preparation of this volume.

Publisher: Frederick G. Ruffner

Executive Vice-President/Editorial: James M. Ethridge

Editorial Director: Dedria Bryfonski

Director, Literature Division: Christine Nasso

Senior Editor, Something about the Author: Adele Sarkissian

Library of Congress Catalog Card Number 72-27107
ISBN 0-8103-2252-8
ISSN 0276-816X
Computerized photocomposition by
Typographics, Incorporated
Kansas City, Missouri
Printed in the United States

Contents

A

B

C

D

E

F

Contents

Y

Z

Introduction

As the only ongoing reference series that deals with the lives and works of authors and illustrators of children's books, *Something about the Author (SATA)* is a unique source of information. The *SATA* series includes not only well-known authors and illustrators whose books are most widely read, but also those less prominent people whose works are just coming to be recognized. *SATA* is often the only readily available information source for less well-known writers or artists. You'll find *SATA* informative and entertaining whether you are:

—a student in junior high school (or perhaps one to two grades higher or lower) who needs information for a book report or some other assignment for an English class;

—a children's librarian who is searching for the answer to yet another question from a young reader or collecting background material to use for a story hour;

—an English teacher who is drawing up an assignment for your students or gathering information for a book talk;

—a student in a college of education or library science who is studying children's literature and reference sources in the field;

—a parent who is looking for a new way to interest your child in reading something more than the school curriculum prescribes;

—an adult who enjoys children's literature for its own sake, knowing that a good children's book has no age limits.

Scope

In *SATA* you will find detailed information about authors and illustrators who span the full time range of children's literature, from early figures like John Newbery and L. Frank Baum to contemporary figures like Judy Blume and Richard Peck. Authors in the series represent primarily English-speaking countries, particularly the United States, Canada, and the United Kingdom. Also included, however, are authors from around the world whose works are available in English translation, for example: from France, Jean and Laurent De Brunhoff; from Italy, Emanuele Luzzati; from the Netherlands, Jaap ter Haar; from Germany, James Krüss; from Norway, Babbis Friis-Baastad; from Japan, Toshiko Kanzawa; from the Soviet Union, Kornei Chukovsky; from Switzerland, Alois Carigiet, to name only a few. Also appearing in *SATA* are Newbery medalists from Hendrik Van Loon (1922) to Robin McKinley (1985). The writings represented in *SATA* include those created intentionally for children and young adults as well as those written for a general audience and known to interest younger readers. These writings cover the spectrum from picture books, humor, folk and fairy tales, animal stories, mystery and adventure, science fiction and fantasy, historical fiction, poetry and nonsense verse, to drama, biography, and nonfiction.

Information Features

In *SATA* you will find full-length entries that are being presented in the series for the first time. This volume, for example, marks the first full-length appearance of Laszlo Acs, Harry Allard, Harvey Dinnerstein, Nat Hentoff, Robert Leeson, Frank Robbins, Ronald Searle, James Stevenson, and Aldren A. Watson, among others. Since Volume 25, each *SATA* volume also includes newly revised and updated biographies for a selection of early *SATA* listees who remain of interest to today's readers and who have been active enough to require extensive revision of their earlier entries. The entry for a given biographee may be revised as often as there is substantial new information to provide. In Volume 42 you'll find revised entries for Barbara Brenner, Scott Corbett, and Margaret Oldroyd Hyde. Brief Entries, first introduced in Volume 27, are another regular feature of *SATA*. Brief Entries present essentially the same types of information found in a full entry but do so in a capsule form and without illustration. These entries are intended to give you useful and timely information while the more time-consuming process of compiling a full-length biography is in progress. In this volume you'll find Brief Entries for Margot Apple, Barbara Bartholomew, Gilda Berger, Joyce Audy dos Santos, Michael Ende, Kathy Jacobi, Ann Jonas, Patricia MacLachlan, and Yuri Salzman, among others.

Obituaries have been included in *SATA* since Volume 20. An Obituary is intended not only as a death notice but also as a concise view of a person's life and work. Obituaries may appear for persons who have entries in earlier *SATA* volumes, as well as for people who have not yet appeared in the series. In this volume Obituaries mark the recent deaths of Jene Barr, Betty Boegehold, Emil Lengyel, Jane Sherrod Singer, Luther L. Terry, Lynd Ward, Betty Youngs, and others.

Each *SATA* volume provides a cumulative index in two parts: first, the Illustrations Index, arranged by the name of the illustrator, gives the number of the volume and page where the illustrator's work appears in the current volume as well as all preceding volumes in the series; second, the Author Index gives the number of the volume in which a person's biographical sketch, Brief Entry, or Obituary appears in the current volume as well as all preceding volumes in the series. These indexes also include references to authors and illustrators who appear in *Yesterday's Authors of Books for Children.* Beginning with Volume 36, the *SATA* Author Index provides cross-references to authors who are included in *Children's Literature Review.* You will also find cross-references to authors in the *Something about the Author Autobiography Series,* starting with Volume 42. This exciting new companion series to *SATA* is described in detail below.

Illustrations

While the textual information in *SATA* is its primary reason for existing, photographs and illustrations not only enliven the text but are an integral part of the information that *SATA* provides. Illustrations and text are wedded in such a special way in children's literature that artists and their works naturally occupy a prominent place among *SATA*'s listees. The illustrators that you'll find in the series include such past masters of children's book illustration as Randolph Caldecott, Kate Greenaway, Walter Crane, Arthur Rackham, and Ernest L. Shepard, as well as such noted contemporary artists as Maurice Sendak, Edward Gorey, Tomie de Paola, and Margot Zemach. There are Caldecott medalists from Dorothy Lathrop (the first recipient in 1938) to Trina Schart Hyman (the latest winner in 1985); cartoonists like Charles Schulz, ("Peanuts"), Walt Kelly ("Pogo"), Hank Ketcham ("Dennis the Menace"), and Georges Rémi ("Tintin"); photographers like Jill Krementz, Tana Hoban, Bruce McMillan, and Bruce Curtis; and filmmakers like Walt Disney, Alfred Hitchcock, and Steven Spielberg.

In more than a dozen years of recording the metamorphosis of children's literature from the printed page to other media, *SATA* has become something of a repository of photographs that are unique in themselves and exist nowhere else as a group, particularly many of the classics of motion picture and stage history and photographs that have been specially loaned to us from private collections.

What a *SATA* Entry Provides

Whether you're already familiar with the *SATA* series or just getting acquainted, you will want to be aware of the kind of information that an entry provides. In every *SATA* entry the editors attempt to give as complete a picture of the person's life and work as possible. In some cases that full range of information may simply be unavailable, or a biographee may choose not to reveal complete personal details. The information that the editors attempt to provide in every entry is arranged in the following categories:

1. The "head" of the entry gives

    —the most complete form of the name,
    —any part of the name not commonly used, included in parentheses,
    —birth and death dates, if known; a (?) indicates a discrepancy in published sources,
    —pseudonyms or name variants under which the person has had books published or is publicly known, in parentheses in the second line.

2. "Personal" section gives

   —date and place of birth and death,
   —parents' names and occupations,
   —name of spouse, date of marriage, and names of children,
   —educational institutions attended, degrees received, and dates,
   —religious and political affiliations,
   —agent's name and address,
   —home and/or office address.

3. "Career" section gives

   —name of employer, position, and dates for each career post,
   —military service,
   —memberships,
   —awards and honors.

4. "Writings" section gives

   —title, first publisher and date of publication, and illustration information for each book written; revised editions and other significant editions for books with particularly long publishing histories; genre, when known.

5. "Adaptations" section gives

   —title, major performers, producer, and date of all known reworkings of an author's material in another medium, like movies, filmstrips, television, recordings, plays, etc.

6. "Sidelights" section gives

   —commentary on the life or work of the biographee either directly from the person (and often written specifically for the *SATA* entry), or gathered from biographies, diaries, letters, interviews, or other published sources.

7. "For More Information See" section gives

   —books, feature articles, films, plays, and reviews in which the biographee's life or work has been treated.

How a *SATA* Entry Is Compiled

A *SATA* entry progresses through a series of steps. If the biographee is living, the *SATA* editors try to secure information directly from him or her through a questionnaire. From the information that the biographee supplies, the editors prepare an entry, filling in any essential missing details with research. The author or illustrator is then sent a copy of the entry to check for accuracy and completeness.

If the biographee is deceased or cannot be reached by questionnaire, the *SATA* editors examine a wide variety of published sources to gather information for an entry. Biographical sources are searched with the aid of Gale's *Biography and Genealogy Master Index*. Bibliographic sources like the *National Union Catalog*, the *Cumulative Book Index*, *American Book Publishing Record*, and the *British Museum Catalogue* are consulted, as are book reviews, feature articles, published interviews, and material sometimes obtained from the biographee's family, publishers, agent, or other associates.

For each entry presented in *SATA*, the editors also attempt to locate a photograph of the biographee as well as representative illustrations from his or her books. After surveying the available books which the biographee has written and/or illustrated, and then making a selection of appropriate photographs and illustrations, the editors request permission of the current copyright holders to reprint the material. In the case of older books for which the copyright may have passed through several hands, even locating the current copyright holder is often a long and involved process.

We invite you to examine the entire *SATA* series, starting with this volume. Described below are some of the people in Volume 42 that you may find particularly interesting.

Highlights of This Volume

C. E. BROCK......a portrait painter and book illustrator who was one of four artistic brothers in a family from Cambridge, England. Brock believed that an artist's personal involvement with his subjects helped to develop the keen powers of observation that are essential for his success. "To the enthusiast," he remarked, "his work is ever present and the delight of studying the things around needs no insisting upon." This attitude led Brock to produce the art work for more than one hundred books by authors such as E. Nesbit, Charles Dickens, James Fenimore Cooper, George Eliot, Jane Austen, and Jonathan Swift. Also featured in this volume is H. M. BROCK, the youngest of the Brock brothers. Like his older sibling, H. M. Brock produced illustrations for over one hundred works by well-known authors. The two brothers collaborated on several books for young readers, including *The Novels of Jane Austen; The Golden Staircase*, compiled by Louey Chisholm; and *The Golden Book of Bible Stories.*

SCOTT CORBETT......an author whose audience includes children and teenagers, especially pre-adolescent boys. "I am a storyteller," he explains, "devoted to the proposition that suspense and humor are a worthwhile combination." For nearly thirty years, Corbett has adeptly blended these elements in many of his sixty-eight juvenile works, including the "Trick" and "The Great McGoniggle" series. He happily observes that his books, such as *Cutlass Island, One by Sea, The Big Joke Game*, and *The Mysterious Zetabet*, "have been widely used in schools to trap reluctant readers." Past winner of both the Edgar Allan Poe and Mark Twain awards, Corbett continues to entice children into the world of reading with his latest endeavor, *Witch Hunt.*

CHARLES J. FINGER......an author and editor who chronicled his life as an adventurer and world traveler in works of fiction for young readers. As a child in England, Finger was enamored of books about adventure in foreign lands. He became a merchant seaman in his late teens and, for fifteen years, lived the life of a wanderer in places like Patagonia and Tierra del Fuego. Finger later drew upon those years when he wrote his Newbery Award-winning book, *Tales from Silver Lands.* As a writer, he observed: "I found myself stuffed full of tales, so full indeed that although I should write for twenty years more . . . I would not have told the half of them." The half that Finger did tell can be found in *Tales Worth Telling, Courageous Companions, When Guns Thundered at Tripoli, Golden Tales from Faraway*, and others.

CHARLES GEER......an artist and illustrator of books for children, including the popular "Miss Pickerell" series by Dora Pantell. Ten years after the death of Ellen MacGregor, originator of the "Miss Pickerell" books, the series acquired not only a new author in Pantell, but a new illustrator as well. Geer followed in the footsteps of Paul Galdone who had illustrated the first four books. As Geer remembers: "The trick was to keep a continuity. I couldn't just copy what had been done before. I had to give the Pickerell books my own flavor." He has accomplished just that in a dozen books of the ongoing series, including *Miss Pickerell on the Moon, Miss Pickerell and the Supertanker*, and *Miss Pickerell and the War of the Computers.* Although he also executes adult book jackets and paints landscapes, Geer knows that "it is important to retain part of your childhood . . . children's books have helped me to do that."

THOMAS HANDFORTH......an author and illustrator who, although born of Irish ancestry, was greatly intrigued as a child by the mysticism of the Orient. Handforth spent his childhood in Tacoma, Washington, where "ever about me was a panorama of sea and islands and mountains. . . .[and] ships sailed forth from the harbor . . . toward Japan, China and the Indies." His fascination with the Eastern culture remained with him throughout his lifetime, influencing his work as a young artist and later leading him on his own sojourns to Japan, India, and China. It was out of the love he developed for the peoples of these lands that Handforth produced his picture books *Mei Li*, a Caldecott Award winner, and *Faraway Meadow.*

ELIZABETH MacKINSTRY......an illustrator, author, sculptor, and violinist. MacKinstry's promising career as a violinist came to an abrupt end when she suffered tuberculosis of the spine in her teens. Undaunted, she turned to her second great love—drawing. In 1925 MacKinstry produced *Puck in Pasture*, with her own illustrations and verse. For her, poetry had taken the place of the music she had lost. "I read it as one would music, write it as one would play. . . .It is the music that is left." As an illustrator, she believed that art "was something gay and myth making . . . something breaking out into decoration as naturally as a tulip breaks out into color. . . ." MacKinstry enhanced the texts of numerous children's works, including Rachel Field's *Eliza and the Elves,* Marie Catherine d'Aulnoy's *The White Cat, and Other Old French Fairy Tales,* and George MacDonald's *The Princess and the Goblin.*

These are only a few of the authors and illustrators that you'll find in this volume. We hope you find all the entries in *SATA* both interesting and useful.

Something about the Author Autobiography Series

Now you can complement the information in *SATA* with the new *Something about the Author Autobiography Series (SAAS),* which provides autobiographical essays written by important current authors and illustrators of books for children and young adults. In every volume of *SAAS* you will find about twenty specially commissioned autobiographies, each accompanied by a selection of personal photographs supplied by the authors. A wide range of contemporary writers and artists will be describing their lives and interests in the new *Autobiography Series:* Joan Aiken, Betsy Byars, Leonard Everett Fisher, Milton Meltzer, Maia Wojciechowska, and Jane Yolen are among the contributors to Volume 1. Though the information presented in the autobiographies is as varied and unique as the authors, you can expect to learn about the people and events that influenced these writers' early lives, how they began their careers, what problems they faced in becoming established in their professions, what prompted them to write or illustrate particular books, what they now find most challenging or rewarding in their lives, and what advice they may have for young people interested in following in their footsteps, among many other subjects.

Autobiographies included in the *SATA Autobiography Series* can be located through both the *SATA* cumulative index and the *SAAS* cumulative index, which lists not only the authors' names but also the subjects mentioned in their essays, such as titles of works and geographical and personal names.

The *SATA Autobiography Series* gives you the opportunity to view "close up" some of the fascinating people who are included in the *SATA* parent series. Now, the combined *SATA* series makes available to you an unequaled range of comprehensive and in-depth information about the authors and illustrators of young people's literature.

Please write and tell us if we can make *SATA* even more helpful to you.

Forthcoming Authors

**A Partial List of Authors and Illustrators Who Will Appear
in Forthcoming Volumes of *Something about the Author***

Abels, Harriette S.
Allen, Agnes B.   1898-1959
Allert, Kathy
Anders, Rebecca
Anderson, Leone C.   1923-
Andrist, Ralph K.   1914-
Appleby, Ellen
Ardley, Neil (Richard)   1937-
Austin, R. G.
Axeman, Lois
Ayme, Marcel   1902-1967
Bains, Rae
Baker, Olaf
Balderson, Margaret   1935-
Bartlett, Margaret F.   1896-
Barton, Harriett
Bassett, Jeni   1960(?)-
Bauer, Caroline Feller   1935-
Bauer, John Albert   1882-1918
Beckman, Delores
Beim, Jerrold   1910-1957
Beim, Lorraine   1909-1951
Bernheim, Evelyne   1935-
Bernheim, Marc   1924-
Betancourt, Jeanne   1941-
Birnbaum, Abe   1899-
Bloom, Lloyd
Boegehold, Betty   1913-1985
Boning, Richard A.
Bonners, Susan
Bourke, Linda
Bowen, Gary
Bracken, Carolyn
Brewton, Sara W.
Bridgman, Elizabeth P.   1921-
Bromley, Dudley   1948-
Bronin, Andrew   1947-
Bronson, Wilfrid   1894-
Brooks, Ron(ald George)   1948-
Brown, Roy Frederick   1921-
Brownmiller, Susan   1935-
Buchanan, William   1930-
Buchenholz, Bruce
Budney, Blossom   1921-
Burchard, Marshall
Burke, David   1927-
Burstein, Chaya M.
Butler, Dorothy   1925-
Butler, Hal   1913-
Calvert, Patricia
Camps, Luis   1928-
Carley, Wayne
Carlson, Nancy L.
Carrie, Christopher

Carroll, Ruth R.   1899-
Cauley, Lorinda B.   1951-
Chang, Florence C.
Charles, Carole
Charles, Donald   1929-
Chartier, Normand
Chase, Catherine
Clarke, Bob
Cline, Linda   1941-
Cohen, Joel H.
Cole, Brock
Cooper, Elizabeth Keyser   1910-
Cooper, Paulette   1944-
Cosgrove, Margaret   1926-
Coutant, Helen
Dabcovich, Lydia
D'Aulnoy, Marie Catherine
   1650(?)-1705
David, Jay   1929-
Davies, Peter   1937-
Davis, Maggie S.   1942-
Dawson, Diane
Dean, Leigh
Degens, T.
Deguine, Jean-Claude   1943-
Dentinger, Don
Deweese, Gene   1934-
Ditmars, Raymond   1876-1942
Drescher, Henrik
Dumas, Philippe   1940-
East, Ben
Edelson, Edward   1932-
Edens, Cooper
Eisenberg, Lisa
Elder, Lauren
Elwood, Roger   1943-
Endres, Helen
Enik, Ted
Eriksson, Eva
Erwin, Betty K.
Etter, Les   1904-
Everett-Green, Evelyn   1856-1932
Falkner, John Meade   1858-1932
Felix, Monique
Fender, Kay
Filson, Brent
Fischer, Hans Erich   1909-1958
Flanagan, Geraldine Lux
Flint, Russ
Folch-Ribas, Jacques   1928-
Foley, Louise M.   1933-
Fox, Thomas C.
Freschet, Berniece   1927-
Frevert, Patricia D(endtler)   1943-

Funai, Mamoru R.   1932-
Gans, Roma   1894-
Garcia Sanchez, J(ose) L(uis)
Garrison, Christian   1942-
Gathje, Curtis
Gelman, Rita G.   1937-
Gemme, Leila Boyle   1942-
Gerber, Dan   1940-
Goldstein, Nathan   1927-
Gould, Chester   1900-1985
Graeber, Charlotte Towner
Gray, J.M.L.
Greenberg, Polly   1932-
Grimm, Cherry Barbara   1930-
Gross, Alan   1947-
Gutman, Bill
Haas, Dorothy F.
Halverson, Lydia
Harris, Marilyn   1931-
Hayman, LeRoy   1916-
Heine, Helme   1941-
Henty, George Alfred   1832-1902
Herzig, Alison Cragin
Hicks, Clifford B.   1920-
Higashi, Sandra
Hockerman, Dennis
Hollander, Zander   1923-
Hood, Thomas   1779-1845
Howell, Troy
Hull, Jessie Redding
Hunt, Clara Whitehill   1871-1958
Hunt, Robert
Inderieden, Nancy
Irvine, Georgeanne
Iwamura, Kazuo   1939-
Jackson, Anita
Jackson, Kathryn   1907-
Jackson, Robert   1941-
Jameson, Cynthia
Janssen, Pierre
Jaspersohn, William
Jenkins, Jean
Johnson, Harper
Johnson, Maud
Johnson, Sylvia A.
Jukes, Mavis
Kahn, Joan   1914-
Kalan, Robert
Kantrowitz, Mildred
Kasuya, Masahiro   1937-
Keith, Eros   1942-
Kiedrowski, Priscilla
Kirn, Ann (Minette)   1910-
Koenig, Marion

13

Kohl, Herbert   1937-
Kohl, Judith
Kredenser, Gail   1936-
Kurland, Michael   1938-
Lawson, Annetta
Leach, Christopher   1925-
Lebrun, Claude
Leckie, Robert   1920-
Leder, Dora
Le-Tan, Pierre   1950-
Lewis, Naomi
Lindgren, Barbro
Lindman, Maj (Jan)
Lines, Kathleen
Livermore, Elaine
Lye, Keith
Mali, Jane Lawrence
Marks, Burton   1930-
Marks, Rita   1938-
Marron, Carol A.
Marryat, Frederick   1792-1848
Marsh, Carole
Martin, Dorothy   1921-
Marxhausen, Joanne G.   1935-
May, Dorothy
Mayakovsky, Vladimir   1894-1930
McKim, Audrey Margaret   1909-
McLoughlin, John C.   1949-
McReynolds, Ginny
Melcher, Frederic G.   1879-1963
Miller, J(ohn) P.   1919-
Milone, Karen
Molesworth, Mary L.   1839(?)-1921
Molly, Anne S.   1907-
Moore, Lilian
Moskowitz, Stewart
Muntean, Michaela
Murdocca, Sal
Nickl, Peter
Nicoll, Helen
Obligado, Lillian Isabel   1931-
O'Brien, John   1953-
Odor, Ruth S.   1926-
Oppenheim, Shulamith (Levey)   1930-
Orr, Frank   1936-
Orton, Helen Fuller   1872-1955
Overbeck, Cynthia
Owens, Gail   1939-

Packard, Edward   1931-
Parker, Robert Andrew   1927-
Paterson, A(ndrew) B(arton)   1864-1941
Patterson, Sarah   1959-
Pavey, Peter
Pelgrom, Els
Peretz, Isaac Loeb   1851-1915
Perkins, Lucy Fitch   1865-1937
Petersen, P(eter) J(ames)   1941-
Peterson, Jeanne Whitehouse   1939-
Phillips, Betty Lou
Plowden, David   1932-
Plume, Ilse
Poignant, Axel
Pollock, Bruce   1945-
Pollock, Penny   1935-
Polushkin, Maria
Porter, Eleanor Hodgman   1868-1920
Poulsson, Emilie   1853-1939
Powers, Richard M.   1921-
Prager, Arthur
Prather, Ray
Pursell, Margaret S.
Pursell, Thomas F.
Pyle, Katharine   1863-1938
Rabinowitz, Solomon   1859-1916
Randall, E.T.
Rappoport, Ken   1935-
Reese, Bob
Reich, Hanns
Reid, Alistair   1926-
Reidel, Marlene
Reiff, Tana
Reiss, Elayne
Reynolds, Marjorie   1903-
Robert, Adrian
Rohmer, Harriet
Rosier, Lydia
Ross, Pat
Roy, Cal
Rudstrom, Lennart
Sadler, Marilyn
Satchwell, John
Schindler, Regine
Schneider, Leo   1916-
Sealy, Adrienne V.
Seidler, Rosalie
Silbert, Linda P.

Slepian, Jan(ice B.)
Smith, Alison
Smith, Betsy Corington   1937-
Smith, Catriona (Mary)   1948-
Smith, Ray(mond Kenneth)   1949-
Smollin, Michael J.
Steiner, Charlotte
Stevens, Leonard A.   1920-
Stine, R. Conrad   1937-
Stubbs, Joanna   1940-
Sullivan, Mary Beth
Suteev, Vladimir Grigor'evich
Sutherland, Robert D.   1937-
Sutton, Jane   1950-
Sweet, Ozzie
Tarrant, Graham
Thaler, Mike
Timmermans, Gommaar   1930-
Todd, Ruthven   1914-
Tourneur, Dina K.   1934-
Treadgold, Mary   1910-
Velthuijs, Max   1923-
Villiard, Paul   1910-1974
Vincent, Gabrielle
Wagner, Jenny
Walker, Charles W.
Walsh, Anne Batterberry
Walter, Mildred P.
Watts, Franklin   1904-1978
Wayne, Bennett
Weston, Martha
Whelen, Gloria   1923-
White, Wallace   1930-
Wild, Jocelyn
Wild, Robin
Winter, Paula   1929-
Winterfeld, Henry   1901-
Wolde, Gunilla   1939-
Wong, Herbert H.
Woolfolk, Dorothy
Wormser, Richard   1908-
Wright, Betty R.
Wright, Bob
Yagawa, Sumiko
Youldon, Gillian
Zaslow, David
Zistel, Era
Zwerger, Lisbeth

In the interest of making *Something about the Author* as responsive as possible to the needs of its readers, the editor welcomes your suggestions for additional authors and illustrators to be included in the series.

Acknowledgments

Grateful acknowledgment is made to the following publishers, authors, and artists
for their kind permission to reproduce copyrighted material.

ADDISON-WESLEY PUBLISHING CO., INC. Illustration by True Kelley from *Let's Give Kitty a Bath!* by Steven Lindblom. Text copyright © 1982 by Steven Lindblom. Illustrations copyright © 1982 by True Kelley. Reprinted by permission of Addison-Wesley Publishing Co., Inc.

AVON BOOKS. Illustration by Maxie Chambliss from *Baby Talk* by D. Leb Tannenbaum. Text copyright © 1981 by Donald Tannenbaum. Illustrations copyright © 1981 by Maxie Chambliss. Reprinted by permission of Avon Books.

ERNEST BENN LTD. Illustration by Charles E. Brock from "The Runaways," in *Oswald Bastable and Others* by E. Nesbit. Reprinted by permission of Ernest Benn Ltd.

BLACKIE & SONS LTD. Frontispiece illustration by H. M. Brock from *The Old Curiosity Shop* by Charles Dickens./ Illustration by Carme Solé Vendrell from *A Bear in the Air* by Leslie Williams. Text copyright © 1979 by Leslie Williams. Illustrations copyright © 1979 by Carme Solé Vendrell. Reprinted by permission of Blackie & Sons Ltd.

BOOK LURES, INC. Illustration by Jerry Warshaw from *Tangles* by Nancy Polette. Copyright © 1983 by Book Lures, Inc. Reprinted by permission of Book Lures, Inc.

CBS EDUCATIONAL & PROFESSIONAL PUBLISHING. Illustration by Charles Geer from *The Marvelous Inventions of Alvin Fernald* by Clifford B. Hicks. Copyright © 1960 by Clifford B. Hicks./ Illustration by Susan Jeschke from *Mia, Grandma and the Genie* by Susan Jeschke. Copyright © 1978 by Susan Jeschke. Both reprinted by permission of CBS Educational & Professional Publishing.

COLLIER MACMILLAN LTD. Illustrations by Harvey Dinnerstein from *At the Back of the North Wind* by George MacDonald. Afterword and illustrations copyright © 1964 by The Macmillan Co. Both reprinted by permission of Collier Macmillan Ltd.

COWARD, McCANN & GEOGHEGAN, INC. Illustration by Elizabeth MacKinstry from "The Emperor's New Clothes," in *Andersen's Fairy Tales* by Hans Christian Andersen. Copyright 1933, renewed © 1961 by Coward, McCann & Geoghegan, Inc./ Illustration by Elizabeth MacKinstry from "The True Princess," in *Andersen's Fairy Tales* by Hans Christian Andersen. Copyright 1933, renewed © 1961 by Coward, McCann & Geoghegan, Inc./ Illustration by Irene Brady from *Have You Ever Heard of a Kangaroo Bird?* by Barbara Brenner. Text copyright © 1980 by Barbara Brenner. Illustrations copyright © 1980 by Irene Brady./ Photograph by Sam Grainger from *The First Words Picture Book* by Bill Gillham. Text copyright © 1982 by Bill Gillham. Photographs copyright © 1982 by Sam Grainger./ Illustration by Victor G. Ambrus from *The Three Brothers of Ur* by J. G. Fyson. Copyright © 1964 by J. G. Fyson. All reprinted by permission of Coward, McCann & Geoghegan, Inc.

CROWN PUBLISHERS, INC. Jacket illustration by Richard Cuffari from *Goalkeepers Are Different* by Brian Glanville. Copyright © 1972 by Brian Glanville./ Illustration by Diane Dawson from *Roger on His Own* by Marcia Keyser. Text copyright © 1982 by Marcia Keyser. Illustrations copyright © 1982 by Diane Dawson. Both reprinted by permission of Crown Publishers, Inc.

DELL PUBLISHING CO., INC. Jacket illustration by Allan Manham from *The Day They Came to Arrest the Book* by Nat Hentoff. Text copyright © 1982 by Marnate Productions, Inc. Jacket illustration copyright © 1982 by Allan Manham. Reprinted by permission of Dell Publishing Co., Inc.

J. M. DENT & SONS LTD. Illustration by C. E. Brock from *A Christmas Carol* by Charles Dickens. Reprinted by permission of J. M. Dent & Sons Ltd.

ANDRE DEUTSCH LTD. Illustration by Peter Rush from *No Pets Allowed and Other Animal Stories* by Margaret Dunnett. Text copyright © 1981 by The Estate of Margaret Dunnett. Illustrations copyright © 1981 by Peter Rush./ Illustration by Sally Long from *Lightning Cliff* by Rodie Sudbery. Copyright © 1975 by Rodie Sudbery. Both reprinted by permission of Andre Deutsch Ltd.

DIAL BOOKS FOR YOUNG READERS. Frontispiece illustration by Robert Andrew Parker from *The Trees Stand Shining: Poetry of the North American Indians,* selected by Hettie Jones. Text copyright © 1971 by Hettie Jones. Illustrations copyright © 1971 by Robert Andrew Parker. Reprinted by permission of Dial Books For Young Readers.

DILLON PRESS, INC. Photograph from *Italy Balanced on the Edge of Time* by Anthony Di Franco. Copyright © 1983 by Dillon Press, Inc./ Photograph from *China: From Emperors to Communes* by Chris and Janie Filstrup. Both reprinted by permission of Dillon Press, Inc.

DODD, MEAD & CO. Photograph by R. W. Lemke from *Earthquakes: Nature in Motion* by Hershell H. Nixon and Joan Lowery Nixon./ Photograph from *Acrobats and Ping-Pong: Young China's Games, Sports, and Amusements* by Isobel Willcox. Copyright © 1981 by Isobel Willcox. Both reprinted by permission of Dodd, Mead & Co.

DOUBLEDAY & CO., INC. Sidelight excerpts and photographs from *Seven Horizons* by Charles J. Finger. Copyright 1930 by Charles J. Finger./ Illustration by Paul Honoré from "The Wonderful Mirror," in *Tales from Silver Lands* by Charles J. Finger. Copyright 1924 by Doubleday & Co., Inc./ Illustrations by Thomas Handforth from *Mei Li* by Thomas Handforth. Copyright 1938 by Thomas Handforth./ Sidelight excerpts from *Writing Books for Boys and Girls,* edited by Helen Ferris. Copyright © 1962 by Doubleday & Co., Inc./ Cover illustration from *This School Is Driving Me Crazy* by Nat Hentoff. Copyright © 1976 by Nat Hentoff./ Cover illustration from *Jazz Country* by Nat Hentoff. Copyright © 1965 by Nat Hentoff./ Cover illustration from *Does This School Have Capital Punishment?* by Nat Hentoff. Copyright © 1981 by Marnate Productions Ltd./ Illustration by Elizabeth MacKinstry from "The Goose Girl," in *The Fairy Ring,* edited by Kate Douglas Wiggin and Nora Archibald Smith. Copyright 1906 by McClure, Phillips & Co. Copyright renewed 1910 by Doubleday & Co., Inc./ Illustration by Elizabeth MacKinstry from "History of Jack the Giant Killer," in *The Fairy Ring,* edited by Kate Douglas Wiggin and Nora Archibald Smith. Copyright 1906 by McClure, Phillips & Co. Copyright renewed 1910 by Doubleday & Co., Inc./ Illustration by Anna Vojtech from *The Star Husband* by Jane Mobley. Text copyright © 1979 by Jane Mobley. Illustrations copyright © 1979 by Anna Vojtech./ Woodblock by Paul Honoré from *Authors and Others* by Anice Page Cooper. Copyright 1927 by Doubleday, Page & Co./ Illustration by Thomas Handforth from *Faraway Meadow* by Thomas Handforth. Copyright 1939 by Thomas Handforth./ Illustration by James Marshall from *There's a Party at Mona's Tonight* by Harry Allard. Text copyright © 1981 by Harry Allard. Illustrations copyright © 1981 by James Marshall. All reprinted by permission of Doubleday & Co., Inc.

E. P. DUTTON, INC. Jacket illustration by Les Morrill from *Dunker* by Ronald Kidd. Copyright © 1982 by Ronald Kidd./ Illustration by Richard Bowen from *Origins* by Richard E. Leakey and Roger Lewin. Copyright © 1977 by Richard E. Leakey and Roger Lewin./ Illustration by C. E. Brock from *A Christmas Carol* by Charles Dickens. All reprinted by permission of E. P. Dutton, Inc.

FABER & FABER LTD. Illustration from *Your Book of Camping* by D. T. Roscoe. Copyright © 1980 by D. T. Roscoe. Reprinted by permission of Faber & Faber Ltd.

FOUR WINDS PRESS. Illustration by Nola Langner from *The Prince and the Pink Blanket* by Barbara Brenner. Text copyright © 1980 by Barbara Brenner. Illustrations copyright © 1980 by Nola Langner. Reprinted by permission of Four Winds Press.

THE GREEN TIGER PRESS. Illustration by Katie Thamer from *The Red Shoes* by Hans Christian Andersen. Reprinted by permission of The Green Tiger Press.

GROSSET & DUNLAP, INC. Jacket illustration by Ponder Goembel from *The Illustrated Treasury of Fairy Tales,* edited by T. A. Kennedy. Copyright © 1982 by Grosset & Dunlap, Inc./ Illustration by Aldren Watson from *Gulliver's Travels* by Jonathan Swift. Copyright 1947 by Grosset & Dunlap, Inc./ Illustration by George Zaffo from *Airplanes and Trucks and Trains, Fire Engines, Boats and Ships, and Building and Wrecking Machines* by George Zaffo. Copyright 1949, 1950, 1951, 1953, © 1958, 1963, 1964, 1966 by Grosset & Dunlap, Inc. All reprinted by permission of Grosset & Dunlap, Inc.

HARCOURT BRACE JOVANOVICH, INC. Illustration by Charles Geer from *Plain Girl* by Virginia Sorensen. Copyright 1955 by Virginia Sorensen./ Illustration by Ronald Searle from *Paris! Paris!* by Irwin Shaw. Text copyright © 1976, 1977 by Irwin Shaw. Illustrations copyright © 1976, 1977 by Ronald Searle. Both reprinted by permission of Harcourt Brace Jovanovich, Inc.

HARPER & ROW, PUBLISHERS, INC. Illustration by Joan Sandin from *A Year in the Life of Rosie Bernard* by Barbara Brenner. Text copyright © 1971 by Barbara Brenner. Illustrations copyright © 1971 by Joan Sandin./ Sidelight excerpts from *We Chose Cape Cod* by

Scott Corbett. Copyright 1953 by Harper & Row, Publishers, Inc./ Illustration by Aldren A. Watson from *The Golden Summer* by Le Claire Alger. All reprinted by permission of Harper & Row, Publishers, Inc.

HOLIDAY HOUSE, INC. Photograph by William Muñoz from *A Picture Book of Cows* by Dorothy Hinshaw Patent. Text copyright © 1982 by Dorothy Hinshaw Patent. Photographs copyright © 1982 by William Muñoz. Reprinted by permission of Holiday House, Inc.

THE HORN BOOK, INC. Illustration from "The Notebooks of Elizabeth MacKinstry," April, 1957 in *Horn Book./* Sidelight excerpts from an article "Moon Bridge in Lily Pond," by Thomas Handforth, May-June, 1939 in *Horn Book./* Sidelight excerpts from *Caldecott Medal Books: 1938-1953,* edited by Bertha Mahony Miller and Elinor Whitney Field. Copyright © 1957 by The Horn Book, Inc./ Sidelight excerpts from *Horn Book,* special issue, October 19, 1950./ Sidelight excerpts from an article "Getting Inside Jazz Country," by Nat Hentoff, October, 1966 in *Horn Book.* Copyright © 1966 by The Horn Book, Inc./ Sidelight excerpts from an article "Elizabeth MacKinstry," by May Massee, April, 1957 in *Horn Book.* Copyright © 1957 by The Horn Book, Inc. All reprinted by permission of The Horn Book, Inc.

HOUGHTON MIFFLIN CO. Illustration by James Marshall from *The Stupids Step Out* by Harry Allard. Text copyright © 1974 by Harry Allard. Illustrations copyright © 1974 by James Marshall./ Illustration by Jan Brett from *St. Patrick's Day in the Morning* by Eve Bunting. Text copyright © 1980 by Eve Bunting. Illustrations copyright © 1980 by Jan Brett./ Frontispiece illustration by Henry C. Pitz from *Our Navy: An Outline History for Young People* by Charles J. Finger. Copyright 1936 by Charles J. Finger./ Illustration by Tom Huffman from *Be a Perfect Person in Just Three Days!* by Stephen Manes. Text copyright © 1982 by Stephen Manes. Illustrations copyright © 1982 by Tom Huffman. All reprinted by permission of Houghton Mifflin Co.

INTERNATIONAL PUBLISHERS CO., INC. Sidelight excerpts by W. E. B. Du Bois from *The Autobiography of W. E. B. Du Bois: A Solioquy on Viewing My Life from the Last Decade of Its First Century.* Copyright © 1968 by International Publishers Co., Inc. Reprinted by permission of International Publishers Co., Inc.

MICHAEL JOSEPH LTD. Illustration by John Ward from *Brown Buck: A Californian Fantasy* by A. L. Rowse. Copyright © 1976 by A. L. Rowse. Reprinted by permission of Michael Joseph Ltd.

ALFRED A. KNOPF, INC. Jacket painting by Richard Hess from *The Kentucky Trace: A Novel of the American Revolution* by Harriette Simpson Arnow. Copyright © 1974 by Harriette Simpson Arnow./ Illustration by Aldren A. Watson from *What Is One?* by Nancy Dingman Watson. Copyright 1954 by Nancy Dingman Watson./ Illustration by Aldren A. Watson from "Sunrise in His Pocket," in *Chanticleer of Wilderness Road: A Story of Davy Crockett* by Meridel LeSueur. Copyright 1951 by Meridel LeSueur. All reprinted by permission of Alfred A. Knopf, Inc.

LIONS. Cover illustration by Mark Thomas from *The Third Class Genie* by Robert Leeson. Reprinted by permission of Lions.

J. B. LIPPINCOTT CO. Jacket illustration by Laura Lydecker from *Early Rising* by Joan Clarke. Copyright © 1974 by Joan Clarke. Reprinted by permission of J. B. Lippincott Co.

LITTLE, BROWN & CO., INC. Illustrations by Ronald Searle from *Ronald Searle's Big Fat Cat Book* by Ronald Searle. Copyright © 1967, 1968, 1969, 1970, 1971, 1972, 1973, 1974, 1975, 1976, 1977, 1978, 1979, 1980, 1981, and 1982 by Ronald Searle./ Illustration by James Marshall from *Mary Alice, Operator Number 9* by Jeffrey Allen. Text copyright © 1975 by Jeffrey Allen. Illustrations copyright © 1975 by James Marshall./ Illustration by H. M. Brock from *Good-bye Mr. Chips* by James Hilton. Copyright 1934 by James Hilton. Copyright renewed © 1962 by Alice Hilton./ Illustration by Bill Ogden from *The Great McGoniggle's Key Play* by Scott Corbett. Text copyright © 1976 by Scott Corbett. Illustrations copyright © 1976 by William Ogden./ Illustration by Geff Gerlach from *The Red Room Riddle: A Ghost Story* by Scott Corbett. Copyright © 1972 by Scott Corbett./ Illustration by Bert Dodson from *Run for the Money* by Scott Corbett. Copyright © 1973 by Scott Corbett./ Illustration by Jon McIntosh from *The Mysterious Zetabet* by Scott Corbett. Text copyright © 1979 by Scott Corbett. Illustrations copyright © 1979 by Jon McIntosh./ Illustration by Paul Frame from *The Case of the Silver Skull* by Scott Corbett. Copyright © 1974 by Scott Corbett./ Illustration by Wallace Tripp from *The Baseball Bargain* by Scott Corbett. Copyright © 1970 by Scott Corbett./ Illustration by Paul Galdone from *The Hangman's Ghost Trick* by Scott Corbett. Copyright © 1977 by Scott Corbett./ Sidelight excerpts from "Preface," in *Home Computers: A Simple and Informative Guide* by Scott Corbett. Copyright © 1980 by Scott Corbett./ Illustration by Marvin Friedman from *Pinch* by Larry Callen. Text copyright © 1975 by Larry Callen./ Jacket illustration by Bob Zeiring from *The Wolfman of Beacon Hill* by Kathleen Kilgore. Copyright © 1982 by Kathleen Kilgore. All reprinted by permission of Little, Brown & Co., Inc.

LOTHROP, LEE & SHEPARD BOOKS. Illustration by Pat Cummings from *My Mama Needs Me* by Mildred Pitts Walter. Text copyright © 1983 by Mildred Pitts Walter. Illustrations copyright © 1983 by Pat Cummings. Reprinted by permission of Lothrop, Lee & Shepard Books.

MACMILLAN, INC. Illustration by C. E. Brock from *Rewards and Fairies* by Rudyard Kipling./ Illustration by C. E. Brock from *Nancy Owlett* by Eden Phillpotts. Copyright 1933 by The Macmillan Co./ Illustration by Charles E. Brock from *Travels into Several Remote Nations of the World by Lemuel Gulliver* by Jonathan Swift. Illustrations copyright by Macmillan Publishers Ltd./ Illustrations by Harvey Dinnerstein from *At the Back of the North Wind* by George MacDonald. Afterword and illustrations copyright © 1964 by The Macmillan Co./ Illustration by Harvey Dinnerstein from *Silently, the Cat, and Miss Theodosia* by Felice Holman. Text copyright © 1965 by Felice Holman. Illustrations copyright © 1965 by The Macmillan Co./ Illustration by Charles Geer from *Katie Kittenheart* by Miriam E. Mason. Copyright © 1957 by The Macmillan Co./ Illustration by Thomas Handforth from *Toutou in Bondage* by Elizabeth Coatsworth. Copyright 1929 by The Macmillan Co. All reprinted by permission of Macmillan, Inc.

ROBERT M. McBRIDE & CO. Illustration by Paul Honoré from *Romantic Rascals* by Charles J. Finger. Copyright 1927 by Robert M. McBride & Co./ Illustration by Paul Honoré from *Highwaymen: A Book of Gallant Rogues* by Charles J. Finger. Copyright 1923 by Robert M. McBride & Co. Both reprinted by permission of Robert M. McBride & Co.

McGRAW-HILL BOOK CO. Illustration by Charles Geer from *Miss Pickerell and the Supertanker* by Ellen MacGregor and Dora Pantell. Copyright © 1978 by McGraw-Hill, Inc./ Illustration by Bill Morrison from *Know About Alcohol* by Margaret O. Hyde. Copyright © 1978 by Margaret O. Hyde. Both reprinted by permission of McGraw-Hill Book Co.

MINTON, BALCH & CO. Illustration by Thomas Handforth from *Tranquilina's Paradise* by Susan Smith. Copyright 1930 by Minton, Balch & Co. Reprinted by permission of Minton, Balch & Co.

WILLIAM MORROW & CO., INC. Illustrations by Henry C. Pitz and Helen Finger from *Foot-Loose in the West* by Charles J. Finger. Copyright 1932 by Charles J. Finger./ Illustration by Charles Geer from *Open Throttle: Stories of Railroads and Railroad Men,* selected by Phyllis R. Fenner. Copyright © 1966 by Phyllis R. Fenner./ Illustration by Susan Yard Harris from *Wild Berry Moon* by John Jiler. Text copyright © 1982 by John Jiler. Illustrations copyright © 1982 by Susan Yard Harris./ Illustration by René Martin from *Life and Death* by Herbert S. Zim and Sonia Bleeker. Copyright © 1970 by Herbert S. Zim and Sonia Bleeker./ Illustration by René Martin from *Armored Animals* by Herbert S. Zim. Copyright © 1971 by Herbert S. Zim./ Illustration by René Martin from *Waves* by Herbert S. Zim. Copyright © 1967 by Herbert S. Zim./ Jacket illustration by Jan Palmer from *The House on the Hill* by Mildred Masters. Copyright © 1979, 1982 by Mildred Carolyn Masters./ Illustration by James Stevenson from *"Could Be Worse!"* by James Stevenson. Copyright © 1977 by James Stevenson. All reprinted by permission of William Morrow & Co., Inc.

FREDERICK MULLER LTD. Illustration by Harry Toothill from *With Whymper in the Alps* by Alan R. Warwick. Copyright © 1964 by Alan R. Warwick. Reprinted by permission of Frederick Muller Ltd.

THOMAS NELSON, INC. Jacket illustration by Lydia Rosier from *That's What Friends Are For* by Ronald Kidd. Copyright © 1978 by Ronald Kidd. Reprinted by permission of Thomas Nelson, Inc.

PETER PAUPER PRESS. Illustration by Aldren A. Watson from *Walden; or, Life in the Woods* by Henry David Thoreau. Copyright © 1966 by Peter Pauper Press. Reprinted by permission of Peter Pauper Press.

PLATT & MUNK PUBLISHERS. Illustration by Aldren Watson from *Uncle Wiggily's Happy Days* by Howard R. Garis. Copyright 1947, © 1976 by Platt & Munk Publishers. Reprinted by permission of Platt & Munk Publishers.

PRENTICE-HALL, INC. Illustration by Dennis Nolan from *Witch Bazooza* by Dennis Nolan. Copyright © 1979 by Dennis Nolan./ Illustration by Tom Morgan from *The Building Book* by Tom Morgan. Copyright © 1979 by Tom Morgan. Both reprinted by permission of Prentice-Hall, Inc.

PUFFIN BOOKS. Illustration by C. E. Brock from *The Railway Children* by E. Nesbit./

Illustration by James Stevenson from *The Sea View Hotel* by James Stevenson. Copyright © 1978 by James Stevenson. Both reprinted by permission of Puffin Books.

G. P. PUTNAM'S SONS. Sidelight excerpts from *The Three Owls* by Anne Carroll Moore. Copyright © 1956 by Anne Carroll Moore. Reprinted by permission of G. P. Putnam's Sons.

RANDOM HOUSE, INC. Illustration by Thomas Handforth from *The Secret of the Porcelain Fish* by Margery Evernden. Copyright 1947 by Random House, Inc. Reprinted by permission of Random House, Inc.

SCHOLASTIC, INC. Illustration by William Hogarth from *101 Elephant Jokes,* compiled by Robert Blake. Copyright © 1964 by Scholastic Magazines, Inc. Reprinted by permission of Scholastic, Inc.

SIMON & SCHUSTER, INC. Illustration by Hilda Offen from "Sam Pig and the Wind," by Alison Uttley in *A Treasury of Animal Stories,* edited by Linda Yeatman. Copyright © 1982 by Kingfisher Books Ltd. Reprinted by permission of Simon & Schuster, Inc.

CHARLES SKILTON LTD. Photographs from *The Brocks: A Family of Cambridge Artists and Illustrators* by C. M. Kelly. Copyright © 1975 by C. M. Kelly. All reprinted by permission of Charles Skilton Ltd.

STEMMER HOUSE PUBLISHERS, INC. Illustration by Carme Solé Vendrell from *A Bear in the Air* by Leslie Williams. Text copyright © 1979 by Leslie Williams. Illustrations copyright © 1979 by Carme Solé Vendrell. Reprinted by permission of Stemmer House Publishers, Inc.

UNIVERSITY OF MASSACHUSETTS PRESS. Photographs from *Against Racism: Unpublished Essays, Papers, Addresses, 1887-1961* by W. E. B. Du Bois. Edited by Herbert Aptheker. Copyright © 1985 by University of Massachusetts Press. Both reprinted by permission of University of Massachusetts Press.

VAN NOSTRAND REINHOLD CO., INC. Sidelight excerpts and illustration from *The Watson Drawing Book* by Ernest W. Watson and Aldren A. Watson. Copyright © 1962 by Ernest W. Watson and Aldren A. Watson. Both reprinted by permission of Van Nostrand Reinhold Co., Inc.

THE VIKING PRESS. Illustration by Aldren A. Watson from *Tommy's Mommy's Fish* by Nancy Dingman Watson. Text copyright © 1971 by Nancy Dingman Watson. Illustrations copyright © 1971 by Aldren A. Watson./ Illustration by Aldren A. Watson from *Annie's Spending Spree* by Nancy Dingman Watson. Copyright © 1957 by Nancy Dingman Watson and Aldren A. Watson./ Illustration by Ronald Searle from *From Frozen North to Filthy Lucre* by Ronald Searle. Copyright © 1961, 1962, 1963, 1964 by Ronald Searle. All reprinted by permission of The Viking Press.

WATSON-GUPTILL PUBLICATIONS. Sidelight excerpts and illustration from *Harvey Dinnerstein: Artist at Work.* Both reprinted by permission of Watson-Guptill Publications.

YOUNG-SCOTT BOOKS. Illustration by Fred Brenner from *The Flying Patchwork Quilt* by Barbara Brenner. Text copyright © 1965 by Barbara Brenner. Illustrations copyright © 1965 by Fred Brenner. Reprinted by permission of Young-Scott Books.

ZENITH BOOKS. Illustration by Harvey Dinnerstein from *Remember the Days: A Short History of the Jewish American* by Milton Meltzer. Reprinted by permission of Zenith Books.

Sidelight excerpts from an article "Ronald Scarle—British Graphic Artist," by Henry C. Pitz, September, 1955 in *American Artist.* Reprinted by permission of *American Artist./* Sidelight excerpts from an article "Aldren A. Watson: Disciple of Walden," by Norman Kent, March, 1946 in *American Artist.* Reprinted by permission of *American Artist./* Sidelight excerpts from an article "Aesop's Fables," by Aldren Watson, November, 1941 in *American Artist.* Reprinted by permission of *American Artist./* Sidelight excerpts from an article "The Saturday Library Matinee," by Nat Hentoff, April, 1976 in *American Libraries.* Copyright © 1976 by The American Library Association. Reprinted by permission of The American Library Association./ Photograph from *Cartoonist Profiles,* Volume 1, number 4, fall, 1969. Reprinted by permission of Cartoonist Profiles, Inc./ Illustration by Thomas Handforth from *The Dragon and the Eagle* by Delia Goetz. Copyright 1944 by Foreign Policy Association, Inc. Reprinted by permission of Foreign Policy Association, Inc./ Illustration by Carol Lawson from *Jenny and the Sheep Thieves* by Griselda Gifford. Illustrations copyright © 1975 by Carol Lawson. Reprinted by permission of Griselda Gifford./ Illustration by Ronald Searle from *The Situation Is Hopeless* by Ronald Searle. Copyright © 1980 by Ronald Searle. Reprinted by permission of Hope Leresche & Sayle./ Illustration from the Sunday comic strip "Johnny Hazard." Copyright 1944 by King Features Syndicate, Inc. Reprinted by permission of King

Features Syndicate, Inc./ Sidelight excerpts and illustration from *The Art of the Illustrator* by Percy V. Bradshaw. Reprinted by permission of The Press Art School./ Photograph by Jeff Foott from *Grizzly Bears* by John L. Weaver. Copyright © 1982 by John L. Weaver. Reprinted by permission of John L. Weaver.

PHOTOGRAPH CREDITS

Harry Allard: Mitzel; Barbara Brenner: George Ancona; Scott Corbett: Jane Corbett; Anthony Di Franco: Timothy Layer; Harvey Dinnerstein (self-portrait): Studio/Nine, Inc.; Susan Jeschke: Max Block; Marcia Keyser: Andrew Partos; Ronald Kidd: Stephen McBrady; Richard E. Leakey: Time-Life Video; Robert Leeson: Pat Mantle; Constance Leonard: Tom Place; Carole Livingston: © 1980 by Thomas Victor; Mildred Masters: Haga Photography; Irwin Math: Jack Magaril; Jim Moore: Gordon Munro; William Muñoz: Sandy Muñoz; Hershell Howard Nixon: Murray Getz; Nancy Polette: Hammond Photography; James Stevenson: Susan Hirschman; Anna Vojtech: Jan Dvorak; John L. Weaver: Franz J. Camenzind; Isobel Willcox: Patricia Bennett.

something About the Author

ACS, Laszlo (Bela)   1931-

PERSONAL: Born May 18, 1931, in Budapest, Hungary; son of János and Margit (Acs) Acs; married second wife (a teacher); children: John Laszlo. *Education:* Academy of Fine Arts, Budapest, diploma, 1956; attended Hornsey College of Art, London, 1959-60. *Home:* Devon, England.

CAREER: Graphic designer and illustrator. Began career in advertising; later served as head of graphic design, Independent Television News, England; free-lance artist and illustrator. Lecturer in graphic design and illustration, Exeter College of Art, 1974—. Executed various commissions, including posters for *The Times,* Council for Health Education, and others, and audio-visual designs for the Schools Council, all in England. Work has been exhibited at the National Gallery, Hungary, Leyden University, Holland, Galerie du Cercle Loisirs, Switzerland, Wakefield, York, and Exeter, England. *Member:* Society of Industrial Artists and Designers.

ILLUSTRATOR—Juvenile nonfiction: Richard John Salter, *Great Moments in Engineering,* Roy, 1964; (with Bernard Blatch) Walter Shepherd, *Electricity,* John Day, 1964; Norman Coats, *Energy and Power,* Weidenfeld & Nicholson, 1967; Jean Haynes, *The Young Keats* (biography), Roy, 1967; Frederick E. Dean, *Bridges and Tunnels,* Golden Press, 1968, revised edition, Hart-Davis, 1974; W. Shepherd, *The Earth's Surface,* Golden Press, 1968; (with George Craig) W. Shepherd, *The Story of Man,* Golden Press, 1968; (with Eric Thomas) Leo Lange, *Germs,* Weidenfeld & Nicholson, 1968; James Muirden, *The Earth's Neighbors,* Golden Press, 1968, revised edition updated by R. G. Lascelles, Hart-Davis, 1975; Alan James, *Hospitals,* Blackwell, 1969; Irmgard Meyer, *Der Uhu* (German textbook), Harrap, 1972; I. Meyer, *Wo ist fips?* (Ger-

LASZLO ACS

21

man textbook), Harrap, 1972; Albert E. Tansley, *Sound Sense* (textbook), three books, E. J. Arnold, 1972; (with Tom Swimmer) Paul Roberson, *Engines,* Hart-Davis, 1973, revised edition, 1975; Margaret C. M. Roberts, *Tapas* (Spanish textbook), four volumes, Harrap, 1975; David Stacey, *Fire in My Bones: Prophets and Prophecy, Then and Now* (textbook), Religious Education Press, 1975; Robert J. Unstead, *Living in Pompeii,* A. & C. Black, 1976.

Juvenile fiction: *Boy's Choice: A New Book of Stories,* Golden Pleasure Books, 1965; René Guillot, *The Troubadour,* translated from the French by Anne Carter, Collins, 1965, McGraw, 1967; Barbara Bingley, *Vicky and the Monkey People,* Abelard, 1966; C. Everard Palmer, *The Cloud with the Silver Lining,* Deutsch, 1966; Allen Aldous, *Bushfire,* Brockhampton Press, 1967, Criterion, 1968; Eleanor Farjeon, *The Wonderful Knight,* Kaye & Ward, 1967; Elizabeth Taylor, *Mossy Trotter,* Harcourt, 1967; Geoffrey Palmer and Noel Lloyd, *Ghosts Go Haunting* (short stories), Roy, 1968; C. E. Palmer, *A Cow Called Boy,* Deutsch, 1973 (Acs was not associated with earlier edition); Hilary Voisey, *Change for the Better,* Chatto & Windus, 1973; C. E. Palmer, *Baba and Mr. Big,* Deutsch, 1974; John Kennett, reteller, *The Sea Shall Not Have Them,* Blackie & Son, 1975; Peggy Appiah, *Ring of Gold,* Deutsch, 1976; Rosemary Sutcliff, *Shifting Sands,* Hamish Hamilton, 1977; Christina Green, *Beetle Boy,* Hamish Hamilton, 1977; William Mayne, *Max's Dreams,* Greenwillow, 1977; Christina Green, *The Logan Stone,* Hamish Hamilton, 1978; David Rees, *The House That Moved,* Hamish Hamilton, 1978; Geoffrey Trease, *When the Drums Beat, and Other Stories,* Pan Books, 1979; Margaret Greaves, *The Abbotsbury Ring,* Methuen, 1979; Geoffrey Kilner, *Joe Burkinshaw's Progress,* Methuen, 1979; Violet Bibby, *The Phantom Horse,* Kaye & Ward, 1979; Winifred Finlay, *Tales of Sorcery and Witchcraft,* Kaye & Ward, 1980; Gillian Hancock, *The Great Volcanoes,* Kaye & Ward, 1982; Bill Gilham, *My Brother Barry,* Deutsch, 1982; Alexander McCall Smith, *The Perfect Hamburger,* Hamish Hamilton, 1982; Frances Thomas, *Secrets,* Hamish Hamilton, 1983; Anne Molloy, *The Christmas Rocket,* F. Watts, 1984; Joan Phipson, *Beryl, The Rainmaker,* Hamish Hamilton, 1984; Barbara Willard, *Smiley Tiger,* MacRae, 1984; (with John Storey) Allen Sharp, *Terror in the Fourth Dimension,* Childrens Press, 1984; Ann Ruffell, *The Bowley Boy,* Hamish Hamilton, 1985.

Other: Leonard Gribble, *Famous Stories of the Wild West,* Barker, 1967, abridged edition, Target, 1973; Herman Melville, *Typee and the Story of Toby,* Heron Books 1968; Somerset Maugham, *The Veil,* Heron Books, 1968; James Hawthorne and others, compilers, *Northern Ireland: Physical Features, Geology, Archeology, Agriculture, Industry, Transport,* British Broadcasting Corporation, 1970; Guy de Maupassant, *Une vie* (novel), translated from the French by Katharine Vivian, Folio Society, 1981; Daphne du Maurier, *The Loving Spirit,* Heron Books, 1982; D. du Maurier, *I'll Never Be Young Again,* Heron Books, 1982; D. du Maurier, *The Progress of Julius,* Heron Books, 1982.

SIDELIGHTS: Acs was born and educated in Budapest, Hungary. He later attended Hornsey College of Art in London, before beginning his professional career in England. "Having left my native country after receiving my diploma in Graphic Design, my professional life has been fully connected with England. Here I first spent three years in advertising, then joined Independent Television News as Head of Graphic Design. Eighteen months later, I was a full-time freelancer working on a wide variety of children's books, both fact and fiction. [I] also designed posters for *The Times,* the Post Office (Savings Bank and Telecommunications), the Council for Health Education, etc. For four years I was engaged in audio-visual design in foreign language teaching for the Schools Council.

"Children's book illustration had gone through a revolutionary development in the early 1960s, chiefly due to a general up-

There was Barry, flat on his face, holding down a struggling rabbit. ■ (From *My Brother Barry* by Bill Gillham. Illustrated by Laszlo Acs.)

surge in the field of communications. Space travel, new technical developments and the realization of a new social relevance of the work of designers all contributed to this new phenomenon, and rich rewards made children's book publishing a challenging and worthwhile territory even for internationally established names. Graphic designers who, in normal circumstances, would hardly have noticed children's books, took up this challenging medium and produced some most striking and engaging solutions. . . . Some of the publishing houses [in England] had been slow to notice the drift but, by the early 1970s everyone wanted to join the bandwagon. While it is enlightening to talk with knowledgeable art editors, some of them still tend to apply the old rigid unenterprising standards to their selection, as they did thirty years ago. . . . One might also add how underpaid illustrators in England are.'' [Lee Kingman and others, compilers, *Illustrators of Children's Books: 1967-1976*, Horn Book, 1978.]

FOR MORE INFORMATION SEE: Lee Kingman and others, compilers, *Illustrators of Children's Books, 1967-1976*, Horn Book, 1978.

ALLARD, Harry G(rover), Jr.   1928-
(Harry Allard)

PERSONAL: Born January 27, 1928, in Evanston, Ill.; son of Harry Grover (in sales) and Gladys (Bedford) Allard. *Education:* Northwestern University, B.S., 1948; Middlebury College, M.A., 1960; Yale University, Ph.D., 1973. *Politics:* "Anarchist. I don't know. Maybe a monarchist." *Religion:* Russian Orthodox. *Home:* 21 Prescott St., Charlestown, Mass. 02129. *Office:* Department of Foreign Languages, Salem State College, 352 Lafayette St., Salem, Mass. 01970.

CAREER: Wabash College, Crawfordsville, Ind., instructor in French, 1959-60; Trinity University, San Antonio, Tex., instructor in French, 1962-65; associated with Yale University, New Haven, Conn., 1965-68; Salem State College, Salem, Mass., 1968—, began as assistant professor, became associate professor of French. Taught English at Berlitz School in Paris; worked as legal translator in Paris. Author and translator of children's books. *Military service:* U.S. Army Signal Corps, 1951-52.

AWARDS, HONORS: The Tutti-Frutti Case was selected as one of the *New York Times*'s best illustrated children's books of the year, 1975; *The Stupids Step Out* was selected for the Children's Book Showcase, 1975, and was included on *School Library Journal*'s list, "Best of the Best 1966-1978," 1979; *Miss Nelson Is Missing!* was a runner-up for the Edgar Allan Poe Award, and was selected as an outstanding book of the year by the *New York Times*, both 1977, received the Georgia Children's Book Award from the University of Georgia, 1980, and the California Young Readers Medal, 1982; Academy Award nomination for best animated film from Academy of Motion Picture Arts and Sciences, 1978, for movie adaptation of *It's So Nice to Have a Wolf Around the House; The Stupids Have a Ball* was selected one of the International Reading Association's "Children's Choices," 1979, and *There's a Party at Mona's Tonight* and *The Stupids Die* were selected, 1982; *I Will Not Go to Market Today* was selected for the American Institute of Graphics Arts Book Show, 1980; *The Stupids Die* was chosen one of *School Library Journal*'s Best Books, 1981, and was runner-up for First Kentucky Bluegrass Award, 1983; Colorado Children's Book Award, 1985, for *Miss Nelson Is Back.*

WRITINGS: Anna de Noailles, Nun of Passion: A Study of the Novels of Anna de Noailles, [New Haven, Conn.], 1973.

For children; under name Harry Allard: (With James Marshall) *The Stupids Step Out* (illustrated by J. Marshall), Houghton, 1974; *The Tutti-Frutti Case: Starring the Four Doctors of Goodge* (illustrated by J. Marshall), Prentice-Hall, 1975; (translator from the German) Luis Murschetz, *A Hamster's Journey,* Prentice-Hall, 1976; *Crash Helmet* (illustrated by Jean-Claude Suarès), Prentice-Hall, 1977; *It's So Nice to Have a Wolf Around the House* (illustrated by J. Marshall; Junior Literary Guild selection), Doubleday, 1977; *Miss Nelson Is Missing!* (illustrated by J. Marshall), Houghton, 1977; (with J. Marshall) *The Stupids Have a Ball* (illustrated by J. Marshall), Houghton, 1978; (adapter and translator from the German) *May I Stay?* (fairy tale; illustrated by F. A. Fitzgerald), Prentice-Hall, 1978; *Bumps in the Night* (illustrated by J. Marshall), Doubleday, 1979; *I Will Not Go to Market Today* (illustrated by J. Marshall; Junior Literary Guild selection), Dial, 1979; (translator from the German) Friedrich Karl Waechter, *Three Is Company* (illustrated by F. K. Waechter), Doubleday, 1980; (with J. Marshall) *The Stupids Die* (illustrated by J. Marshall) Houghton, 1981; *There's a Party at Mona's Tonight* (illustrated by J. Marshall; Junior Literary Guild selection), Doubleday, 1981; *Miss Nelson Is Back* (illustrated by J. Marshall), Houghton, 1982; *Miss Nelson Has a Field Day* (illustrated by J. Marshall), Houghton, 1985.

ADAPTATIONS: "It's So Nice to Have a Wolf Around the House" (full-length television cartoon feature), Learning Corporation of America, 1978; "Miss Nelson Is Missing" (motion picture), Learning Corporation of America, 1979, (film-

HARRY G. ALLARD, JR.

"I'm your Aunt Gertrude, Mona," she said. "Don't you recognize me, dear?" ■ (From *There's a Party at Mona's Tonight* by Harry Allard. Illustrated by James Marshall.)

strip), Weston Woods, 1984; ''Miss Nelson Is Back'' (TV segment; introduced by LeVar Burton and narrated by Ruth Buzzi), Reading Rainbow, 1983; ''I Will Go to Market To-day'' (five filmstrips), Random House, 1984.

WORK IN PROGRESS: Miss Nelson Meets Her Match; In a Spanish Inn; a novel for children; *Lullaby,* an adult horror novel; translation of an adult novel from the French.

SIDELIGHTS: Allard shares the same birthday, January 27, with another famous children's author, Lewis Carroll. ''I was born in Evanston, Illinois. I now look upon sharing a birthday with the creator of *Alice* as a good omen.

''I went to high school in Chicago. My favorite subject was Latin. I majored in art at Northwestern University, and was graduated from there in 1949 with a B.S. A limbo of misdirected efforts followed, from which I was at last saved by the Korean War (Signal Corps in Japan and in Korea). Chicago again, but only for one year. To shake the dust of Chicago from my heels forever, I went to live in Paris for four years. When I came back to the U.S.A. the only thing I could do was teach French, so I taught French. . . . To make it official I got an M.A. from Middlebury College in 1960 and a Ph.D. in French from Yale in 1973.''

Since 1968 Allard has taught at Salem State College in Salem, Massachusetts. After his move to Charlestown, Massachusetts, Allard met author-illustrator James Marshall. It was Marshall's art that was the inspiration for Allard's first book, *The Stupids Step Out*. ''I gave him *The Stupids Step Out* and he took it to Houghton Mifflin. I never had a hard time beginning. It's a strange thing; I feel almost guilty. You know, you hear about people writing letters and sending manuscripts in. I never had to do anything. It was always easy.''

Allard commented on the reasons for the success of *The Stupids*. ''I hate anything with a message. For a while everyone was hooked on stories about death or old people. Who wants to hear about that! You have enough time to learn about that when you grow old. . . . When you're little, you can think of other things.

''I think it's because children are always under the thumb of somebody—adults, whether they are parents or priests or nuns or whatever—and here the children can make fun of adults and feel superior to them and know more than they do. Also because the Stupids are such a wild family, you know, there's something anarchistic about them. And as I was saying, so many books seem to be socially manipulative. They're either telling children to love children of other races or to respect old people or to understand blind people and dying people. There are too many messages. With the Stupids there is no message at all. They just seem to do what they want to do.''

"Bath time!" said Mrs. Stupid.

"Everyone into the tub," ordered Mr. Stupid.

"But where's the water?" asked Petunia.

■ (From *The Stupids Step Out* by Harry Allard. Illustrated by James Marshall.)

The Stupids Step Out was followed by *Miss Nelson Is Missing!*, which was a runner-up for a 1977 Edgar Allan Poe Award.

"James Marshall and I work very closely together and we fight a lot about things. I've only worked with two other illustrators, and those books didn't work. I don't think it was because of the illustrators, but those books were failures, so now I am a little superstitious about it. It's hard to get top-notch people; people like Sendak only work for Sendak. I admire Tomi Ungerer very much, but I think he has gone back to Europe and doesn't want to do children's books anymore.

"It's text first, but then we work a lot on the illustrations. I make suggestions, and of course anything that's in the drawing gets deleted from the text. I have to redo the text because I don't want it to say what the picture is already saying, so the text gets shorter and smaller. Sometimes if I have an idea for a visual gag I bracket it in the text and suggest a visual idea.

"Once I get the idea, I write in a white heat, like [one] night . . . when I got up at three. It was all done by seven or eight and then I went to Cambridge to have it photocopied. But if something is accepted, if it is going to become a book, then I keep doing it, doing it, doing it. And I think the polishing shows, because it's always obviously towards simplicity, to make the sentences as simple and almost transparent as possible. There's no way to show off in children's books. You know, you're not showing off your vocabulary. The only thing you can really work with is rhythm, as in the sense of the English Bible. The words are so simple, but very often the rhythm is mysterious and beautiful.

"When I get an idea, I want to write immediately. I might not have an idea for a long time, so then I do other things. I'm writing a book for adults now and I write in my diary and I write a lot of letters; I'm always writing something. I suppose if I lived exclusively from this I would get up every morning

"Keep your mouths shut," said Miss Swamp.

"Sit perfectly still," said Miss Swamp.

"And if you misbehave, you'll be sorry," said Miss Swamp.

■ (From *Miss Nelson Is Missing* by Harry Allard. Illustration from animated film adaptation. Released by Learning Corporation of America, 1979.)

(From the animated film "It's So Nice to Have a Wolf Around the House." Released by Learning Corporation of America, 1979.)

and sit down at nine o'clock to write, whether I was inspired or not. I don't really believe in inspiration. I think you just do it, that's all. If you wait for inspiration you might wait forever.''

Allard has also taught English for the Berlitz School in Paris, has been a legal translator of French to English, translator of

three children's books from German to English, and has made a career of teaching French on the college level. His interest in languages ''was always there. I remember when I went to high school in 1942 I took Latin. The first day I took Latin I absolutely loved it; I still do. All languages, all words, fascinate me. If I hear a word or see a word in any language that I know well or know even vaguely, I can't wait until I've looked it up in the dictionary and written it down and thought about it. I saw a chamber opera, . . . *The Lighthouse,* by Peter Maxwell Davies. It's about a true story that happened circa 1900: Three lighthouse keepers vanish in the north of Scotland, and one of the possible explanations is that the selkies got them. I looked up *selkies* and it's a word in Scottish mythology for half-seals, half-men. I didn't know that. I love that idea. I think it would make a wonderful ghost story for older children—about fifth or sixth grade, so they wouldn't be terrified. Say a boy from Florida or California goes to visit somebody in the north of Scotland. . . . That could be so spooky.''

Besides writing children's books, Allard enjoys translating them from German to English. ''I enjoy that very, very much. I'm only sorry that my German isn't as adequate as my French, but I can always figure it out. You read a sentence and then you ask yourself what you would have said as a child, or what a child from a cultivated milieu where they spoke correctly would have said in a given situation. It's really a recreation, and that's wonderful.

''I did one called *Three Is Company.* The title wasn't my idea and I don't like it; it's from the television program 'Three's Company.' But the book itself was beautifully done, written and illustrated by a German author-illustrator, Friedrich Karl Waechter, and I was really proud of that book. You know, you don't get much money when you translate—it's just a flat fee of something like five hundred dollars—and no one pays much attention to you, but I like doing it. Oddly enough, I've never had any French work at all. When I did German books, the German economy was going very well and there was a lot of creative energy in Germany, not only in books but in films.''

HOBBIES AND OTHER INTERESTS: Drawing, reading, listening to classical music, and learning languages.

FOR MORE INFORMATION SEE: Martha E. Ward and Dorothy A. Marquardt, *Authors of Books for Young People,* 2nd edition, Scarecrow, 1971; *New York Times Book Review,* May 5, 1974, April 17, 1977, November 6, 1977, November 13, 1977, May 21, 1978, April 22, 1979, April 12, 1981, April 26, 1981, November 14, 1982; *Washington Post Book World,* May 19, 1974, July 12, 1981; *New Yorker,* December 2, 1974; *New York Times,* December 12, 1974, December 8, 1977; *Newsweek,* July 18, 1977, December 19, 1977, December 6, 1982; *Commonweal,* November 11, 1977; *Saturday Review,* May 27, 1978; Sally Holmes Holtze, editor, *Fifth Book of Junior Authors and Illustrators,* H. W. Wilson, 1983.

ALLEN, Jeffrey (Yale)   1948-

PERSONAL: Born September 3, 1948, in Detroit, Mich.; son of Bernard (an advertising salesman, factory representative and co-owner of warehouse) and Laura (Sitorsky) Allen. *Education:* Attended Michigan State University, 1966-70; University of Michigan, B.A., 1971. *Religion:* Judaism. *Residence:* San Francisco, Calif. *Agent:* c/o Little, Brown & Co., 34 Beacon St., Boston, Mass. 02129; Viking Penguin, Inc., 40 West 23rd St., New York, N. Y. 10010.

CAREER: Detroit Free Press, Detroit, Mich., copyboy, 1967-68; *Boston Globe,* Boston, Mass., editorial assistant, 1974-76; *Chronicle,* Willimantic, Conn., reporter and editor, 1976-79; California Delta Newspapers, Pittsburg, Calif., reporter and editor, 1979-82; writer. Swimming coach and teacher.

Member: United States Masters Swimming Association, University of Michigan Alumni Association, American Swimming Coaches Association. *Awards, honors:* Children's Book Council selected *Bonzini! The Tattooed Man* for the Children's Book Showcase, 1977.

WRITINGS—All for children: *Mary Alice, Operator Number Nine* (illustrated by James Marshall), Little, Brown, 1975; *Bonzini! The Tattooed Man* (illustrated by J. Marshall), Little, Brown, 1976; *The Secret Life of Mr. Weird* (illustrated by Ned Delaney), Little, Brown, 1982; *Nosy Mrs. Rat,* Viking Penguin, 1985.

WORK IN PROGRESS: Several manuscripts for a series of self-illustrated picture books; a sequel to *Mary Alice, Operator Number Nine* entitled, *The Return of Mary Alice, Operator Number Nine.*

SIDELIGHTS: ''I was born the youngest of two sons and raised in Detroit, Michigan to a small, middle-class Jewish family. I was introduced at an early age to publishing by my uncle, a newspaper publisher, for whom my father worked as an advertising salesman.

''One vivid recollection of my rather mundane childhood is visiting my Uncle Harry's newspaper office with its dark oak walls, and smell of rubber cement and copy paper. The typewriters fascinated me, and I enjoyed playing with the keys.

''I was educated in the Detroit public schools. It wasn't until high school that I realized I had some writing talent. An English teacher required that we keep a daily journal in which we could write about whatever subject we chose. I received enormous satisfaction in recording my thoughts and opinions, from the civil rights fervor of the day to the death of a school chum in an automobile accident.

''My interest in writing was reinforced when I won a gold key and dictionary in a city-wide writing contest sponsored by the *Detroit News.*

''I dropped out of college during my junior year and found a job working as a copyboy for the *Detroit Free Press.* It gave me a first-hand look at the operations of a metropolitan daily, and I decided to become a newspaper reporter. I eventually returned to college, resuming studies in journalism and political science. In 1971, I graduated with a B.A. in liberal arts from the University of Michigan.

''After graduation, I lived briefly in San Francisco, but wound up in Boston where I worked as an editorial assistant with the *Boston Globe.* It was also in Boston where I met James Marshall who was to have an enormous influence on my career. I became good friends with Jim, who in 1974 was beginning to make a name for himself as an author and illustrator with his book *George and Martha,* a delightful children's book about two hippos.

''One day, Jim and I decided to see a movie matinee. I called the time service on the telephone to synchronize our watches, and jokingly mentioned that a duck had answered. I decided to write a story about this duck with the time service. Jim liked the manuscript, drew a few illustrations, and we took the package to John Keller, children's book editor at Little, Brown. A contract was drawn up, and my career as an author had begun.

''I was pleased when the book, *Mary Alice, Operator Number Nine* became a critical and commercial success. Imogene Coca,

Mary Alice felt bad about leaving her job. "Don't worry," clucked Boss Chicken. "I'll find someone to take your place. . . ." Mary Alice felt even worse. ■ (From *Mary Alice, Operator Number 9* by Jeffrey Allen. Illustrated by James Marshall.)

the comedienne, narrated the story on 'Captain Kangaroo.' I narrated the story for public educational television. The book went on to become published in Japanese and French and the paperback version was selected for Scholastic Book Service's Book Club.

"In 1976, Jim and I collaborated on a second book, *Bonzini! The Tattooed Man*. Although it didn't receive the commercial acclaim of *Mary Alice*, it was selected by the Children's Book Council in New York as one of the best-designed books of the year. It toured the United States on the Bicentennial Train as part of an exhibit of children's books.

"Jim and I are now working on a sequel to *Mary Alice*, appropriately called *The Return of Mary Alice, Operator Number Nine*.

"I've been encouraged by several people to illustrate my own text. I'm excited by the possibility of illustrating my own stories and creating a new dimension to my career. I've already started sketching for a series of books.

"I consider myself a storyteller first and not a 'children's book author.' My stories are for everyone, regardless of age. I'm not interested in becoming a moralist. If any of my stories have a moral or a lesson to be learned, it's incidental. I'm only interested in telling a good story, whatever its outcome."

HOBBIES AND OTHER INTERESTS: Competitive swimming. "I still compete in the Masters swimming program, and coach two swim teams of children, ages six through seventeen."

APPLE, Margot

BRIEF ENTRY: Born in Detroit, Mich. Illustrator of books for children. Apple is the product of an artistic household; her father was a musician and her mother an illustrator. A free-lance illustrator since she graduated from Pratt Institute, Margot Apple has provided illustrations for over twenty books by authors like Paul Fleischman, Dick King-Smith, and Jean Van Leeuwen. Her black-and-white line drawings have been described by critics as "delicate and deft" and "appropriately light-hearted." In a review of Van Leeuwen's humorous yet wistful *Benjy and the Power of the Zingies* (Dial, 1982), *Horn Book* observed that Apple's "soft pencil illustrations skillfully complement the mood and tone of the story, capturing the stance and expressions of the characters." Among Apple's other works are Jean Thompson's *Don't Forget Michael* (Morrow, 1979), Linda Allen's *Lionel and the Spy Next Door* (Morrow, 1980), King-Smith's *The Mouse Butcher* (Viking, 1982), and Fleischman's *Phoebe Danger, Detective, in the Case of the Two-Minute Cough* (Houghton, 1983). She has also illustrated 1979 editions of Beatrix Potter's *The Tale of Peter Rabbit* (Troll Associates) and Patrick Skene Catling's *The Chocolate Touch* (Morrow). In addition to illustrating, Apple enjoys sewing, knitting, gardening, and exploring flea markets. She and her husband reside in western New England.

ARNOW, Harriette (Louisa Simpson) 1908-

PERSONAL: Born July 7, 1908, in Wayne County, Ky.; daughter of Elias Thomas (a teacher, farmer, and oil well driller) and Mollie Jane (a teacher; maiden name, Denney) Simpson; married Harold B. Arnow (publicity director for Michigan Heart Association), March 11, 1939; children: Marcella Jane, Thomas Louis. *Education:* Berea College, student, 1924-26; University of Louisville, B.S., 1931. *Home:* 3220 Nixon Rd., R. Route 7, Ann Arbor, Mich. 48105.

CAREER: Author. *Member:* Authors Guild, American Civil Liberties Union, Women's International League for Peace and Freedom, PEN, Phi Beta Kappa (honorary). *Awards, honors:* Friends of American Writers award, an honorary degree from Albion College, Berea College Centennial award, *Woman's Home Companion* Silver Distaff award for "unique contribution by a woman to American life," all 1955, all for *The Dollmaker;* commendation from Tennessee Historical Commission and award of merit of American Association for State and Local History, both 1961, both for *Seedtime on the Cumberland; Tennessee Historical Quarterly* prize for best article

HARRIETTE ARNOW

of the year, 1962; Outstanding Alumni award, 1979, from the University of Louisville, College of Arts and Sciences; an honorary degree from Transylvania College, 1979, and University of Kentucky, 1981.

WRITINGS—Of interest to young adults: *Mountain Path* (novel), Covici-Friede, 1936; *Hunter's Horn* (novel), Macmillan, 1949; *The Dollmaker* (novel), Macmillan, 1954; *Seedtime on the Cumberland* (nonfiction), Macmillan, 1960; *Flowering of the Cumberland* (nonfiction), Macmillan, 1963; *The Weedkiller's Daughter* (novel), Knopf, 1970; *The Kentucky Trace: A Novel of the American Revolution*, Knopf, 1974; *Old Burnside* (nonfiction), University of Kentucky Press, 1978. Author of short stories in the 1930s, two of them anthologized in *O. Henry Memorial Award Prize Stories*. Contributor of articles and reviews to magazines.

SIDELIGHTS: "The greatest pleasure of my young life began before I was old enough to go to school. My sister, Elizabeth, and I looked forward to evenings when our father was home from work; after reading the daily paper, he had time to tell some of the many stories he knew. Several were handed-down tales from the Revolution and other wars, or stories of a grandfather's boyhood or his own. He was a great teller of ghost tales that made us shiver with fright as did his version of *Jack and the Beanstalk* during which we were for a time certain the giant with his roaring 'Fee fi fo fum' would catch Jack. We heard humorous stories, but some were so sad, tears would start dripping off my chin before he was finished. Thinking about a sad tale heard during the evening, I would cry myself to sleep.

"However, I soon began to imagine happy endings for the sad stories and stopped crying. That is how I began writing. I could even change a grandmother's blood-chilling tales of a family on the western borders of Virginia during the French and Indian war so that it had a happy ending.

"Elizabeth, though only two years older than I, read many stories to me: *King of the Golden River*, and others I wanted to hear over and over to reach that happy ending. There were only three children when we moved to the hill, but at the end of several years three more had been born.

"Our childhood home was on a level bench of wooded land on the side of a hill adjacent to the small town of Burnside in south central Kentucky. The family after moving from the country had lived in Burnside for several months while the home on the hill was being built. I was sorry to leave the lower town, a busy, noisy, exciting place with lumber mills, and log booms in the Cumberland near the mouth of Big South Fork. Best of all was the wharf where the paddle wheel steamboats from Nashville stopped to unload or take on cargo. The Southern Railway tracks, after crossing Cumberland River on a high bridge, came along the top of a steep hillside adjacent to the lowland.

"Past the railway, the land was level to rolling. Here were more homes, four churches, and the grade and high school in one building. During my first months on the hill, the only times I visited Burnside was on our weekly trips to Sunday School and church.

"I was soon enjoying life on the hill. Many trees had to be cut to make way for a yard, garden, orchard, and a 'view' for our mother. Our side of the hill faced west; we could see a part of Burnside, and farmland for miles beyond the river. We

William David, as usual when being carried, was quiet, and he meant for him to stay that way until the right time came. ■ (Jacket illustration by Richard Hess from *The Kentucky Trace: A Novel of the American Revolution* by Harriette Simpson Arnow.)

could hear the sounds of Burnside that had so annoyed our mother, but on the hill they were muted, even the roar of fast freights. The steamboat whistles were as music. I enjoyed wandering in the woods, especially in spring when the wild flowers were in bloom. Sometimes I climbed all the way to the top of the hill. Looking east, I could see nothing but other hills rising, higher than our own. I had heard of the 'backhills' and wanted to live among them and their people.

"The beginning of school in September left less time for wandering in the woods. The best parts of school were the stories our teacher read to us each day. Soon, I was able to read stories in the first reader. Shortly after Christmas, our mother decided I should be writing letters to my grandmothers. She helped me with spelling. I rather enjoyed writing letters, but often thought I would rather be writing stories. There were so many untold stories in the world."

Most of Arnow's books were written after her marriage to Harold Arnow. "I hope to be able to give most of my time to writing. Life in exurbia has been a trial both in the amount of time and mind that must go into such a complicated way of life, and the loss of casual contacts with people—housewife writers have little time for social lives."

FOR MORE INFORMATION SEE: New York Times, May 28, 1949; *Commonweal,* June 10, 1949; *New York Herald Tribune,* April 25, 1954; *New Yorker,* May 1, 1954; *Library Journal,* June 15, 1960, December 1, 1963, April 15, 1970; *Christian Science Monitor,* November 20, 1963; *Saturday Review,* November 23, 1963; *New York Times Book Review,* March 22, 1970.

BARKIN, Carol
(Beverly Hastings, a joint pseudonym)

BRIEF ENTRY: A graduate of Radcliffe College, Barkin and her husband have traveled extensively in Europe, the Far East, and the United States. It was while she was living on the West Coast that Barkin met author Elizabeth James. In the mid-1970s the two authors began a partnership that has produced over twenty nonfiction books for children and young adults. In an informative yet casual writing style, the Barkin-James team has covered a wide variety of topics. A sampling of their titles includes *Slapdash Alterations: How to Recycle Your Wardrobe* (Lathrop, 1977), *How to Keep a Secret: Writing and Talking in Code* (Lothrop, 1978), *How to Grow a Hundred Dollars* (Lothrop, 1979), *How to Write a Term Paper* (Lothrop, 1980), and *The Scary Halloween Costume Book* (Lothrop, 1983). Under the joint pseudonym Beverly Hastings, Barkin and James are the authors of three adult thrillers: *Don't Talk to Strangers, Rated X,* and *Secret.* Barkin has also edited and written for a children's periodical and has been employed as an editor in the United States and England.

There was an Old Man with a beard,
Who said, 'It is just as I feared!—
    Two Owls and a Hen,
    Four Larks and a Wren,
Have all built their nests in my beard!'

—Edward Lear

BARR, Jene   1900-1985
(Jene Barr Cohen)

OBITUARY NOTICE—See sketch in *SATA* Volume 16: Born July 28, 1900, in Kobrin, Russia (now U.S.S.R.); died April 5, 1985, in San Jose, Calif. Educator and author. Barr was a physical education instructor in the Chicago Public Schools for more than thirty years before her retirement in 1964. She was the author of numerous books for children, including *Ben's Busy Service Station, Mike the Milkman, Texas Pete, Little Cowboy, Mr. Mailman, Little Circus Dog,* and *Baker Bill.* Among the awards she received throughout her career were the Children's Reading Round Table Award and the Citation for Meritorious Service in the Field of Juvenile Literature from Friends of American Writers.

FOR MORE INFORMATION SEE: Authors of Books for Young People, Scarecrow, 1964; *Contemporary Authors,* Volumes 5-8, revised, Gale, 1969. Obituaries: *Chicago Sun-Times,* April 10, 1985; *Chicago Tribune,* April 11, 1985.

BARTHOLOMEW, Barbara   1941-

BRIEF ENTRY: Born in 1941. Author of fiction for young adults. Bartholomew is a native of Oklahoma who graduated from the Oklahoma School of Journalism. Among her seven young adult romance novels, all published by Signet Vista, are *Anne and Jay* (1982), *Mirror Image* (1983), *Someone New* (1984), and *Lucky at Love* (1985). Bartholomew's novel *Julie's Magic Moment* was chosen best teen romance novel of 1983 by Romance Writers of America and also received the Golden Medallion award for best young adult romance novel of 1983-84. In addition to romance novels, Bartholomew has written *The Great Gradepoint Mystery* (Macmillan, 1983) and two "Making Choices" books, *The Cereal Box Adventures* (1981) and *Flight into the Unknown* (1982), published by Chariot Books. Her most recent work is a fantasy trilogy in which four young adults discover a pathway through time. The titles of their adventures are *The Timeskeeper, Child of Tomorrow,* and *When Dreamers Cease to Dream* (all Signet Vista, 1985). Bartholomew is also a well-known contributor of short stories to magazines, including *Seventeen.* She is married to a computer system analyst, and they have one child. *Residence:* Dallas, Texas.

BERGER, Gilda

BRIEF ENTRY: A teacher of special education, Berger is the author of more than twenty nonfiction books for young adults. Among the varied topics her books explore are physical disorders, geography, animals, holidays, and religion. In *Addiction: Its Causes, Problems, and Treatments* (F. Watts, 1982), she examines the abuse of legal and illegal substances such as drugs, tobacco, alcohol, caffeine, and food. *Booklist* observed that she handled the subject "with customary thoroughness and control," and *Appraisal* stated that "all in all, this book has much to recommend it as a sober, reasoned introduction to the subject of addiction. . . ." She was also lauded for *The Southeast States* (F. Watts, 1984) which *School Library Journal* called an "excellent introduction to the area."

Berger has written several books with her husband, Melvin Berger. *Booklist* described the husband-and-wife team as "prolific and reliable authors of nonfiction books for young

people." Between them, the Bergers have produced more than seventy books. A number of them have been selected as Outstanding Trade Books by the National Science Teachers Association and the Children's Book Council. In addition the books have received awards from the Child Study Association, the Library of Congress, and the New York Public Library. Among the Bergers' joint works are *"Fitting in": Animals in Their Habitats* (Coward, 1976), *The New Food Book: Nutrition, Diet, Consumer Tips, and Foods of the Future* (Crowell, 1978), and *The Whole World of Hands* (Houghton, 1982). Gilda Berger's own works include *Home Economics Careers* (F. Watts, 1977), *Mountain Worlds: What Lives There* (Coward, 1978), *The Gifted and Talented* (F. Watts, 1980), *Easter and Other Spring Holidays* (F. Watts, 1983), and *PMS: Premenstrual Syndrome* (F. Watts, 1984). *Home:* 18 Glamford Rd., Great Neck, N.Y. 11023.

BLAKE, Robert   1949-

PERSONAL: Born May 10, 1949, in Paterson, N.J.; son of Harris an oral surgeon and Bernice (a schoolteacher; maiden name, Hack) Blake. *Education:* University of Pennsylvania, B.A., 1972. *Politics:* "Uncommitted." *Religion:* Jewish. *Home:* Shmuel Hanagid St. #8, Jerusalem, Israel.

CAREER: Musician.

WRITINGS: 101 Elephant Jokes (paperback; illustrated by William Hogarth), Scholastic Book Services, 1964.

SIDELIGHTS: "I wrote and compiled *101 Elephant Jokes* at the age of fourteen when I was a junior high school student.

ROBERT BLAKE

How do you fit six elephants in your car?
Three in the back; three in the front!

■ (From *101 Elephant Jokes,* compiled by Robert Blake. Illustrated by William Hogarth.)

Now, twenty years later, it is still in print and remains popular among today's youth. My real vocation, however, is music. I play the piano and sing popular songs here in Jerusalem where I have made my home. I have more than one thousand songs in my repertory. Next time you're in the neighborhood, stop in to see me and I'll sing your favorite songs!''

BOEGEHOLD, Betty (Doyle) 1913-1985 (Donovan Doyle)

OBITUARY NOTICE: Born September 15, 1913, in New York, N.Y.; died of an apparent heart attack, April 7, 1985, in Bronxville, N.Y. Educator, librarian, editor, and author. Boegehold's career included positions as a teacher, librarian, assistant principal, workshop director, and remedial reading specialist. She was the author of over a dozen books for children, including *Three to Get Ready, Pippa Mouse,* and *In the Castle of Cats.* Under the pseudonym Donovan Doyle, she wrote *Gray Gull, Bugs,* and *The Woman Who Couldn't Keep a Secret.* In her most recent works, Boegehold dealt with situations faced by many children in today's society: *You Can Say ''No'': A Book about Protecting Yourself,* written with Carolyn Bracken, and *Daddy Doesn't Live Here Anymore: A Book about Divorce.*

FOR MORE INFORMATION SEE: Contemporary Authors, New Revision Series, Volume 12, Gale, 1984. Obituaries: *New York Times,* April 9, 1985.

'Tis an old said saw. Children and fools speak true.
—John Lyly

BRENNER, Barbara (Johnes) 1925-

PERSONAL: Born June 26, 1925, in Brooklyn, N.Y.; daughter of Robert Lawrence (a real estate broker) and Marguerite (Furboter) Johnes; married Fred Brenner (an illustrator), March 16, 1947; children: Mark, Carl. *Education:* Seton Hall College (now University), student, 1942-43; extension courses at Rutgers, The State University, 1944-46; studies painting at New York University, 1953-54; also attended New School for Social Research, 1960-62. *Politics:* Independent. *Religion:* Jewish. *Home:* Box 1826, Hemlock Farms, Hawley, Pa. 18428.

CAREER: Prudential Insurance Co., Newark, N.J., copywriter, 1942-46; free-lance artist's agent, 1946-52; free-lance writer, mainly of juvenile works, 1957—; Bank Street College of Education, Publications Division, writer-consultant, 1962—; Bank Street College, instructor, 1974-80. Parson's School of Design, New York, N.Y., instructor, 1980-81. Committee for a Sane Nuclear Policy, county chairman, 1960-61. Associate Editor for Bank Street College Media Group. *Member:* Authors Guild, P.E.N., National Audubon Society. *Awards, honors: New York Herald Tribune* Children's Spring Book Festival honor book award, 1961, for *Barto Takes the Subway; Book World* Children's Spring Book Festival honor book award, 1970, for *A Snake-Lover's Diary; New York Times* selected *A Snake-Lovers Diary* as one of the best children's books, 1970; Outstanding Science Book award from the National Science Teachers Association and the Children's Book Council, 1974, for *Baltimore Orioles,* 1975, for *Lizard Tails and Cactus Spines,* 1977, for *On the Frontier with Mr. Audubon,* 1979, for *Beware! These Animals Are Poison,* and 1980, for *Have You Heard of a Kangaroo Bird?: Fascinating Facts about Unusual*

BARBARA BRENNER

Once I saw her standing on the doghouse with a balloon tied around her. ■ (From *The Flying Patchwork Quilt* by Barbara Brenner. Illustrated by Fred Brenner.)

Birds; On the Frontier with Mr. Audubon was selected one of *School Library Journal's* Best Books, 1977.

WRITINGS—Juvenile, except as noted: *Somebody's Slippers, Somebody's Shoes,* W. R. Scott, 1957; *Barto Takes the Subway* (photographs by Sy Katzoff), Knopf, 1961; *A Bird in the Family* (illustrated by husband, Fred Brenner; Junior Literary Guild selection), W. R. Scott, 1962; *Amy's Doll* (photographs by S. Katzoff), 1963; *The Five Pennies* (illustrated by Erik Blegvad), Knopf, 1963; *Careers and Opportunities in Fashion* (a young adult), Dutton, 1964; *The Flying Patchwork Quilt* (illustrated by F. Brenner; Junior Literary Guild selection), W. R. Scott, 1965; *Beef Stew* (illustrated by John E. Johnson), Knopf, 1965; *Mr. Tall and Mr. Small,* (illustrated by Tomi Ungerer), W. R. Scott, 1966; *Nicky's Sister* (illustrated by J. E. Johnson), Knopf, 1966; *Summer of the Houseboat* (illustrated by F. Brenner), Knopf, 1968.

A Snake-Lover's Diary (illustrated with photographs; ALA Notable Book), W. R. Scott, 1970; *Faces* (illustrated with photographs by George Ancona), Dutton, 1970; *A Year in the Life of Rosie Bernard* (illustrated by Joan Sandin), Harper, 1971, revised edition, Avon, 1983; *Is it Bigger than a Sparrow?: A Book for Young Bird Watchers* (illustrated by Michael Eagle), Knopf, 1972; *Mystery of the Plumed Serpent* (illustrated by Blanche Sims), Houghton, 1972; *Bodies* (illustrated with photographs by G. Ancona), Dutton, 1973; *If You Were an Ant* (illustrated by F. Brenner), Harper, 1973; *Hemi, a Mule* (illustrated by J. Winslow Higginbottom), Harper, 1973; (reteller) *Walt Disney's "The Three Little Pigs,"* Random House, 1973; (reteller) *Walt Disney's "The Penguin That Hated the*

Cold", Random House, 1973; *Baltimore Orioles* (illustrated by J. W. Higginbottom), Harper, 1974; *Lizard Tales and Cactus Spines* (illustrated with photographs by Merritt S. Keasey III), Harper, 1975; *Tracks,* Macmillan, 1975; *Pen Pal from Another Planet,* Macmillan, 1975; *Cunningham's Rooster* (illustrated by Anne Rockwell), Parents Magazine Press, 1975.

Little One Inch (illustrated by F. Brenner), Coward, 1977; *On the Frontier with Mr. Audubon* (illustrated with photographs and historic paintings), Coward, 1977; *We're Off to See the Lizard* (illustrated by Shelley Dieterichs), Raintree, 1977; *The Color Bear,* Center for Media Development, 1978; *Ostrich Feathers* (two-act play; first produced off-Broadway, 1965; illustrated by Vera B. Williams), Parents Magazine Press, 1978; *Wagon Wheels* (illustrated by Don Bolognese; ALA Notable Book), Harper, 1978; *Beware! These Animals Are Poison* (illustrated by Jim Spanfeller), Coward, 1979; (with May Garelick) *The Tremendous Tree Book* (illustrated by F. Brenner), Four Winds Press, 1979.

The Prince and the Pink Blanket (illustrated by Nola Langner), Four Winds Press, 1980; *Have You Ever Heard of a Kangaroo Bird?: Fascinating Facts about Unusual Birds* (illustrated by Irene Brady), Coward, 1980; *A Killing Season,* Four Winds Press, 1981; *Mystery of the Disappearing Dogs* (illustrated by B. Sims), Knopf, 1982; *A Dog I Know* (illustrated by F. Brenner), Harper, 1983; *Love and Discipline* (adult), Ballantine, 1983; *Bank Street's Family Guide to Home Computers* (adult), Ballantine, 1984; *The Gorilla Signs Love,* Lothrop, 1984; *The Snow Parade* (illustrated by Mary Tara O'Keefe) Crown, 1984; (with Betty Boegehold and Joanne Oppenheim) *Raising a Confident Child* (adult), Pantheon, 1985.

Editor: Edward Turner and Clive Turner, *Frogs and Toads,* Raintree, 1976; Ralph Whitlock, *Spiders,* Raintree, 1976. Contributor of articles to periodicals, including *Cricket* and *Sierra Club.*

WORK IN PROGRESS: A sequel to *A Year in the Life of Rosie Bernard,* which will take Rosie up to age sixteen and the beginning of World War II; a book for parents on choosing appropriate books for children of various ages, written with Joanne Oppenheim.

SIDELIGHTS: "My mother died when I was a year old and I was brought up in a household of loving aunts, uncles, grandparents and cousins my age. We lived in Brooklyn, which still has a special quality for me.

"When I was a little girl I had four books—*The Tale of Peter Rabbit* by Beatrix Potter; *When We Were Very Young* by A. A. Milne; *Pinocchio* by Collodi; *Blackie's Children's Annual,* an anthology of Blackie & Sons. I still remember those books vividly. I wish I still had them. They taught me to fantasize. They taught me to read. They taught me how wonderful books can be. I think they may have been somewhat responsible for my becoming a writer of children's books. Anyway, I know that books can make a difference in your life.

"I have always been interested in the aura of places. As I grew older and moved around, first to New Jersey, then, when I was married, to New York City and its suburbs, I was still affected, eye and mind, by where I was. I think this shows clearly in my work."

A teacher in grade school was the first person who encouraged Brenner to write stories. "I have been interested in writing since I was nine years old, although I took almost every detour one could imagine before I got to doing what I wanted to do. But I guess you finally write because you can't help it, and I started working at it seriously when I was about twenty-five. I write for young people because I feel a special sense of communications with them. What I hope I'm saying in all my books, beneath the obvious theme or plot, is that the world is a vastly interesting and exciting place, that it is good to be curious, that biologically we are part of a vast and remarkable chain of life.

"All this may seem vague, but I think that if you read my work it speaks to these ideas rather consistently. I am particularly interested in nature and so several of my books have themes related to nature and natural science.

"Most of my books have a natural history component; I write about what I like—snakes, spiders, mules, roosters, dogs, cats, ants, gorillas, bears—all of these creatures have found their way into my work.

"I am also interested in the education of both parents and children. Several of my books are directed to parents—*Love and Discipline, Bank Street's Family Computer Book,* and *Raising a Confident Child.* In particular, my work for Bank Street College of Education has been mainly in the area of reading books for urban children with special focus on literature for minority groups.

"My job as editor at Bank Street College has enabled me to get another perspective on children, parents, and on children's learning, as well as on some of the new forms of communication available to kids. I now write material for computer software and for other electronic media, as well as continuing my work as an author of children's and adult books. Presently we are designing computer software and teacher guides that will maximize its effectiveness in the classroom. I consider this new direction a tremendous learning experience for me and an opportunity to keep up with a world that is changing all the time."

Brenner's ideas for books come from many sources, including: "My own reading and my hobbies and interests. I read a couple of books a week. My children's interests very often spark an idea, and I also have a group of young friends who can usually be depended upon to contribute ideas.

"Let's go in the water right away."

"No, let's go on some rides first. Then we'll go in the water." ■ (From *A Year in the Life of Rosie Bernard* by Barbara Brenner. Illustrated by Joan Sandin.)

One day the King was feeling especially cranky. So when Prince Hal strolled past the throne room with his blanket dragging and his thumb in his mouth, King Hal the First flew into a *royal* rage!

(From *The Prince and the Pink Blanket* by Barbara Brenner. Illustrated by Nola Langner.)

A tropical bird called the *finfoot* has been nicknamed the *kangaroo bird*. . . . The male carries the young in pockets under its wings. ■ (From *Have You Ever Heard of a Kangaroo Bird?* by Barbara Brenner. Illustrated by Irene Brady.)

"I consider writing books for children a very difficult and challenging art form. Because writing has been such a tremendous 'kick' for me, I spend a great deal of time helping teachers to help children to express themselves through writing.

"I also enjoy very much talking with children about their own writing. I'm really happy to see that more and more schools are focusing on children's writing and that kids are beginning to make their own books, with illustrations. Fred [Brenner's husband] and I love to go to schools and share with young people our common experiences in doing a book. We find that the process is very much the same—that is, amateur or professional, you're still faced with that blank page and the need to put your thoughts and ideas in order. Children should be comforted by the fact that we writers and illustrators struggle with the same things they struggle with."

A Bird in the Family was the first of many of Brenner's books to be illustrated by her husband, Fred. It was a Junior Literary Guild selection and a "more than slightly autobiographical" account of a family who lived with a parakeet in a New York City apartment.

"The idea for *The Flying Patchwork Quilt* took shape when my son Carl went through what is referred to in our house as a 'flying stage.' During this time he tried constantly and unsuccessfully to become airborne. Since this was the second time I had encountered this phase (my older boy, too, had a flying stage), I decided there must be something fairly typical in it. When I sat down to write *Quilt,* it practically wrote itself. I had never before written a story that unfolded so completely as I wrote it.

"The quilt of the story is modeled after an old patchwork quilt that I bought several years ago. The children have always been fond of it, and for that reason I thought it would be interesting to use it as the focal point of a fantasy.

"When the time came to do the drawings, Fred researched the neighborhood thoroughly for the proper kind of setting into which to put the family. Many of the scenes in the book are authentic sketches of West Nyack sites. A little girl we know posed for the Ellen of the story, and a young man of our acquaintance was the model for Carl. You might say that *The Flying Patchwork Quilt* was a community project, in a sense. That is, it's an authentic story of something that never happened!

"In 1977, my husband and I moved to a wonderful house that overlooks a wild lake in Pennsylvania. He is an artist-illustrator and both of us have found a great deal of satisfaction in our work in this lovely spot. It's wildflower walks and blueberry-picking, swimming, canoeing, tennis. Lovely."

HOBBIES AND OTHER INTERESTS: Organic gardening, yoga, sports, travel, fossil hunting, bird-watching, and animal behavior. "I play the recorder (badly), enjoy cooking, hate housework, adore my husband and family, and write because there's nothing that gives me more satisfaction. My problem is that I enjoy everything. And there's not time for it all!"

FOR MORE INFORMATION SEE: Library Journal, July, 1968, May 15, 1970; *Horn Book,* August, 1970; Doris de Montreville and Elizabeth D. Crawford, editors *Fourth Book of Junior Authors and Illustrators,* H. W. Wilson, 1978.

BRETT, Jan 1949-
(Jan Brett Bowler)

PERSONAL: Born December 1, 1949, in Hingham, Mass.; daughter of George (a sales engineer) and Jean (Thaxter) Brett; married Daniel Bowler, February 27, 1970 (divorced, 1979); married Joseph Hearne (a musician), August 18, 1980; children: (first marriage) Lia. *Education:* Attended Colby-Sawyer College, 1968-69, Boston Museum of Fine Arts School, 1970. *Home:* 132 Pleasant St., Norwell, Mass. 02061.

CAREER: Painter; author and illustrator of books for young people. *Awards, honors:* Parent's Choice Award for illustration in children's books, Parent's Choice Foundation, 1981, for *Fritz and the Beautiful Horses* and *St. Patrick's Day in the Morning; In the Castle of Cats* and *Fritz and the Beautiful Horses* were chosen as "Children's Choices" by the International Reading Association, 1982; Ambassador of Honor, English-Speaking Union of the United States, 1983, for *Some Birds Have Funny Names;* Gene Shalit NBC Television Best of the Year Award, 1983, for calendar for Sunrise Publication.

WRITINGS—For children; self-illustrated: *Fritz and the Beautiful Horses,* Houghton, 1981; *Good Luck Sneakers,* Houghton, 1981; *Annie and the Wild Animals,* Houghton, 1985.

Illustrator; all for children: (Under name Jan Brett Bowler) Stephen Krensky, *Woodland Crossings,* Atheneum, 1978; Mary Louise Cuneo, *Inside a Sand Castle and Other Secrets,* Houghton, 1979; Seymour Simon, *The Secret Clocks: Time*

JAN BRETT

Outside, the mountains were as green as cats' eyes. Clouds hung in tatters around their tops. ■
(From *St. Patrick's Day in the Morning* by Eve Bunting. Illustrated by Jan Brett.)

Senses of Living Things, Viking, 1979; Eve Bunting, *St. Patrick's Day in the Morning,* Clarion Books, 1980; Mark Taylor, *Young Melvin and Bulger,* Doubleday, 1981; Betty Boegehold, *In the Castle of the Cats,* Dutton, 1981; Diana Harding Cross, *Some Birds Have Funny Names,* Crown, 1981; Ruth Krauss, *I Can Fly,* Golden Press, 1981; E. Bunting, *The Valentine Bears,* Clarion Books, 1983; D. H. Cross, *Some Plants Have Funny Names,* Crown, 1983; M. Taylor, *The Great Rescue,* Parker Brothers, 1984; Jennifer Perryman, *Where Are All the Kittens?,* Random House, 1984; E. Bunting, *Old Devil Is Waiting,* Harcourt, 1985. Also illustrator of a calendar for Sunrise Publication, 1983.

ADAPTATIONS: "The Great Rescue" (cassette), Parker Brothers, 1984.

SIDELIGHTS: Brett lives in a seacoast town in Massachusetts close to where she grew up. During the summer her family moves to a cabin in the Berkshire Mountains. It is there that her husband plays with the Boston Symphony at Tanglewood and Brett paints. She finds the beautiful music, birds, wild animals and the shimmering lake make a perfect place to work.

As a child, Brett decided to be an illustrator and spent many hours reading and drawing. "I remember the special quiet of rainy days when I felt that I could enter the pages of my beautiful picture books. Now I try to recreate that feeling of believing that the imaginary place I'm drawing really exists. The detail in my work helps to convince me, and I hope others as well, that such places might be real."

Brett says that all her ideas come from her memory. As a student at the Boston Museum School she spent many hours in the Museum of Fine Arts. "It was overwhelming to see roomsize landscapes and towering stone sculpture, and then moments later to refocus on delicately embroidered kimonos and ancient porcelain. I'm delighted and surprised when fragments of these beautiful images come back to me in my painting."

BROCK, C(harles) E(dmund)   1870-1938

PERSONAL: Born February 5, 1870, in Holloway, London, England; died February 28, 1938, in Cambridge, England; son of Edmund Brock; married Annie Dudley Smith. *Education:* Studied art under sculptor, Henry Wiles. *Residence:* Cranford, Cambridge, England.

CAREER: Book illustrator and portrait painter. Work exhibited at the Royal Academy and the Royal Institute, 1910, 1911, 1913-15, 1933-34, 1936. *Member:* Royal Institute of Painters in Water Colours.

ILLUSTRATOR: J. R. Johnson, *The Parachute and Other Bad Shots* (verse), Routledge, 1891; Canon Atkinson, *Scenes in Fairyland,* Macmillan (London), 1892; Edwin S. Hartland, *English Fairy and Folk Tales,* W. Scott, 1893; James Barr, editor, *The Humour of America,* Sharon Hill, 1893; Hans Casenov, *The Humour of Germany,* W. Scott, 1893; Thomas Hood, *Humorous Poems,* Macmillan (London), 1893; J. R. Johnson, *The Knight of Grazinbrook,* Routledge, 1893; Jonathan Swift, *Travels into Several Remote Nations of the World by Lemuel Gulliver,* Macmillan (London), 1894, facsimile reprint published as *Gulliver's Travels,* 1980; (with brother, Henry M. Brock) *History Readers: Book II,* Macmillan (London), 1894.

John Galt, *Annals of the Parrish and the Ayrshire Legatees,* Macmillan (London), 1895; Hedley Peek, *Nema and Other Stories,* Chapman & Hall, 1895; Jane Austen, *Pride and Prejudice,* Macmillan (London), 1895, new edition, Dent, 1907; (with others) H. Peek, editor, *The Poetry of Sport,* Longmans, Green, 1896; William Canton, *W. V.: Her Book, and Various Verses,* Isbister, 1896; Charles Kingsley, *Westward Ho!,* two volumes, Macmillan (London), 1896; W. Canton, *The Invisible Playmate* [*and*] *W. V.: Her Book,* Isbister, 1897; Sir Walter Scott, *Ivanhoe,* Service & Paton, 1897 [another edition illustrated with H. M. Brock, two volumes included in *The Temple Classics for Young People,* Dent, 1899]; William Cowper, *The Diverting History of John Gilpin,* Aldine House, 1898; Sir Walter Scott, *The Lady of the Lake,* Service & Paton,

C. E. BROCK

1898; Daniel Defoe, *The Life and Adventures of Robinson Crusoe*, Service & Paton, 1898; *Second French Book*, Dent, 1898; (with H. M. Brock) J. Austen, *The Novels of Jane Austen*, ten volumes, edited by R. Brimley Johnson, Dent, 1898; Oliver Goldsmith, *The Vicar of Wakefield*, Service & Paton, 1898, new edition, Dent, 1904; G. J. Whyte-Melville, *M or N*, Thacker, 1899; Agnes Hohler, *The Bravest of Them All: A Story for Young People*, Macmillan (London), 1899.

James Fenimore Cooper, *The Pathfinder; or, The Inland Sea*, Macmillan, 1900; *Une Joyeuse Nichée*, Dent, 1900; Kate D. Wiggin, *Penelope's English Experiences*, Houghton, 1900, later edition published as *Penelope's Experiences in England*, A. & C. Black, 1930; Charles Lamb, *The Essays of Elia*, Dent, 1900, Dutton, 1929; K. D. Wiggin, *Penelope's Experiences in Scotland*, Houghton, 1900; J. F. Cooper, *The Prairie: A Tale*, Macmillan, 1900; K. D. Wiggin, *A Cathedral Courtship*, Houghton, 1901; C. Lamb, *The Last Essays of Elia*, two

volumes, Scribner, 1901; K. D. Wiggin, *Penelope's Irish Experiences*, Houghton, 1902; William Makepeace Thackeray, *The Prose Works of William Makepeace Thackeray*, edited by W. Jerrold, Dent, 1902; C. Lamb, *The Works of Charles Lamb*, twelve volumes, edited by William Macdonald, Dutton, 1903; Elizabeth C. Gaskell, *Cranford*, Dent, 1904, Dutton, 1926; C. Lamb and Mary Ann Lamb, *Mrs. Leicester's School*, Wells Gardner, 1904; Mary R. Mitford, *Our Village*, Dent, 1904.

George Eliot (pseudonym of Mary Ann Evans), *Silas Marner*, Dent, 1905; (with H. R. Millar) Edith Nesbit, *Oswald Bastable and Others* (short stories), Wells Gardner, 1905, reprinted, Dover, 1960; Washington Irving, *The Keeping of Christmas at Bracebridge Hall*, Dutton, 1906, reprinted, 1927; Anne Manning, *The Household of Sir Thomas More*, Dent, 1906; E. Nesbit, *The Railway Children*, Wells Gardner, 1906, Macmillan, 1915, reprinted, Penguin, 1970; J. Austen, *Northanger Abbey*, Dent, 1907; *Atlas Reminiscent*, Dent, 1908;

Margaret S. Masters, *The Knights of Compassion*, Wells Gardner, 1908; J. Austen, *Mansfield Park*, Dent, 1908, Dutton, 1928; J. Austen, *Sense and Sensibility*, Dent, 1908, Dutton, 1928; J. Austen, *Emma*, Dent, 1909; *A Day Book for Girls*, Hodder & Stoughton, 1909; Lucas Malet, *Little Peter*, Hodder & Stoughton, 1909; J. Austen, *Persuasion*, Dent, 1909.

(With Charles E. Brittan) Richard D. Blackmore, *Lorna Doone: A Romance of Exmoor*, Sampson Low, 1910; W. Irving, *The Sketch Book*, Cassell, 1910; W. Irving, *Tales from the Alhambra*, adapted by Josephine Brower, Houghton, 1910; T. H. Orpen, *The Rain Children*, Society for the Propagation of Christian Knowledge, 1910; Rudyard Kipling, *Rewards and Fairies*, Macmillan (London), 1910, reprinted, Pan Books, 1975; May Byron, *The Garden of Love*, Hodder & Stoughton, 1910; Juliana H. Ewing, *Mrs. Overtheway's Remembrances*, Hodder & Stoughton, 1911; Dinah Maria Craik, *John Halifax, Gentleman*, Cassell, 1911; Charles J. Lee, *The Widow Woman*, Dent, 1911; Maurice Clare (pseudonym of May Clarissa Gillington), *Days with the Great Writers*, Hodder & Stoughton, 1911; John J. Farnol, *The Broad Highway*, Sampson Low, 1912, A. L. Burt, 1920; Violet Bratby, *The Capel Cousins*, Hodder & Stoughton, 1912; M. S. Masters, *The King's Scout*, Wells Gardner, 1912; Walter Raymond, *Tryphena in Love* [and] *Young Sam and Sabina*, Dutton, 1912; Samuel R. Crockett, *Sweethearts at Home*, Hodder & Stoughton, 1912; J. J. Far-

Frank carried me piggy-back to my aunt's house. ■ (From *Rewards and Fairies* by Rudyard Kipling. Illustrated by C. E. Brock.)

The battle was brief, for Childers lacked the other's reach and knowledge of the noble art. ■ (From *Nancy Owlett* by Eden Phillpotts. Illustrated by C. E. Brock.)

nol, *The Honourable Mr. Tawnish*, Sampson Low, 1913; Ian Hay, *Happy Go Lucky*, Blackwood, 1913; Mrs. H. de la Pasteur (pseudonym of E. M. Delafield), *The Unlucky Family*, Hodder & Stoughton, 1914; Arthur Quiller-Couch, *Troy Town*, Dent, 1914; Frank Stockton, *Rudder Grange*, Dent, 1914; J. J. Farnol, *The Amateur Gentleman*, Sampson Low, 1916; O. Goldsmith, *She Stoops to Conquer*, Ginn, 1917; Alpha of the Plough (pseudonym of Alfred George Gardiner), *Pebbles on the Shore*, Dent, 1917.

Henry C. Cook, *Littleman's Book of Courtesy*, Dent, 1920; Herbert Strang, *Bright Ideas*, Humphrey Milford, 1920; Brenda Girvin, *Jenny Wren*, Humphrey Milford, 1920; Eleanor Farjeon, *Martin Pippin in the Apple Orchard*, Collins, 1921; Richard Bird, *The Rival Captains*, Hodder & Stoughton, 1922; Hylton Cleaver, *The Old Order*, Humphrey Milford, 1922; H. Strang (pseudonym of George Herbert Ely and C. J. L'Estrange) *Winning His Name*, Humphrey Milford, 1922; Moses Gaster, *Children's Stories from Rumanian Legends and Fairy Tales*, R. Tuck, 1923; H. Strang, *True as Steel*, Humphrey Milford, 1923; Annette Reid, *Off the High Road: Stories of English Village Life*, W. Heffer, 1923; Ethel Corkey, *The Magic Circle*, Blackie & Son, 1924; Frances H. Burnett, *Little Lord Fauntleroy*, F. Warne, 1925; (with others) Edric Vredenburg, editor, *The Book for Boys*, R. Tuck, 1927; (with H. M. Brock) Louey Chisholm, compiler, *The Golden Staircase*, T. C. &

E. C. Jack, 1928; Robert L. Stevenson, *Catriona*, Macmillan (London), 1928; (with W. R. Flint) William Gilbert, *The Mikado*, Macmillan (London), 1928, Mayflower Books, 1979; C. Lamb, *The Collected Essays of Charles Lamb*, two volumes, Dent, 1929; (with W. R. Flint) W. Gilbert, *The Yeoman of the Guard*, Macmillan (London), 1929, reprinted, Mayflower Books, 1979.

Annie Keary and Eliza Keary, *The Heroes of Asgard: Tales from Scandinavian Mythology*, Macmillan (London), 1930, reprinted, Mayflower Books, 1979; Mary L. Molesworth, *The Cuckoo Clock*, Macmillan (London), 1931, Penguin, 1941, reprinted, Mayflower Books, 1980; George Mills, *Meredith and Company*, Oxford University Press, 1933; Eden Philpotts, *Nancy Owlett*, R. Tuck, 1933; J. J. Farnol, *Way Beyond*, Little, Brown, 1933; (with H. R. Millar) Rudyard Kipling, *All the Puck Stories*, Macmillan (London), 1935; John Galt, *The Works of John Galt*, ten volumes, edited by D. S. Meldrum and William Roughead, John Grant, 1936; (with H. M. Brock) Theodora Wilson-Wilson, *Through the Bible*, Collins, 1938; (with H. M. Brock) *The Golden Book of Bible Stories: Favorite Stories from the Old and New Testaments Retold for Children*, Grosset, 1941; (with H. M. Brock) Margaret Tempest and Kathleen Fryer, *Stories from the Bible*, Collins, 1955; M. Tempest and K. Fryer, *Stories from the Old Testament*, Collins, 1955; (with H. M. Brock and Irene Mountford) Lucy Diamond, *Bible Story*, Collins, 1957.

All written by Charles Dickens: *The Holly Tree* [and] *The Seven Poor Travellers*, Lippincott, 1900; *A Christmas Carol: In Prose, Being a Ghost Story for Christmas*, Dutton, 1905, reprinted, 1960; *The Chimes*, Dent, 1905; *The Cricket on the Hearth: A Fairy Tale of Home*, Dutton, 1905; *Christmas Books* (contains *The Cricket on the Hearth*, *A Christmas Carol*, *The Battle of Life*, *Haunted Man*, and *The Chimes*), Dutton, 1905; *The Battle of Life*, Dutton, 1907; *The Haunted Man* [and] *The Ghost's Bargain: A Fancy for Christmas Time*, Dutton, 1907; *Doctor Marigold*, T. N. Foulis, 1908; *A Christmas Tree*, Hodder & Stoughton, 1911; *Christmas Stories* (contains *A Christmas Carol*, *The Chimes*, *The Cricket on the Hearth*, *Mugby Junction*, and *The Seven Poor Travellers*), Ginn, 1927; *The Posthumous Papers of the Pickwick Club*, Dodd, 1930; *The Life and Adventures of Nicholas Nickleby*, Dodd, 1931; *The Life and Adventures of Martin Chuzzlewit*, Harrap, 1932, Dodd, 1935; *A Christmas Carol: In Prose, Being a Ghost Story for Christmas* [and] *The Cricket on the Hearth: A Tale of Home*, Dutton, 1963.

Also illustrator of (frontispiece) Leo Tolstoi, *The Vow*, 1909; E. Phillips Oppenheim, *Jeanne of the Marshes*, 1909; *Stories from the Classics*, Houghton; *Tales That Thrill*, R. Tuck, circa 1930; (with others) *The Book of Adventure and Sport*, R. Tuck, circa 1930; *The Glowing Bird and the Grey Wolf*, R. Tuck; Sharpe, *The Youngest Girl in School*, Macmillan; Sharpe, *Who Was Jane?*, Macmillan; (covers and frontispieces) *Herbert*

I was in the utmost astonishment, and roared so loud, that they all ran back in a fright.... ■
(From *Travels into Several Remote Nations of the World by Lemuel Gulliver* by Jonathan Swift. Illustrated by C. E. Brock.)

C. E. Brock, about 1928.

Strang's Library of Children's Classics. Illustrated book jackets of most of the popular editions of J. J. Farnol's books. Contributor of illustrations to periodicals, including *Punch, Graphic, Bookman,* and *Captain.*

SIDELIGHTS: Born **February 5, 1870** in Holloway, London, England, Brock was the eldest of a quartet of artist brothers: Charles, Richard, Tom, and Harry. The Brocks worked together in a studio built in the garden of their old home.

Biographer C. M. Kelly [*The Brocks: A Family of Cambridge Artists and Illustrators,* Skilton, 1975.¹] discovered that "by a very remarkable coincidence there was a separate family of Brocks who were also artists and sculptors, and exactly contemporary with the Brocks of Cambridge. They were Londoners; Sir Thomas Brock, sculptor, had a son called, above all things, Charles Edmond Brock, who painted portraits. He lived in Cavendish Avenue, NW8, and the confusion between this man and Charles Edmund Brock of Cambridge, who also painted portraits, can be imagined ... they even found themselves paying each other's bills! Finally they came to an agreement that the Cambridge one would stop using the Edmund, and the London one would stop using the Charles. It seemed certain that there must be a common ancestry leading to the use of those particular Christian names—but there is no link between them this side of 1740, at any rate.

"What is certain is that the artistic ability came from the mother's side. She was a Pegram and the Pegrams were notable artists. There was Alfred Bertram Pegram (1873-1941) sculptor, creator of 'numerous works decorative and monumental in Britain and the United States.' There was Henry Pegram,

R.A., sculptor (1862-1937), who not only received medals for works shown at the Paris and Dresden exhibitions—groups with titles such as 'Labour,' 'The Last Song,' 'By the Waters of Babylon'—but was responsible for the Great Candelabra in St. Paul's, the statues of Sir Thomas Browne and Nurse Cavell at Norwich, Sir John Campbell at Auckland, and Cecil Rhodes at Cape Town. There was Fred Pegram, R.I. (1870-1937), exact contemporary of cousin C. E. Brock and an equally celebrated pen and ink illustrator in the world of magazines, at one time on the staff of the *Pall Mall Gazette.* There was also Amy Pegram, quite unknown to *Who's Who* but with considerable artistic talent, if her most irreverent pencil sketch of her Uncle Alfred is anything to go by.''

Brock graduated from the Higher Grade School, Cambridge and studied under the tutelage of sculptor Henry Wiles. That was to be the extent of his formal education as an artist.

His entrance into the world of book illustration occurred at the age of twenty when a friend showed some of his illustrations to a member of the Macmillan staff. Shortly thereafter Macmillan commissioned the young artist to execute his first book illustrations.

Brock's beginnings as an illustrator were not punctuated by struggle. His popularity, in fact, was well established after publication of his illustrations for *Hood's Humorous Poems* in 1893.

"Here is your prize," said Oswald, with feelings of generous pride. ■ (From "The Runaways," in *Oswald Bastable and Others* by E. Nesbit. Illustrated by C. E. Brock.)

Scrooge crept towards it, trembling as he went; and following the finger, read upon the stone of the neglected grave his own name, "Ebenezer Scrooge." ■ (From *A Christmas Carol* by Charles Dickens. Illustrated by C. E. Brock.)

To youthful students of art, he advised: "I'm afraid that I have nothing particularly fresh to put forward concerning drawing for Illustration, but I might perhaps say that, to me, the cultivation of the powers of observation seems *very* important, and likely to have great effect on one's work. If one gets into a habit of looking at, and noticing with a little effort of memory, the things and people round about, one's work is bound to be very greatly improved by it.

"To get a satisfactory result in Illustration or interpretative work, much more is needed than a careful drawing of any model that one may pose, and my experience is that a constant 'looking-about,' from the point of view of the artist, is absolutely necessary. After all, this, I suppose, is another way of saying that one needs enthusiasm, and if one has that, the habit of observation naturally follows. To the enthusiast his work is ever present and the delight of studying the things around needs no insisting upon.

"Another thing I would say is, don't make *Style* the first thing—important though it may be, and indeed, is. There is so much drawing nowadays that is more Style than anything else. Such work has a sort of superficial and spurious masterliness with nothing to back it up, and it becomes merely annoying to those

PART II Air Throne, the Dwarfs and the light Elves

(From *The Heroes of Asgard* by A. and E. Keary. Illustrated by C. E. Brock.)

who have any feeling for drawing. The deficiencies are only too evident, in spite of the splashes and boldness which are meant to conceal them.

"I should recommend the student to do a good deal of drawing in the truth and sincerity of which he is so engrossed that he forgets all about the question of Style, and lets the technique come naturally out of the subject. This is the way to develop individuality and originality of expression, and to avoid the danger of depending too much on ready-made devices founded on other people's work. It is not a good habit to have an invariable recipe for drawing certain things, and this is only to be avoided by constant reference to Nature.

"One finds it so easy to get into a bad habit and so difficult to get out of it, especially as, very often, there is not too liberal an allowance of time for work that one may be doing. To keep your drawing fresh should be a constant aim, though I know full well how hard it is to avoid the little hackneyed tricks that save time and thought, but gradually reduce work to a monotonous level.

"With regard to materials—the nibs I generally use in my work are Brandauers, 518 and 515, with, just occasionally, a thicker pen of some sort. The first mentioned is very flexible, and, though fine, can be made to give a very fat line when necessary. As to pencils—anything that comes along. I have got into the way of working on Bristol Board because of its whiteness, although this surface is perhaps rather slippery.

"The pen is rather an exacting tool, and I find it advisable to lay down a fairly firm pencil foundation before beginning with the pen. Alterations or changes are not so possible in the ink stage, and the student mustn't be discouraged if he finds that he has to start a pen drawing more than once because of something which goes wrong and can't well be altered.

In one hand she carried a large tin can, and in the other a thick slice of bread and butter. "Afternoon tea," she announced proudly. . . . ■ (From *The Railway Children* by E. Nesbit. Illustrated by C. E. Brock.)

"I believe that, if work has good in it, sooner or later the Editor or Publisher will be found who is able to appreciate its quality—and use your drawings." [Percy V. Bradshaw, *The Art of the Illustrator*, The Press Art School (London), 1917.²]

February 28, 1938. Died in Cambridge, England. *The Times* read: "Mr Charles Edmund Brock, the artist, died yesterday at his residence, 38 Grange Road, Cambridge. He had been in ill-health for some time. . . . He spent most of his life in Cambridge. After leaving the Higher Grade School there, he went for three or four years into the Cambridge studio of Mr Henry Wiles, the sculptor. His experience there, and some lessons at an art school, were the only training he received; he was practically self-taught.

"He was chiefly known as a water-colour artist and book-illustrator. He had been a member of the Royal Institute of Painters in Water Colours for many years. He was largely interested in eighteenth-century and early Victorian studies. Among the novels he illustrated were those of Jane Austen and Dickens.

"In the early days of the present century he did a fair amount of work for *Punch* at the invitation of its then editor, Burnand, who had noticed Mr Brock's drawings in a book. Several examples of his work as a portrait painter hang in Cambridge colleges, for he painted a number of Cambridge worthies, including Professor Cowell, Dr. Campion of Queen's, and Dr Robert Sinker of Trinity. Several of these were exhibited at the Royal Academy.

"Mr Brock was the brother of Mr H. M. Brock, who is also a well-known artist and lives in Cambridge."[1]

FOR MORE INFORMATION SEE: A. E. Johnson, "The Line Drawings of Charles E. Brock, R. I.," *International Studio,* August, 1916; Percy V. Bradshaw, *The Art of the Illustrator,* Press Art School, 1917; Stanley J. Kunitz and Howard Haycraft, editors, *Junior Book of Authors,* 2nd edition, H. W. Wilson, 1951; Brian Doyle, editor, *Who's Who of Children's Literature,* Schocken, 1968; C. M. Kelly, *The Brocks: A Family of Cambridge Artists and Illustrators,* Skilton, 1975; Nick Meglin, "Pen and Ink," *American Artist,* November, 1979.

BROCK, H(enry) M(atthew)   1875-1960

PERSONAL: Born July 11, 1875, in Cambridge, England; died July 21, 1960, in Cambridge, England; son of Edmund (reader for Cambridge University Press specializing in medieval and oriental languages) and Mary Anne (Pegram) Brock; married cousin, Doris Joan Pegram, in 1912; children: one son, two daughters. *Education:* Attended Cambridge School of Art. *Residence:* Woodstock, Storey's Way, Cambridge, England.

CAREER: Book illustrator and watercolor artist. First illustrations were published in 1893. Exhibited work at the Royal Academy, 1901; the Royal Institute of Painters in Water-Colours, 1901, 1904-12, 1914, 1916, 1921, 1923, 1926-27, 1929, 1933-36, 1950; the Walker Art Gallery, 1904, 1906-10, 1912, 1915-16; and the Sketch Society, 1910.

ILLUSTRATOR: (With brother, Charles E. Brock) *History Readers: Book II,* Macmillan (London), 1894; Frederick Marryat, *Jacob Faithful,* Macmillan (London), 1895; F. Marryat, *Japhet in Search of a Father,* Macmillan (London), 1895; Robert Pollok, *Tales of the Covenanters,* Oliphant Anderson, 1895; William Makepeace Thackeray, *Ballads and Songs,* Cassell, 1896; Samuel Lover, *Handy Andy,* Macmillan (London), 1896; A. G. T. Watson, *Racing and Chasing,* Longmans, 1897; Lilly G. Frazer, *Macmillan's Illustrated Primary Series of French and German Readings,* six volumes (includes *Scenes of Child Life,* 1898, and *Scenes of Familiar Life,* 1898), Macmillan (London), 1896-1899; Elizabeth C. Gaskell, *Cranford,* Service & Paton, 1898, new edition, 1912; (with brother,

H. M. Brock, age 35.

C. E. Brock) Jane Austen, *The Novels of Jane Austen,* ten volumes, edited by R. Brimley Johnson, Dent, 1898; John W. Fortescue, *The Drummer's Coat,* Macmillan (London), 1899; (with C. E. Brock) Sir Walter Scott, *Ivanhoe,* two volumes included in *The Temple Classics for Young People,* Dent, 1899; William Shakespeare, *The Swan Shakespeare: Richard II,* Longmans, Green, 1899; W. Scott, *Waverley,* Service & Paton, 1899; G. J. Whyte-Melville, *Black But Comely,* Thacker, 1899; G. J. Whyte-Melville, *Songs and Verses,* Thacker, 1899.

James Fenimore Cooper, *The Deerslayer: A Tale,* Macmillan, 1900; J. F. Cooper, *The Last of the Mohicans,* Macmillan, 1900; L. G. Frazer, *Asianthe,* Dent, 1900; G. J. Whyte-Melville, *Digby Grand,* Thacker, 1900; Mabel E. Wotton, *The Little Browns,* Blackie & Son, 1900; John Bunyan, *The Pilgrim's Progress,* Pearson, 1900; M. C. E. W., *All about All of Us: Some Higgledy-Piggledly Memories of a Happy Childhood,* Dent, 1901; G. J. Whyte-Melville, *Sister Louise,* Thacker, 1901; G. J. Whyte-Melville, *Cerise,* Thacker, 1901; Charles Dickens, *The Old Curiosity Shop,* Gresham, 1901; G. J. Whyte-Melville, *Kate Coventry,* Thacker, 1901; J. F. Cooper, *The Pioneers; or, The Sources of the Susquehanna,* Macmillan (London), 1901; Mabel C. Bradley, *Private Bobs and the New Recruit,* Dent, 1901; Johann D. Wyss, *Swiss Family Robinson,* Pearson, 1902; Oliver Wendell Holmes, *The Autocrat of the Breakfast Table,* Houghton, 1902; William M. Thackeray, *History of Henry Esmond,* Pearson, 1902, another edition (with Lancelot Speed) published as *Henry Esmond,* Bowman, 1909; Lew Wallace, *Ben Hur,* Pearson, 1902; Mary Blundell, *North, South, and over the Sea,* George Newnes, 1902; *Siepmann's Primary French Course,* Macmillan (London), 1902; O. W. Holmes, *The Poet at the Breakfast Table,* Houghton, 1902; George Eliot (pseudonym of Mary Ann Evans), *The Mill on the Floss,* Nisbet, 1902; O. W. Holmes, *The Professor at the Breakfast Table,* Houghton, 1902; Douglas W. Jerrold, *The*

Essays of Douglas Jerrold, edited by grandson, Walter J. Dent, Dent, 1903; James H. L. Hunt, *The Essays of Leigh Hunt,* edited by Arthur Symons, Dent, 1903; Charles Kingsley, *Westward Ho!,* Pearson, 1903; Louisa May Alcott, *Little Women [and] Good Wives,* Pearson, 1904; James G. Frazer, *An Historical Sketch and Argument of Molière's ''Les Femmes Savantes'',* Heffer, 1904; Daniel Defoe, *The Life and Adventures of Robinson Crusoe,* Pearson, 1904; Grace Aguilar, *The Days of Bruce: A Story from Scottish History,* Pearson, 1905; Hans Christian Andersen, *Fairy Tales and Stories,* Pearson, 1905, Bowman, 1909, published as *Andersen's Fairy Tales and Stories,* Seeley, 1910; Miguel de Cervantes Saavedra, *The Life and Adventures of Don Quixote de la Mancha,* Pearson, 1905; *Sir Roger de Coverley, and Other Essays from the ''Spectator'',* Dent, 1905; W. E. Mallett, *An Introduction to Old English Furniture,* George Newnes, 1906; Dinah Marie Craik, *John Halifax, Gentleman,* Pearson, 1906; Thomas Hughes, *Tom Brown's School Days,* Oxford University Press, 1907, another edition (with L. Speed), Seeley, 1911; (with others) *Envelope Books,* T. N. Foulis, 1907; *The Fairy Library,* George Newnes, 1907; Desmond Coke, *The House Prefect,* Hodder & Stoughton, 1908; Emmuska Orczy, *The Emperor's Candlesticks,* Greening, 1909; Washington Irving, *The Old English Christmas,* T. N. Foulis, 1909; E. Orczy, *The Man in the Corner,* Dodd, 1909, facsimile reprint, International Polygon-

(From *The Old Curiosity Shop* by Charles Dickens. Illustrated by H. M. Brock.)

When he stood... to take call-over

Some of those names . . . recurred to him ever afterward without any effort of memory. . . . Ainsworth, Attwood, Avonmore, Babcock, Baggs, Barnard. . . . ■ (From *Good-bye Mr. Chips* by James Hilton. Illustrated by H. M. Brock.)

ics, 1977 (published in England as *The Old Man in the Corner,* Greening, 1909); D. Coke, *The Bending of a Twig,* Hodder & Stoughton, 1909.

D. Coke, *The School Across the Road,* Hodder & Stoughton, 1910; L. G. Frazer, *Histoire de Monsieur Blanc,* Macmillan, 1910; E. Orczy, *The Scarlet Pimpernel and I Will Repay,* Greening, 1910; C. Dickens, *A Christmas Tree,* Hodder & Stoughton, 1911; C. Dickens, *The Holly-Tree Inn,* Hodder & Stoughton, 1911; E. Orczy, *Nest of the Sparrow Hawk,* Greening, 1911; Norman J. Davidson, editor, *A Knight Errant and His Doughty Deeds: The Story of Amadis of Gaul* (based on the version by Robert Southey), Seeley, 1911; (with W. T. Horton) H. Rider Haggard, *The Mahatma and the Hare,* Holt, 1911; Otto Siepmann, *A Primary German Course,* Macmillan (London), 1912; Thomas W. Harding, *Tales of Madingley,* Bowes, 1912; Oliver Goldsmith, *The Vicar of Wakefield,* Seeley, Service, 1912; W. Bourne Cook, *The Cragsmen: A Story of Smuggling Days,* Cassell, 1913; Juliana H. Ewing, *Jackanapes, and Other Tales,* G. Bell, 1913; L. G. Frazer, *Victor et Victorine,* Macmillan (London), 1913; *The Old Fairy Tales,* F. Warne, 1913-16, Volume I: *Puss in Boots [and] Jack and the Beanstalk,* Volume II: *Hop-o'-My-Thumb [and] Beauty and the Beast,* Volume III: *Valentine and Orson [and] Jack the*

Giant Killer, all titles also published separately, Volume I and II published as *The Book of Fairy Tales*, 1914; L. G. Frazer, *La Maison aux panonceaux*, Cambridge University Press, 1914; D. Coke, *The Worst House at Sherborough*, Hodder & Stoughton, 1915; Violet Bratby, *Judy and Others*, Hodder & Stoughton, 1916; *Brave Boys and Girls in War Time*, Blackie & Son, 1918; *H. M. Brock's Picture Book of Fairy Tales*, Warne, 1919; Kenelm Foss, *"Till Our Ship Comes In": Chapters in the Life of Two Poor Dears*, Grant Richards, 1919; D. Coke, *Youth, Youth!* (short stories), Chapman & Hall, 1919.

Hylton Cleaver, *Captains of Harley*, Humphrey Milford, 1921; Alfred Judd, *The School on the Steep*, T. Nelson, 1924; (with Arthur A. Dixon) W. Irving, *Tales of the Alhambra*, edited by Edric Vredenburg, R. Tuck, 1924; James G. Frazer, *Leaves from the Golden Bough*, Macmillan (London), 1924; J. Winsford, *The Secret of Sampson's Farm*, Cassell, 1926; Robert Louis Stevenson, *Master of Ballantrae*, Macmillan (London), 1928; R. L. Stevenson, *Kidnapped*, Macmillan (London), 1928; R. L. Stevenson, *The Black Arrow*, Macmillan (London), 1928; (with C. E. Brock) Louey Chisholm, compiler, *The Golden Staircase* (poetry), T. C. & E. C. Jack, 1928; Marc Ceppi, *New French Picture Cards*, C. Bell, 1928; *Un Peu de Francais* (textbook), G. Bell, 1928; *French for Young Beginners* (textbook), G. Bell, 1928; John Drinkwater, *All about Me: Poems for a Child*, Collins, 1928; C. Kingsley, *The Heroes; or, Greek Fairy Tales for My Children*, Macmillan (London),

(From *The Children's Omnibus*, edited by J. Keir Cross. Illustrated by H. M. Brock.)

1928, reprinted, Mayflower Books, 1980; R. L. Stevenson, *Treasure Island*, Macmillan (London), 1928; J. Drinkwater, *More about Me: Poems for a Child*, Collins, 1929; Eleanor Farjeon, *The Tale of Tom Tiddler*, Collins, 1929.

L. G. Frazer, *The Singing Wood*, A. & C. Black, 1931; Flora Klickmann, *The Lady with the Crumbs*, Putnam, 1931; F. Klickmann, *Mystery in Windflower Wood*, Putnam, 1932; C. Dickens, *Christmas Tales*, Harrap, 1932; Paul Meyer, *Bell's German Picture Cards*, G. Bell, 1932; George H. Borrow, *Lavengro: The Scholar, the Gypsy, the Priest*, T. Nelson, 1932; (with Walter Crane) Henry F. B. Gilbert, *Robin Hood and the Men of the Greenwood*, T. Nelson, 1932; D. Coke, *A Schoolboy Omnibus*, Oxford University Press, 1934; *The Book of Nursery Tales*, F. Warne, 1934 (contains "The Old Fairy Tales," with "Tom Thumb," "Cinderella," "Snowdrop," "Sleeping Beauty," "Little Red Riding Hood," and "Dick Whittington and His Cat"); John B. Nichols, compiler, *A Book of Old Ballads*, Hutchinson, 1934; C. Dickens, *A Christmas Carol*, Dodd, 1935; James Hilton, *Goodbye, Mr. Chips*, Little, Brown, 1935; J. G. Frazer and L. G. Frazer, *Pasha the Pom: The Story of a Little Dog*, Blackie & Son, 1937; (with C. E. Brock) Theodora Wilson-Wilson, *Through the Bible*, Collins, 1938; Florence Gunby Hadath, *More Pamela*, Collins (London), 1939; Amy Steedman, *My Bible Pictures and Stories*, T. Nelson, 1939; Jeffrey Havilton, *Study Thirteen in a Tangle*, Blackie & Son, 1939.

F. G. Hadath, *Pamela Calling*, Collins (London), 1940; J. Havilton, *School Versus Spy*, Blackie & Son, 1940; (with C. E. Brock) *The Golden Book of Bible Stories: Favorite Stories from the Old and New Testaments Retold for Children*, Grosset, 1941; C. Dickens, *Martin Chuzzlewit*, Dodd, 1944; J. Havilton, *George Goes One Better*, Blackie & Son, 1944; Theo Wilson, *Into the Arena*, Collins, 1944; (with Tom Curr, Lucy Gee, and G. A. Neilson) *Bible Pictures to Paint*, Pickering & Inglish, 1945; *The Bible Book of Golden Deeds*, R. A. Publishing, 1946; F. D'Amico, *Golden Eagle and Other Tales*, Hutchinson, 1947; *Hans Andersen's Fairy Tales*, Peter Lunn, 1947; Dorothy M. Stuart, *The Young Clavengers*, University of London Press, 1947; J. Keir Cross, *The Children's Omnibus*, Peter Lunn, 1947; L. J. Caunter, *The Children's Pilgrim's Progress*, Hutchinson, 1950; (with C. E. Brock) Margaret Tempest and Kathleen Fryer, *Stories from the Bible*, Collins, 1955; (with C. E. Brock and Irene Mountford) Lucy Diamond, *Bible Story*, Collins, 1957; (with Ralph Caldecott) J. H. Ewing, *Lob Lie-by-the-Fire; or, The Luck of the Lingborough [and] The Story of a Short Life*, reissue, Dutton, 1964.

Also illustrator of W. Bourne Cook, *Smugglers All*, 1953; *Stories of Legendary Heroes*, Houghton; H. B. Davidson, *The Makeshift Patrol*, Sheldon Press; Uncle Raymond, *The Bible Story*, Charles F. Kimball; Irene Martyn, *Learning to Spell*, Harper of Holloway; *Herbert Strang's Library of Children's Classics;* and *Out of School*, *The Luck of Study*, and *Harold Comes to School*, all by J. Havilton, all published by Blackie & Son.

Contributor of illustrations to periodicals, including *Punch*, *Graphic*, *Sketch*, *Little Folks*, *Boy's Own Paper*, *The Captain*, *Strand*, *Sphere*, *Cassell's Family Magazine*, *Quiver*, *Good News*, *Fry's Magazine*, *Chums Annual*, and *Fun*.

SIDELIGHTS: Born on **July 11, 1875,** in Cambridge, England. H. M. Brock was educated at the Higher Grade School five years after his older brother, C. E. Brock, had attended it. He then attended the Cambridge School of Art before joining his brother's studio.

And the King ate and drank, and declared that he had never met with as good [a] cook. ▪ (From
"Puss in Boots," in *The Fairy Library*. Illustrated by H. M. Brock.)

H. M. Brock, age 78, in his studio.

1914. Served in the L.D.V. (equivalent of the Home Guard) during World War I.

Mr. W. J. Samuel, a fellow volunteer with H. M. in the L.D.V., remembered how proud they were to have "a *Punch* artist" in their platoon. "No doubt we gave him a few ideas, with our antics. In fact I remember seeing some recognizeable [sic] at the time. . . . He was a gentleman, you know, that was the thing . . . very pleasant, quiet, prepared to do anything required . . . well-built chap, stocky . . . we had some silly things to do, I suppose . . . guarding haystacks and the like, for fear somebody set fire to them . . . we did have an aeroplane to guard once, a fighter that appeared in a field . . . nobody in it . . . never found out what had happened . . . yes, he was a nice chap . . . seemed old to me then, of course—he was about forty, and I wasn't thirty—your ideas change on that subject, don't they?" [C. M. Kelly, *The Brocks: A Family of Cambridge Artists and Illustrators,* Skilton, 1975.[1]]

Doris Brock recalled her husband as an observant, gentle and compassionate man. "Harry had a wonderful memory for faces. I have recognized faces in the streets of Cambridge that had appeared in his drawings. They never knew. People don't recognize themselves, you know.

"But he would never have caricatured anybody. He couldn't have hurt anyone. He was really *too* kind-hearted. He was victimized at times."

She recalled a children's storybook for which he had provided many pictures—and in the end received only eight guineas. "There was a man came here once when Harry was ill. Not long before he died, in fact. He wouldn't go away. I knew what he was after—he wanted a picture—and for nothing. . . . Harry just couldn't say No. . . . [The Brocks] were so quiet, so reserved. And modest. . .really terribly shy. . . ."[1]

July 21, 1960. Died in Cambridge, England. *The Times* responded: "Mr. H. M. Brock, whose drawings were regularly seen in *Punch* for many years, died at Cambridge on Thursday. He was 85.

"He was a pleasant and highly successful illustrator and draughtsman, somewhat in the Hugh Thomson tradition of lightly humorous, skilfully controlled and clear-cut pen drawing.

"Like him, he did many illustrations for reprints of old books, which demanded an historical knowledge of costume—the works of Thackeray, Whyte Melville and O. W. Holmes among them. . . ."[1]

The *Cambridge Daily News* added their tribute. "There came in this week a tribute to the late H. M. Brock, R.I., for many years a well-known *Punch* contributor, book-illustrator and painter in water-colours, whose recent death saddened his many friends.

"He was the last of the four sons, all artists, of Edmund Brock, who was born in Shepreth, educated in London, and was for many years Reader in Oriental Languages at the Cambridge University Press. Born in Cambridge, H. M. Brock had lived and worked here all his life.

"The following lines have been written by one of the many people who knew and loved him—

"Here lies Thy servant, Harry Brock,
Sprung from ancient yeoman stock;
He manifests, if any can,
The aristocracy of man.
Ages of duty, stern and good,
Flowed in his generous Cambridge blood;
And all his life fulfilled his birth
In homage to the English earth.
With hands that might have held a plough
Or nursed an ewe, or milked a cow,
With eyes that might have watched the dawn
O'er many a harvest deep in corn,
His dedication was to draw
For all, the loveliness he saw.

"He painted us the world he knew
Still innocent and wet with dew,
And birds and beasts and human kind
Bright from the mintage of his mind;
From corners of the earth and sky
The little people cocked an eye,
But even they were gay and bland
Like everything that left his hand,
For every creature he would bless
With something of his kindliness.

"Industrious as a field of bees
He gathered his felicities;
His life a page of gentle art
Drawn from the colours of his heart,
Strong as the hill that shields the lamb
And placid as our smiling Cam,
He was the genius of the place
And bore for us its special grace;
But first and always, to the end,
Was brother, father, man and friend.

"Unsigned, but by his niece Barbara Noel Scott."[1]

FOR MORE INFORMATION SEE: Bertha E. Mahony and others, compilers, *Illustrators of Children's Books: 1744-1945,* Horn Book, 1947; Stanley J. Kunitz and Howard Haycraft, editors, *Junior Book of Authors,* 2nd edition, H. W. Wilson, 1951; Brian Doyle, editor, *Who's Who of Children's Literature,* Schocken, 1968; C. M. Kelly, *The Brocks: A Family of Cambridge Artists and Illustrators,* Skilton, 1975. Obituaries: *Times* (London), July 25, 1960.

BROWN, (Robert) Fletch 1923-

PERSONAL: Born May 28, 1923, in New York, N.Y.; son of Harry C. (a foreman) and Lillian (a homemaker; maiden name, Carheart) Brown; married Laura DeLong (a nurse), November 28, 1949; children: Diane Brown Spotts, Craig Alan. *Education:* Northwestern Technical Institute, B.S., 1947. *Politics:* Independent. *Religion:* Evangelical. *Home:* 16924 Northeast 14th St., Bellevue, Wash. 98008.

CAREER: The Boeing Co., Seattle, Wash., engineer, 1952-85. National ski patrolman, 1949-74. *Military service:* United States Navy, 1942-45, Motor Machinist's Mate, 3rd class. *Awards, honors:* Named Writer of the Year for juvenile fiction, 1981, by the Warner-Pacific College Christian Writers Conference.

WRITINGS—Fiction; for young readers: *Street Boy,* Moody, 1980; *Street Boy Returns,* Moody, 1982. Editor, *Ski Patrol Newsletter,* 1955-62.

WORK IN PROGRESS: An adult romance/fantasy novel, based on a bicycle trip through England; a novel based on his experiences as a flight test engineer; short stories.

SIDELIGHTS: "I have always made my living as an engineer. Most of my time, almost thirty years, has been with The Boeing Company. I started out as a structural engineer, worked as a hydraulic systems test engineer, and then began a fifteen-year stint in the Flight Test Department where I tested new airplanes, from the 707 through the 747. After that I was a maintenance instructor, followed by two and a half years in Bombay, India, as a field service engineer. Now I'm back in Flight Test flying test airplanes once again.

"Back in 1975 I was laid off for a while, so I tried writing—something I always wanted to do. After four months I sold one piece for $25.00. I didn't consider $6.50 a month a living wage, so I went back to engineering. However, the writing bug had bit. It was the old routine of before dawn paper pounding, writing classes at the local vocational school, writers conferences, the whole thing. Eventually, *Street Boy* came out and then *Street Boy Returns.* I was a writer. The trip to India slowed things down a bit with all the new sights and sounds, but I soon learned that early morning was the nicest time of day in Bombay, and I was back at the machine with my new novel.

"In my engineering career I have written hundreds of engineering documents from test reports to sales proposals and training manuals. After all that experience, I found the transition to fiction quite easy. The same techniques apply: 1. Gather your facts; 2. Arrange them so they sound logical; 3. Write them in a way that won't put the reader to sleep. That last item is hard in technical writing, but is excellent training for fiction. Technical writing also produces good work habits. You write that report today whether you want to or not, and you have it finished Friday. There is no waiting for the Muse.

"While stationed in Bombay I traveled all over the East, from Tokyo to Tel Aviv and from Kathmandu to Nairobi. There should be lots of stories there but they haven't popped out yet.

"Having to waste eight hours a day working slows the writing something fierce. I look forward to the day I can become a full-time writer. All it takes is money."

HOBBIES AND OTHER INTERESTS: Community theater, sports car racing, scuba diving, amateur radio, wood carving, and bicycling.

Soap and education are not as sudden as a massacre, but they are more deadly in the long run.
—Mark Twain
(pseudonym of Samuel Langhorne Clemens)

JOSEPH BRUCHAC III

BRUCHAC, Joseph III 1942-

PERSONAL: Surname is pronounced Brew-shack; born October 16, 1942, in Saratoga Springs, N.Y.; son of Joseph E. (a taxidermist) and Flora (Bowman) Bruchac; married Carol Worthen, June 13, 1964; children: James Edward, Jesse Bowman. *Education:* Cornell University, A.B., 1965; Syracuse University, M.A., 1966; graduate study at State University of New York at Albany, 1971-73; Union Graduate School, Ph.D., 1975. *Religion:* Animist. *Home address:* R.F.D., Greenfield Center, N.Y. 12833. *Agent:* Julie Fallowfield, McIntosh & Otis, Inc., 475 Fifth Ave., New York, N.Y. 10017. *Office:* Greenfield Review Press, Greenfield Center, N.Y. 12833.

CAREER: Keta Secondary School, Ghana, West Africa, teacher of English and literature, 1966-69; Skidmore College, Saratoga Springs, N.Y., instructor in creative writing and in African and black literatures, 1969-73, teacher of creative writing at Great Meadows Institute, Comstock Prison, 1972—; Greenfield Review Press, Greenfield Center, N.Y., publisher and editor of *Greenfield Review*, 1969—. *Member:* Poetry Society of America, P.E.N., National Association of Metis Indians, National Wildlife Federation.

AWARDS, HONORS: New York State Arts Council grant, 1972; Vermont Arts Council grant, 1972; monthly poetry prize from Poetry Society of America, February, 1972; New York State CAPS poetry fellowship, 1973, 1982; poetry fellowship, National Endowment for the Arts, 1974; editors' fellowship, Coordinating Council of Literary Magazines, 1980; Rockefeller Foundation Humanities fellowship, 1982-83.

*WRITINGS—*Poetry, except as indicated: *Indian Mountain and Other Poems*, Ithaca House, 1971; (editor with William Witherup) *Words from the House of the Dead: An Anthology of Prison Writings from Soledad*, Greenfield Review Press, 1971; *The Buffalo in the Syracuse Zoo*, Greenfield Review Press, 1972; *The Poetry of Pop*, Dustbooks, 1973; *Flow*, Cold Mountain Press, 1975; *Turkey Brother and Other Iroquois Folk Tales*,

Crossing Press, 1976; *The Road to Black Mountain*, Thorp Springs Press, 1976; *This Earth Is a Drum*, Cold Mountain Press, 1977; *The Dreams of Jesse Brown* (novel), Cold Mountain Press, 1977; *Stone Giants and Flying Heads: Adventure Stories of the Iroquois* (illustrated by Kahionhes Brascoupe and Clayton Brascoupe), Crossing Press, 1978; *Entering Onondaga*, Cold Mountain Press, 1978; *There Are No Trees inside the Prison*, Blackberry Press, 1978; (translator from Iroquois) *The Good Message of Handsome Lake*, Unicorn Press, 1979.

Ancestry, Great Raven, 1980; *Translator's Son*, Cross-Cultural Communications, 1981; *Remembering the Dawn*, Blue Cloud, 1983; (editor) *Songs from This Earth on Turtle's Back* (anthology), Greenfield Review Press, 1983; (editor) *The Light from Another Country* (anthology), Greenfield Review Press, 1984; (editor) *Breaking Silence* (anthology), Greenfield Review Press, 1984; *Iroquois Stories: Tales of Heroes and Heroines, Monsters and Magic*, The Crossing Press, 1985; *The Wind Eagle and Other Abenaki Stories* (illustrated by Kahionhes), Bowman Books, 1985; *No Telephone to Heaven* (novel), Cross-Cultural Communications, 1986.

Work represented in numerous anthologies, including: *New Campus Writing*, edited by Nolan Miller, McGraw, 1966; *Syracuse Poems, 1963-1969*, edited by George P. Elliott, Syracuse University Press, 1970; *Our Only Hope Is Humor: Some Public Poems*, edited by Robert McGovern and Richard Snyder, Ashland Poetry Press, 1972; *From the Belly of the Shark: A New Anthology of Native Americans*, edited by Walter Lowenfels, Vintage, 1973; *The Remembered Earth*, edited by Geary Hobson, University of New Mexico, 1979; *The Pushcart Prize Anthology, 1980-81*, Pushcart Press, 1981; *From A to Z: 200 Contemporary Poets*, Swallow Press, 1981; *Editors' Choice*, Spirit That Moves Us, 1981; *Peace Is Our Profession*, East River Anthology, 1981.

Also author of *Peter Davis*, an album of songs which has been recorded. Contributor of poetry to over four hundred periodicals, including *New Letters, Paris Review, Akwesasne Notes, Hudson Review, American Poetry Review*, and *Contact II.* Assistant editor, *Epoch*, 1964-65; contributing editor, *Nickel Review*, 1967-71, and *Studies in American Indian Literature*, 1983—; contemporary music editor, *Kite*, 1971—; editor, *Prison Writing Review*, 1976—.

WORK IN PROGRESS: Border Crossing, poems and translations from West Africa; two collections of Iroquois folk tales; *The Broken Rainbow* and *Foxy*, both novels.

SIDELIGHTS: "Much of my writing and my life relates to the problem of being an American. While in college I was active in Civil Rights work and in the anti-war movement. . . . I went to Africa to teach—but more than that to be taught. It showed me many things. How much we have as Americans and take for granted. How much our eyes refuse to see because they are blinded to everything in a man's face except his color. And most importantly, how human people are everywhere—which may be the one grace that can save us all.

"My writing is informed by several key sources. One of these is nature, another is the native American experience (I'm part Indian). . . . I like to work outside, in the earthmother's soil, with my hands . . . but maintain my life as an academic for a couple of reasons: it gives me time to write (sometimes) and it gives me a chance to share my insights into the beautiful and all too fragile world of human life and living things we have been granted. Which is one of the reasons I write—not to be a man apart, but to share.''

FOR MORE INFORMATION SEE: Albany Times Union, June 1, 1980.

CARRIS, Joan Davenport 1938-

BRIEF ENTRY: Born August 18, 1938, in Toledo, Ohio. An author of fiction for young readers, Carris found her niche in life as a student at Iowa State University. Prior to that time, as she humorously reveals, her life was a constant discovery of ''the vast number of things I couldn't do. . . . I couldn't do a handstand, jump rope past 'pepper,' skate without bloodying my entire body, or dance.'' Things changed in college when she ''discovered that I could understand literature, really understand it. I could diagram sentences and spell—of all things.'' Although Carris entered the university as an art major, she graduated in 1960 with a degree in English, speech, and French education and spent the following five years teaching those subjects to high school students in Iowa. After a voluntary ten-year hiatus (during which time she concentrated on raising three children), Carris found her desire to return to teaching impeded by an overabundance of English teachers in her field. Writing became her recourse. Since 1974 she has also worked as a private tutor of English in Princeton, N.J.

Carris's first book, *The Revolt of 10-X* (Harcourt, 1980), a Junior Literary Guild selection, was followed by *When the Boys Ran the House* (Crowell, 1982), its sequel *Pets, Vets, and Marty Howard* (Lippincott, 1984), and the fantasy *Witch-Cat* (Lippincott, 1984). She is also coauthor of *SAT Success* (Peterson's Guides, 1982), a study guide for college entrance examinations. Although an advocate of ''trying to teach young people to love and emulate good English,'' Carris confesses that ''writing children's books is my delight. . . . It is the hardest work . . . , the loneliest, the least rewarding financially, and the most frustrating.'' She adds: ''I wouldn't trade it for anything.'' Carris has written a one-act play entitled ''The Revolution Continues'' and is a contributor to magazines and newspapers. *Address:* Box 231, 48 Princeton Ave., Rocky Hill, N.J. 08553.

FOR MORE INFORMATION SEE: Contemporary Authors, Volume 106, Gale, 1982.

CHESSARE, Michele

BRIEF ENTRY: Illustrator. A graduate of the Rhode Island School of Design, Chessare's pen-and-wash and watercolor drawings have appeared in eight books for children. These include Clyde Robert Bulla's *My Friend the Monster* (Crowell, 1980), *Lion to Guard Us* (Crowell, 1981), and *The Cardboard Crown* (Crowell, 1984), as well as X. J. Kennedy's *The Owlstone Crown* (Atheneum, 1983). Chessare has been a regular contributor of drawings to *New York Times Book Review* and magazines like *Saturday Review, Rolling Stone*, and *Rocky Mountain*. *Residence:* Upper Montclair, N.J.

...he who pleases children will be remembered with pleasure by men.

—James Boswell

This is the story of Erica, from the time she first remembered anything at all to the time she was sixteen and refused her first offer of marriage. ▪ (Jacket illustration by Laura Lydecker from *Early Rising* by Joan Clarke.)

CLARKE, Joan 1921-

PERSONAL: Born in 1921 in England. *Home:* 55 Silverdale Rd., Yealand Redmayne, Cannforth, Lancashire, U.K.

CAREER: Pediatrician; biographer and author of books for young readers.

WRITINGS—All of interest to young readers; all fiction: *The Happy Planet* (illustrated by Anthony Maitland), J. Cape, 1963, Lothrop, 1965; *Foxon's Hole* (illustrated by Pat Marriot), J. Cape, 1969; *Early Rising* (illustrated by Pauline Martin), J. Cape, 1974, Lippincott, 1976.

SIDELIGHTS: Among Clarke's three novels are two works of science fiction. In *The Happy Planet*, two children from the planet Tuan return to Earth on an exploratory mission one thousand years after it has been destroyed by a shower of meteorites. *Foxon's Hole* details an experiment in time travel whereby a Neanderthal boy, Mick, is brought from the Ice Age into the twentieth century. *Times Literary Supplement* called *Foxon's Hole* ''an excellent and highly enjoyable book,'' adding that ''there is a strong comic element to offset the more chilling implications of the story.''

Clarke's third novel, *Early Rising*, is a fictionalized biography based on the life of Erica, one of five children growing up in an English vicarage during the late Victorian period. "Erica dominates the book," commented *Junior Bookshelf*, "and her progress from a fidgety seven-year old to an impetuous adolescent, still stubborn but brimming with laughter, is charted with convincing and faithful detail." *School Library Journal* also took note of Clarke's ability to focus on moments of Erica's life "with a sharpness that turns seemingly mundane events . . . into memorable vignettes."

FOR MORE INFORMATION SEE: Times Literary Supplement, December 4, 1969; *Junior Bookshelf,* April, 1975; *School Library Journal,* October, 1976; D. L. Kirkpatrick, editor, *Twentieth-Century Children's Writers,* St. Martin's, 1978.

COONEY, Nancy Evans 1932-

PERSONAL: Born September 9, 1932, in Northfork, W. Va.; daughter of Earl B. (a banker) and Grace (Howard) Evans; married John Mason Cooney (a university administrator), June 5, 1955; children: James, Carolyn, Christine, Mark. *Education:* University of North Carolina, B.A., 1954; Marshall University, M.A., 1956. *Home:* 691 Red Lion Way, Bridgewater, N.J. 08807.

CAREER: Northfork-Elkhorn Junior High School, Northfork, W.Va., teacher, 1954-55; West Windsor Elementary School, Dutch Neck, N.J., teacher and guidance counselor, 1956-57; Princeton Seminary, Princeton, N.J., librarian, 1957-58; Philip's Bookstore, Cambridge, Mass., general assistant, 1958-59; writer, 1978—. *Member:* Society of Children's Book Writers, Children's Literature Association, Authors Guild. *Awards, honors: The Blanket That Had to Go* was nominated for California Reading Association's Young Readers Medal, 1984-85.

WRITINGS: The Wobbly Tooth (illustrated by Marilyn Hafner), Putnam, 1978; *The Blanket That Had to Go* (illustrated by Diane Dawson), Putnam, 1981; *Bad Luck Follows Shrimp,* Putnam, in press; *Sky High,* Putnam, in press.

WORK IN PROGRESS: More picture books and short-chapter books for young readers.

SIDELIGHTS: Cooney was reared in Northfork, a small town in the coal-mining region of southern West Virginia. "I never planned to be a writer, though as I look back on my life, I find that words were always important to me. I began by reading everything I could find. My father, a quiet and gentle man, had a great sense of humor; he would often make my two sisters and me laugh with his stories and tall tales.

"Once in a while on weekends at my grandfather's house, we three sisters would join our cousins to write plays. We would rehearse and then perform these wonders for the grown-ups, a captive audience. I attended school in Northfork and on at least one occasion I remember being one of the writers who devised a play for Assembly. But despite these efforts and a rare, secret poem or two, I never thought of being a writer. Music and drawing competed with reading as my major preoccupations."

Attended the University of North Carolina in Greensboro where Cooney switched her major from voice to English literature. She earned her B.A. and taught school at West Virginia junior high. After her marriage to John Cooney, she continued her education, earning an M.A. in educational guidance and counseling from Marshall University. She taught school, worked

in a library, and in a bookstore. Cooney stopped teaching to rear her children Jim, Carolyn, Christine, and Mark.

"*The Blanket That Had to Go* was partly inspired by my youngest, Mark, whose devotion to his blanket was especially strong. . . . I like to use a theme that is universal in my stories and try to make it very particular. My children have given me ideas for stories, but I find when writing that I draw on my own memories, my own feelings and sensations. I suppose each children's book writer is still very much in touch with the child within."

Cooney's book *The Blanket That Had to Go* has been read on the "Captain Kangaroo" television program.

HOBBIES AND OTHER INTERESTS: Singing with performing groups.

CORBETT, Scott 1913-

PERSONAL: Born July 27, 1913, in Kansas City, Mo.; son of Edward Roy and Hazel Marie (Emanuelson) Corbett; married Elizabeth Grosvenor Pierce, 1940; children: Florence Lee. *Education:* Kansas City Junior College, Associate of Art, 1930-32; University of Missouri, B.J., 1934. *Religion:* Episcopalian. *Home:* 149 Benefit St., Providence, R.I. 02903. *Agent:* Curtis Brown Ltd., 575 Madison Ave., New York, N.Y. 10022.

CAREER: Writer. Moses Brown School, Providence, R.I., English teacher, 1957-65. *Military service:* U.S. Army, 1943-46; became sergeant; army correspondent and editor, continental edition, *Yank. Member:* Authors Guild, Authors League of America. *Awards, honors:* Edgar Allan Poe Award, Mystery Writers of America, 1963, for *Cutlass Island;* Mark Twain Award, Missouri Library Association, 1976, and Golden Archer Award, University of Wisconsin, 1978, both for *The Home Run Trick.*

WRITINGS—All juvenile, except as noted; all published by Atlantic-Little, Brown, except as noted: *The Reluctant Land-*

SCOTT CORBETT

Fox Face would be surprised to know where he was now! ■ (From *Run for the Money* by Scott Corbett. Illustrated by Bert Dodson.)

lord (adult), Crowell, 1950; *Sauce for the Gander* (adult), Crowell, 1951; *We Chose Cape Cod* (adult), Crowell, 1953; *Cape Cod's Way: An Informal History* (adult), Crowell, 1955; (with Manuel Zora) *The Sea Fox: The Adventures of Cape Cod's Most Colorful Rumrunner* (adult), Crowell, 1956; *Susie Sneakers* (illustrated by Leonard Shortall), Crowell, 1956; *Midshipman Cruise,* 1957; *Tree House Island* (illustrated by Gordon Hanson; Junior Literary Guild selection), 1959.

Dead Man's Light (illustrated by L. Shortall), 1960; *Danger Point: The Wreck of the Birkenhead,* 1962; *Cutlass Island* (illustrated by L. Shortall; Junior Literary Guild selection), 1962; *What Makes a Car Go?* (illustrated by Leonard Darwin), 1963; *One by Sea* (illustrated by Victor Mays; Junior Literary Guild selection), 1965; *What Makes TV Work?* (illustrated by L. Darwin), 1965; *The Cave above Delphi* (illustrated by Gioia Fiammenghi), 1965; *What Makes a Light Go On?* (illustrated by L. Darwin; Junior Literary Guild selection), 1966; *Pippa Passes* (illustrated by Judith Gwyn Brown), Holt, 1966; *The Case of the Gone Goose* (illustrated by Paul Frame), 1966; *Diamonds Are Trouble,* Holt, 1967, new edition published as *The Trouble with Diamonds,* Dutton, 1985; *What Makes a Plane Fly?* (illustrated by L. Darwin), 1967; *Cop's Kid* (illustrated by Jo Polseno), 1968; *The Case of the Fugitive Firebug* (illustrated by P. Frame), 1969; *Ever Ride a Dinosaur?* (illustrated by Mircea Vasiliu), Holt, 1969; *Rhode Island* (adult), Coward, 1969; *Diamonds Are More Trouble,* Holt, 1969.

The Baseball Bargain (illustrated by Wallace Tripp), 1970; *What Makes a Boat Float?* (illustrated by V. Mays), 1970; *The Mystery Man* (illustrated by Nathan Goldstein), 1970; *Steady, Freddie!* (illustrated by Lawrence B. Smith; Junior Literary Guild selection), Dutton, 1970; *The Case of the Ticklish Tooth* (illustrated by P. Frame), 1971; *The Red Room Riddle* (illustrated by Geff Gerlach), 1972; *Dead before Docking* (illustrated by P. Frame), 1972; *The Big Joke Game* (illustrated by M. Vasiliu; Junior Literary Guild selection), Dutton, 1972; *Run for the Money* (illustrated by Bert Dodson), 1973; *Dr. Merlin's Magic Shop* (illustrated by Joe Mathieu), 1973; *What about the Wankel Engine?* (illustrated by Jerome Kühl), Four Winds Press, 1973; *Here Lies the Body* (illustrated by G. Gerlach), 1974; *The Case of the Silver Skull* (illustrated by P. Frame), 1974; *The Great Custard Pie Panic* (illustrated by J. Mathieu), 1974; *Take a Number,* Dutton, 1974; *The Case of the Burgled Blessing Box* (illustrated by P. Frame), 1975; *The Boy with Will Power* (illustrated by Ed Parker), 1975; *The Boy Who Walked on Air* (illustrated by E. Parker), 1975; *Captain Butcher's Body* (illustrated by G. Gerlach), 1976; *The Hockey Girls,* Dutton, 1976; *The Foolish Dinosaur Fiasco* (illustrated by Jon McIntosh), 1978; *Bridges* (illustrated by Richard Rosenblum, ALA Notable Book), Four Winds Press, 1978; *The Discontented Ghost,* Dutton, 1978; *The Mysterious*

Standing as stiff as a corpse in that tiny black pantry, which indeed seemed no larger than a coffin, Roger waited to find out. ■ (From *The Case of the Silver Skull* by Scott Corbett. Illustrated by Paul Frame.)

An important-looking man came out and stood in front of Zack with his arms folded. ■ (From
The Mysterious Zetabet by Scott Corbett. Illustrated by Jon McIntosh.)

Zetabet (illustrated by J. McIntosh; Junior Literary Guild selection), 1979; *The Donkey Planet* (illustrated by Troy Howell), Dutton, 1979.

Jokes to Read in the Dark (illustrated by Annie Gusman), Dutton, 1980; *Home Computers: A Simple and Informative Guide*, 1980; *The Deadly Hoax*, Dutton, 1981; *Grave Doubts*, 1982; *Jokes to Tell to Your Worst Enemy*, (illustrated by A. Gusman), Dutton, 1984; *Down with Wimps* (illustrated by Larry Ross), Dutton, 1984; *Witch Hunt*, Atlantic-Little, Brown, 1985.

"Trick" series; all illustrated by Paul Galdone; all published by Atlantic-Little, Brown: *The Lemonade Trick* (Junior Literary Guild selection), 1960; *The Mailbox Trick*, 1961; *The Disappearing Dog Trick*, 1963; *The Limerick Trick* (Junior Literary Guild selection), 1964; *The Baseball Trick*, 1965; *The Turnabout Trick*, 1967; *The Hairy Horror Trick*, 1969; *The Hateful Plateful Trick*, 1971; *The Home Run Trick*, 1973; *The Hockey Trick*, 1974; *The Black Mask Trick*, 1976; *The Hangman's Ghost Trick*, 1977.

"The Great McGoniggle" series; all illustrated by Bill Ogden; all published by Atlantic-Little, Brown: *The Great McGoniggle's Gray Ghost*, 1975; *The Great McGoniggle's Key Play*, 1976; *The Great McGoniggle Rides Shotgun*, 1977; *The Great McGoniggle Switches Pitches*, 1980.

Contributor to periodicals, including *Saturday Evening Post*, *Atlantic Monthly*, and *Good Housekeeping*.

ADAPTATIONS: "Love Nest" (movie), based on *The Reluctant Landlord*, Twentieth Century-Fox, 1950; "The Great McGoniggle's Gray Ghost" (recording), Listening Library, 1980; "The Red Room Riddle" (movie), screenplay by Stephen Manes, ABC-TV, 1983.

SIDELIGHTS: **July 27, 1913.** Born in Kansas City, Missouri.

1930-1932. Attended Kansas City Junior College. "The first piece of writing I ever sold was written on a trolley car in Kansas City on my way from junior college to my afternoon job at a branch public library. *College Humor* paid six dollars for my parody verse, a princely sum in those depression days, and I felt certain I had hit the road which would soon widen out into Easy Street.''

Corbett's next sales were cartoon ideas and two-line jokes to small magazines at two dollars each. During his senior year at the University of Missouri he began selling to the ''Post Scripts'' page of the *Saturday Evening Post.*

1934. Graduated with a bachelor's degree in journalism from the University of Missouri.

May 11, 1940. Married Elizabeth Grosvenor Pierce.

1950. First book published. ''At that time TV was beginning to loom up as a threat to the movies, and the movie industry was terrified. Where an average of 600 properties (books and stories) had been bought each year in the past, in 1950 somewhere between twelve and fifty were bought. Fortunately, *The Reluctant Landlord* was one of them, a fact that gave us a running start in moving to Cape Cod. It was bought by Twentieth Century-Fox, and appeared the next year under the title, ''Love Nest,'' a pretty sexy title for a true story about a couple

Kerby and Fenton were staring dumbfounded at Waldo's nose. Waldo was squinting at it cross-eyed. ▪ (From *The Hangman's Ghost Trick* by Scott Corbett. Illustrated by Paul Galdone.)

who had been married ten years. The film was one of the earliest to feature Marilyn Monroe, and still turns up from time to time on TV, usually late at night.''

1951. Moved from New York City to Cape Cod with his wife and daughter. ''One thing we often said in our own defense during our last months in New York—and we were given plenty of opportunities to defend our position—was that if we had been uneasy about having to live to ourselves for awhile, we would not have considered moving, unknown, unheralded, unsung, and unconnected, to a place like Cape Cod.

''Everybody told us people would scarcely speak to us for at least six months. We believed them and were undisturbed. I was in the midst of writing a book, and Elizabeth had plans enough for fixing up the house to keep her busy indefinitely. We even hoped that, left to ourselves, we would actually get something done for a change.

''When we arrived in February, business was very quiet on Quivet Neck. The sole business establishment there was D. H. Sears' Grocery Store, and D. H. was keeping it open out of pure sociability as much as anything else. After sixty-four years, running the store had become something of a habit with him.

''David Henry, who was eighty-six years old, was the first old Cape Codder we really became acquainted with. We dropped in to subscribe to the local newspaper, the Cape Cod *Standard-Times*, and D. H. scribbled our name on a card under one of

With every step the bag of groceries came more and more to resemble a sack of cement. ▪ (From *The Baseball Bargain* by Scott Corbett. Illustrated by Wallace Tripp.)

the pigeon-holes where he stuck the papers. There were about twenty other names, mostly Sears. . . .

''At first the Cape Codders' attitude toward outsiders annoyed us. They could not have lived without the tourist trade; newcomers who became permanent residents tended to increase their prosperity; and yet, even when they tried to conceal it, we knew that they secretly resented every outsider who came pushing his way across the bridge onto the sacred soil of their beloved Cape. There was a saying about the native attitude concerning what they would really have liked to see the outsiders do: 'Leave your money on the bridge and go home.'

''This attitude seemed downright disgusting. Who were they to bite the hand that fed them? It took us awhile to realize the truth—that tourism was still a comparatively new thing on Cape Cod. For nearly three hundred years, Cape Codders had managed on their own. . . .'' [Scott Corbett, *We Chose Cape Cod,* Crowell, 1953.[1]]

1956. First book for children was published. ''My first book for children had for its setting the Cape Cod village in which I was then living, and the story was based on an actual situation involving my niece. Two of my stories, *Diamonds Are*

Panting and sniffing, came the biggest, ugliest bulldog we had ever seen. ■ (From *The Red Room Riddle: A Ghost Story* by Scott Corbett. Illustrated by Geff Gerlach.)

Trouble and *The Mystery Man,* take place at country inns that closely resemble a real inn on Cape Cod, with an innkeeper who looked and acted very much like the real innkeeper.

''Since my wife and I like to travel, especially on freighters, several of my books have been written at sea. *The Turnabout Trick* was written during a trip round the world. I started it in the Pacific Ocean, rewrote it in the Indian Ocean, and finished it in the Atlantic Ocean. *The Mystery Man* was finished and *Steady, Freddie!* was started during a three-months' trip round South America.

''During one of our longest continuous freighter trips, I decided to go up on deck for a few minutes to start the long process of getting an idea—the hardest part of writing stories. Before we had left home, my Dutton editor had urged me to consider writing a funny story for girls. For some reason I started thinking about how we all had to go door-to-door once a year selling cookies when I was a Boy Scout. I thought about how much I hated it, and what a poor salesman I was. Suddenly I was thinking, why not Girl Scout, and how about having a pet frog end up in one of the boxes of cookies—and no way of knowing which one? It was one of the few times in my life I got a workable idea in five minutes' time. It may not sound very workable, but it turned out to be *Steady, Freddie!*

''Oddly enough, though I have written several books that had a lot to do with the sea, I have never written a story while at sea that was not firmly based on land.''

1957. Moved from Cape Cod to Providence, R.I. ''Our daughter's elementary school had been excellent, but the local high school was not teaching kids how to study, and we decided Janie had better learn how, if she was to be accepted by a good college. She didn't want to go off to boarding school, and we didn't want her to, either—even if we could have afforded it—so we decided we'd all move. A first-rate girl's school in Providence made the choice of cities for us. We expected to stay there four years. We have now lived in Providence longer than anywhere else, despite the fact that since I returned to writing full-time, in 1965 it no longer matters *where* we are. In the old days, when we used to drive up to the Cape from New York City, the highway took us through all the drabbest parts of Providence. At that time I considered it the last place in the country I'd ever live in. But it turned out to be a great place to live. At the same time, we've never lost our ties with Cape Cod.''

1963. Awarded the Edgar Allan Poe award for *Cutlass Island.* Corbett's numerous books for children include several series of books for teenagers, boys, and younger children. ''I am a storyteller devoted to the proposition that suspense and humor are a worthwhile combination. My books, especially the 'Trick' books, have been widely used in schools to trap reluctant readers and get them started on books. My most successful efforts . . . have been ghost stories of a slightly more modern flavor than those Victorian chillers which today are not only period pieces but, all too often, semi-colon pieces. The 'What Makes It Work' books are successful in explaining difficult subjects to beginning readers—mainly because I started with no knowledge of the subjects myself and thus did not make the expert's mistake of assuming too much basic understanding on the part of his readers. *What Makes a Car Go?* was published in an Arabic edition, not for children but as a workable introduction to the internal combustion engine for adult Arabs. Perhaps this was a mistake—I may have let something slip about the importance of all that oil.'' [D. L. Kirkpatrick, *Twentieth Century Children's Writers,* St. Martin's Press, 1978.[2]]

1965. *One by Sea,* a book that combined the author's love for travel and history, was published. "Every time I cross the Atlantic Ocean I wish I could have made the voyage in a sailing ship. When Boston Harbor was a forest of tall masts, it must have been quite a place to bring a square-rigger into after a good run from some port an ocean away.

"And then, there's Cape Cod. On many a beach and back road, I did my best to recapture the feeling of the bleak, hardy, earthy Cape Cod of a century earlier, when thousands of blue-water skippers called it home, even though they spent more time on the China Seas than they did in their Cape villages.

"All these hankerings to turn back the clock for a look at the past combined to produce *One by Sea.* I was glad to meet up along the way with young Nye Gorham, because by starting from England in his company I was able to take in all the sights I have mentioned. The only trouble was, some of his adventures kept me from inspecting the scenery along the way quite as closely as I would have in other circumstances. A person can't travel at too leisurely a pace when he's being tracked by a scoundrel like Red-Eye Pell."

1972. *The Big Joke Game* was the ninth of his books to be chosen as a Junior Literary Guild selection. "*The Big Joke Game* gave me the chance to use limericks again as part of a story, which is the way I most enjoy writing them. It was a special pleasure to follow Ozzie Hinkle through his unusual adventures, because when I was his age I had the same weakness for jokes. I loved to read joke books and think up jokes of my own. All too often I was probably just as obnoxious as Ozzie, but fortunately my jokes never got me in quite as much trouble. And yet, why do I say that? I think that for the pleasure of knowing Beelzebub, his guardian devil, I would gladly have undergone all of Ozzie's trials and tribulations.

"It was also fun to give the great Trojan hero Aeneas his lumps on behalf of my daughter, Florence. In her senior year in high school she studied Virgil, which of course involved reading the *Aeneid* in Latin. She felt Aeneas was the most pompous and tiresome hero on record. She never forgave him for his treatment of poor Dido. I might add that since then she has married and provided our family with a new hero who is neither pompous nor tiresome: our grandson, Gavin Lonsdale McKee."

1976. Awarded the Mark Twain Award for *The Home Run Trick.*

1980. Fascinated by new gadgets, Corbett purchased a home computer, and turned this learning experience into a book. "The only way to learn the simple facts about home computers, I decided, was to live with one and learn how to use it myself. For over a year I have known the agony and ecstasy of this new existence—the agony a computer can put a person through when it isn't working right, and the ecstasy it can provide when it starts accomplishing wonders.

"At times I have felt like a pioneer in the wilderness. After its most recent trip back from the serviceman's bench, which it had left working all right, I hooked my video terminal to the computer, turned it on, and found it would print everything—but only in the space of one short line, writing everything over and over that one line. I turned it off and did something I had never done in the course of our love-hate relationship—I raised my hand to it. I jiggled it! Then I turned it on again, and now the cursor, the little bright underline that indicates where the next printed character will appear, showed

"I'm looking for the cop that works here in the station. Fat man with white hair." ■ (From *The Great McGoniggle's Key Play* by Scott Corbett. Illustrated by Bill Ogden.)

up in the middle of the screen. Now the lines marched down the screen in perfect order—but only the left half of them showed on the screen.

"For some reason connected with desperation I lifted the left edge of the terminal, tilting it sideways. The cursor flickered out and reappeared in its proper place, on the left-hand side of the screen! From then on the terminal worked . . . most of the time. This terminal, however, is already obsolete. I have replaced it with a new 'smart' terminal, which has its own microprocessor and is far superior in performance to the earlier model, even when it was working right." [Scott Corbett, "Preface," *Home Computers: A Simple and Informative Guide,* Little, Brown, 1980.[3]]

1984. Corbett and his wife have travelled widely, although they still return to their home in Providence. "In March we flew from San Francisco to Singapore to board an American President Lines freighter for a month. Our first port was Columbo, the capital of Sri Lanka. Next, Fujairah, one of the United Arab Emirates. We were supposed to go to Dubai, but Dubai is just inside the Persian Gulf, and at that time there was some shooting going on in the Gulf. Our Navy did not want American ships to come through the Strait of Hormuz. Fujairah is just outside, and directly across from Dubai, only fifty miles by road, so we went there, and the cargo we unloaded for Dubai was transshipped in a German freighter. After return stops at Colombo and Singapore we went on to our final port, Kaohsiung on the southern tip of Taiwan, then back once more to disembark at Singapore.

"[Recently] two friends and I finally managed to do something we've been trying to do: go up in a hot air balloon. We three and the balloonist took off in northern Rhode Island and landed eighteen miles and one hour and a quarter later in southern Massachusetts, so I now sign my name, 'Scott Corbett, I.A.'—'Interstate Aerialist.' (Only kidding about that, but we thought the title would be impressive.) Taking off is easy, sliding along above the trees is a job—sometimes at 2000 feet, then coming down and skimming the treetops just for fun; it's getting down again that provides the adventure. When we were ready to come down, suddenly there were all kinds of suitable open fields on both sides of us, but nothing but forest in front of us. Then a big gravel pit appeared. There was a nice patch of level space with one boulder in front of it. Naturally we touched down exactly in front of the boulder, but our balloonist skimmed us neatly over the top of it. 'Just flex your knees a bit,' was his instruction for absorbing the impact of the basket on *terra firma*. We flexed, and bumped together as the basket tilted this way and that after touching down, but soon the eighty-foot balloon was deflated and everything under control. It was a magnificent experience I'd recommend to anybody physically able to climb into the basket, stand there, and take a little bit of shaking upon landing.''

HOBBIES AND OTHER INTERESTS: Reading, travel, tennis, chess, fishing, boats, islands, the sea, and New England fishing villages.

FOR MORE INFORMATION SEE: Scott Corbett, *We Chose Cape Cod*, Crowell, 1953; *Times Literary Supplement*, May 29, 1959; *Saturday Review*, November 12, 1960, May 27, 1978; Huck and Young, *Children's Literature in the Elementary School*, Holt, 1961; *Atlantic Monthly*, December, 1962; *Christian Science Monitor*, August 8, 1963; *New York Times Book Review*, November 7, 1965, July 16, 1972, April 30, 1978, April 27, 1980; *Books for Children: 1960-1965*, American Library Association, 1966; *Horn Book*, February, 1967; Nancy Larrick, *A Parent's Guide to Children's Reading*, 3rd edition, Doubleday, 1969: *Book World*, May 4, 1969; *Science Books*, September, 1970; *Commonweal*, November 19, 1971; *America*, December 2, 1972; *Booklist*, May 1, 1974; *Parents' Magazine*, October, 1975; *Children's Literature Review*, Volume I, Gale, 1976; *Language Arts*, September, 1976; *West Coast Review of Books*, September, 1977; Doris de Montreville and Elizabeth D. Crawford, editors, *Fourth Book of Junior Authors and Illustrators*, H. W. Wilson, 1978; D. L. Kirkpatrick, *Twentieth-Century Children's Writers*, St. Martin's Press, 1978; Scott Corbett, *Home Computers: A Simple and Informative Guide*, Little, Brown, 1980.

CUMMINGS, Pat   1950-

PERSONAL: Born November 9, 1950, in Chicago, Ill.; daughter of Arthur B. (a management consultant) and Christine M. (a librarian; maiden name, Taylor) Cummings; married Chuku Lee (a lawyer), February, 1975. *Education:* Pratt Institute, B.F.A., 1974. *Home and office:* 28 Tiffany Pl., Brooklyn, N.Y. 11231.

CAREER: Free-lance illustrator, 1975—. *Exhibitions:* Restoration Corporation, Brooklyn, N.Y., 1974; Black Enterprise Gallery, New York, N.Y., 1980; CRT Gallery, Hartford, Conn., 1981; Master Eagle Gallery, New York, N.Y., 1984, 1985; Akbaw Gallery, Mt. Vernon, N.Y., 1985. *Member:* Black Art Directors Group of New York, Graphic Artists Guild. *Awards, honors:* Coretta Scott King honorable mention, 1983, for *Just*

Us Women; Coretta Scott King Award, 1984, for *My Mama Needs Me.*

WRITINGS: Jimmy Lee Did It (self-illustrated), Lothrop, 1985; *C.L.O.U.D.S* (self-illustrated), Lothrop, 1986.

Illustrator: Eloise Greenfield, *Good News,* Coward, 1977; Trudie MacDougall, *Beyond Dreamtime: The Life and Lore of the Aboriginal Australian,* Coward, 1978; Cynthia Jameson, *The Secret of the Royal Mounds,* Coward, 1980; Jeanette Caines, *Just Us Women,* Harper, 1982; Mildred Pitts Walter, *My Mama Needs Me,* Lothrop, 1983; Cathy Warren, *Fred's First Day,* Lothrop, 1984; J. Caines, *Chilly Stomach,* Harper, 1986; Cathy Warren, *Playing with Mama,* Lothrop, 1986.

WORK IN PROGRESS: Illustrations for two books, *Why Me Teddy?* and *Lunchbox* by Jeanette Caines.

SIDELIGHTS: "I began free lancing with children's theatre groups doing posters, flyers, ads and even, at times, costumes and sets. I remember some of my early children's books and the fantasy and limitless imagery always appealed to me. The illustrations were close to music. Sometimes, now, before starting a new book, I'll read the story to some kids to see what they see and, invariably, they have illustrated the whole story in their minds.

"I like to incorporate personal things: people I know, things I use around the house or places I've been. It draws me into the story a bit more.

"I like to travel a great deal and was raised as an army brat in Okinawa and Japan. I speak some French and Italian and usually try to pick up enough to travel with. I've studied Jap-

PAT CUMMINGS

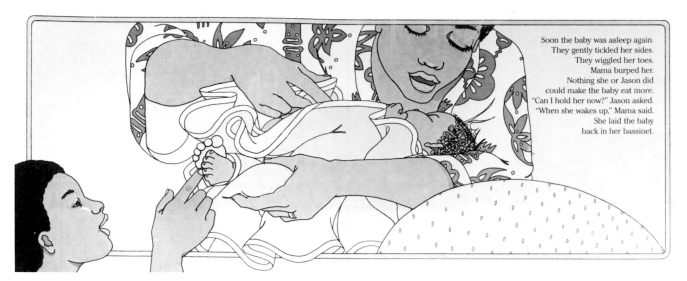

Soon the baby was asleep again.
They gently tickled her sides.
They wiggled her toes.
Mama burped her.
Nothing she or Jason did
could make the baby eat more.
"Can I hold her now?" Jason asked.
"When she wakes up," Mama said.
She laid the baby
back in her bassinet.

(From *My Mama Needs Me* by Mildred Pitts Walter. Illustrated by Pat Cummings.)

anese, Spanish, Swahili, and Greek as well but with disastrous results.

"I work in mixed media for full color books. Black and white books in pencil, ink and gouache. I try to see the story from inside the potential reader and the subject. I prefer graphic compositions and try to use color to reflect the mood of the book.

"I've been impressed with the work of Tom Feelings, Leo and Diane Dillon, Henrik Drescher, Nicole Claveloux, Michel Guire Vaka, and Chris Van Allsburg, among others."

ANTHONY Di FRANCO

Di FRANCO, Anthony (Mario) 1945-
(Anthony deFrance)

PERSONAL: Born August 29, 1945, in New York, N.Y.; son of Theodore J. (a lawyer) and Josephine (Greco) Di Franco; married Adrienne De Luccia (a college administrator), July 13, 1968; children: Allyson, Elizabeth, Dorothea, William. *Education:* Fordham University, B.A., 1966, M.A., 1969; St. John's University, professional diploma, 1972. *Residence:* Ft. Salonga, N.Y. *Agent:* Esther Newberg, International Creative Management, Inc., 40 West 57th St., New York, N.Y. 10019. *Office:* Department of English, Suffolk Community College, 533 College Rd., Selden, N.Y. 11784.

CAREER: Holy Family Diocesan High School, South Huntington, N.Y., head of English department and administrator, 1967-74; Suffolk Community College, Selden, N.Y., assistant professor of English, 1974—. Advisor, *Compass* (campus newspaper), 1977-82, *Reflections* (campus yearbook), 1981-84; chairman, Publications Board, Suffolk Community College, 1978—. *Member:* ARBA SICULA (national Sicilian-American cultural organization). *Awards, honors:* First prize, Catholic Press Association, 1982, for short story "The Brave."

*WRITINGS—*All for children: *Italy: Balanced on the Edge of Time,* edited by Tom Schneider, Dillon, 1983; *Pope John Paul II: Bringing Love to a Troubled World,* edited by T. Schneider, Dillon, 1983; (with JoAnn Di Franco) *Mister Rogers: Good Neighbor to America's Children,* Dillon, 1983.

Adult: *Streets of Paradise,* Bantam, 1984; *Ardent Spring,* Bantam, 1986.

Also contributor of about one dozen short stories (some under pseudonym Anthony deFrance) to national religious periodicals and literary magazines; editor, *Long Pond Review,* 1978—.

SIDELIGHTS: "I started writing at about age ten, mostly because I liked reading and was taken with the invented worlds in books and with the idea of conceiving and controlling them. The first real short story I wrote, at eighteen, was published, but I wrote for many years before I could do so in confidence of publication. The large religious magazines, like *Columbia* and *St. Anthony Messenger,* became regular outlets for me when I realized that writing with a strong moral dimension—

These young people are learning to drive at a government run auto-driving school in a Rome park. ■ (From *Italy Balanced on the Edge of Time* by Anthony Di Franco.)

writing whose main purpose was to make intelligible the meaning of important human actions and decisions—had found its home there; these magazines now print the sort of domestic-conflict, crisis of personal faith or courage type stories that the good commercial magazines used to—when they used to print fiction.

"I began writing for children when I became interested in the subject of Italian-Americans. To write for young readers is a challenge to every writing skill one has struggled to master, and I suspect that it's as much more difficult than writing for adults as teaching grade school is more difficult than teaching college. One advantage to me is the 'test audience' near at hand, since my children range in age from nine to fifteen years. They sampled my chapters as the heritage book on Italy was in progress.

"The world is probably filled with English teachers who are striving to be novelists . . . the Kingdom of First Novels must be as fantastic and elusive as any imagined world in children's literature, and may call for the same qualities of romanticism. I'm glad that my passage into that world was won with a manuscript on the lives of southern Italian immigrants to the

U.S., for their experience has been greatly under-represented or distorted in popular fiction.

"I think it necessary for writers to be re-builders, to continue to find and express the value of life, its beauty, its purpose and coherence; whether the subject matter be civilization itself, the values of capitalism or democracy or any other human system, the personal conflicts of love, divorce, or death, the writer is the counter-agent to entropy and the pervasive sense of the corruption of purpose which the media and the sea of human troubles around us assail us with. He does this by keeping in mind what the reader wants and needs when he picks up a book: something *good* for his insides. This is the answer I give to young writers who ask what sort of fiction I favor for *Long Pond Review*. In sum, I'm saying 'anything which isn't *ugly*.' I suppose that some ugly writing and some ugly world-views have been of use to our culture, but a little of it goes a long way, and to encourage it would be misleading.

"I live in a rather secluded house surrounded by tall old trees. It's rarely quiet inside, though, with all the kids. Until recently I typed on a seventeen-year-old Olivetti manual. Somehow, it stood up under thousands of manuscript pages. My latest adventure has been making the transition to a word processor, which I find a delight.''

HOBBIES AND OTHER INTERESTS: ''I jog, ride, ice skate, and swim. I grew up in mid-town Manhattan, and my chief enjoyment is actually taking walks, either in the preserves or arboretums on Long Island, or as a repatriate on Manhattan streets.''

DINNERSTEIN, Harvey 1928-

PERSONAL: Born April 3, 1928, in Booklyn, N.Y.; son of Louis and Sarah (Kobilansky) Dinnerstein; married Lois Behrke (an art historian), May 24, 1951; children: Rachel, Michael. *Education:* Studied art privately under Moses Soyer, 1944-46; attended Art Students League, 1946-47; Tyler Art School, Temple University, certificate of art, 1950. *Home and office:* 933 President St., Brooklyn, N.Y. 11215. *Agent:* (Paintings) Sindin Galleries, 1035 Madison Ave., New York, N.Y. 10021.

CAREER: Artist and illustrator. Instructor in drawing and painting, School of Visual Arts, 1965-80, National Academy of Design, 1975—, Art Students League, 1980—. *Exhibitions*—One-man: Davis Galleries, New York, N.Y., 1955, 1960, 1961, 1963; Kenmore Galleries, Philadelphia, Pa., 1964, 1966, 1969, 1970; FAR Galleries, New York City, 1972, 1979; Capricorn Gallery, Bethesda, Md., 1980; Sindin Galleries, New York City, 1984. Group: Whitney Museum of American Art, New York City, 1955, 1964; Childe Hassam Award Exhibition, American Academy and Institute of Arts and Letters, New York City, 1974; New York Cultural Center, 1976; Bicentennial Exhibition of American Illustrators, New York Historical Society, 1976; and elsewhere. Work is also represented in the permanent collections of the Metropolitan Museum of Art, New York City, Whitney Museum of American Art, New York City, Martin Luther King Labor Center, New York City, Fleming Museum at the University of Vermont, Burlington, New Britain Museum of American Art, New Britain, Conn., and in numerous private collections. *Military service:* U.S. Army, 1951-53.

MEMBER: National Academy of Design (academician, 1974), Audubon Artists, Allied Artists of America. *Awards, honors:* Louis Comfort Tiffany Foundation Grant, 1948, 1961; Temple Gold Medal, Pennsylvania Academy of Fine Arts, 1950; National Book Award finalist, Association of American Publishers, 1975, for *Remember the Days: A Short History of the Jewish American;* Allied Artists of America Gold Medal, 1977; President's Award, Audubon Artists, 1978.

WRITINGS: Harvey Dinnerstein: Artist at Work (self-illustrated), Watson-Guptill, 1978.

Illustrator; all for children: Arthur Conan Doyle, *Tales of Sherlock Holmes,* Macmillan, 1963; George MacDonald, *At the Back of the North Wind,* Macmillan, 1964; Felice Holman, *Silently, the Cat, and Miss Theodosia,* Macmillan, 1965; Milton Meltzer, *Remember the Days: A Short History of the Jewish American,* Zenith Books, 1974.

Other: *A Portfolio of Drawings,* Kenmore Press, 1968. Also contributor of articles and illustrations to periodicals such as *Esquire* and *Art News.*

SIDELIGHTS: ''An artist's work develops out of need, compassion, and commitment. Technique and craft are essential,

but the expressive power of a pictorial image is ultimately shaped by the intensity of the artist's personal vision.

''I have worked in various places over the years; they range from a converted garage with a wall of windows overlooking landscape and sky, to a view of ancient walls in Rome. I have also worked in transient quarters and motel rooms, with a chair or dresser improvised as an easel. My present studio is on the top floor of a brownstone in Brooklyn. I can close the door to the studio when I desire privacy, but I also am in contact with the flow of life of my family in the rest of the house. There is a human activity in the street outside, and a great variety of different kinds of people in the neighborhood whom I use as models.

''. . . My workshop has a quality that I view as organized chaos, though a visitor might characterize it in other terms. There is a mannikin draped with a dashiki, a butcher's apron over a fruit crate, balloons and flowers, a skeleton, and an arrangement of butterflies pinned to a board. Also a white rat in a cage. A radio plays Bach, jazz, or Yiddish music, according to the pleasure of the model posing or the rhythm of my work.

''. . . I usually work on a number of related projects at the same time. There are several upright easels, and also a French folding easel for work outside. I have a lifesize mirror that I refer to continually while working in order to get a fresh view and check the progress of the painting.

''My major light source is an overhead north skylight, which I supplement with fluorescent tubes. . . . I prefer to work with a natural north light, which enables me to discern the greatest

Harvey Dinnerstein, self-portrait. (Collection of the National Academy of Design.)

range of color. The light will vary slightly according to sky and cloud conditions, but it is the most constant, evenly balanced light source. I find it a pleasant light to work with, even though the painting will lose some of the qualities I strive for if it is exhibited under floodlights in a gallery or reproduced by mechanical means on a printing press. My skylight is rather small, and I supplement it with fluorescent tubes balanced to a color range comparable to north light. . . . The fluorescent tubes do not have exactly the same quality as natural north light, but they come quite close to it; and, used together with natural light, they work very well. I also like to pose the model under this soft diffused overhead light, as it helps to mold and reinforce the forms. Sometimes I find that I want to vary the light on the subject, and I have windows facing south that I can open to allow sun to enter the room. I also have floodlights available, if I want to illuminate the subject with a strong direct light source. In either case, I try to place my canvas under the skylight. If this is not physically possible, I check the painting under the skylight from time to time, to get a truer reading of the color. . . .

"I usually stand while working. I feel more agile and alert to the task, and I can move back easily to view the work from a distance. Occasionally, I sit on a chair to fix my eye level; I have chairs and stools of different heights for this purpose. When I want to elevate the position of the model, I have four wooden platforms . . . which I can stack at different levels." [*Harvey Dinnerstein: Artist at Work*, Watson-Guptill, 1978.[1]]

Dinnerstein believes that the solutions to painting problems must ultimately come from a study of life. ". . . But I look to the lessons of the past for sustenance and inspiration. . . . The direct encounter with a great artist's mind and hand, one that reaches across the centuries, is the most vivid and exciting lesson of all. Public museums today make available a vast treasure of art that in other times could only have been viewed in private collections. I often think that there is far more to be learned by studying these great paintings than from anything an instructor might say in school. Of course there is much information that you can derive in the classroom and from reading, but there is absolutely nothing like confronting the

original work of art. Many of the answers to our problems are there—answers to questions of scale and paint surface, movement, gesture, and how to achieve luminosity in the shadows. You can study the brushwork that embraces the form, and the magic that transforms ordinary materials into an illusion of light, air, and space.

"To draw is to seek out the essence of forms in nature. It is the basic factor in creating a visual image. From the initial sketch to the fully developed painting, your drawing abilities will provide the foundation and structure of all your work.

"Each and every problem has a unique solution, but there is a general approach that I follow in all my drawings. I am after a visual image that I respond to. Sometimes I arrive at it on my first encounter with the subject. At other times, I have to study the subject for a long time, until I see something that interests me. If I am working from the figure, I might try various poses, or the model might suggest an interesting gesture when resting. I try to stay alert to unexpected possibilities that present themselves. I might approach a subject from all angles, circling about, considering the spatial possibilities from a certain distance, or close up. Light is an important element. A strong dramatic light will set up tonal patterns of one kind, as opposed to the shapes that develop when the same subject is in a flat gray light. Shifting my view in relation to the light sets up still another kind of pattern. In considering the total image, all the elements are equally important: shapes, volumes, and the negative spaces in-between—all merit the same consideration.

". . . I always carry a sketchbook with me. It is more than a desire to keep my hand in practice, it reflects my deep need to make contact with life. I never know what observation will spark a visual idea.

"The drawings in my sketchbook range from studies of friends and family, to sketches of street life, and notations from museum visits. I draw in New York City subways, Roman markets, or the Louvre, wherever I happen to be. I might go out to a particular location with a specific object in mind, though

She and Roger and Silently and the mouse all sat quietly at the edge of the moonlight, eating jam and listening to the Night Birds calling. ■ (From *Silently, the Cat, and Miss Theodosia* by Felice Holman. Illustrated by Harvey Dinnerstein.)

He sat, while the horse ate, wondering how he was to reach the ground. ■ (From *At the Back of the North Wind* by George MacDonald. Illustrated by Harvey Dinnerstein.)

In the alcove at the far end of my studio is a small domed skylight that allows the sun to enter. . . .
■ (From *Harvey Dinnerstein: Artist at Work* by Harvey Dinnerstein. Illustrated by the author.)

I often simply wander about, looking for visual possibilities. There are times when I do not expect to work, but carry a sketchbook anyway for that unexpected moment when a striking visual image presents itself. Many of the drawings in sketchbooks I have accumulated over the years have no particular purpose beyond the sheer delight of recording visual perceptions. But in going over these haphazard notes, I often find information that is useful to me in a current project.

"I employ various tools and materials in drawing. I might use a brush and wash, for example, to study tonal masses of foliage and landscape, or pen and ink for a detailed portrait

(From *Remember the Days: A Short History of the Jewish American* by Milton Meltzer. Illustrated by Harvey Dinnerstein.)

study. I might also use a variety of materials to explore the same subject. One approach results in a broad view of structure, while another medium yields an image that is related in form, but provides another kind of insight. . . .

"In my first pass over the drawing, I sweep directly across the page, setting up the general proportions and directions. I look for a variety of shapes, contrasting patterns of light and dark value, or a broad tonal area against an elegant line. In designing the drawing, I try to make every part of the image function, considering the forms and the space around them. . . .

"In depicting the dramatic action of a figure composition, my primary concern is to establish the role of each of the figures, and their relationship to one another in the context of the total image. I usually block in the drawing very broadly from memory or from imagination, and then have a model approximate the poses that I have in mind. Or I may pose two models together for various groupings of figures. Sometimes, after indicating the concept in a broad sketch, I photograph the model in order to explore the possibilities of various gestures. A Polaroid camera is very helpful, in this case. In establishing the gesture from a photographic reference, I am wary of distortions of the camera lens, and the distraction of nonessential details. I usually use the photograph to set up generalized shapes, and then work directly from the model for a more meaningful resolution of the forms. Sometimes I use myself in a mirror to work out a gesture, or information on structure and drapery.

"Occasionally, I derive a theme from another work of art, perhaps a classical relief of figures in battle, and have a model assume related poses. Working from the model is important in all these approaches, as it enables me to work out the convincing structure of the figure. Even when I am not after a portrait of a particular individual, the model provides me with some information or direct contact with life that I feel makes the final image more effective. At the same time that I touch on the specific, however, I try to remain fully aware of the broad concept and rhythmic flow that unify the picture.

"Though I paint directly from nature most of the time, I often add some touches after the model has left the studio. In developing paintings of landscape or city views outdoors, I often resolve the forms back in the studio, in order to integrate all the diverse effects of nature into a unified concept. I usually work a long time on a painting; starting with a broad overall view, building a complexity to the structure, then simplifying the forms again, trying to arrive finally at an image that includes both specific and universal aspects of the subject.

". . . Most people look, but do not see. [I feel one should] develop the consciousness that encompasses the awe and wonder of a child's initial encounter with the world, and the perception of one viewing the earth for the last precious moment. It is this kind of insight that will shape the intensity and conviction of your work.

"... I often go outside to gather information for paintings.... I usually work in early morning or late afternoon, when the sun projects strong dramatic shadows, and I make note of the time of day so that if I want to return to the spot I have the same quality of light. I also like to work under a gray sky that does not break up the form, and casts a soft glow in light and shadow. Sometimes after I have established the overall patterns of light on a sunny day, I might return to the spot on an overcast day to work out certain forms within the shadow, and then study the subject in sunlight again in order to retain the original concept of light. I always carry extra panels or papers on which I can note unexpected changes of light or jot down ideas for other images. A sudden shift of light through an overcast sky or the twilight after a sunset may suggest a visual idea that I had not anticipated, and want to use.

"For the past three or four years, I have been working on studies for a series of paintings, *The Seasons*.... As I worked on the studies, I tried to intensify certain qualities beyond the naturalistic aspect of the scene, so that the tunnel became a passage, with all the connotations that implies. *The Seasons* refers to the human condition as well, and I started to make studies from memory and imagination, using the studies of tunnels to stage figure compositions.

"At present, I am planning a series of four large paintings on this theme. I hope that the pictorial images that develop reflect aspects of everyday life as well as universal concepts. I hesitate to be more explicit about a complex work in progress;

"Do read that one," said Diamond.... "It sounded very nice. I am sure it is a good one." ■ (From *At the Back of the North Wind* by George MacDonald. Illustrated by Harvey Dinnerstein.)

there is always an element of the unpredictable in the creative process. The studies that were undertaken as an exploration of a particular place, Prospect Park, are developing other implications.

"... There are many fundamental aspects of creativity that cannot be fully articulated. Many intuitive responses are involved in developing a visual idea, and the relationship of all the small decisions that affect the final work often are apparent only in retrospect.

"... Only a limited amount of information can be taught in art schools or gathered from books.... It is essentially up to ... the artist, to reflect upon [his] experience and shape an image that is true to [his] own personal view."[1]

FOR MORE INFORMATION SEE: American Artist, October, 1964, May, 1973, August, 1983; Harvey Dinnerstein, *Harvey Dinnerstein: Artist at Work,* Watson-Guptill, 1978; Susan E. Meyer, *Twenty Figure Painters and How They Work,* Watson-Guptill, 1979.

dos SANTOS, Joyce Audy

BRIEF ENTRY: Free-lance illustrator and author. A former student of the Massachusetts College of Art and the Harvard Graduate School of Design, dos Santos's past employment has included teaching art to children. Now a full-time illustrator, she has written and illustrated four books for children. Her first, *Sand Dollar, Sand Dollar* (Lippincott, 1980), was described by *Publishers Weekly* as a "rollicking story about the child Peter and his dog Urchin who share a wonder-filled day at the beach," accompanied with "dazzling silkscreen pictures in blue and gold...." *Horn Book* further observed: "Simply and effectively designed, the illustrations show wide expanses of yellow sand and blue sky, frothy waves, and the teeming life under the surface of the sea." Dos Santos's second and third books are simple stories based on French-Canadian folklore. *The Diviner* (Lippincott, 1980) is an adaptation of tales told to dos Santos by her grandmother, while *Henri and the Loup-Garou* (Pantheon, 1982) evolves around the werewolf of Canadian legendry.

In *Giants of Smaller Worlds: Drawn in Their Natural Sizes* (Dodd, 1983), dos Santos explores the world of arthropods, including exotica like the Goliath beetle, the Queen Alexandra birdwing butterfly, and walkingsticks. She invites young readers to place their hands next to her pictures for an accurate comparison of size. *Publishers Weekly* considered the book "preeminent among works that educate and entertain," labeling dos Santos "a scientist and fine artist." In addition to her own books, dos Santos has provided illustrations for Joanne Oppenheim's *Mrs. Peloki's Snake* (Dodd, 1980), Shirley Climo's *Piskies, Spriggans, and Other Magical Beings: Tales from the Droll-Teller* (Crowell, 1981), Ron Roy's *Million Dollar Jeans* (Dutton, 1983), Stephen Mooser's *Orphan Jeb at the Massacree* (Random House, 1984), and others. *Residence:* Merrimac, Mass.

Learn to live, and live to learn,
Ignorance like a fire doth burn,
Little tasks make large return.

—Bayard Taylor

Du BOIS, W(illiam) E(dward) B(urghardt) 1868-1963

PERSONAL: Born February 23, 1868, in Great Barrington, Mass.; immigrated to Ghana, 1960; became Ghanian citizen, 1963; died August 27, 1963, in Accra, Ghana; buried in Accra; son of Alfred and Mary (Burghardt) Du Bois; married Nina Gomer, 1896 (died, 1950); married Shirley Graham (an author), 1951 (died, 1977); children: Burghardt (deceased), Yolande Du Bois Williams (deceased). *Education:* Fisk University, B.A., 1888; Harvard University, B.A. (cum laude) 1890, M.A., 1891, Ph.D., 1896; graduate study at University of Berlin, 1892-1894. *Politics:* Joined Communist Party, 1961.

CAREER: Wilberforce University, Wilberforce, Ohio, professor of Greek and Latin, 1894-96; University of Pennsylvania, Philadelphia, assistant instructor in sociology, 1896-97; Atlanta University, Atlanta, Ga., professor of history and economics, 1897-1910; National Association for the Advancement of Colored People (NAACP), New York City, director of publicity and research and editor of *Crisis,* 1910-1934; Atlanta University, professor and chairman of department of sociology, 1934-1944; NAACP, director of special research, 1944-48; Peace Information Center, New York City, director, 1950. Co-founder and general secretary of Niagra Movement, 1905-09. Organizer of the Pan-African Congress, 1919. Vice-chairman of the Council of African Affairs, 1949. American Labor Party candidate for U.S. Senator from New York, 1950. *Awards, honors:* Spingarn Medal from NAACP, 1932; elected to the National Institute of Arts and Letters, 1943; Lenin International Peace Prize, 1958; Knight Commander of the Liberian Humane Order of African Redemption conferred by the Liberian Government; Minister Plenipotentiary and Envoy Extraordinary conferred by President Calvin Coolidge; LL.D. from Howard University, 1930, and Atlanta University, 1938; Litt.D., Fisk University, 1938; L.H.D., Wilberforce University, 1940; honorary degrees from Morgan State College, University of Berlin, and Charles University (Prague).

WRITINGS—Novels: *The Quest of the Silver Fleece,* A. C. McClurg, 1911, reprinted, Kraus Reprint, 1974; *Dark Princess: A Romance,* Harcourt, 1928, reprinted, Kraus Reprint, 1974; *The Ordeal of Mansart* (first novel in trilogy; also see below), Mainstream Publishers, 1957; *Mansart Builds a School* (second novel in trilogy; also see below), Mainstream Publishers, 1959; *Worlds of Color* (third novel in trilogy; also see below), Mainstream Publishers, 1961; *The Black Flame* (trilogy; includes *The Ordeal of Mansart, Mansart Builds a School, Worlds of Color*), Kraus Reprint, 1976.

Poetry: *Selected Poems,* Ghana University Press, c. 1964, reprinted, Panther House, 1971.

Also author of pageants, "The Christ of the Andes," "George Washington and Black Folk: A Pageant for the Centenary, 1732-1932," and "The Star of Ethiopia."

Works edited in conjunction with the annual Conference for the Study of Negro Problems; all originally published by Atlanta University Press: *Mortality Among Negroes in Cities,* 1896, reprinted, Octagon, 1968; *Social and Physical Condition of Negroes in Cities,* 1897, reprinted, Octagon, 1968; *Some Efforts of American Negroes for Their Own Social Benefit,* 1898, reprinted, Octagon, 1968; *The Negro in Business,* 1899, reprinted, AMS Press, 1971; *The College-Bred Negro,* 1900, reprinted, Octagon, 1968; *A Select Bibliography of the American Negro: For General Readers,* 1901; *The Negro Common School,* 1901, reprinted, Octagon, 1968; *The Negro*

W. E. B. Du BOIS

Artisan, 1902, reprinted, Octagon, 1968; *The Negro Church,* 1903, reprinted, Arno Press, 1968; *Some Notes on Negro Crime, Particularly in Georgia,* 1904, reprinted, Octagon, 1968; *A Select Bibliography of the Negro American,* 1905, reprinted, Octagon Books, 1968; *The Health and Physique of the Negro American,* 1906, reprinted, Octagon, 1968; *Economic Cooperation Among Negro Americans,* 1907, reprinted, Russell & Russell, 1969; *The Negro American Family,* 1908, reprinted, M.I.T. Press, 1970; *Efforts for Social Betterment Among Negro Americans,* 1909, reprinted, Russell & Russell, 1969; (with Augustus Grandville Dill) *The College-Bred Negro American,* 1910, reprinted, Russell & Russell, 1969; (with A. G. Dill) *The Common School and the Negro American,* 1911, reprinted, Russell & Russell, 1969; (with A. G. Dill) *The Negro American Artisan,* 1912, reprinted, Russell & Russell, 1969; (with A. G. Dill) *Morals and Manners Among Negro Americans,* 1914, reprinted, Russell & Russell, 1969.

Other: *The Suppression of the African Slave Trade to the United States of America, 1638-1870,* Longmans, Green, 1896, reprinted, Kraus Reprint, 1973; *The Conservation of Races,* American Negro Academy, 1897, reprinted, Arno Press, 1969; *The Philadelphia Negro,* University of Pennsylvania, 1899, reprinted, Kraus Reprint, 1973; *The Souls of Black Folk: Essays and Sketches,* A. C. McClurg, 1903, reprinted, Dodd, 1929; (with Booker Taliaferro Washington) *The Negro in the South: His Economic Progress in Relation to His Moral and Religious Development* (lectures), G. W. Jacobs, 1907, reprinted, Metro Books, 1972; *John Brown* (biography), G. W. Jacobs, 1909, reprinted, Kraus Reprint, 1973; *The Negro,* Holt, 1915, reprinted, Kraus Reprint, 1975.

Darkwater: Voices from Within the Veil (semi-autobiographical), Harcourt, 1920, reprinted, Kraus Reprint, 1975; *The Gift of Black Folk: The Negroes in the Making of America,* Stratford Co., 1924, reprinted, Kraus Reprint, 1975; *Africa: Its Geography, People and Products* (also see below), Haldeman-Julius Publications, 1930; *Africa: Its Place in Modern History,* Haldeman-Julius Publications, 1930, reprinted in a single volume with *Africa: Its Geography, People and Products,* KTO Press, 1977; *Black Reconstruction: An Essay Toward a History of the Part Which Black Folk Played in the Attempt to Reconstruct Democracy in America, 1860-1880,* Harcourt, 1935, reprinted, Kraus Reprint, 1976; *Black Folk, Then and Now,* Holt, 1939, reprinted, Kraus Reprint, 1975; *Dusk of Dawn: An Essay Toward an Autobiography of a Race Concept,* Harcourt, 1940, reprinted, Kraus Reprint, 1975; *Color and Democracy: Colonies and Peace,* Harcourt, 1945, reprinted, Kraus Reprint, 1975; *The World and Africa: An Inquiry into the Part Which Africa Has Played in World History,* Viking, 1947, reprinted, Kraus Reprint, 1976; (editor) *An Appeal to the World: A Statement on the Denial of Human Rights to Minorities in the Case of Citizens of Negro Descent in the United States of America and an Appeal to the United Nations for Redress,* [New York], 1947; *In Battle for Peace: The Story of My 83rd Birthday* (autobiography), Masses and Mainstream, 1952, reprinted, Kraus Reprint, 1976.

An ABC of Color: Selections from Over a Half Century of the Writings of W.E.B. Du Bois, Seven Seas Publishers (Berlin), 1963; *The Autobiography of W.E.B. Du Bois: A Soliloquy on Viewing My Life from the Last Decade of Its First Century,* International Publishers, 1968; *W.E.B. Du Bois Speaks: Speeches and Addresses,* edited by Philip S. Foner, Pathfinder Press, 1970; *The Selected Writings of W.E.B. Du Bois,* edited by Walter Wilson, New American Library, 1970; *W.E.B. Du Bois: A Reader,* edited by Meyer Weinberg, Harper, 1970; *The Seventh Son: The Thought and Writings of W.E.B. Du Bois,* edited by Julius Lester, Random House, 1971; *A W.E.B. Du Bois Reader,* edited by Andrew G. Paschal, Macmillan, 1971; *W.E.B. Du Bois: The Crisis Writings,* edited by Daniel Walden, Fawcett Publications, 1972; *The Emerging Thought of W.E.B. Du Bois: Essays and Editorials from "The Crisis,"* edited by Henry Lee Moon, Simon & Schuster, 1972; *The Correspondence of W.E.B. Du Bois,* edited by Herbert Aptheker, University of Massachusetts Press, Volume I, 1973, Volume II, 1976; *The Education of Black People: Ten Critiques, 1906-1960,* edited by H. Aptheker, University of Massachusetts Press, 1973; *The Writings of W.E.B. Du Bois,* edited by Virginia Hamilton, Crowell, 1975; *Book Reviews,* edited by H. Aptheker, KTO Press, 1977; *Against Racism: Unpublished Essays, Papers, Addresses, 1887-1961,* edited by H. Aptheker, University of Massachusetts Press, 1985.

Columnist for newspapers, including *Chicago Defender, Pittsburgh Courier, New York Amsterdam News,* and *San Francisco Chronicle.* Contributor to numerous periodicals, including *Atlantic Monthly* and *World's Work.* Founder and editor of numerous periodicals, including *Moon,* 1905-06, *Horizon,* 1908-10, *Brownies' Book,* 1920-21, and *Phylon Quarterly,* 1940. Editor in chief of *Encyclopedia of the Negro,* 1933-46. Director of *Encyclopaedia Africana.*

SIDELIGHTS: **February 23, 1868.** "I was born by a golden river and in the shadow of two great hills, five years after the Emancipation Proclamation, which began the freeing of American Negro slaves. The valley was wreathed in grass and trees and crowned to the eastward by the huge bulk of East Mountain, with crag and cave and dark forests. Westward the hill was gentler, rolling up to gorgeous sunsets and cloud-swept storms. The town of Great Barrington, which lay between these mountains in Berkshire County, Western Massachusetts, had a broad Main Street, lined with maples and elms, with white picket fences before the homes. The climate was to our thought quite perfect.

"In 1868 on the day after the birth of George Washington was celebrated, I was born on Church Street, which branched east from Main in midtown. The year of my birth was the year that the freedmen of the South were enfranchised, and for the first time as a mass took part in government.

Conventions with black delegates voted new constitutions all over the South, and two groups of laborers—freed slaves and poor whites—dominated the former slave states. It was an extraordinary experiment in democracy. Thaddeus Stevens, the clearest-headed leader of this attempt at industrial democracy, made his last speech, impeaching Andrew Johnson of February 16, and on February 23 I was born.

"The house of my birth was quaint, with clapboards running up and down, neatly trimmed; there were five rooms, a tiny porch, a rosy front yard, and unbelievably delicious strawberries in the rear. A South Carolinian, lately come to the Berkshire Hills, owned all this—tall, thin, and black, with golden earrings, and given to religious trances. Here my mother, Mary Burghardt, and my father, Alfred Du Bois, came to live temporarily after their marriage ceremony in the village of Housatonic, which adjoined Great Barrington on the north. Then after a few years my father went east into Connecticut to build a life and home for mother and me.

"Work for black folk which would lead to a more prosperous future was not easy to come by. Just why this was so it is difficult to say; it was not solely race prejudice, although this played its part; it was lack of training and understanding, re-

W. E. B. Du Bois, 1907.

The graduating class at Fisk University in 1888: Du Bois is seated at left.

luctance to venture into unknown surroundings, and fear of a land still strange to family mores which pictured travel as disaster. In my family, I remember farmers, barbers, waiters, cooks, housemaids and laborers. In these callings a few prospered.'' [W.E.B. Du Bois, *The Autobiography of W.E.B. Du Bois: A Soliloquy on Viewing My Life from the Last Decade of Its First Century,* International Publishers, 1969.[1]]

1873. ''I entered public school at the age of about five or six. For ten years I went regularly to school, from nine o'clock until noon, and one o'clock until four each day, five days a week, ten months a year. The teachers were mature women, most of them trained in State Normal Schools and invariably white American Protestants.

''Gradually I became conscious that in most of the school work my natural gifts and regular attendance made me rank among the best, so that my promotions were regular and expected. I look back upon my classmates with interest and sharpened memory. They were boys and girls of town and country, with

a few Irish and never but once another colored child. My rapid advancement made me usually younger than my classmates, and this fact remained true in high school and at college and even when I began my life work it influenced my attitudes in many ways. I was often too young to lead in enterprises even when I was fitted to do so, but I was always advising and correcting older folk.

''My schoolmates were invariably white; I joined quite naturally all games, excursions, church festivals; recreations like coasting, swimming, hiking and games. I was in and out of the homes of nearly all my mates, and ate and played with them.

''I knew nevertheless that I was exceptional in appearance and that this riveted attention upon me. Less clearly, I early realized that most of the colored persons I saw, including my own folk, were poorer than the well-to-do whites; lived in humbler houses, and did not own stores. None of the colored folk I knew were so poor, drunken and sloven as some of the lower class Americans and Irish. I did not then associate poverty or ignorance with color, but rather with lack of opportunity; or more often with lack of thrift, which was in strict accord with the philosophy of New England and of the 19th century."[1]

1884. Became the first of his family to graduate from high school. "In the Summer of 1884, after my graduation from high school, there loomed the problem as to where I was to go to college. The fact that I was going had been settled in my own mind from the time that my school principal . . . had recommended my high school course. . . . He suggested, quite as a matter of course, that I ought to take the college preparatory course which involved algebra, geometry, Latin and Greek . . . comparatively few of my white classmates planned or cared to plan for college—perhaps two or three in my class of 13. I became therefore a high school student preparing for college and thus occupied an unusual position among whites in the town.

"I collected catalogues of colleges and over the claims of Williams and Amherst, nearest my home, or of Yale not much further, I blithely picked Harvard. . . .

". . . In my mind there was no doubt but that I was going to college. The whole matter was subtly taken out of my hands and a sort of guardianship of family and white friends were quietly established. I was advised that after all I was rather young to go directly to college; and also our high school was below the standard of Harvard entrance requirements. It might then be wise for me to work and study a year and then enter college in the Fall of '85. There followed an unexpected change when in the Fall of 1884 my mother died."[1]

1885. Attended Fisk University in Nashville, Tennessee on a scholarship. "At Fisk I began my writing and public speaking. I edited the *Fisk Herald*. I became an impassioned orator and developed a belligerent attitude toward the color bar. I was determined to make a scientific conquest of my environment, which would render the emancipation of the Negro race easier and quicker. The persistence which I had learned in New England stood me now in good stead. Because my first college choice had been Harvard, to Harvard I was still resolved to go.

"It was a piece of unusual luck, much more than my own determination, that admitted me to Harvard. There had been arising in Harvard at that time a feeling that the institution was becoming too ingrown, too satisfied with a sense of its New England sufficiency. A determined effort was made in 1884 and later to make Harvard a more national institution, with good students from the South and West. I saw advertisements of scholarships which were to be offered and I made application. In my favor were my New England elementary education, and the fact that I was studying in the South and that I was colored. There had been hitherto very few colored students at Harvard.

"I was immediately accepted on condition that I enter as a Junior, even after receiving my Fisk A.B. This was not altogether unfair, since my own high school in New England was somewhat behind Harvard's requirements and Fisk, because of the wretched Southern common school system, still further behind. However, all this made little difference to me. I wanted to go to Harvard because of what it offered in opportunity for wide learning."[1]

1890. Graduated cum laude from Harvard University. The following year Du Bois received his masters degree from Harvard.

1892-1894. Awarded a Slater Fund Fellowship for graduate study abroad. Did graduate work at the University of Berlin. "In the days of my formal education, my interest became concentrated upon the race struggle. My attention from the first was focused on democracy and democratic development; and upon the problem of the admission of my people into the freedom of democracy. This my training touched but obliquely. We studied history and politics almost exclusively from the point of view of ancient German freedom, English and New England democracy, and the development of the white United States. Here, however, I could bring criticism from what I knew and saw touching the Negro.

"Europe modified profoundly my outlook on life and my thought and feeling toward it, even though I was there but two short years with my contacts limited and friends few. . . . In Germany in 1892, I found myself on the outside of the American world, looking in. With me were white folk—students, acquaintances, teachers—who viewed the scene with me. They did not always pause to regard me as a curiosity, or something sub-human; I was just a man of the somewhat privileged student rank, with whom they were glad to meet and talk over the world; particularly, the part of the world whence I came.

"I found to my gratification that they, with me, did not regard America as the last word in civilization. Indeed, I derived a certain satisfaction in learning that the University of Berlin did not recognize a degree even from Harvard University, no more than Harvard did from Fisk. Even I was a little startled to realize how much that I had regarded as white American, was white European and not American at all; America's music is German, the Germans said; the Americans have no art, said the Italians; and their literature, remarked the English, is mainly English. All agreed that Americans could make money and did not care how they made it. . . . Sometimes their criticism got under even my anti-American skin, but it was refreshing on the whole to hear voiced my own attitude toward so much that America had meant to me."

1894. "I returned to the United States at 26 years of age and after 20 years of study to look for a job and begin work. I wrote [a friend] in London: 'You know I landed in New York in June, 1894, with $2 plus my fare home up in Berkshire. It was not altogether a happy homecoming. . . .'"[1]

Accepted a position as a professor of Greek and Latin at Wilberforce University in Ohio. "I went to Wilberforce with high ideals. I wanted to help build a great university. I was willing to work night as well as day, and taught full time. I helped in student discipline, took part in the social life, and began to write books. But I found myself against a stone wall. Nothing stirred before my impatient pounding! Or if it stirred, it soon slept again.

"The African Methodist Church was the greatest social institution of American Negroes. Wilberforce was its largest school. This school therefore became the capital of a nation-wide institution. Its large body of trustees were interested in the church organization, not the college. The bishops and would-be bishops gathered here in force on each commencement where elders and ministers waylaid them in long conferences. The teachers also found it expedient to make powerful acquaintances at these occasions; I in my independence met no one but walked off into the woods as the hosts talked."[1]

1896. Married Nina Gomer. Awarded a Ph.D. degree from Harvard. Became an assistant instructor in sociology at the University of Pennsylvania in Philadelphia. "With my bride of three months, I settled in one room in the city over a cafeteria run by a College Settlement, in the worst part of the Seventh Ward. We lived there a year, in the midst of an atmosphere of dirt, drunkenness, poverty, and crime. Murder sat on our doorsteps, police were our government, and philanthropy dropped in with periodic advice.

"The world seized and whirled me. I hardly knew what was important, what negligible; somehow I remember life, curiously enough, chiefly as a succession of homes; the settlement at Philadelphia at Seventh and Lombard in the slums where kids played intriguing games like 'cops and lady bums'; and where in the night when pistols popped, you didn't get up lest you find you couldn't."[1]

1897-1910. Became a professor of history and economics at Atlanta University in Georgia. "My real life work was begun at Atlanta for 13 years, from my 29th to my 42nd birthday. There were years of great spiritual upturning, of the making and unmaking of ideals, of hard work and hard play. Here I found myself. I lost most óf my mannerisms. I grew more broadly human, made my closest and most holy friendships, and studied human beings. I became widely acquainted with the real condition of my people. I realized the terrific odds which faced them. I saw the Atlanta riot.

"The main significance of my work at Atlanta University, during the years 1897 to 1910, was the development at an American institution of learning, of a program of study on the problems affecting the American Negroes, covering a progressively widening and deepening effort designed to stretch over the span of a century."

1903. Wrote *The Souls of Black Folk,* a portrayal of the hypocrisy, hostility, and brutality of white America toward black America.

1910-1934. Director of publicity and research for the National Association for the Advancement of Colored People (NAACP) and editor of *Crisis.* "I was still fighting the battle of liberalism against race prejudice; trying to adjust war and postwar problems to the question of racial justice; trying to show from the injustices of war time what the new vision must encompass; fighting mobs and lynchings; encouraging Negro migration; helping woman suffrage; encouraging the new rush·of young blacks to college; watching and explaining the political situation and traveling and lecturing over thousands of miles and in hundreds of centers.

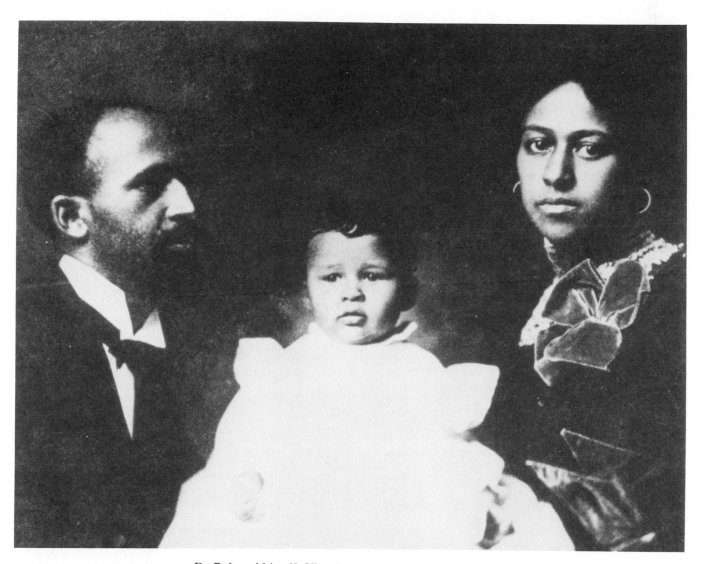

Du Bois and his wife Nina Gomer with their son, Burghardt.

Harlem storefront office of the N.A.A.C.P., about 1945, during the time Du Bois was director of special research.

"In addition to this I was encouraging the writing of others and trying to help develop Negro art and literature. Besides editing *The Crisis* continuously, I published *Darkwater* in 1920; *The Gift of Black Folk* in 1924. This Georgia fought bitterly to keep from appearing. . . . I also wrote the concluding chapter in *The New Negro* edited by Alain Locke in 1925, besides a number of magazine articles. Most of the young writers who began what was called the renaissance of Negro literature in the 20's saw their first publication in *The Crisis* magazine.

"Above all in these days I made two efforts toward which I look back with infinite satisfaction: the two-year attempt in the *Brownie's Book* to furnish a little magazine for Negro children . . . ; and most especially my single-handed production of the pageant 'The Star of Ethiopia.' The pageant was an attempt to put into dramatic form for the benefit of large masses of people, a history of the Negro race. It was first attempted in the New York celebration of Emancipation in 1913; it was repeated with magnificent and breath-taking success in Washington with 1,200 participants; it was given again in Philadelphia in 1916; and in Los Angeles in 1924."[1]

From 1934 to 1944, Du Bois returned to Atlanta University as professor and chairman of the sociology department.

1948. Campaigned for the Progressive Party in the national elections. His radical political stance provoked some run-ins with the United States government from time to time.

1950. Following the death of his first wife, Du Bois married author Shirley Graham, a year later.

1951. Indicted and tried for "failure to register as an agent of a foreign principle." Although he was acquitted, Du Bois was denied a passport on the grounds that it was not in "the best interest of the United States" for him to journey abroad. "I have faced during my life many unpleasant experiences; the growl of a mob; the personal threat of murder; the scowling distaste of an audience. But nothing has so cowed me as that day, . . . when I took my seat in a Washington courtroom as an indicted criminal. I was not a criminal. I had broken no law, consciously or unwittingly. Yet I sat with four other American citizens of unblemished character, never before accused even of misdemeanor, in the seats often occupied by murderers, forgers and thieves; accused of a felony and liable to be sentenced before leaving this court to five years of imprisonment, a fine of $10,000 and loss of my civil and political rights as a citizen, representing five generations of Americans.

"The publication of my story of this persecution in my book *In Battle for Peace;* the collaboration of Shirley Graham; my open thanks to the Communists of the world for their help in my defense; and my clear stand in favor of the Soviet Union intensified the enmity of those who rule. My defense of the Rosenbergs in speech and writing and my denunciation of the hounding and imprisonment of the Communists as unjust and barbarous did the same.

"All this made my enemies and the Federal government take a determined stand to insure my destruction. The secret police swarmed in my neighborhood asking about my visitors; whether I entertained and whom. When we entertained a Soviet diplomat, his wife and daughter, and Paul Robeson, the whole borough of Brooklyn was declared 'out of bounds' for Soviet diplomats. My manuscripts and those of Shirley Graham were refused publication by reputable commercial publishers. My mail was tampered with or withheld. Negro newspapers were warned not to carry my writings nor mention prominently my name. Colleges ceased to invite my lectures and Negro colleges no longer asked for my lectures or my presence at Commencement exercises. From being a person whom every Negro in the nation knew by name at least and hastened always to entertain or praise, churches and Negro conferences refused to mention my past or present existence. The white world which had never liked me but was forced in the past to respect me, now ignored me or deliberately distorted my work. A whispering campaign continually intimated that some hidden treason or bribery could be laid at my door if the government had not been lenient. The central office of the NAACP refused to let local branches invite me or sponsor any lectures. I was refused the right to speak on the University of California campus because of NAACP protest. In fine I was rejected of men, refused the right to travel abroad and classed as a 'controversial figure' even after being acquitted of guilt by a Federal court of law.

"It was a bitter experience and I bowed before the storm. But I did not break. I continued to speak and write when and where I could. I faced my lowered income and lived within it. I found new friends and lived in a wider world than ever before—a world with no colored line. I lost my leadership of my race. It was a dilemma for the mass of Negroes; either they joined the current beliefs and actions of most whites or they could not make a living or hope for preferment. Preferment was possible. The color line was beginning to break. Negroes were getting recognition as never before. Was not the sacrifice of one man, small payment for this? Even those who disagreed with this judgment at least kept quiet. The colored children ceased to hear my name."[1]

1958. Following the Supreme Court's decision that allowed Du Bois and his wife to leave the country, the two spent several months traveling in Europe, the U.S.S.R. and China. "... My long travel was beginning to tell on me and I was in a Soviet sanitarium near Moscow. I prepared to leave for Africa, but the council of physicians advised against the trip as too taxing. I had prepared three messages for Africa. One I delivered at Tashkent, one I sent by my wife Shirley, who attended the conference at Accra, and the last I broadcast later from Peking on my 91st birthday."[1]

1961. Joined the Communist Party. Moved to Ghana at the invitation of President Nkrumah.

August 27, 1963. Died in Accra, Ghana at the age of ninety-five. "I have lived a good and full life. I have finished my course. I don't want to live this life again. I have known its pain, suffering and despair. I am tired, I am through. For the souls who follow me, . . . I bequeath all that waits to be done, and Holy Time what a task, forever!"[1]

FOR MORE INFORMATION SEE: W.E.B. Du Bois, *Darkwater: Voices from Within the Veil,* Harcourt, 1920, reprinted, Kraus Reprint, 1975; *Springfield Republican,* May 28, 1928; *Boston Transcript,* June 24, 1939; *Saturday Review of Literature,* July 29, 1939, June 23, 1945; W.E.B. Du Bois, *Dusk of Dawn: An Essay Toward an Autobiography of Race Concept,* Harcourt, 1940, reprinted, Kraus Reprint, 1975; *New York Times,* March 9, 1947; W.E.B. Du Bois, *In Battle for Peace: The Story of My 83rd Birthday,* Masses and Mainstream, 1952, reprinted, Kraus Reprint, 1976; Robert A. Bone, *The Negro Novel in America,* Yale University Press, revised edition, 1965; Elliott M. Rudwick, *W.E.B. Du Bois: Propagandist of the Negro Protest,* Atheneum, 1968; W.E.B. Du Bois, *The Autobiography of W.E.B. Du Bois: A Soliloquy on Viewing My Life from the Last Decade of Its First Century,* International Publishers, 1968.

Leslie Alexander Lacy, *The Life of W.E.B. Du Bois: Cheer the Lonesome Traveler,* Dial, 1970; Rayford W. Logan, editor, *W.E.B. Du Bois: A Profile,* Hill & Wang, 1971; Emma Gelders Sterne, *His Was the Voice: The Life of W.E.B. Du Bois,* Crowell-Collier, 1971; Shirley Graham Du Bois, *His Day Is Marching On: A Memoir of W.E.B. Du Bois,* Lippincott, 1971; Houston A. Baker, Jr., *Black Literature in America,* McGraw, 1971; *Newsweek,* August 23, 1971; *Contemporary Literary Criticism,* Gale, Volume 1, 1972, Volume 2, 1974; *New Republic,* February 26, 1972; *Ebony,* August, 1972, August, 1975; *New York Review of Books,* November 30, 1972; Hugh Hawkins, editor, *Booker T. Washington and His Critics: Black Leadership in Crisis,* Heath, 1974; Arnold Rampersad, *Art and Imagination of W.E.B. Du Bois,* Harvard University Press, 1976; Allison Davis, *Leadership, Love and Aggression,* Harcourt, 1983; Herbert Aptheker, editor, *Against Racism: Unpublished Essays, Papers, Addresses, 1887-1961,* University of Massachusetts Press, 1985.

Although Linda called it an express, the train did stop every now and then, at dimly lit stations. ■ (From *No Pets Allowed and Other Animal Stories* by Margaret Dunnett. Illustrated by Peter Rush.)

MARGARET DUNNETT

DUNNETT, Margaret (Rosalind)   1909-1977

PERSONAL: Born May 15, 1909, in Tunbridge Wells, England; died in 1977; married George Dunnett; children: one son, three daughters. *Education:* Received diploma from London University. *Home:* Basings Cottage, Furnace Lane, Cowden, Kent, England.

CAREER: Writer of children's novels and stories. Also served as local government councillor, 1955-66. *Member:* Society of Authors.

WRITINGS—All juvenile; all published by Deutsch: *The People Next Door* (illustrated by Maurice Bartlett), 1965; *Has Anyone Seen Emmy?*, 1968; *The Gypsy's Grand-daughter*, 1970; *Max-a-Million*, 1972; *The Boy Who Saw Emmy*, 1973; *Ladies and Gentlemen* (illustrated by Jill Gardiner), 1976; *No Pets Allowed and Other Animal Stories,* (illustrated by Peter Rush) 1981. Contributor of stories for children to periodicals and programs.

Children are entitled to their otherness, as anyone is; and when we reach them, as we sometimes do, it is generally on a point of sheer delight, to us so astonishing, but to them so natural.

—Alastair Reid
(from *Places, Poems, Preoccupations*)

EDWARDS, Linda Strauss

BRIEF ENTRY: Born in White Plains, N.Y. An author and illustrator of books for children, Edwards received her B.F.A. from Syracuse University School of Art. She illustrated a number of books written by others before writing and illustrating one of her own entitled *The Downtown Day* (Pantheon, 1983). Edwards' story follows the shopping trip of stubborn young Linda, who yearns for a red sweater with buttons down the front, and her two aunts, who are looking for "sensible" school clothes. *School Library Journal* observed: "The family love portrayed in this city story is colorfully supplemented by the use of warm hues in soft wash illustrations. . . ." Among Edwards' illustrated works are Barbara Williams' *So What If I'm a Sore Loser?* (Harcourt, 1981), Jamie Gilson's *Thirteen Ways to Sink a Tub* (Lothrop, 1982) and *4B Goes Wild* (Lothrop, 1983), Jill Ross Klevin's *The Turtle Street Trading Co.* and *Turtles Together Forever!* (both Delacorte, 1982), and Betty Bates' *Call Me Friday the Thirteenth* (Holiday House, 1983). Edwards is married to a physician's assistant and is the mother of two children. *Residence:* Lowville, N.Y.

ENDE, Michael   1930(?)-

BRIEF ENTRY: Born about 1930, in Garmisch-Partenkirchen, Bavaria, Germany (now West Germany). German novelist, author of books for children, and poet. Ende is best known for his international bestseller *Unendliche geschichte* (1979), translated and published in America as *The Neverending Story* (Doubleday, 1983). Most appropriately described as a book-within-a-book, this fantasy novel begins with the ten-year-old hero Bastian reading a book also titled "The Neverending Story." As he reads, Bastian follows the adventurous quest of a young hunter named Atreyu and learns that Fantasiana (or Fantastica) is being destroyed by the Nothing, symbolic of humankind's lost interest in the magic of fantasy. The crossover between reality and fantasy occurs when Bastian bursts into Fantasiana to save the land from destruction and its ailing childlike Empress from death. The original book design of *The Neverending Story* includes a silk cover and two-color type— red for Bastian's or the "real" story and green for the fantasy he is reading.

Unintended by Ende, *The Neverending Story* gained great popularity among antinuclear activists in West Germany, remaining at the top of the country's bestseller list for more than three years. A movie adaptation, simultaneously filmed in German and English, was released in 1984. Although commercially successful, the movie was panned by Ende who demanded that his name be removed from the credits. Ende has received numerous European awards for his book, including Germany's Buxtehuder Bulle and Wilhelm-Hauff-Preis, Italy's Premio Europeo "Provincia di Trento," and Poland's International Janusz Korczak Prize.

Ende's career as a writer began during post-World War II days when, an aspiring actor, he began creating satiric sketches for Munich cabarets. He went on to write film and theater reviews for Munich radio before the publication of his first book in 1961. *The Neverending Story,* translated into twenty-five languages, was the first of Ende's works to appear in America. In 1985 Doubleday published a translation of his fantasy novel *Momo. Residence:* Near Rome, Italy.

FOR MORE INFORMATION SEE: Publishers Weekly, May 28, 1982; *People Weekly,* August 27, 1984; *Contemporary Literary Criticism,* Volume 31, Gale, 1985.

EZZELL, Marilyn   1937-

PERSONAL: Surname is accented on second syllable; born March 11, 1937, in Teaneck, N.J.; daughter of Paul Herbert and Thelma (a secretary; maiden name, Hoagland) Ezzell. *Education:* St. Luke's Hospital, New York, N.Y., R.N., 1958; attended Columbia University, 1964-65. *Religion:* Christian. *Residence:* New York, N.Y.

CAREER: Has worked as a nurse in a hospital, a doctor's office and as an instructor of nursing, as well as a typist and secretary. Writer.

WRITINGS—"Susan Sand Mystery" series; for young people; all published by Pinnacle Books: *The Mystery at Hollowhearth House,* 1982; *The Secret of Clovercrest Castle,* 1982; *The Clue in Witchwhistle Well,* 1982; *The Riddle of Raggedrock Ridge,* 1982; *The Phantom of Featherford Falls,* 1983; *The Password to Diamondwarf Dale,* 1983.

WORK IN PROGRESS: The Search for the Snowship Songs, and *The Mystery of Beggarbay Bluff.*

HOBBIES AND OTHER INTERESTS: Classical music (especially *lieder* of Franz Schubert), walking, swimming, reading, games, cats.

FINGER, Charles J(oseph)   1869(?)-1941

PERSONAL: Born December 25, 1869 (some sources cite 1871), in Willesden, Sussex, England; came to the United States in 1887, became naturalized citizen in 1896; died following a heart attack, January 7 (some sources cite January 8), 1941, near Fayetteville, Ark.; son of Charles H. and Julia (Connolly) Finger; married Nellie B. Ferguson, June 7, 1902; children: Hubert Philip, Mrs. Felix Helbling, Charles Joseph, Mrs. Robert A. Leflar, Herbert Eric. *Education:* Attended King's College, London and studied music at Frankfurt am Main, Germany. *Religion:* Episcopalian. *Residence:* Fayetteville, Ark.

CAREER: Author and editor. In his late teens, Finger became a merchant seaman and traveled to South America, where he roamed for ten years; later traveled to Mexico, Canada, and Alaska, where he was a prospector in the Klondike Gold Fields; about 1900, became director of the Conservatory of Music, San Angelo, Tex.; in 1906 entered the railroad business, beginning as a boilermaker's helper in Alamogordo, N.M., and then moving to Ohio where he worked until 1920 and became an auditor and eventually a general manager for the Ohio Southeastern System; about 1920, became editor and then owner of the magazine *Reedy's Mirror* (renamed *All's Well, or, The Mirror Repolished*), a one-man journal which ran until 1935; beginning in 1933, worked as a managing editor for the Bellows-Reeve Co., Chicago, Ill.; from 1936, employed as an editor for Newbery Press.

MEMBER: Scarab Club (Detroit). *Awards, honors:* Newbery Medal, American Library Association, 1925, for *Tales from Silver Lands;* Longmans, Green & Co. Prize for best adventure story, 1929, for *Courageous Companions;* D. Litt., Knox College, 1931; LL.D., University of Arkansas, 1933; *Give a Man a Horse* was named an honor book in the older children's category of the Spring Book Festival Awards by the *New York Herald Tribune,* 1938.

WRITINGS—Juvenile; fiction, except as noted: *Tales from Silver Lands* (folktales; illustrated by Paul Honoré), Doubleday, Page, 1924; *Tales Worth Telling* (folktales; illustrated by P. Honoré), Century, 1927; *David Livingstone: Explorer and Prophet* (biography), Doubleday, Page, 1927, revised edition (illustrated by Arthur Zaidenburg), Doubleday, Doran, 1930; *The Spreading Stain: A Tale for Boys and Men with Boys' Hearts* (illustrated by P. Honoré), Doubleday, Page, 1927; (editor) *Heroes from Hakluyt* (illustrated by P. Honoré), Henry Holt, 1928; *Courageous Companions* (historical romance; illustrated by James H. Daugherty), Longmans, Green, 1929; *A Paul Bunyan Geography* (folktale; illustrated by daughter, Helen Finger), privately printed, 1931; *The Magic Tower* (illustrated by H. Finger), Kings Arms Press, 1933; *A Dog at His Heel: The Story of Jock, an Australian Sheep Dog, and What Befell Him and His Companions on a Great Drive* (illustrated by Henry C. Pitz), John C. Winston, 1936; *Our Navy: An Outline History for Young People* (nonfiction; illustrated by H. C. Pitz), Houghton, 1936.

When Guns Thundered at Tripoli (illustrated by H. C. Pitz), Holt, 1937; *Bobbie and Jock and the Mailman* (illustrated by H. Finger), Holt, 1938; *Give a Man a Horse* (illustrated by H. C. Pitz), John C. Winston, 1938; *Cape Horn Snorter: A Story of the War of 1812, and of Gallant Days with Captain Porter of the U.S. Frigate, Essex* (illustrated by H. C. Pitz), Houghton, 1939; *Golden Tales from Faraway* (folktales; illustrated by H. Finger), John C. Winston, 1940; *The Yankee Captain in Patagonia* (illustrated by H. C. Pitz), Grosset, 1941; *High Water in Arkansas* (illustrated by H. C. Pitz), Grosset, 1943.

Other principal writings: (Editor) *The Choice of the Crowd* (poetry anthology), Golden Horseman Press, 1922; *In Lawless*

Charles J. Finger. Woodblock by Paul Honoré.

Charles J. Finger on an ornithology trip.

Lands (short stories), M. Kennerley, 1924; *Highwaymen: A Book of Gallant Rogues* (illustrated by P. Honoré), R. M. McBride, 1924; *Bushrangers* (illustrated by P. Honoré), R. M. McBride, 1924; *Ozark Fantasia* (short stories; illustrated by P. Honoré), compiled and edited by Charles M. Wilson, Golden Horseman Press, 1927; (compiler) *Frontier Ballads* (songs; illustrated by P. Honoré), Doubleday, Page, 1927; *Romantic Rascals* (illustrated by P. Honoré), R. M. McBride, 1927; *A Man for a'That: The Story of Robert Burns*, Stratford, 1929; *Seven Horizons* (autobiography), Doubleday, Doran, 1930; *Adventure under Sapphire Skies* (travel; illustrated by H. Finger), Morrow, 1931; *The Affair at the Inn as Seen by Philo the Innkeeper and the Taxgatherer of Rome*, privately printed, 1931; *Foot-Loose in the West, Being the Account of a Journey to Colorado and California and Other Western States* (illustrated by H. Finger), Morrow, 1932; *After the Great*

Companions: A Free Fantasia on a Lifetime of Reading, Dutton, 1934; *The Distant Prize: A Book about Rovers, Rangers, and Rascals*, D. Appleton-Century, 1935; *Valiant Vagabonds*, D. Appleton-Century, 1936.

Also author of *Fighting for Fur*, 1940. Author of additional publications in the "Ten Cent Pocket" series, including *Hints on Writing Short Stories*, 1922, *The Tragic Story of Oscar Wild's Life*, 1923, (editor) Jules Verne, *A Voyage to the Moon*, 1923, (compiler) *Sailor Chanties and Cowboy Songs*, 1923, and in the "Little Blue Book" series, including *Hints on Writing One-Act Plays*, 1923, (compiler) *Book of Real Adventures*, 1924, published by Haldeman-Julius; author of songs; member of editorial board, *Story Parade;* contributor to periodicals, including *Century, Youth's Companion, American Boy, Smart*

Set, American Mercury, Nation, St. Nicholas, Classmate, Red Cross Magazine, and *New York Herald Tribune.*

ADAPTATIONS: "Tales from Silver Lands" (filmstrip with phonodisc or phonotape and teacher's notes), Miller-Brody, 1972; "The Magic Ball and Other Tales from Silver Lands" (based on *Tales from Silver Lands;* filmstrip with phonodisc or phonotape and teacher's notes), Miller-Brody, 1972; "Tale of the Lazy People" (based on *Tales from Silver Lands;* 16mm film), Miller-Brody, 1976.

Recordings: "Tales from Silver Lands" (dramatization; contains "The Magic Ball," "Na-Ha the Fighter," and "The Tale of the Lazy People"), incidental music by Herb Davidson, Newbery Award Records, 1970; "The Calabash Man and Other Tales from Silver Lands" (record or cassette), Miller-Brody, (n.d.).

SIDELIGHTS: **Christmas Day, 1869.** Born in Willesdon, Sussex, England. The exact year of Finger's birthdate is vague—some biographical sources list 1869, while others list 1871. Nevertheless, it is universally agreed that Finger grew up in London, and was educated at private schools and at King's College in London. For a brief time, he also studied music at Frankfurt am Main in Germany. ". . . Glorious were the festivals in my boyhood. As if it were yesterday I see, with my mind's eye, the glittering tree, thickly hung with shining things, and the wonders at its foot. Christmas Eve had been the time of expectation when we put our plates under the bare pine tree, our names written on paper slips for the guidance of the mysterious bringer of gifts. And as we stole downstairs in the gray dawn, anxious, expectant, we wondered whether our misdeeds in the year past had been noted, and, as punishment, we would go empty–handed. But always the Fates were kind. The mysterious giver had overlooked our shortcomings with delicate tact, and there were the gifts to dazzle and bewilder us. Poor would have been the Christmas that did not bring a new Jules Verne, a Boy's Annual, a Henty, a Kingstone, or some other glorious book vividly illustrated.

"Year after year other gifts came—a magic lantern with colored slides; clockwork trains; model yachts that would sail, tack, and return to the owner; an ingenious balloon that rose, loosed a parachute, and had to be retrieved from the stratosphere, which was the ceiling; humming tops, rocking horses, boxes of paints, and boxes of tools; microscopes, telescopes, skates, puppet theaters, boxing gloves—all according to age and requirements." [Helen Ferris, editor, *Writing Books for Boys and Girls,* Doubleday, 1952.[1]]

Very early in his life, he became interested in going to sea, and read books about foreign lands and adventure. "I adventured into a many-hued land of enchantment. I came to know every bookshop, new and second-hand, in the West End of London, as well as in other towns to which I frequently went. The day was barren on which I did not have a book in hand, and I read riding, walking in crowded streets, at mealtimes. Captain Marryat took me by storm and I read everything of his that I could lay hands on. Then Mayne Reid captured me, and upon what glorious crusade I entered when I came to know his sun-tanned, alkali-dusted scalp hunters. Incidentally hundreds of western tales by writers of lesser caliber delighted me, but I abandoned them when I found Bret Harte. In his characters I first made acquaintance with living, illumined human beings and with fictional folk that made distinct impressions. . . .

". . . Harte's poems were the first poems I read with understanding and interest, and, strangely, through them my horizon became widened for I came across his *Dickens in Camp* and so came to Dickens by way of *Oliver Twist.* Next came the *Pickwick Papers* which I read avidly and with shouts of laughter. . . . I reveled in all those odd people whom I found to be far more interesting than the constrained folks of the real world. . . ." [Charles J. Finger, *Seven Horizons,* Doubleday, Doran, 1930.[2]]

1890s. The lore of adventure and travel led Finger to a life as a merchant seaman during his late teenage years. From England, Finger travelled to South America and Africa, followed Magellan's route from Belen to the Pacific, explored the Andes, lived in Patagonia and in Tierra del Fuego. For fifteen years he lived a life of adventure. "I wanted to set foot in Patagonia. I wanted to know something of Tierra del Fuego. The living there might be hard, but one would have lived at first hand. It would be getting away from all my entanglements with the past. . . .

"With it you may see the hidden spirit of other people, seeing through the mask they wear." ▪
(From "The Wonderful Mirror," in *Tales from Silver Lands* by Charles J. Finger. Woodcuts by Paul Honoré.)

The frigate *Constitution*. ■ (From *Our Navy: An Outline History for Young People* by Charles J. Finger. Illustrated by Henry C. Pitz.)

"... There were a thousand paths to be trodden and I found myself free to choose. I could aim at fullness of life and not vacuity. I could come to deserve my own respect because I would earn my own living at first hand, somehow. I would leave behind all that debris among which I had been wandering, all that quoting of other men, all that following of beaten tracks, all that gush about the welfare of my fellow man, all that humiliating obedience to constituted authority. I would live life on my own terms. I would find by study of myself and of the ground I stood on what my combined inward and outward capability was.

"The idea of becoming a cogwheel in the world's machinery stuck in me, but I wanted to be a wheel, not a point on the rim of one. That is why, at San Julian Bay, I chose to go without any purpose other than to wander to the foothills of the Andes, rather than to ship to Europe in the *Bootle*, a barkentine that lay there loading wool, and hides, and tallow. I jerked myself out of a great desire to walk from San Julian to Santa Cruz, and then south to where Magellan's *Santiago* suffered shipwreck. . . .

"I jerked myself out of that desire, as I say, and went to work with an odd company, bossing the loading of the *Bootle,* and, with the money thus earned, I bought a couple of horses and gear. So the way lay open for limitless adventure, and much of that adventure I have told in my books, with a certain amount of imaginative trimmings. I have elaborated and transmuted because I could not help doing so; and I could not help doing so because almost unconsciously, some particle in my

brain insisted that to foreshorten here, and to color there, here to add and there to diminish, would make for a sort of completeness. If you drag something from its context you must needs trim edges, satisfying yourself with the comforting and uplifting conclusion that Art betters Nature.

"There were, during those . . . years and more, happenings that I thought to be cardinal events in my life, but which soon paled into insignificance. There was my enlistment in the Chilean army during the Balmaceda-Montt trouble and my desertion two days later. There was a silly gesture when I thought to make myself important in a political way by writing furious pamphlets against those who offered a bounty for the ears of Indians, and all that came of it was a jail sentence by a very nonchalant young deputy governor who smoked cigarettes and drank wine while he questioned me, not so much curious about the case in hand as about myself, and my opinions, and my hopes and aims and expectations."[2]

From South America, Finger travelled to Mexico, Canada and Alaska. In San Angelo, Texas he became director of the San Angelo Conservatory of Music from 1898 to 1900. ". . . I had marched to horizons to see other horizons. From the youthful horizon of respectability I had seen the horizon of altruism. From the horizon of altruism I had seen the far line of independence and of living for self. There had been the narrow horizon of love. Now I began to see distant heights, affairs of business, or economic activity. Yet to wrench myself out of all that freedom and into any kind of servitude seemed a huge task.

". . . I went to Canada, first Montreal, then Ottawa; next in a great jump to Port Arthur where I met with a party of pro-

A Patagonian. ■ (From *Foot-Loose in the West* by Charles J. Finger. Illustrated by Henry C. Pitz.)

spectors and with them went north in search of minerals. There was a kind of interlude when I paddled about the many lakes west of Fort William and north of Savannah, and joined for a while a party of lumberers. I turn the leaves of my diary to find a record of joyful weeks in pine woods, of hunting and fishing, of days when I canoed alone, of hearty French-Canadian companions who ate tremendously and laughed tremendously and enjoyed life to the full. And one day, being near Winnipeg, I heard the tale of construction work in the Rockies at Crow's Nest Pass, so that seemed the chance I sought to get into the economic machine that seemed to have no place for me. There was Edmonton, and an attempt to get to the Klondike by the overland route, and failure because of cold. Next I headed east and worked for a while on a fishing steamer that plied between Duluth and Fort William, until, with something of money in hand, I again made my way to Texas and one fine day my violinist and I started our School of Fine Arts.

"It prospered beyond expectations, for we threw ourselves heartily into the work, found plentiful support, organized subsidiary activities such as elocutionary classes, singing, orchestra and all that kind of thing. . . . The fundamental weakness in the field of music teaching was that people were not satisfied to have young ones learn to appreciate and to love music as a means of elevating and enriching life, but took it for granted that everyone should become a performer, which is, in effect, much as though one should learn to read not for private pleasure of reading and all that may grow out of that pleasure, but to the end that one might become an elocutionist.

"In the midst of a certain measure of success there came upon me the old restlessness. I tried to combat it by bicycling south

With a ragged army Jorgenson marched north. ■
(From *Romantic Rascals* by Charles J. Finger. Woodcuts by Paul Honoré.)

(From *Foot-Loose in the West* by Charles J. Finger. Illustrated by Helen Finger.)

to San Antonio and to Laredo, north to New Mexico, but those trips were as drops of water to a thirsting dog. With my violinist friend and a singer, I made a restricted concert tour, but it whetted my appetite for further travel. I engaged with a stock-man, dressed in overalls, and took a trainload of sheep to Chicago, but the yearning remained. And, being again in Texas, one day I sat under a pecan tree with a pencil and paper because the idea of a story had come to mind. I wrote it, mailed it to *Youth's Companion* and in time received a check of twenty-five dollars and a pleasant letter from the editor asking me for more. So that was my first literary effort, but many years elapsed before I tried again, for between the time of the sending of the story and the receipt of the check I had joined forces with a friend, closed my music school, and had become a very happy man buying this and that for a cross-country ride that should end when I found employment to please me. The employment, I decided, should be one in which I might identify myself with the economic machinery of the world. It should be no blind alley, but an open road offering advancement. It should have something to do with things moving and not static. But lacking trade and profession, whatever that employment might be I must start at the lowest rung. So the world was open for adventure once more, and I set off with a blithe heart, slept at night under the stars, and, like the pilgrim, 'when I awoke I sang.'"[2]

1906. Entered the railroad business. ". . . My years in the untamed lands served to train me for the part I took in commercial life. I entered the business field with no knowledge of the economic life, without prepossessions, and what is better, unhampered by taboos and conventions, so everything was interesting and sometimes exciting. I had no special qualifications, as qualifications were counted by efficiency engineers, but the life I had lived made for an alertness that stood me in good stead. Thrown among men in whom those habits and qualities existed in me, and with those men often lax because of their many years of monotonous toil, it became an easy matter to pass competitors.

"As I have said, I was unhampered by conventions. Perhaps it would be better to say that I walked a middle way, going between humility and pride, though unconsciously. . . .'"[2]

Finger moved to Ohio, where he became a railroad auditor and then a general manager for the Ohio Southeastern System. "By one lucky stroke and another . . . I became general manager. By renting out waste lands, making new interline traffic arrangements, stepping outside the true functions of railroading, and, where electric lines were concerned, renting power to towns for light; by one means and another as well as by a certain saving in administration and a narrow scrutiny of ex-

All eyes were turned to see Blueskin wrestling furiously with Wild, the Thief-taker. ■ (From *Highwaymen: A Book of Gallant Rogues* by Charles J. Finger. Illustrated by Paul Honoré.)

pense accounts, the loss side of the balance sheet began to show more favorably. The loss presently turned into a gain, though a slight one, when I bought a tract of rockbearing land and a couple of stone-crushers and went into the quarrying business so that the roads should reap the benefit of the freight. But there were strikes and stealing to combat; there were floods and fires and minor mishaps; there were state railroad commissioners who insisted on certain schedules on the just plea of the people living along the line, and who ordered stations to be built, and who sometimes commanded that freakish things be done. But there was also the burden of debt because of the ancient monster graft. Also steadily growing there was automobile traffic, an evolution in transportation that obviously must, some day in the near future, work as much havoc in railroad affairs as the advent of the steam engine had worked among holders of turnpike stock that once paid its six per cent. . . .''[2]

1919. Began to contribute to the weekly magazine, *Reedy's Mirror*. Became editor until 1920 when Reedy died.

1920. Moved to Fayetteville, Arkansas, where he wrote and published a one-man monthly magazine, *All's Well*. ''In a manner of speaking, a sense of uneasiness made me leave the world of economic activity to march toward a new horizon and, after a time, literary fields. A sort of uneasiness possessed me because life seemed a dull performance if man did not live in touch with the natural beauty of the earth. Then there was a marked loneliness. I went hither and yon in trains and automobiles, my affairs being spread over a wide territory, but I knew no friendship worthy of the name. There were men for whom I had tremendous respect, and I saw evidences of similar respect existing between other men, but friendship among men seemed to have gone from the world. There were few to whom I could talk without strain or effort. It was rare to discover anyone who seemed to have contact with or interest in the higher side of knowledge, as with things literary, or musical, or with philosophical questions. . . .

''I repeat that what I most deplored during those years of successful activity was the absence of true companionship among men of affairs. Having entered the economic world I seemed to have closed the door upon something which had made me glad and grateful to meet men. The very letters I received from associates in the business world were cold and distant as if the writers of them feared that an appearance of friendship might mean loss of dignity. There was no end of expensive hospitality, there were generosities, there were long hours during train rides and auto rides when I sat side by side or face to face with men that I liked, but always there were stone walls of separation and very little earnest enjoyment. And in many of the homes of successful men it was very apparent that whatever companionship once existed between men and their wives had long since become diluted. The very fact of success kept men more and more occupied with other men and away from their homes, and the women turned more and more to social affairs. Children of age were sent away to boarding schools, or, being too young for them, found attractions away from home because commercial interests worked one way to disrupt the family as a social and educational institution. . . .

''. . . It came to me with all the force of a blow that my five children were growing up, and, except for seeing them at the week-end, I was a stranger to them. But I saw more in a confused way. I saw that there was danger of the children making individual pleasure the guide of conduct. There was too much dependence upon the automobile, upon social functions, upon commercialized amusements. There was a taking for granted that the mere fact of going to school would solve

Finger, while editor of *Reedy's Mirror*.

problems of character, would automatically make for discipline, would ensure a taste for knowledge. Schools, I knew, could do none of those. They could not so much as make for efficiency and power of concentration because a foolish curriculum necessitated short cuts on the part of the children.

''Obviously the man with children had a duty other than money making. I had seen, in my own experience, that the physical or material world was not very difficult one to fight. But there were other worlds. There was a world moral and a world intellectual. Money, pleasure and position were easily gained or cultivated. It was not so easy to cultivate one's self. Strength of body and control of hand came easily. Self-discipline came hard. . . . I wrestled mightily with the problem and could not help but come back to the decision that I must give up everything in the way of money making and turn to character making. The family would have to be turned into a social and educational institution because education as left to the schools seemed to have become very much like a social affair. As for the church—for there were some slight bonds of allegiance to the Episcopal denomination (though I very rarely attended church, except to play the organ occasionally)—that struck me as being very much like a social organization from which nothing at all could be demanded or expected in actual achievement, when achievement was taken to mean the aiming to model human character upon an ideal character.

''Suddenly I saw a solution, and in seeing the general scheme of things numberless cogs fitted together with a click. The sincere study of worth-while literature! There was the answer. The young mind seizes upon an ideal character and imitates it. In my youth I had tried to model myself upon an hundred or more fictional characters, good, bad and indifferent. I had found righteousness and heroism in Hereward the Wake and in Danton and in John Ball and in Paul Jones. I had burned to alleviate suffering with Damien, and to explore with Livingstone, and to stand for liberty and right with Lincoln; to be independent with Robinson Crusoe and Thoreau; to be noble and excellent with Jack Oakhurst; and to be strong and fearless with John Ridd. I was a bundle of qualities, theoretically, taken from warriors, poets, kings, patriots, outlaws, barbarians, peasants and masters of men.

"We went to northwest Arkansas to live on a run-down farm that I had bought, which was situated three miles from the university town of Fayetteville. There came a time of vivid activity, what with repairing the old house and building a new one, with fencing the land, ditching and draining, plowing and planting, trimming the orchard and putting in a vineyard, gathering together sheep and cattle and horses. But, whether because of my ignorance of farming processes, or because of general agricultural conditions, or because of expensive tastes, or because of a mixture of all those, after a couple of years it became manifest that farming meant early financial ruin.

There was the giant holding the sailor high. . . . ▪ (From *Courageous Companions* by Charles J. Finger. Illustrated by James H. Daugherty.)

Therefore I turned to writing as a means of support. . . . If I had not turned to writing I would have turned to something else, to general contracting, or to operating a line of motor cars, or to sheep raising on a considerable scale after renting surrounding vacant farms, of which there were a few.''[2]

1921. Urged by a fellow author to record his early adventures in books for young readers, Finger devoted much of his time to serious writing. During the next twenty years he contributed greatly to juvenile literature.

1924. ''My first bound book was *In Lawless Lands*. It was brought out by that extraordinary publicist, Mitchell Kennerley, a close friend of Reedy's, a man with an eye for a beautiful book. But before the manuscript reached Kennerley, it had been lost for six months by another publisher who has since gone bankrupt. Kennerley published with no regard to marketing and only because he liked a piece of work. He concerned himself not at all with advertising or boosting. When he had made a book it had to take care of itself, falling or standing upon its own merits. He would make no contract, would not even promise a date of appearance, however much the author might plead, threaten, abuse, be lofty, solemn, or try to excite a lachrymose sympathy. In the case of *In Lawless Lands* I ran the entire gamut. But with the manuscript he tampered not at all, and no author could lay praise or blame upon the publisher for excellences or shortcomings. As to my book, which sold well enough without a line of advertising, it is a collection of short stories that grew out of remembered incidents or experiences; the scenes of action were laid, for the most part, in South America. In my mind, when writing, the qualities of vigor and interest were uppermost. The most brutal and bloody scenes were not inventions, but were founded on fact. That romantic incidents connected with women form so small a part of the tales is due to the fact that I have a lively sense of incongruity. There were few women in Patagonia, and those were uninteresting. . . .

"Close on the heels of *In Lawless Lands* appeared the book *Highwaymen*, which McBride brought out. I enjoyed tremendously the writing of the stories that composed it, for I took romantic and criminal characters and flung them into a contemporary world among circles literary and artistic and social into which they could never have entered. I reveled in doing that. I introduced Pepys, Walpole, Pope, DeFoe and other characters that had interested me, and I strove heartily for verisimilitude. It was an experiment in fictionalized history carried out with zeal. It was an attempt to do something in the style of the writers who had charmed me in my boyhood, but with their scheme lifted to a higher plane. I had no suspicion that the effort would be taken seriously by anyone. Yet it was.''[2]

1925. Awarded the Newbery Medal for *Tales from Silver Lands*. Four years later *Courageous Companions* won the Longmans Green Juvenile Fiction Prize. ''. . . There was adventure when *Tales from Silver Lands* was awarded the Newbery Medal and I went to Seattle as a guest of Doubleday, Page and Company to receive the honor. There was adventure when *Courageous Companions* . . . was adjudged the winner of the two-thousand-dollar prize offered by Longman's. It opened a way for a visit to Europe.

"I do not list such things in any spirit of boasting, nor in any foolish spirit of glow suffusion, as one might say. There were clouds aplenty, disappointments, annoyances, worries. There were cramped financial conditions. There were days without incitement to effort. There were silly distractions. But here is the main thing: I was tied to work in life and always have been, saw to it that I was. Indeed, I would never indulge indolence, nor, I hope, ever shall. For a man has to cultivate somehow a sort of zest. He has to be interested. He must go through life with a lilt, not trudge along. Above all, he must believe in himself, not seeing failure in what are, after all, mere stumbling blocks and quite in the routine of things, but trying his experiment to the end."[2]

1931. Awarded an honorary Litt.D. degree from Knox College. Two years later he was awarded an honorary LL.D. from the University of Arkansas. "Now there have been gentlemen of critical ability who found occasion, in reviewing, to take me to task for too active production, but what would they have? I found myself stuffed full of tales, so full indeed that although I should write for twenty years more at the rate I have written for the five years past I would not have told the half of them. Besides, I cannot separate enjoyment from writing. Also vigor has been and is part and parcel of my life. Nor do I find it hopeless drudgery to revise. It is fun searching for an apt phrase or a quietly humorous one, trying experiments in diction, endeavoring to do vigorous writing, aiming to the best of my ability to do honest work. If anything more needs be said, then I add that as I choose to do, so I do; and it has been tremendous fun to write this or that, and to read it aloud to the family. It has been good and wholesome and invigorating to hear the outspoken criticisms of my own children and to accept and reject accordingly. The game of activity has been worth while in this corner of the field as in others, and the only shadow on it, as on other fields, has been when people have imposed their moods and ill-tempers."[2]

January 7 (some sources cite January 8), **1941.** Died of a heart attack in Fayetteville, Arkansas. "It seems to me that my life's duty fines down to a commonplace simplicity. To achieve order in my immediate vicinity: that comes first. To resist invasion: that is second and tremendously important. And last: to assume such obligations as shall enure to the physical and intellectual welfare of my children, to the end that they may become happy warriors fit to engage in the battle of life. That's all. That last is my seventh horizon and I can expect no more than to see it, and to march toward it, stumbling and slow perhaps because of the long journey, but the gods helping, going on and on, somewhat tired perhaps at sunset, but never sitting down to wail in despair by the wayside."[2]

HOBBIES AND OTHER INTERESTS: Sailing, riding, poolplaying.

FOR MORE INFORMATION SEE: Anice Page Cooper, *Authors and Others,* Doubleday, Page, 1927; Charles J. Finger, *Seven Horizons* (autobiography), Doubleday, Doran, 1930; Stanley Kunitz and Howard Haycraft, editors, *Junior Book of Authors,* H. W. Wilson, 1934; Helen Ferris, editor, *Writing Books for Boys and Girls,* Doubleday, 1952; Bertha E. Miller and E. W. Field, editors, *New Medal Books: 1925-1955,* Horn Book, 1955; Martha E. Ward and D. A. Marquardt, *Authors of Books for Young People,* Scarecrow, 1964; *Anthology of Children's Literature,* 4th edition, Houghton, 1970; *Twentieth-Century Children's Writers,* 2nd edition, St. Martin's Press, 1983. Obituaries: *New York Times,* January 8, 1941; *Publishers Weekly,* January 25, 1941; *Wilson Library Bulletin,* February, 1941.

It is books that teach us to refine our pleasures when young, and to recall them with satisfaction when we are old.

—Leigh Hunt

FRANK, Anne   1929-1945(?)

BRIEF ENTRY: Born June 12, 1929, in Frankfort on the Main, Germany (now West Germany); died in March, 1945 (some sources cite 1944), near Bergen, Germany (now West Germany). German diarist. Anne Frank, a German-born Jewish girl whose family sought refuge in the Netherlands from Nazi persecution during World War II, kept a diary while in hiding with her family in an Amsterdam warehouse. On August 4, 1944, after the Frank family had been in seclusion for two years, they were discovered by the Gestapo and arrested. Anne was subsequently sent to Belsen, a concentration camp, where she died in March 1945, just before the end of World War II.

Anne's father, who survived, returned to the Amsterdam warehouse after the war's end and found his daughter's diary. It was later published and translated into thirty-two languages. *Anne Frank: The Diary of a Young Girl* (1952) was dramatized for the stage and screen as "The Diary of Anne Frank." A collection of Frank's other writings, including reminiscences, fairy tales, and a short story, was published in English as *Anne Frank's Tales From the Secret Annex* (1983).

FOR MORE INFORMATION SEE: Piccolo Book of Heroines (juvenile), Pan Books, 1974; *Encyclopedia of the Third Reich,* McGraw, 1976; *Her Way: Biographies of Women for Young People,* American Library Association, 1976; Angela Bull, *Anne Frank* (juvenile), Hamish Hamilton, 1984; *Los Angeles Times,* April 13, 1984.

FRIEDMAN, Marvin   1930-

PERSONAL: Born September 26, 1930, in Chester, Pa.; son of Myer (a musician) and Frances (an artist; maiden name, Bookman) Friedman; married Sonya Graboyes (a teacher); children: Marcy, Michele, Steven, Barry. *Education:* Attended Philadelphia Museum School of Art, 1948-52. *Home:* 17 Montague Ave., West Trenton, N.J. 08628.

CAREER: Illustrator for magazines and of books for children. Lecturer in illustration at Rhode Island School of Design, 1974-76, Pratt Institute, 1976, Philadelphia College of Art, 1972-79, and Trenton State College, 1979. Exhibition of work at various locations, including Philadelphia (Pa.) Art Alliance, 1971, Princeton Art Association, 1971, New Jersey Artists, Philadelphia Museum of Art, Academy of Fine Art (Philadelphia), Pittsburgh Museum, Brandywine Museum (Delaware), and Pennsylvania Representational Artists. Work is represented in the permanent collections of the Chicago & Ford Motor Co., Dearborn, Ill.; Boy Scouts of America, Dallas, Tex.; National Broadcasting Co., New York, N.Y.; and American Legion, New Jersey; Library of Congress, Washington, D.C.; Smithsonian Institution, Washington, D.C.; Philadelphia Museum of Art; Columbia University, New York, N.Y.; University of Pennsylvania. *Awards, honors:* Society of Illustrators Annual Award, 1969, for "Picture Thieves"; Gold Medal from New Jersey Art Directors, 1972, for Ciba Pharmaceuticals; Gold Medal from Society of Illustrators, 1981, for artwork.

ILLUSTRATOR—All for children: Jerry Seibert, *Amelia Earhart: First Lady of the Air,* Houghton, 1960; Josephine Hemphill, *Fruitcake and Arsenic,* Little, Brown, 1962; Martha Shapp and Charles Shapp, *Let's Find Out about Thomas Alva Edison,* F. Watts, 1966; John Clarke, *Roar of Engines,* Doubleday, 1967; *The Jago Secret,* Follett, 1967; Doris Faber, *Rose*

Greenhow: Spy for the Confederacy, Putnam, 1968; Ruth P. Harnden, *Runaway Raft,* Houghton, 1968; Marie Elizabeth Pitcher, *Shadow of a Crow,* Doubleday, 1968; Marie Thoger, *Shanta,* translated by Eileen Amos, Follett, 1968; Gerry Turner, *The Silver Dollar Hoard of Aristotle Gaskin,* Doubleday, 1968; Molly Cone, *Annie, Annie,* Houghton, 1969; Evelyn S. Lampman, *The Bandit of Mok Hill,* Doubleday, 1969; Charles Raymond, *Enoch,* Houghton, 1969.

M. Cone, *Simon,* Houghton, 1970; R. P. Harnden, *Next Door,* Houghton, 1970; M. Cone, *You Can't Make Me If I Don't Want To,* Houghton, 1971; M. Shapp and C. Shapp, *Let's Find Out about Jewish Holidays,* F. Watts, 1971; Bianca Bradbury, *Those Traver Kids,* Houghton, 1972; M. Cone, *Dance Around the Fire,* Houghton, 1974; Barbara Brooks Wallace, *Can Do, Missy Charlie,* Follett, 1974; Larry Callen, *Pinch,* Little, Brown, 1975; Genevieve S. Gray, *Varnell Roberts, Super-Pigeon,* Houghton, 1975; Norma E. Lee, *Chewing Gum,* Prentice-Hall, 1976; L. Callen, *Sorrow's Song,* Little, Brown, 1979; Bert Metter, *Bar Mitzvah, Bat Mitzvah: How Jewish Boys and Girls Come of Age,* Clarion, 1984; Miriam Chaikin, *Shake a Palm Branch: The Story and Meaning of Sukkot,* Clarion, 1984; Miriam Chaikin, *Ask Another Question,* Clarion, 1985.

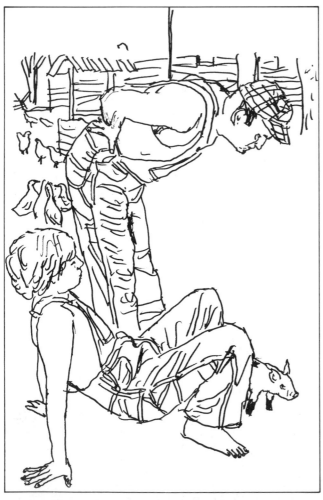

"Mmmm," he said and kept staring. He walked around me and took a look at the pig from another direction. ■ (From *Pinch* by Larry Callen. Illustrated by Marvin Friedman.)

Also illustrator for periodicals such as *Good Housekeeping, Cosmopolitan, Ladies' Home Journal, Changing Times, Redbook, Ford Times, Better Homes and Gardens, Gourmet, Fortune, Boys' Life, New York Times, Playboy* and others.

WORK IN PROGRESS: Two picture essays—one on the Vietnam Memorial in Washington, and the other on Ellis Island and immigration—for *Boys' Life;* an ongoing commission of portraits of Jewish entertainers for Theodore Mann, Museum of Israel: "I'm presently researching Jack Benny, Al Jolson, and Louie B. Mayer."

SIDELIGHTS: "Except for selected book assignments from Clarion and a monthly feature for *Gourmet* magazine, I concentrate primarily on portraits these days."

FOR MORE INFORMATION SEE: Walt Reed, editor and compiler, *Illustrators in America, 1900-1960s,* Reinhold, 1966.

FYSON, J(enny) G(race)   1904-

PERSONAL: Born October 3, 1904, in Bromley, Kent, England; daughter of Cholmondeley (a local government administrator of education) and Jenny Maud (Mann) Harrison; married Christopher Fyson, March, 1939 (deceased); children: Charles. *Education:* Educated by a governess at home, in a private village school, and at St. Swithun's, Winchester, England, 1918-1921. *Politics:* "No party." *Religion:* Ecumenical. *Home:* Near Maidstone, Kent, England.

CAREER: Painter, 1921-37; playwright, 1934-38; author of children's books. *Awards, honors:* Carnegie Medal runner-up, 1965, for *The Three Brothers of Ur,* and 1966, for *The Journey of the Eldest Son.*

*WRITINGS—*Juvenile: *The Three Brothers of Ur* (illustrated by Victor Ambrus), Oxford University Press, 1964, Coward, 1966; *The Journey of the Eldest Son* (illustrated by V. Am-

J. G. FYSON

**And what had happened to the—the Sacred Image?...
It lay broken in two on the floor.** ■ (From *The Three Brothers of Ur* by J. G. Fyson. Illustrated by Victor G. Ambrus.)

brus), Oxford University Press, 1965, Coward, 1967; (contributor) Edward Blishen, editor, *Miscellany V,* Oxford University Press, 1968; *Friend Fire and the Dark Wings* (illustrated by Annabel Large), Oxford University Press, 1983.

WORK IN PROGRESS: Let the Waters Bring, a book about God and evolution—mainly the evolution of awareness; *Father Pierre: A True Story Told as a Myth.*

SIDELIGHTS: Kept out of school by poor health in her late teens, Fyson fell back on painting, reading, and literature. "It was then, that Darwin's *Origin of Species* and Bernard Shaw came like earthquakes, upsetting accepted and unquestioned philosophy. Gibbon interested me in the past and Frazer's

Golden Bough provided a solution for the sacrifice of Isaac. Abraham was a brave man throwing off the shackles of an old custom. So I wrote two books about the world in which Abraham lived as a child, drawing on archaeological discoveries for information.

"My most recent book, *Friend Fire and the Dark Wing,* is about primitive man and the ancestral fear that makes men see in their enemies the center of all evil. Until we can understand this unconscious inheritance, we cannot get rid of war."

HOBBIES AND OTHER INTERESTS: Evolution, Jung, archaeology, the causes of war, gardening.

GEER, Charles   1922-

PERSONAL: Born August 25, 1922, on Long Island, N.Y.; children: four. *Education:* Attended Dartmouth College and Pratt Institute. *Address:* Box 127, Neavitt, Md. 21652.

CAREER: Author and free-lance illustrator of children's books. Served as member and president of Readington Township Board of Education, 1960-64. *Military service:* U.S. Navy, World War II; served on a destroyer.

WRITINGS—For young people; self-illustrated: *Dexter and the Deer Lake Mystery,* Norton, 1965; *Soot Devil,* Grosset, 1971.

Illustrator; all for young people: Louis Wolfe, *Clear the Track: True Stories of Railroading,* Lippincott, 1952; Dustin C. Scott (pseudonym of Verne Chute), *The Return of Mojave Joe,* Knopf, 1952 (Geer was not associated with earlier edition); Virginia Sorensen, *Plain Girl,* Harcourt, 1955; Helen Rushmore, *Chief Takes Over,* Harcourt, 1956; Kenneth Gilbert, *Wolf Dog Valley,* Holt, 1956; Gwendolyn Bowers, *The Lost Dragon of Wes-*

CHARLES GEER

sex, Oxford University Press, 1957; Mary Beery, *Young Teens Talk It Over*, Whittlesey House, 1957; Helen Oakley, *The Ranch by the Sea*, Knopf, 1959; Hazel Wilson, *Jerry's Charge Account*, Little, Brown, 1960; (with Sally Tate) James Whitcomb Riley, *Joyful Poems for Children*, Bobbs-Merrill, 1960; Clifford B. Hicks, *The Marvelous Inventions of Alvin Fernald*, Winston, 1960; Lilla Stirling, *The Pipe Organ in the Parlor*, Thomas Nelson, 1960; Adeline McElfresh, *Summer Change*, Bobbs-Merrill, 1960; Maurine H. Gee, *Timothy and the Snakes*, Morrow, 1960.

Ursula M. Williams, *The Earl's Falconer*, Morrow, 1961; M. H. Gee, *Jeff and the River*, Morrow, 1961; Audrey McKim, *Lexy for Short*, Abingdon, 1961; Alice P. Miller, *Make Way for Peggy O'Brien!*, Lippincott, 1961; Margaret Pitcairn Strachan, *Mennonite Martha*, Ives Washburn, 1961; Sydney Taylor, *Mr. Barney's Beard*, Follett, 1961; Hazel Krantz, *One Hundred Pounds of Popcorn*, Vanguard Press, 1961; An Rutgers van der Loeff-Basenau, *Oregon at Last!*, translated by Roy Edwards, Morrow, 1961; Florence Wightman Rowland, *Pasquala of Santa Ynez Mission*, Walck, 1961; Barbee O. Carleton, *The Secret of Saturday Cove* (Junior Literary Guild selection), Holt, 1961; Molly Cone, *The Trouble With Toby*, Houghton, 1961; Dale White (pseudonym of Marian Place), *Young Deputy Smith*, Viking, 1961; M. P. Strachan, *Dolores and the Gypsies*, Ives Washburn, 1962; Hildreth Tyler Wriston, *The Oom-Pah Horn*, Abingdon, 1962; Robert J. Antonacci and Jene Barr, *Physical Fitness for Young Champions*, Whittlesey House, 1962; Martha Robinson, *The Twins at Thatchem Quickett*, Ives Washburn, 1962.

Phyllis R. Fenner, editor, *Dark and Bloody Ground: Stories of the American Frontier*, Morrow, 1963; Edwin Palmer Hoyt, *From the Turtle to the Nautilus: The Story of Submarines*, Little, Brown, 1963; Margaret Scherf, *The Mystery of the Velvet Box*, F. Watts, 1963; M. Cone, *Reeney*, Houghton, 1963; Gordon R. Dickson, *Secret Under Antarctica*, Holt, 1963; M. P. Strachan, *Summer in El Castillo*, Ives Washburn, 1963; Marjorie B. Paradis, *Too Many Fathers*, Atheneum, 1963; Jean Horton Berg, *The Wee Little Man*, Follett, 1963; P. R. Fenner, editor, *Behind the Wheel: Stories of Cars on Road and Track*, Morrow, 1964; Bianca Bradbury, *Circus Punk*, Macrae, 1964; H. Krantz, *Free-style for Michael*, Vanguard Press, 1964; Helga Sandburg, *Gingerbread*, Dial, 1964; Gerald Raftery, *The Natives Are Always Restless*, Vanguard Press,

Miss Pickerell, with Pumpkins sitting sideways in the basket, started the ride down the mountain. ■ (From *Miss Pickerell and the Supertanker* by Ellen MacGregor and Dora Pantell. Illustrated by Charles Geer.)

(From *Open Throttle: Stories of Railroads and Railroad Men*, selected by Phyllis R. Fenner. Illustrated by Charles Geer.)

1964; Richard Edward Wormser, *Ride a Northbound Horse*, Morrow, 1964; G. R. Dickson, *Secret under the Caribbean*, Holt, 1964; A. McKim, *That Summer with Lexy*, Abingdon, 1964.

P. R. Fenner, editor, *Danger Is the Password: Stories of Wartime Spies*, Morrow, 1965; Babbis Friis Baastad, *Kristy's Courage*, translated by Lise Somme McKinnon, Harcourt, 1965; Bertrand R. Brinley, *The Mad Scientists' Club*, Macrae, 1965; Dora Pantell, *Miss Pickerell on the Moon* [Ellen MacGregor was the originator of the "Miss Pickerell" series], McGraw, 1965; Marjory Schwalje, *Mystery at Redtop Hill*, Whitman Publishing, 1965; Verne T. Davis, *The Runaway Cattle*, Morrow, 1965; H. Krantz, *The Secret Raft*, Vanguard Press, 1965; Farley Mowat, *The Curse of the Viking Grave*, Little, Brown, 1966; Elizabeth P. Witheridge, *Dead End Bluff*, Atheneum, 1966; M. H. Gee, *Flood Hazard*, Morrow, 1966; Richard Parker, *M for Mischief*, Duell, 1966; D. Pantell, *Miss Pickerell Goes on a Dig*, McGraw, 1966; P. R. Fenner, compiler, *Open Throttle: Stories of Railroads and Railroad Men*, Morrow, 1966; M. Beery, *Young Teens Away from Home*, McGraw, 1966; B. Bradbury, *Sam and the Colonels*, Macrae, 1966.

Eve Hanley, *A Blazing Torch*, Ives Washburn, 1967; P. R. Fenner, editor, *Contraband: Stories of Smuggling the World Over*, Morrow, 1967; Helen F. Daringer, *Just Plain Betsy*, Harcourt, 1967; Barbara Goolden, *Trouble for the Tabors*, Ives Washburn, 1967; Laurence Hyde, *Captain Deadlock*, Houghton, 1968; E. P. Hoyt, *Deadly Craft: Fireships to PT Boats*, Little, Brown, 1968; M. H. Gee, *Firestorm*, Morrow, 1968; P. R. Fenner, compiler, *The Hunter and the Hunted: Stories of Forest and Field*, Morrow, 1968; D. Pantell, *Miss Pickerell Harvests the Sea*, McGraw, 1968; B. R. Brinley, *The New Adventures of the Mad Scientists' Club*, Macrae, 1968; Roy Simpson Marsh, *Tundra, Arctic Sled Dog*, Macrae, 1968; Jessie Hosford, *An Awful Name to Live Up To*, Meredith Press, 1969; E. P. Hoyt, *Destroyers: Foxes of the Sea*, Little, Brown, 1969; P. R. Fenner, compiler, *Finders Keepers: Stories of Treasure Seekers*, Morrow, 1969; Molly Lefebure, *Scratch and Company: The Great Cat Expedition*, Meredith Press, 1969; Anthony Fon Eisen, *the Magnificent Mongrel*, World Publishing, 1970; P. R. Fenner, compiler, *Perilous Ascent: Stories of Mountain Climbing*, Morrow, 1970; Arthur J. Beckhard, *The Story of Dwight D. Eisenhower*, Grosset, 1970.

P. R. Fenner, compiler, *Desperate Moments: Stories of Escapes and Hurried Journeys*, Morrow, 1971; D. Pantell, *Miss Pickerell and the Weather Satellite*, McGraw, 1971; P. R. Fenner, compiler, *Where Speed Is King: Stories of Racing Adventure*, Morrow, 1972; P. R. Fenner, compiler, *Consider the Evidence: Stories of Mystery and Suspense*, Morrow, 1973; D. Pantell, *Miss Pickerell Meets Mr. H.U.M.*, McGraw, 1974; D. Pantell, *Miss Pickerell Takes the Bull by the Horns*, McGraw, 1976; D. Pantell, *Miss Pickerell to the Earthquake Rescue*, McGraw, 1977; D. Pantell, *Miss Pickerell and the Supertanker*, McGraw, 1978; D. Pantell, *Miss Pickerell Tackles the Energy Crisis*, McGraw, 1980; D. Pantell, *Miss Pickerell on the Trail*, McGraw, 1982; D. Pantell, *Miss Pickerell and the Blue Whales*, McGraw, 1983; D. Pantell, *Miss Pickerell and the War of the Computers*, F. Watts, 1984.

SIDELIGHTS: "I was born on August 25, 1922 at Point O'Woods, Long Island, which is almost in the ocean. That may account for my love of the water. I spent wonderful summers sailing up and down the New England Coast on the family sailboat.

"One of my earliest memories is lying on the floor in our home, copying pictures out of newspapers. My mother read to us a great deal, and it was an important part of my growing up. *Mutiny on the Bounty* and *Treasure Island* and all the other old classics were memorable. The whole family, including my father, would lie about listening, completely absorbed in these fantasy worlds.

"I always wanted to be an artist. I was the first one in my family to pursue such an interest. Art was not regarded as a very good way to earn a living, so while my parents encouraged and supported me, they were surprised and a little alarmed when I wanted to make a career of it."

Attended school in Bellerose, Long Island. "I took every art course available during my school years. I worked hardest at reading, drawing, and playing football. After high school, I attended Dartmouth, where, for a while, I sidestepped into economics for several years before realizing that what I really wanted to be doing was drawing and painting pictures. I chose economics as a major because it required less course work than other majors, leaving me more time for my drawing and painting. Art courses for credit, other than art appreciation, were not available at Dartmouth, but I studied with artist-in-residence Paul Sample, who offered extra-curricular drawing classes. My work with Sample was very important for me.

"After college I joined the Navy. I was on a destroyer for four years, and I saw the Mediterranean, the Atlantic and the Pacific. Strangely, this was one of the most productive times in my life, when I became very disciplined about drawing. I

(From *Plain Girl* by Virginia Sorensen. Illustrated by Charles Geer.)

**"I would have enjoyed this day better at school,"
thought Katie. She looked at the splashing rain. ■**
(From *Katie Kittenheart* by Miriam E. Mason. Illustrated by Charles Geer.)

did so much sketching and had so much time to think things
over that I realized I should make illustrating my full-time
work. I filled sketch book after sketch book with life drawings
and watercolors—not exactly what the Navy had in mind for
me. There were several other would-be artists onboard as well.
We were never openly reprimanded for drawing, but the Navy
checked our sketch books as they were sent home to make
sure we hadn't revealed any war secrets!

"After the war, I attended Pratt Institute in Brooklyn to study
illustration and I've been illustrating ever since. I studied with
excellent teachers, and many of the students were war veterans
like myself. We were all very enthusiastic. After graduation I
started illustrating what were called "The Pulps"—cheap
cowboy magazines—a good way to get started in those days.
I did many, many ten dollar black and white illustrations to
make a living—or a non-living! Then I drifted into children's
books."

Illustrated his first "Miss Pickerell" book, *Miss Pickerell on
the Moon* in 1965. "The first several books of 'The Pickerell'

series were illustrated by Paul Galdone who was very important to the development of Miss Pickerell. I picked up on his
visualization of her and gradually changed and added things
as the series went along. The trick was to keep a continuity.
I couldn't just copy what had been done before. I had to give
the Pickerell books my own flavor. I think the series now
reflects my sensibility and my style. It's been an interesting
experience to see my development over a number of years.
I've learned a lot about putting pictures together. You never
stop learning. For every job I do, I have to face a blank piece
of paper and I always learn something. I think I have become
more perceptive and better able to look at my work critically.

"I haven't any particular favorite of the Pickerell series. I
enjoy them all. They are equally mad and wonderful. Each
illustration, as well as the jacket, the frontispiece, and the
'spots' has its own job to do. The little spots sprinkled here
do their job as accents, while the bigger illustrations work for
a particular page or chapter. The jacket or frontispiece has to
capture the feeling of the whole book. You have to be thinking
of a nice balance of all this as you illustrate a book."

Miss Pickerell's popularity, Geer believes, came about because "she is unusual and does unexpected things. Miss Pickerell is a little old lady facing tremendous adventures that make
the stories marvelously surprising. People love new views of
things, and Pickerell is certainly a refreshing view of what
kids think of as a 'granny' type.

"One of the editors at McGraw-Hill suggested that I try using
thought balloons in the Pickerell books. I was rather tentative,
because it was unlike anything I had ever done before. I just
loved it! The balloons with the question marks, the exclama-
tion points, and little pictures of what the characters including
the cat, are thinking sparked things up. It was liberating to
finally discover that I didn't have to be so *literal*. Bringing in
a little cartooning—which I think Miss Pickerell needed because she isn't a literal, rational, straight-forward character—
made for more fun and, I think, improved the illustrations a
lot.

"The on-the-spot sketching in the Navy and after the war was
helpful in developing my skills. I used to ride the subway in
New York and sketched people for hours. That called for a
quick, economical means of portraying things. I learned quickly
to jot stuff down, and I learned about human gesture and
movement. A line or two can reveal much about a person—
and that is the heart of illustration."

Extensive research is part of Geer's illustration technique. "I
research whatever the story calls for. Dora Pantell is marvelously inventive in the situations she gets Miss Pickerell into.
I never know what I'm going to have to research! I use the
New York Public Library picture collection as well as my own
collection of *National Geographic* magazines, which dates back
to 1918. I've also clipped magazines throughout my career,
so I have my own personal picture collection, and if that doesn't
suffice, I go somewhere else. Things must be authentic—readers sense if they are not."

As a rule Geer's working relationship with an author is an
independent one, but in the case of the Miss Pickerell books,
"I do my rough sketches on thin tracing paper in pencil and
then meet with Dora Pantell and the editor. We spend half a
day going over the rough drawings, making sure that I caught
all the little details and nuances. Between us, we usually come
up with new touches or corrections.

"For the Miss Pickerell books, I do a lot of groundwork. I read the book very carefully, and make three or four pages of tightly written notes, chapter by chapter. Then I go over my notes and pick out what I want to illustrate. I have to take care that I am not repeating or choosing similar situations to illustrate. If there is research, and there usually is, I surround myself with the material and then I sit down and start to think about drawing. I stare at the paper for quite awhile, gathering my thoughts, before I start with tentative little marks . . . then the drawing slowly comes from my head, through my hands, to the paper.

"I don't use models for the Pickerell books. For my paperback jackets which demand more reality and detail, I do a very complete rough sketch and after the sketch is approved by the publisher, I book models and go to a photographer in New York who specializes in working with illustrators. We pose the models according to my sketch and the photographers give me the necessary detail. I often rent costumes of the period from a costume supplier in New York. All quite different from doing children's books!

"The action of the figures in my books is great fun to do. When I draw Miss Pickerell running or whatever, I move with her. I really get into it and sort of act things out to get the feeling of her gestures and movement.

"I use pen and ink and often a wash to help pull things together. On the Navy destroyer, pen and ink was a very simple way to work under those conditions. All I needed was a pen, a little watercolor pan and a pad and I was in business. I still paint and sketch just for myself, and I often use pen and ink, and watercolor."

Aside from work in the field of children's books, Geer has also done many adult book jackets. "It's good to try other things to keep yourself stirred up. Book jackets are enjoyable, and they also tend to pay more than children's books, which can be rather important! They also enable me to work in full color which I like. I have recently done historical novels and family sagas for authors like Cynthia Freeman and Stephen Birmingham. I make every effort to get a copy of the manuscript so that I can read it closely. Sometimes, with book jackets, I am only given a one-paragraph summary, which is difficult to work from. I like to immerse myself in the material. That's a carry over from my children's book work, where I *have* to read a manuscript and come up with many illustrations. For my adult jackets, as well, it's important for me to read the story to find the psychological threads which relate the characters.

"I usually work straight through the week when I'm committed to a lot of projects. Saturdays, Sundays, holidays are all the same. I work all day and at night, but when things let up, I'm free to do other things. I set my own schedules and I'm my own boss, which is nice.

"I listen to classical music a lot while I work. In the conceptual stage, however, it has to be really quiet. Even the music is too distracting. I have to become very single-minded when I am facing a blank piece of paper. Once I get my idea and the general layout is conceived, then I can relax a little."

Geer lives in an old house on the Chesapeake in Maryland. "Our four children are grown and scattered all over the country. One is a boat builder in Maine, one's a recreational therapist and potter in Minnesota, one's a furniture maker, wood

High in the air, high above the peak of the roof, the paper unfolded with a snap, and pages went fluttering in all directions. ■ (From *The Marvelous Inventions of Alvin Fernald* by Clifford B. Hicks. Illustrated by Charles Geer.)

carver, and house builder in Santa Fe, and one is a mother in Rochester. While our kids were at home, I had a separate studio, outside the log cabin we built in New Jersey. My wife and I have since moved to Maryland, because we like to sail and I now have a studio in our home. My wife, a social worker now in private practice as a family therapist, is a great book person and has been very supportive.

"I enjoy sailing and hiking and building things. I built our boat myself in my spare time. It took five years! It's only twenty-two feet long, but it has a cabin and bunks, so we are able to stock up and just live on the boat, sailing around the Chesapeake Bay for days at a time. I feel a marvelous change, in this other world.

"I also paint landscapes and love drawing people. I made little portraits of my children while they were growing up, and this gave me great pleasure. The time I spend sailing and on illustration has taken away from my own painting, but it's something I want to get back to."

To aspiring artists Geer suggests, "You can't really ask somebody else if you should or shouldn't pursue art. That must come from inside yourself. Just work very hard, and find out what is special within you. When the time comes, look to the kinds of work you'd like to do, such as magazines, or book illustration. If you want to be an illustrator, find out whom to see, call up for an appointment, show your work, and you will soon find your own particular way.

"They say that it is important to retain part of your childhood, and I think children's books have helped me to do that. I sit, all alone, doing my work, involving myself in it, without worrying about any outside influences aside from the story itself. Of course, I want to please my audience, but while I'm drawing, I am working to please myself. I know when my work is good. Nobody has to tell me. It is an enormous pleasure to have done a good picture."

FOR MORE INFORMATION SEE: Lee Kingman and others, compilers, *Illustrators of Children's Books: 1957-1966*, Horn Book, 1968; *Illustrators of Books for Young People*, Scarecrow, 1975.

GIFFORD, Griselda   1931-
(Mary Macdonald)

PERSONAL: Born May 26, 1931, in Monte Carlo, Monaco; daughter of James A. and Jill (Denton) Willoughby; married Paul Julian David Gifford (a sales executive), March 18, 1955; children: Mark Richard, Nicola Jane. *Education:* Attended schools in England. *Religion:* Anglican. *Home:* Holly Lodge, Weathercock Lane, Woburn Sands, Milton Keynes MK17 8NY, England.

CAREER: Has worked as a secretary for various British businesses and organizations, including the Foreign Office, London, 1950-53, the Festival of Britain, 1951, A. M. Heath & Co., Ltd., London, 1955, and Constable & Co.; writer. Adult education teacher of writing, 1980—. *Member:* Amnesty International, International P.E.N.

*WRITINGS—*For children: *The Youngest Taylor* (illustrated by Victor Ambrus), Bodley Head, 1963; (with Helen Calre) *The Mystery of the Wooden Legs*, Bodley Head, 1964; *Ben's Expedition* (illustrated by Robert Micklewright), Bodley Head,

1965; *The Story of Ranald* (historical novel; illustrated by Edward Gage), Bodley Head, 1968; *Jenny and the Sheep Thieves* (illustrated by Carol Lawson), Gollancz, 1975; *Mirabelle's Secret* (illustrated by Jael Jordon), Gollancz, 1976; *Because of Blunder* (illustrated by Mary Rayner), Gollancz, 1977; *Cass the Brave* (illustrated by M. Rayner), Gollancz, 1978; *The Rescue*, Gollancz, 1980; *Silver's Day* (illustrated by M. Rayner), Gollancz, 1980; *Earwig and Beetle* (illustrated by Jill Bennett), Gollancz, 1981; *The Magic Mitre* (illustrated by Sally Holmes), Hamish Hamilton, 1982; *Pete and the Doodle-bug and other Stories* (illustrated by P. Rush), Macmillan, 1983; *Two of a Kind*, Macmillan, 1985.

Contributor of adult fiction to magazines under pseudonym, Mary Macdonald.

WORK IN PROGRESS: Stories for Macmillan Education.

SIDELIGHTS: "I had always wanted to write, and when the British Broadcasting Corporation aired my short stories seventeen years ago, I was encouraged to write my first book for children. This was based on my mother's family, but I brought it up-to-date. Many of my ideas have come from experience; from meeting an old lady, for instance, who kept a herd of sheep and knew them all by name or from the legends about a fig tree that grew against a small Cornish church.

"I suppose being an only child is often a little lonely (though friends and reading and outdoor activities filled most of the gaps), so most of my stories are about families, except for one in which a mother and daughter live in a basement flat, just as I once did, and my novel *Earwig and Beetle*, about a boy whose parents divorce. I am more interested in my characters than in the plot, although, of course, this is obviously important. In *Cass the Brave* I wondered what it would be like to be an identical twin and yet want to assert oneself as an individual.

GRISELDA GIFFORD

It felt so early that she was surprised to find Grandpa in the kitchen. . . . ■ (From *Jenny and the Sheep Thieves* by Griselda Gifford. Illustrated by Carol Lawson.)

"I think girls can be leaders just as well as boys, so several of my stories have girl heroines. I try to be a Christian, and I feel that right and wrong and the joy of life should be shown in books, but without any kind of preaching. And children can be shown how to be sympathetic towards people with problems. I also think children's books should have plenty of humor, because I like laughing!

"What I find most difficult is disciplining myself to work. There are so many distractions—running the house, looking after the family, friends, going for walks, reading, church and other meetings—that I do admire those writers who settle down, come what may, and do a specified number of hours each day.

"I used to be a 'bookworm' and very much enjoyed many American books: including those by Mark Twain, as well as *Little Women, What Katy Did, Daddy Longlegs, Rebecca,* and *The Burgess Big Book of Green Meadow Stories.* Unfortunately I have never visited the United States—our holiday travels have been to France, which I love, and I have been to Holland and Germany. I moved from Monte Carlo at the age of eighteen months, so I can't remember it!

"I live in a very friendly neighbourhood, on the edge of a city and join in many community activities—both purely social and those in aid of charities—or just help by visiting anyone lonely, though I don't do nearly enough in this way.

"We have had many animals—and I even took white mice into the shelter in the War! Now I have two Lhasa apso dogs and two cats, although I used to have lots of rabbits, guinea pigs, and other animals. As a child I rode ponies which are included in two of my books.

"At present I am teaching at an adult education centre once a week, a course on creative writing. I have recently been involved with a festival in a newly-formed arts association. We

ran a workshop for adults, and I also did several children's writing workshops, partly funded by the Arts Council.

"I very much enjoy reading modern children's books as well as adult fiction—and am well known as a constant visitor to our local library!

"I love classical music and some jazz: particularly John Dankworth and his wife, Cleo, who live quite near and have a small theatre on their grounds. We used to go to the London theatre quite often and the ballet sometimes.

"I belong to a friendly, lively church and attend weekly prayer meetings or Bible study. I am a theoretical pacifist, but do not belong to CND [Campaign for Nuclear Disarmament]. I am concerned, as many are by the nuclear arms race, by world poverty and also want to remain living in a democracy (which is why I joined Amnesty whose aim is to help all 'prisoners of conscience')."

Ben's Expedition and *The Mystery of the Wooden Legs* have been published in Sweden and Germany. Two of Gifford's children's stories and three of her adult stories have been broadcast by the British Broadcasting Company.

HOBBIES AND OTHER INTERESTS: Community activities, animals, jazz and classical music, reading modern children's books and adult fiction, adult educational classes on creative writing, and art.

FOR MORE INFORMATION SEE: Times Literary Supplement, September 19, 1975, July 16, 1976, March 25, 1977; *Times Educational Supplement,* March 12, 1982.

GILLHAM, William Edwin Charles   1936-
(Bill Gillham)

PERSONAL: Born January 21, 1936, in Southampton, England; son of Bertram (a merchant seaman) and May (Gurd) Gillham; married Judith Downing (a schoolteacher), July 27, 1963; children: Charles William Anthony, George Edwin Arthur. *Education:* University of Hull, B.A., 1960; University College, London, diploma, 1965; University of Nottingham, Ph.D., 1981. *Politics:* "Pale pink merging into pale blue." *Religion:* "None." *Home:* Glebe House, Cottesmore, Oakham, Rutland, Leicestershire LE15 7AN, England. *Agent:* Elizabeth Stevens, Curtis Brown Ltd., 1 Craven Hill, London W2 3EP, England. *Office:* Department of Psychology, University of Strathclyde, Turnbull Bldg., 155 George St., Glasgow G1 2RD, Scotland.

CAREER: Schoolteacher in Yorkshire, England, 1961-64; educational psychologist in Leicestershire, England, 1965-71; University of Nottingham, Nottingham, England, lecturer in psychology, 1971-84; University of Strathclyde, Glasgow, Scotland, senior lecturer in psychology, 1984—. *Military service:* Royal Air Force, 1954-56; became leading aircraftsman. *Member:* British Psychological Society.

*WRITINGS—*For children; all under name Bill Gillham: *Septimus Fry F.R.S.; or, How Mrs. Fry Had the Cleverest Baby in the World* (fiction; illustrated by Steve Augarde), Deutsch, 1980; *My Brother Barry* (fiction; illustrated by Lazlo Acs), Deutsch, 1981; *The First Words Picture Book* (illustrated with photographs by Sam Grainger), Coward, 1982; *A Place to Hide* (illustrated by Maria Majewska), Deutsch, 1983; *The*

Early Words Picture Book (photos by Sam Grainger), Coward, 1983; *Home Before Long* (illustrated by Francis Mosley), Deutsch, 1983; (with Susan Hulme) *Let's Look for Shapes* (photos by Jan Siegieda), Coward, 1984; (with S. Hulme) *Let's Look for Numbers* (photos by J. Siegieda), Coward, 1984; (with S. Hulme) *Let's Look for Opposites* (photos by J. Siegieda), Coward, 1984; (with S. Hulme) *Let's Look for Colours* (photos by J. Siegieda), Coward, 1984; *The Rich Kid* (illustrated by F. Mosley), Deutsch, 1984; *What Happens Next?* (photos by J. Siegieda), Methuen, 1985; *Spencer's Spaghetti* (illustrated by Margaret Chamberlain), Methuen, 1985; *Our Baby Bites* (illustrated by M. Chamberlain), Methuen, 1985; *Awful Arabella* (illustrated by M. Chamberlain), Methuen, 1985; *Candy's Camel* (illustrated by M. Chamberlain), Methuen, 1985; *What's the Difference?* (photos by Fiona Horne), Methuen, 1986; *Where Is It?* (photos by F. Horne), Methuen, 1986; *Where Does It Go?* (photos by F. Horne), Methuen, 1986; *What Can You Do With It?* (photos by F. Horne), Methuen, 1986.

Other; under name William Edwin Charles Gillham, except as indicated: *Teaching a Child to Read*, University of London Press, 1974; (editor) *Psychology Today* (paperback), Hodder & Stoughton, 1975, revised edition published as *Psychology for Today* (paperback), 1981; (translator) Eliane Vurpillot, *The Visual World of the Child*, Allen & Unwin, 1976; (editor, under name Bill Gillham) *Reconstructing Educational Psychology*, Croom Helm, 1978; (under name Bill Gillham) *The First Words Language Programme: A Basic Language Programme for Mentally Handicapped Children*, Allen & Unwin, 1979; (editor, under name Bill Gillham) *Problem Behaviour*

in the Secondary School: A Systems Approach, Croom Helm, 1981; (editor, with C. I. Howarth) *The Structure of Psychology*, Allen & Unwin, 1981; (with Kim M. Plunkett, under name Bill Gillham) *Child Psychology: The Child to Five Years*, Hodder & Stoughton, 1982; (under name Bill Gillham) *Problems of Adjustment and Learning*, Open University Press, 1982; (under name Bill Gillham) *Two Words Together: A First Sentences Language Programme*, Allen & Unwin, 1983; *Mental Arithmetic*, Hodder & Stoughton, 1983.

Contributor: A. Burton and J. Radford, editors, *Thinking in Perspective*, Methuen, 1978; A. Gobell and G. Upton, editors, *The Challenge of Adolescent Behaviour in School*, University College Cardiff, 1980; N. Frude and H. Gault, editors, *Disruptive Behavior in Schools*, John Wiley, 1984. Also author of series of educational tests published by University of London Press and Hodder & Stoughton, 1970-80, and learning development materials including picture and sentence cards; editor of series dealing with specific topics of remediation, Croom Helm, 1981—. Contributor to professional journals such as *Special Education, Bulletin of the British Psychological Society,* and *New Behaviour*.

WORK IN PROGRESS: Handicapping Conditions in Children, publication by Croom Helm.

SIDELIGHTS: "I grew up in wartime England—in Southampton where nightly raids made the war a reality. Early in the war I was evacuated to rural Dorset (or so it seemed to us) and acquired a taste for the English countryside, which is perhaps why I now live in one of the remotest parts of rural England in an old farmhouse. Evacuation and the war have provided the background for one of my novels for children *(Home Before Long).*

"For a working class boy like myself, the post-war period in England was a time of great educational opportunity. I won a place at Taunton's Grammar School in Southampton and entered a different world. There I developed the ambitions that have carried me through to the present day and still drive me—intellectual ambitions to master an area of knowledge and the ambition to write. To write well—simply and powerfully—has always seemed to me to be one of the greatest of human achievements.

"I was badly thrown by the death of my mother in 1952 when I was sixteen. Her faith in me was a powerful support which I took for granted, and it was gone, so to speak, overnight.

"National Service, for two years from the age of eighteen, gave me the necessary time to readjust. I set to work to make something of myself. It was my good fortune, on the base to which I was posted, to have as Education Officer the poet Edward Lucie-Smith. For eighteen months he acted as my personal tutor. I completed my university entrance, gained a place, and read enormously. I have never looked back—and never do—since past achievements soon fade. Your drive comes from the things you have to do.

"Creative writing had to wait until I had secured my position as an academic writer. Academic writing has the effect of making you careful in your choice of words. It can mean that one becomes pedantic but *no* writer who seeks a precise effort can afford to be careless in his use of words to the slightest degree.

"So, I was forty-two before I wrote my first children's book—scribbled out when on holiday in Cornwall. I was fortunate in

WILLIAM EDWIN CHARLES GILLHAM

Jenny is giving the dog his dinner. ■ (From *The First Words Picture Book* by Bill Gillham. Photograph by Sam Grainger.)

getting it published since it encouraged me to try out other ideas I had.

"I think we underestimate children's sophistication, so I like to write themes that are not conventional—the fantasy child in *Septimus Fry,* the mentally handicapped boy in *My Brother Barry.*

"I must say that I write to satisfy myself. A form which children can understand and enjoy sets the boundaries; the task is to get something worthwhile into that mold."

O for one hour of youthful joy!
Give back my twentieth spring!
I'd rather laugh, a bright-haired boy,
Then reign, a gray-beard King.
                    —Oliver Wendell Holmes

Blessings on thee, little man,
Barefoot boy, with cheek of tan!
With thy turned-up pantaloons,
And thy merry whistled tunes.
                    —John Greenleaf Whittier

GLANVILLE, Brian (Lester) 1931-

PERSONAL: Born September 24, 1931, in London, England; son of James Arthur (a dentist) and Florence (Manches) Glanville; married Elizabeth Pamela de Boer Manasse (a journalist), March 19, 1959; children: Mark Brian James, Toby John and Elizabeth Jane (twins), Josephine Sarah. *Education:* Attended Charterhouse School, 1945-49. *Home:* 160 Holland Park Ave., London W. 11., England. *Agent:* John Farquharson Ltd., 162 Regent St., London, W.1., England.

CAREER: Journalist and author, 1949—. *Sunday Times,* London, England, sports columnist, 1958—. Literary advisor, The Bodley Head Ltd., London, 1958-62. Soccer columnist for the *New York Times. Awards, honors:* First prize at Berlin Film Festival for script of British Broadcasting Corp. television documentary, "European Centre Forward," 1963.

WRITINGS: The Reluctant Dictator, Laurie, 1952; *Henry Sows the Wind,* Secker & Warburg, 1954; *Soccer Nemesis,* Secker & Warburg, 1955; *Along the Arno,* Secker & Warburg, 1956; *The Bankrupts,* Doubleday, 1958; *After Rome, Africa* (suspense novel), Secker & Warburg, 1959.

A Bad Streak (stories), Secker & Warburg, 1961; *Diamond,* Farrar, Straus, 1962; *The Director's Wife* (stories), Secker & Warburg, 1963; *The Rise of Gerry Logan,* Secker & Warburg, 1963, Delacorte, 1965; *Goalkeepers Are Crazy: A Collection*

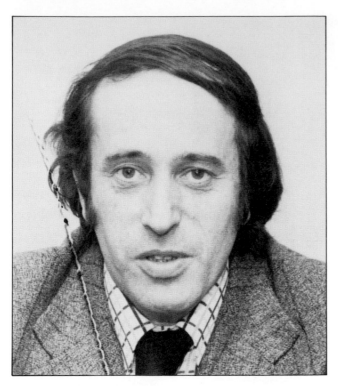

BRIAN GLANVILLE

of Football Stories, Secker & Warburg, 1964; *The King of Hackney Marshes, and Other Stories,* Secker & Warburg, 1965; *A Second Home,* Delacorte, 1966; *A Roman Marriage* (novelette), Coward, 1967; *The Artist Type,* J. Cape, 1967, Coward, 1968; *People in Sport,* Secker & Warburg, 1967; *Soccer,* Crown, 1968; *The Olympian* (novel), Coward, 1969; *A Betting Man* (short stories), Coward, 1969.

Puffin Book of Football, Puffin, 1970; *A Cry of Crickets* (novel), Coward, 1970; *Money Is Love,* Doubleday, 1972 (published in England as *The Financiers,* Secker & Warburg, 1972); *Goalkeepers Are Different* (juvenile), Crown, 1972; *The Thing He Loves* (short stories), Secker & Warburg, 1973; *The Comic,* Stein & Day, 1975; *The Dying of the Light,* Secker & Warburg, 1976; *A Bad Lot and Other Stories,* Penguin, 1977; *The Puffin Book of Footballers,* Puffin, 1978; *Target Man,* Macdonald, 1978; *The Puffin Book of Tennis,* Puffin, 1979; *A Book of Soccer,* Oxford University Press (New York), 1979; *Never Look Back,* M. Joseph, 1980; *Kevin Keegan,* Hamish Hamilton, 1981; *Puffin Book of the World Cup,* Puffin, 1984; *The History of the World Cup,* Faber, 1984; *Kissing America* (novel), Anthony Blond, 1985; *Love Is Not Love* (short stories), Anthony Blond, 1985. Also co-author of ''Underneath the Arches'' (musical), Prince of Wales Theatre (London), 1982, and author of ''A Visit to the Villa'' (play), Chichester Festival Studio Theatre, 1982.

Original contributor to British Broadcasting Corp. television program, ''That Was the Week That Was''; author of commentary for ''Goal!,'' film of 1966 World Cup matches; editor and compiler, *World Football Handbook* (an annual), 1964-76. Contributor of short stories and articles to *Mademoiselle, Gentleman's Quarterly, Saturday Evening Post, Sports Illustrated, Holiday,* and other magazines.

WORK IN PROGRESS: Screenplay, ''The Great St. Bernard''; screenplay of *A Roman Marriage,* for production by Seven Arts, Columbia Pictures.

SIDELIGHTS: ''I began my first sporting journalism as soon as I left Charterhouse [school], at the age of seventeen, and wrote my first published novel at eighteen. At twenty-one, I went to live in Italy, taking to heart E. M. Forster's dictum that every young English writer needs Continental experience.

''I lived for two years in Florence, one in Rome, which was an enormously fecund and germinal time. English public (preparatory) schoolboys of that time had led cloistered lives. One came into contact not only with the enormously different and infinitely exciting world of Italian life, but with those splendid Americans who were living out their last years on the G.I. Bill of Rights; exciting and unexpected people for a young Englishman to meet.

''Soccer was a help again, not only enabling me, as it always has done, to earn a living without having to compromise on my fiction, but in opening an infinity of doors into the closed world of Italian society. When I was twenty-two, and living in Florence, I wrote *Along the Arno,* my third novel but the first to have real critical acclaim. I've written two other novels about Florence, *A Cry of Crickets* and, the latest of all, *Kissing America,* which is also set in the middle 1950s.

''In 1981, having written a play called 'A Visit to the Villa,' which Chichester Festival Theatre wanted to put on, I was lucky enough to be asked to collaborate on writing a musical called, 'Underneath the Arches,' about the lives of a famous Cockney double act, Flanagan and Allen.

''The show transferred with great success from Chichester to the Prince of Wales Theatre in the West End of London, running fifteen months and winning the admiration, among others, of the Italian film director, Federico Fellini.

''Comics and comedians have long been a passion of mine; hence my novel about a comedian, *The Comic.*

''As for children's books, I have written only a handful, but *Goalkeepers Are Different* seems to have a vigorous life of its own. When my youngest child went to Oxford University, she found undergraduates who swore by it and could even quote the last paragraph verbatim, which is more than I could ever do!

''Ring Lardner's work showed me the way to write short stories about the world of professional soccer, something I've been doing for many years. Lately I have read many of them myself on BBC Radio—I can reproduce most English accents, but know that this if the nearest I'll ever get to being a 'performer.'

''For choice, like so many other novelists, I'd now prefer to write for theatre. But the frustrations are infinite.''

Many of Glanville's adult novels have been published in the United States and he has contributed to such magazines as *Sports Illustrated, Saturday Evening Post,* and *Holiday.* His hobby is playing soccer. ''I co-founded the Chelsea Casuals football club in 1957 and have played some 850 games for them, mostly at leftback. It is a little Sunday team which has had many useful amateur players; and some who actually played major league. I myself have always been a tower of solid mediocrity.''

Glanville wrote and helped edit *Goal!,* the official film of the 1966 World Cup. The movie won the British equivalent of the Oscar for best documentary of 1967 and was highly praised in the United States. His adult novel, *The Rise of Gerry Logan,*

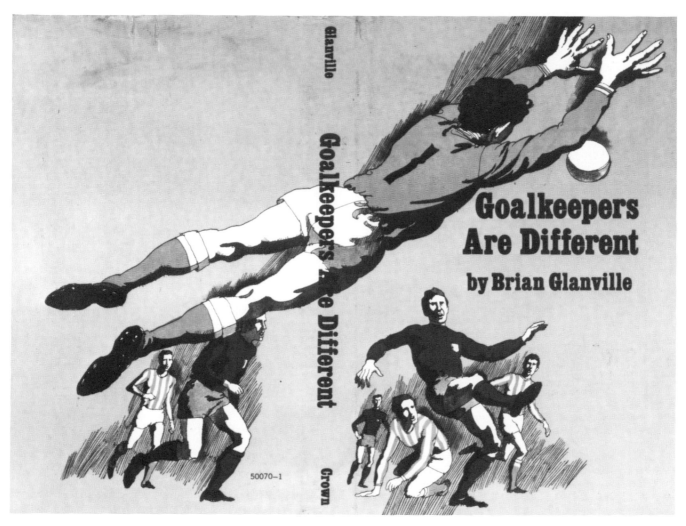

Some people say goalkeepers are crazy, but to me they're not crazy, they're different. ■ (Jacket illustration by Richard Cuffari from *Goalkeepers Are Different* by Brian Glanville.)

is especially popular with players, and was called by Franz Beckenbauer, once Germany's star footballer, "the best book of soccer ever written."

About *Goalkeepers Are Different*, Glanville says: "I wanted to write a soccer book for boys which was wholly authentic and would enable them to 'live' the story for themselves. So the hero is a young goalkeeper, an exceptional athlete but a typical London boy of his age and period. At the same time I wanted to avoid the old patronizing, basically uninformed boys' book about football, which tends to be written without inside knowledge and to insult the reader's capacity and intelligence. Boys want to 'know it like it is' and I feel that *Goalkeepers Are Different* tells them. I made my hero a goalkeeper because they *are* special. My first fiction about soccer, published and anthologized all over the world, was the story, *Goalkeepers Are Crazy*. If *Goalkeepers Are Different* can do something to promote the sport and satisfy the curiosity of young Americans about how it's played, how footballers think, behave, and react, then I'll be happy."

HOBBIES AND OTHER INTERESTS: Soccer, as reporter and player.

FOR MORE INFORMATION SEE: London Magazine, April, 1961; William Walsh, *A Human Idiom,* Chatto & Windus, 1964; *New York Times,* May 22, 1969, June 13, 1969; *Newsweek,* June 23, 1969; *Times Literary Supplement,* July 17, 1969, October 24, 1980; *New York,* April 18, 1970; *Contemporary Literary Criticism,* Volume 6, Gale, 1976.

GRAHAM-BARBER, Lynda   1944-
(Linda Barber)

PERSONAL: Born December 12, 1944, in Pittsburgh, Pa.; daughter of Emerson C. and Mary Jane (Billick) Graham; married Ray Charles Barber (a graphic designer and professor), June 3, 1967. *Education:* Indiana University of Pennsylvania, B.A., 1967; also attended New School for Social Research and Juilliard School. *Religion:* Protestant. *Home:* 295 Washington Ave., Brooklyn, N.Y. 11205. *Agent:* Edite Kroll, 31 East 31st St., Apt. 2E, New York, N.Y. 10016.

CAREER: American Field Service, New York City, area supervisor, 1967-69; Crown Publishers, Inc., New York City, editorial assistant, 1969-70; Western Publishing Co., Inc., New York City, free-lance associate editor, 1972-74; William Morrow & Co., Inc., New York City, associate editor of junior books, 1976-78; free-lance writer, 1978—.

LYNDA GRAHAM-BARBER

WRITINGS: The Kit Furniture Book (Literary Guild selection), Pantheon, 1981; *Round Fish, Flatfish, and Other Animal Changes* (juvenile; illustrated by Pamela Carroll), Crown, 1982; *Personality Decorating,* Ballantine, 1986.

Under name Linda Barber: *Who Lives Inside?* (juvenile), Grosset, 1976.

Contributor to magazines, including *Ladies' Home Journal, Family Circle, Travel and Leisure, Ms., Cosmopolitan, Redbook,* and *Mademoiselle,* and newspapers.

WORK IN PROGRESS: Two picture books for children.

SIDELIGHTS: "As an editor for eight years, I became increasingly motivated to work on my own projects. Twice I quit work to try my hand at free-lance writing, and both times I returned to a full-time position and the security that comes with a job. In my case, the third time was charmed—the *New York Times* bought one of my articles, and that turned into a book. The subject was kit furniture; my husband and I had just assembled an apartment full of antique reproductions from kits. This book was—as are all my books and articles—the outgrowth of a personal interest and venture that I wanted to share with a general readership.

"Any measure of success I've had as a writer can be attributed to two factors: alert antennae and an ability to translate ideas lucidly, with care and enthusiasm. Editors appreciate eager awareness. I hope to continue to write for both adult and juvenile audiences."

GRAND, Samuel 1912-

PERSONAL: Born August 28, 1912, in New York, N.Y.; son of Meyer (a tailor) and Rose (Bronstein) Grand; married Tamar Slavin (a writer), June 14, 1942; children: Deborah, David. *Education:* City College of New York (now of the City University of New York), B.A., 1932; Jewish Theological Seminary of America, B.J.P., 1933; Columbia University, M.A., 1933, Ph.D., 1958; attended Hebrew University, Jerusalem, 1938. *Home and office:* 90-59 56th Ave., Elmhurst, N.Y.

CAREER: Teacher at Hebrew and public schools, New York, N.Y., 1931-36; Forest Hills Jewish Center, Forest Hills, N.Y., principal, 1936-37; Park Avenue Synagogue, New York City, principal, 1938-41; American Association for Jewish Education, New York City, executive secretary, 1941-42; served in Civilian Public Service, Middletown, Conn., 1942-46; Jewish Education Committee, New York City, consultant, 1946-52; Union of American Hebrew Congregations, New York City, director of department of experimental education and audio-visual aids, 1951-64; free-lance writer and producer of audio-visual aids, 1964—. Executive board member, National Council on Jewish Audio-Visual Materials, 1949—; producer and director of numerous educational filmstrips on Judaism, 1949—; producer of record albums for Jewish schools, 1952-56. *Member:* Labor Zionist Organization of America, Jewish Peace Fellowship, Educational Film Library Association, Film Council of America, National Conference of Jewish Communal Service (vice-president, 1956-58), National Conference for Jewish Education (vice-president, 1974-76).

WRITINGS: Palestine in the Jewish School, Jewish Education Committee of New York, 1948; *First Steps in Audio-Visual Education in the Jewish Religious School,* Union of American Hebrew Congregations, 1952; *The Jews Settle in New Amsterdam 1654* (picture book), Union of American Hebrew Congregations, 1955; (with Moshe Genser) *Hebrew, the Audio-Lingual Way,* Ktav, 1962; *Hebrew Prayer Skills,* Behrman House, 1966; (with wife, Tamar Grand) *The Children of Israel* (juvenile; with teacher's guide and activity book), Union of American Hebrew Congregations, 1972; (with wife, T. Grand) *Jews in Distant Lands,* Union of American Hebrew Congregations, 1977.

Also author of unpublished Ph.D. dissertation, "A History of Zionist Youth Organizations in the United States," 1958. Contributor of articles to educational and religious periodicals, including *Jewish Education, Pedagogic Review,* and *Principal.*

WORK IN PROGRESS: Educational filmstrips related to contemporary Israeli and Jewish history.

SIDELIGHTS: "My writing for children has been influenced by years of involvement in visual aids. At least fifty percent of the average page of my books is devoted to visuals, either photographs or illustrations. I often write with a visual in mind."

HOBBIES AND OTHER INTERESTS: Photography and philately.

We are by nature most tenacious of those things which we notice in childhood, just as the flavor with which new vessels are imbued remains in them.
—Seneca

It is better to be a young June-bug than an old bird of paradise.
—Mark Twain
(pseudonym of Samuel Langhorne Clemens)

GREGORY, Diana (Jean)   1933-

BRIEF ENTRY: Born April 27, 1933, in Pasedena, Calif. Author. Gregory describes her reading audience as being in "the change-over from childhood to young adulthood." Prior to the publication of her first novel, Gregory confesses that she wrote two nonfiction books "to get a toehold inside the doorway of fiction." She was literally at home with the topics of these books, *Dairy Goats* and *Owning a Horse: A Practical Guide,* as a breeder of goats and horses on her California ranch between 1971 and 1976. Her varied career has also included work in advertising and as a Hollywood associate producer, a children's theatre director, and an actress. A full-time writer since 1976, Gregory now has more than five novels to her credit. She explores topics that touch the lives of many preadolescents in today's society such as relocating to a new city in *I'm Boo . . . That's Who!* (Addison-Wesley, 1979), when a parent remarries in *There's a Caterpillar in My Lemonade* (Addison-Wesley, 1980), and when parents divorce in *The Fog Burns Off by Eleven O'Clock* (Addison-Wesley, 1981). "All my novels," Gregory affirms, "will be aimed at that particular age group who is asking questions, sometimes silently, and receiving too few answers." *Agent:* Dorothy Markinko, McIntosh & Otis, Inc., 475 Fifth Ave., New York, N.Y. 10017.

FOR MORE INFORMATION SEE: Contemporary Authors, Volumes 97-100, Gale, 1981.

HANDFORTH, Thomas (Schofield)   1897-1948

PERSONAL: Born September 16, 1897, in Tacoma, Wash.; died October 19, 1948, in Los Angeles, Calif.; son of Thomas Jefferson and Ruby Edwardine (Shera) Handforth. *Education:* Attended University of Washington; National Academy of Design; Art Students League; Charles Hawthorne's Summer School; École des Beaux Arts; Academie Delacluse; Academie Colarossis; Academie de la Grande Chaumiere. *Residence:* Wilmington, Del.

CAREER: Artist, illustrator, and author. Went to Paris, 1920, where he lived until about 1926; later travelled to North Africa; spent a year in Mexico, 1930; went to the Orient, 1931; lived in Peking, China for seven years; also travelled in India for one year; returned to the United States, 1939; following World War II, taught art at Seeman School for mentally retarded boys. *Exhibitions:* Work appeared in the group shows "Fifty Prints of the Year," 1926-29, and "Fine Prints of the Year," 1926-37; and is also represented in the permanent collections of the Metropolitan Museum of Art, New York, N.Y.; Library of Congress, Washington, D.C.; Carnegie Institute, Pittsburgh, Pa.; Bibliotheque Nationale, Paris, France; Victoria and Albert Museum, London, England; New York Public Library, New York City; Fogg Art Museum, Cambridge, Mass.; Pennsylvania Museum, Philadelphia; Omaha Art Museum, Omaha, Neb.; Baltimore Museum of Art, Baltimore, Md.; Boston Museum of Fine Arts, Boston, Mass.; Honolulu Academy of Arts, Honolulu, Hawaii. *Military service:* U.S. Army, 1918-19, medical department; became sergeant; U.S. Army Air Corps, 1942-43; private.

MEMBER: Society of American Etchers, Chicago Society of Etchers, Zeta Psi. *Awards, honors:* Emil Fuchs prize, Brooklyn Society of Etchers, 1927; Charles M. Lea prize, Philadelphia Society of Etchers, 1929; Guggenheim fellowship, 1931,

for study in the Far East; Caldecott Medal, 1939, for *Mei Li;* Middle Honor, Spring Book Festival, 1947, for *The Secret of the Porcelain Fish.*

WRITINGS: Mei Li (juvenile; self-illustrated), Doubleday, 1938, reprinted, 1963; *Faraway Meadow* (juvenile; self-illustrated), Doubleday, 1939.

Illustrator: Elizabeth Coatsworth, *Toutou in Bondage,* Macmillan, 1929; Susan Cowles Smith, *Tranquilina's Paradise,* Minton, 1930; Delia Goetz, *The Dragon and the Eagle,* Foreign Policy Association, 1944; Margery Evernden, *The Secret of the Porcelain Fish,* Random House, 1947.

Also author and illustrator of *Sleeping Arrow,* 1941; illustrator of Pierre Coalfleet's (pseudonym of Frank C. Davison) *Sidonie,* 1921; and contributor of work to the periodicals *Forum* and *Asia,* as well as to publications of the Foreign Policy Association.

SIDELIGHTS: **September 16, 1897.** Born in Tacoma, Washington. "That the Orient was to be my destination was determined, I feel sure, not so much by the stars as by the auspicious background of my birthplace and childhood in Tacoma, Washington, and in the Puget Sound country. Ever about me was a panorama of sea and islands and mountains leading my fancy through its vistas, out toward the Pacific Ocean and beyond.

"Ships sailed forth from the harbor below our home toward Japan, China and the Indies, and even the canoes of the Indians, venturing out from our inland sea toward Alaska and farther west, seemed to be trying to maintain a link with the lands of the Mongols and Manchus. The great conical rocks

THOMAS HANDFORTH

on the Olympic Coast, jutting up from a foam-flecked sea and wreathed in mist, seemed to be a continuation of a Chinese landscape. Near Tacoma was the entrance to a Chinese smugglers' cave into which I used to peer with childish fascination. The cave was said to continue through the hills to the sea, perhaps to China itself. At that stage when all boys turn to building model battleships and brigs and barquentines, I was making Chinese junks and sampans for travel on the Yellow River.

"It may have been because of my imaginative Irish ancestry that I became aware very early of the magic in symbolic forms. The symbols to which I reacted were, for the most part, Oriental. My favorite expedition as a three-year-old was to be taken to the rustic moon bridge in one of our city parks. The perilous ascent and descent of that slippery arc should have been excitement enough, but for me the great experience was the sight of the arc's circle. It was the circle of the Yin and Yang, Chinese symbol of the universe, soon to be well known to me through its prosaic use as the insignia of the Northern Pacific Railroad.

"At the age of eight, when I was already recording pictorially the real and the surreal; the Yin and Yang symbol occurs on one of the first pages of my drawing book, followed by a copy of Hokusai's Blue Wave, a sweeping segment of the circle continuing out beyond the frame and tempting one toward unknown realms, a quality characteristic of Eastern compositions not only in pictures but in landscape gardening. Then in the drawing book comes a page of dragons, and after that a sketch of blue-gowned, pigtailed Chinamen, a record of a visit to the Chinatown in Victoria, British Columbia.

"The smooth and subtly smiling faces of Japanese dolls were fixed in the imagery of my childhood, and Japanese fairy tales were dearer to me than those of Andersen or the Brothers Grimm. Masks were made for play, flat faces with slanting eyes, suggested, perhaps, by the West Coast Indian masks which I had seen in the museum in Victoria; masks which, I was to learn much later, had close affinity not only with the Noh masks of classical Japanese drama and the painted faces of the Chinese theatre, but with the Mayan stone carved faces on our own side of the Pacific.

"While I was still in High School I had decided that art was to be my profession. . . ." [Thomas Handforth, "Moon Bridge in Lily Pond," *Horn Book*, May-June, 1939.[1]]

She hurried down the street and found him at the Bridge of Wealth. Under the Bridge of Wealth hung a little bell, and under the bell lay a skinny wrinkled priest who mumbled, "Ring the bell with a penny, and you will have money for all the year." ■ (From *Mei Li* by Thomas Handforth. Illustrated by the author.)

"New rejoicing, Mrs. Ugly Pig!" she said, bowing politely. "New rejoicing, stupid Mr. Duck!" she said, again bowing politely. ■ (From *Mei Li* by Thomas Handforth. Illustrated by the author.)

1915. "After graduating from high school and before my one year at the University of Washington I had decided upon my profession and was trying to learn to paint. It was a rather precious period of jade and ivory towers and yellow furniture; one admired especially Edmund Dulac and Aubrey Beardsley and Kay Nielsen and the then modern Viennese decoration. During this period I painted my one and only mural—a Chinese fantasy with much Dulac influence, and produced my one and only ballet, based on the Babylonian story of Ishtar and Tamuz. I not only did the sets and costumes and arranged the choreography but danced in the chorus. It was one of my few reprehensible outbursts in this form of expression—an urge which I have since managed to preserve discreetly in the category of a suppressed desire. To the dance of others, however, I have remained one of the most ardent of devotees . . . investigating its various forms in India.

"After the mural and the Babylonian ballet I went to the San Francisco Fair of 1915 upon which legend has bestowed the epithet: the most beautiful of all expositions. For me, sentiment if not justice will always concede it that distinction. New realms of European and American art were opened up before me. However, I find myself still most absorbed in things Oriental; my notebooks record: in water color, the great green and gold Dibutsu of the Japanese pavilion against a hot blue sky; *motifs* of Chinese design see here and there, and the curved roofs of San Francisco's Chinatown.'' [Bertha Mahony Miller and Elinor Whitney Field, editors, *Caldecott Medal Books: 1938-1953*, Horn Book, 1957.²]

1916. Moved to New York City, where he studied at the National Academy of Design, and the Art Students League. "Of the two principal techniques in Chinese painting one is called Hsieh Y, 'to write the meaning.' It is a technique related to the calligraphic and is employed by poets and therefore considered the highest form. The brush is used freely as in writing, the very pressure of the brush upon the paper, the shape of the stroke of ink, expressing the quality of the subject. Again, as in the theatre, it is the essence rather than the representation of a specific object that is being sought.

"When Kenneth Hayes Miller, with whom I studied painting for a brief time, used to urge us to paint 'the cosmic essence of white' or our 'inner consciousness of blue,' perhaps he was trying to lead us toward the same goal. But at the age of twenty I couldn't digest a precept in that form. I just didn't get it. It was easier for me to understand another of my teachers, Mahonri Young, when he said, 'Draw the space about the figure rather than the figure itself.' ''²

1920. Went to Paris to study painting, and attended, among other schools, the École des Beaux Arts, where he stayed for six years. "Most of my training in draughtsmanship in New York and at the École des Beaux Arts in Paris was completely academic. Each week one did a charcoal drawing of a nude model on a large sheet of paper, beginning at 9 o'clock on Monday morning, with the head at the top of the page and finishing at the bottom of the page with the feet at exactly noon on Saturday. I often wonder how I survived it. I used to flee from the *ateliers* of Paris to the Cathedral at Chartres, seeking consolation in those quixotic faces of Gothic sculpture, smooth and subtly smiling faces, now of Madonnas instead of Japanese dolls; in those elongated figures of Gothic sculpture with tenuous flowing lines of drapery which were quickened into flame-like shapes of fresh exaltation; sharp flaming movements which come to one again in the fifth century Wei sculpture of China when Buddhism made its first impact upon the Far East.

"In Paris, the Expressionists, the Cubists and the Dadaists, who were the parents of the Surrealists, were holding the center of the stage. The tender pathetic boy Harlequins of Picasso's 'blue period' appealed to me especially—adolescent, supple bodies balancing upon spheres, or stepping out from groups of circus people, or in compositions with strong prancing horses. The cool sharp line of some of the modern French engravers I admired too, but I suspected many of the Modernists of being preoccupied with their manner rather than with the animating spirit. And so I welcomed the opportunity of hearing the opinions of an unbiased critic: Dr. James Cousins, who had just come from India. . . . A large part of his life had been devoted

At midnight when the old bells in the cathedral tower struck the hour, Tranquilina stirred her gold wings. . . . ▪ (From *Tranquilina's Paradise* by Susan Smith. Illustrated by Thomas Handforth.)

to encouraging the so-called new renaissance in India, but for sixteen years he had been completely out of touch with the European trend. He had come to Paris to assemble a collection of contemporary Western painting for the Maharaja of Mysore, but the names and styles of even the better known Modernist painters were unknown to him. I was enlightened by his reactions, for he was always able to select without guidance examples of those painters of the ultramodern school who were recognized as significant by the West, since, he said, they had

something fundamentally in common in their abstract qualities with the great traditions of the East.

"However, my interests were in present aspects of life, call it journalistic if you will, and not with the abstract or theories concerning it.

"The first painter with whom I came in contact who was able to interpret successfully the living scene, using an Eastern style of painting, was a Georgian friend of mine named Goudiach-vili, which means radish. He reveled in the life of the moment, in the scenes of the cafés, in the festivities of the people, in the cabbies and their carriages and the girls of his native town of Tiflis. Yet he painted these scenes in his traditional native style which had come directly from Persia.''[2]

1926. Went to North Africa. ''With Mr. Radish [Goudiachvili] in mind, and Persia, and also thinking of the adventures in ports, and of what a life was that of a sailor, and a lot of other ideas muddled in my head, I sailed from Marseilles to Tunis. I had intended to go to Ragusa but I missed the boat. It really did not matter where I went. I hoped to be amused. I was hilariously so, especially while trying to etch it all on copper. From Tunis I went to Morocco. Then I jumped back to the Great Northwest, to the somber silent coast of Vancouver Island and I recalled my first love, Hokusai. Then to Mexico, breathtakingly magnificent and barbaric—and I found that Diego Rivera was doing on a grand scale and in his own manner what Hokusai had achieved in his little wood block prints. I started to do a series of etchings which were to have been called The One Hundred Views of Mt. Popocatepetl. Eleven of them were completed when I was awarded . . . a Guggenheim Fellowship for travel in the Orient.''[2]

1931. Traveled to the Orient. ''I sailed on a freighter which took a month and a day from New York to Yokohama and the one other passenger on board was a baker from Trenton. There were long hours to hang over the rail and wonder what I was going to do with the Orient or what it would do with me. . . . I had, during my grasshopper leaps, dropped into a good many ports, both on the Atlantic and on the Pacific shores, in the Mediterranean and on the North African Coast. A collection of sketches of these ports had begun to accumulate and it seemed to me that it would be a worthy aim to continue on

(From *The Secret of the Porcelain Fish* by Margery Evernden. Illustrated by Thomas Handforth.)

the same sort of theme, making a sequence of impressions of Ports of the World. Also I wanted to see more of the Dances of the World: In Java, Bali, and India. I would stop in Japan only long enough to corroborate the knowledge which I thought I already had of that country's arts.

''Japan, with its passion for the perfection of arrangement, turned out to look exactly as it was expected to appear. Aside from its blatant scars of western modernization, every view in front of one, or behind, might be of Hiroshige's pictures. After all, too much was enough. Such perfectly ordered and regulated nature was unreasonable.

''In the homes of the potters of Kyoto, where each family for generations had specialized in the manufacture of some special ware, one sat for restive hours while the brothers and the cousins and the fathers and the aunts discussed the decoration on a simple dish; whether the stroke of the flower stem should turn slightly more toward the right or slightly more toward the left. For business reasons, of course, it was important, because the dish was to be sold as an original Chinese piece of the 11th century!''[2]

Settled in Peking, China, where he stayed for six years. ''Within the thick walls of Peking is a city which . . . is inexhaustible. Mystery, intrigue and international modernity mingle with its crumbling culture. Fabulous Ming palaces are hidden behind new little Japanese shops. A cloud of black crows flies over the yellow roofs of the Forbidden City, while cosmopolites dance on the roof garden of the French hotel to the American music of the Russian orchestra. On the dance floor might be seen a boyish Chinese woman dressed in dinner jacket and trousers from Bond Street, or in military uniform. She had become a major in the army of the notorious war lord Chang Sung-ch'iang for her services as procuress of concubines. Below on the broad avenue by the hotel, among the motor cars

Thomas Handforth, self-portrait.

and rickshas, pass camels and herds of sheep and squealing pigs, and near the avenue in the hollow of a tree live two old wrinkled beggars. The smell of the dust of the Gobi Desert is in the air, the smell of caravans and of trade routes to Mongolia, Turkestan and India.

"All the houses in Peking face south. They consist of separate one-story pavilions built around courtyards, the number of courtyards depending upon the size or wealth of the family. I rented a section, which in itself consisted of several courtyards, of one of these large old houses. The last Chinese occupant had been an official who had been active in the Boxer uprising. He had been obliged to flee and the house had been turned over by the Chinese government to an English mission school for the blind. From the mission it had been purchased by an English resident of Peking. It was a handsome house but in an advanced stage of decay. For six years I made it my home. Then came the China Incident.

"For several seasons Japanese war planes had been swooping down over the houses of the city. Japanese troops had been indulging in sham battles at the most unexpected hours in the most unexpected places on the streets and the populace had courteously refrained from showing its feelings. Then the cannons began to rumble, and the rumble came closer and closer to the walls. Streets were sandbagged and trenches dug and the Chinese soldiers courteously retired from the city, leaving their dying and wounded to be picked up and washed and bandaged by the ladies and gentlemen of the foreign colony. With the streets lined by Japanese school children and hired coolies waving red-spotted white flags, the victorious army of the Mikado entered the Celestial City.

"Then the most unworthy Peace Preservation Corps of the Autonomous State of Hopei and Chihli courteously massacred the entire honorable Japanese colony of four hundred men, women and children at T'ung Cho twenty miles from Peking. After that we knew little of what was happening; newspapers were suppressed, there was no rail, telegraph or radio communication even with the port of Tientsín: when trains did reach Tientsín they took twenty hours instead of the normal two and a half. It seemed to me it was a very good time to take that long-postponed trip to India, and so, sealing my etching and lithograph presses into a hidden passageway in the six-foot-thick wall of my house, I went to Japan to catch a boat for India.

"My departure from Japan was delayed because instead of going to the steamship office I went each day to sit on padded matting floors before the golden screens of the Buddhist temples of Kyoto, golden screens which told a story of centuries of tender, warm communion between man and nature. Here on these gold leaf screens were the chrysanthemum and the cicada, the flight of heron, the tiger drinking at the pool, the pine tree and eagle, the fish in the spray of the waterfall.

"Now I was about to go to the source of these symbols and to the source of Buddhistic art. At the steamship office I bought a passage to Colombo, southern port of India."[2]

Handforth traveled in India for one year. ". . . In Jaipur, I hunted tiger with the Raj and painted a portrait of the Maharaja's son. On the northwest frontier of India, I lived in a barracks with British troops. I was about to make a journey with some wild tribesmen of those sinister hills when I was laid low by a sunstroke.

"As fast as a rattling bus could take me, I hurried away from those furnace-hot plains and up to the cooler altitudes of Kashmir. Then I traveled still higher, by pony and by foot, until under the eerie glaciers I reached the Faraway Meadow. As I sat in my tent and looked over the beauty of the vast scene, I felt that the meadow was a grassy stage and my friends puppets waiting for the strings to be pulled to make them come to life. Well, I could pull the strings and put them into a fantastic nonsense tale." [Helen Ferris, editor, *Writing Books for Boys and Girls,* Doubleday, 1952.[3]]

Lalla was delighted and started at once to pose. ■ (From *Faraway Meadow* by Thomas Handforth. Illustrated by the author.)

(From *The Dragon and the Eagle* by Delia Goetz. Illustrated by Thomas Handforth.)

1938. First juvenile book, *Mei Li,* published with Handforth's own illustrations. The book was based on his experiences in China.

"The surest way of winning the confidence and cooperation of these already cheerful people was to serve them plenty of tea, and to jolly them along with some foolish clownish acts, such as a Charlie Chaplin walk, or slapstick farce. It always brought a laugh even when performed by an odd foreigner who made drawings.

"I wanted to bring all these friends of mine together in a picture book for children, but could not decide who should play the leading rôle. Then I met Mei Li. She assumed such importance, which she rightly deserved, as the leading lady, that she crowded many of my other friends out of the story. She was that kind of a girl.

"During the famine in Anhwei Province, Mei Li, then an infant, had been left on the doorstep of a missionaries' home, and had spent the second year of her life in an American mission foundling asylum. Then she was adopted by a rich American lady-bountiful, and lived for two years in a luxurious home in Peking.

"When the American lady found it necessary to come to the United States for a year she sensibly realized that it was an opportune moment, since Mei Li would have to spend most of her life in China anyway, to give the child a season of hardening to immune her from the dangers of Chinese germs, before she was reclaimed for her life of luxury and American sanitation.

"Mei Li was left in the care of the wife of a poor gardener to play in the dust of a tiny courtyard, and to sleep on the large brick Kang which was used by the whole family. The house was seldom heated, even in the bitter cold of the North China winter, except by the clay cook stove in the one room of the house. And did Mei Li thrive on it! Sheathed in her thick padded garments, the cold and the brick bed had no terrors for her.

"Often I went to see her, and, at the gate in the gray wall on the narrow lane in which she lived, Mei Li's pets, a dusty little duck and a pinkish white little dog, would greet me, standing together with just their heads peeping over the gate-sill. Whatever the hour of the day, tea was offered me by Mei Li's nurse and I stayed to gossip with her friends and neighbors who might be there: the wife of the ricksha man, the cabbage-vendor and the night watchman. When the coalman stopped, Mei Li had intent conversations with his camels, when he didn't she talked to her dusty duck. But most of her time was spent in managing the large family upon whom she had been deposited. No Empress Dowager was ever more determined than she. A career is surely ordained for her, other than being the heroine of a children's book.

"Mei Li needed no urging to play this star rôle. Before long she was running the whole show. She brought her own little girl friends to be drawn, and the small boy San Uy, son of the ricksha man, and her pinkish white puppy, but if they ever weakened in this job of posing she would give them a piece of her mind.

"For a long time I searched for just the right type of woman who might have been Mei Li's mother. At last after my servant too had made many futile efforts to find a person such as I described, he brought to the house a peasant woman who had just that day come from the country looking for employment. She was exactly what I wanted, but most women of her kind would have been too shy or modest to have even entered the house of a foreigner. It was Mei Li who made her feel at home, and gave her hints on behavior in an artist's studio.

"The old priest in the picture book was my own lucky discovery. I noticed him just as he was disappearing in a crowd near one of the city gates. In his crazy-quilt robes, with his thick horn-rimmed spectacles slipping down his thin nose, and a large glass jewel in his black hat, he seemed to have just stepped out of an ancient Chinese scroll. He was too good to be true. As he stared vacantly at the sky, and dreamily waved his horsehair fly brush, he was like a mythical being, far, too far removed from earthly matters to ever find the address on the card which I gave him. But he arrived at my house the next day, hours before he was expected, pleased as a child, to have his picture drawn.

"The toys with which Mei Li plays are personages from Chinese folklore, among them the eight immortals. There is a ninth immortal too, but no one knows what he looks like, for each time that he visits the earth to go about amongst the people, he assumes a different guise. If one is polite to him he will bring that person good luck. If one is discourteous, misfortune follows. It behooves one to be courteous to everybody.

"And so my little models were always polite. They asked me my honorable name, my honorable age, and the honorable cost of everything in the house."[2]

1939. Returned to the West Coast. Awarded Caldecott Medal for *Mei Li.*

Faraway Meadow, Handforth's second self-illustrated juvenile book, was published. "Faraway Meadow is a small meadow, like a saddle between two peaks. At an altitude of 8000 feet it is sometimes below the clouds, but it is just as often above them; and sometimes it is blotted out, as by the fog during the battle of the story in *Faraway Meadow.*

"The ponies belong to the Kashmiri farmers, and they are left to graze on the meadow as long as there is no snow. The buffaloes are brought there only in the summer, by Gujar herdsmen from the plains of India, when the grass in the South is burned by the heat. The buffaloes and ponies do not quarrel, as I have pretended they do in the book. On the contrary, when a panther is about, the buffaloes form a circle around the foals as well as their calves, facing out from the center with horns lowered, to protect the young.

"I made the buffaloes and the ponies in my fable behave as human beings do because they looked as if they might have personalities like those of my friends who were camping there, and of other people I knew.

"At our camp was a dear old Scotch lady whom I portrayed as Grannie Nud, dressing her in the comical costume worn by the Gujar women.

"Alas, although I have been truthful about the costume, my picture of the banquet hall is utter fancy. The only houses on the meadow are hovels of logs, with earth floors and mud roofs and no furniture. Nevertheless, under the stars, around great bonfires, we did feast merrily with the Gujar folk while their herd grazed on that Faraway Meadow."[3]

1945. Taught art at Seeman School. Handforth stated his artistic goals and described his work in the following statement:

(From *Toutou in Bondage* by Elizabeth Coatsworth. Illustrated by Thomas Handforth.)

"My goal in etching and lithography is to do, without imitating its technical manner, a Western *Hsie-y,* i.e., 'to write the meaning.' (The Chinese *Hsie-y* is closely related to Chinese calligraphy.)

". . . The rhythm of *Hsie-y* is not contained within the frame. What is visible is only like the fragment of melody carried in and out of the picture frame toward infinity on a two-dimension plane.

"From this approach the Picture Book seems to me to present possibilities analogous to those of the Chinese scroll: giving a larger segment of 'melody' with variations and with a definite progression in time from beginning to end.

"*Realistic*—yes, in detail; but not in composition.

"My detail work is akin to the Chinese *Kung-pi,* 'the work brush,' i.e., meticulous craftsmanship.

"My composition is dominated by the *Hsie-y* concept: attempting to give meaning to the fragmentary melody by imbuing it with the reality of the whole. The method of my composition could be called one of abbreviating reality. If I had to express the quality of *Hsie-y* in Western terminology I should call it 'mythical'—inasmuch as the real myth is an abbreviated reality.

"So, in a restatement of the dominant elements of my work, I should call them *melodious,* instead of 'decorative,' and *mythical,* instead of 'realistic.'" [*Horn Book,* special issue, October 19, 1950.⁴]

October 19, 1948. Died in Pasadena, California.

October 19, 1950. *Horn Book* magazine honored Handforth with a special issue devoted to his life and as an appreciation of his work. His work is included in the Kerlan Collection at the University of Minnesota.

FOR MORE INFORMATION SEE: Thomas Handforth, "Moon Bridge in Lily Pond," *Horn Book,* May-June, 1939; *Horn Book,* special issue, October 19, 1950; Stanley J. Kunitz and Howard Haycraft, editors, *Junior Book of Authors,* 2nd edition, Wilson, 1951; Helen Ferris, editor, *Writing Books for Boys and Girls,* Doubleday, 1952; Thomas Handforth, "Personal Progress toward the Orient," in *Caldecott Medal Books: 1938-1957,* edited by Bertha Mahony Miller and Elinor Whitney Field, Horn Book, 1957; B. M. Miller, and others, compilers, *Illustrators of Children's Books: 1946-1956,* Horn Book, 1958. Obituaries: *Art Digest,* January 1, 1949.

HEALEY, Larry   1927-

BRIEF ENTRY: Born November 10, 1927, in Boston, Mass. An author of novels for young adults, Healey graduated from Harvard College in 1949 and worked in sales until the late 1970s. His first book *The Claw of the Bear* (F. Watts) appeared in 1978, followed by *The Town Is on Fire* (F. Watts, 1979) and *The Hoard of the Himalayas* (Dodd, 1980). Each of these novels features a teenage hero who becomes embroiled in mysterious and deadly occurrences. As *Booklist* observed: "Healey successfully employs the trappings of the adult high-adventure novel, in which characterization is subordinate to pace and action." His latest work, *Angry Mountain* (Dodd, 1983), retains the fast-paced action of the other novels as a sixteen-year-old boy learns a lesson in self-centeredness amidst the catastrophe of a volcanic eruption. While *Booklist* called it "an exciting, if grim, story . . . leavened by a touch of romance," *School Library Journal* assured that an "abundant supply of action and humor should keep most adventure fans pleased." All of Healey's novels are suitable for high/low readers. *Home:* 68 Fifth Ave., New York, N.Y. 10011.

FOR MORE INFORMATION SEE: Contemporary Authors, Volume 101, Gale, 1981.

HENTOFF, Nat(han Irving)   1925-

PERSONAL: Born June 10, 1925, in Boston, Mass.; son of Simon (a salesman) and Lena (Katzenberg) Hentoff; married Margot Goodman (a writer), August 15, 1959; children: (previous marriage) Jessica, Miranda; (present marriage) Nicholas, Thomas. *Education:* Northeastern University, B.A. (with highest honors), 1946; graduate study at Harvard University, 1946, and Sorbonne, 1950. *Home:* 25 Fifth Ave., New York, N.Y. 10003.

CAREER: WMEX (radio station), Boston, Mass., writer, producer, and annnouncer, 1944-53; *Downbeat,* New York City, associate editor, 1953-57; reviewer, *New York Herald Tribune Book Week, Peace News* (London), *The Reporter,* and *Hi Fi Stereo Review; Village Voice,* New York City, columnist, 1958—; *New Yorker,* New York City, staff writer, 1960—; *Washington Post,* columnist, 1984—. Adjunct associate professor, New York University. Lecturer at schools and colleges.

Member: Authors League of America, American Civil Liberties Union, American Federation of Television and Radio Artists, New York Civil Liberties Union, Reporters Committee for Freedom of the Press (member of steering committee), Freedom to Write Committee of P.E.N. *Awards, honors:* Nancy Bloch Memorial Award and *New York Herald Tribune* Spring Book Festival Award, both 1965, and Woodward Park School Annual Book Award, 1966, all for *Jazz Country;* Golden Archer Award, 1980, for *This School Is Driving Me Crazy;* Hugh M. Hefner First Amendment Award, 1981, for *The First Freedom: The Tumultuous History of Free Speech in America; The Day They Come to Arrest the Book* was included on the Acton Public Library Cranberry Award List, 1983.

WRITINGS: (Editor with Nat Shapiro) *Hear Me Talking to Ya: The Story of Jazz by the Men Who Made It,* Rinehart, 1955; (editor with N. Shapiro) *The Jazz Makers,* Rinehart, 1957, reprinted, Greenwood, 1975; (editor with Albert McCarthy) *Jazz: New Perspectives on the History of Jazz by Twelve of the World's Foremost Jazz Critics and Scholars,* Rinehart, 1959, reprinted, Da Capo Press, 1975; *The Jazz Life,* Dial, 1961, reprinted, Da Capo Press, 1978; *Peace Agitator: The Story of A. J. Muste,* Macmillan, 1963; *The New Equality,* Viking, 1964; *Our Children Are Dying,* Viking, 1966; (editor) *The Essays of A. J. Muste,* Bobbs-Merrill, 1967; *A Doctor among the Addicts,* Rand McNally, 1967; (contributor) Edward E. Davis, editor, *The Beatles Book,* Cowles, 1968; *Journey into Jazz* (illustrated by David S. Martin), Coward, 1968; *A Political Life: The Education of John V. Lindsay,* Knopf,

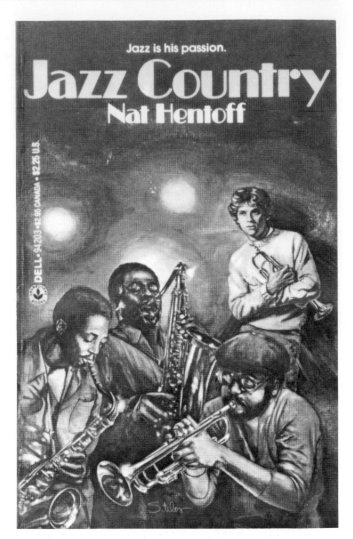

Each musician had entered into his own flashbacks while improvising around Godfrey's backgrounds....
■ (Cover illustration from *Jazz Country* by Nat Hentoff.)

NAT HENTOFF

1969; (author of introduction) *The London Novels of Colin MacInnes,* Farrar, Straus, 1969; (author of introduction) *Black Anti-Semitism and Jewish Racism,* Schocken, 1970; (with others), *State Secrets: Police Surveillance in America,* Holt, 1973; *Jazz Is,* Random House, 1976; *Does Anybody Give a Damn?: Nat Hentoff on Education,* Knopf, 1977; *The First Freedom: The Tumultuous History of Free Speech in America,* Delacorte, 1980.

Novels: *Jazz Country,* Harper, 1965; *Call the Keeper,* Viking, 1966; *Onwards!,* Simon & Schuster, 1967; *I'm Really Dragged But Nothing Gets Me Down,* Simon & Schuster, 1967; *In the Country of Ourselves,* Simon and Schuster, 1971; *This School Is Driving Me Crazy,* Delacorte, 1975; *Does This School Have Capital Punishment?,* Delacorte, 1981; *The Day They Came to Arrest the Book* (ALA Notable Book), Delacorte, 1982; *Blues for Charlie Darwin,* Morrow, 1982.

Contributor to *Progressive, Inquiry, School Library Journal, Civil Liberties Review, Student Press Law Center Report, Wall Street Journal,* and other periodicals. Former associate editor, *Liberation.*

(Jacket illustration by Allan Manham from *The Day They Came to Arrest the Book* by Nat Hentoff.)

WORK IN PROGRESS: The Man from Internal Affairs for Mysterious Press; *The Freedom Fighters: Students and Librarians in American Schools* for young adults.

SIDELIGHTS: "When I was growing up in Roxbury (part of Boston), the nearest public library was twelve long blocks away. It was attached to a fortress-like high school, and by contrast with the multifariously inviting contemporary libraries I've seen recently, our library was forbidding. The rule of silence was so zealously enforced that a Trappist monk could have stayed there for years without being tempted to break his vows. There were no audiovisual sections, booths for listening to recordings, or recordings. The librarians were efficient but hardly outgoing, not at all like what I consider to be the new breed of librarian of the past fifteen years or so—these quite remarkably cheerful people who appear to like what they do for a living more than most people do.

"Nonetheless, I looked forward to my Saturday library visits almost as much as I did to the Saturday afternoon picture show, the nearly four-hour long cornucopia every week—a double feature, strings of shorts and previews, and the literally cliff-hanging serials. The library too was a cornucopia, and I never ceased marveling at the continual surprises that came with my first library card. And unlike school, the library was—and still is—a place where one can find and keep on finding one's own surprises.

"Nobody, for instance, had told me when I was eight about the Andrew Lang books of fairy tales—the *Red Book* and the *Blue Book* and all those other color books. But I found them, and I read them all. Then I found the sea tales of Howard Pease, and all kinds of novels that could never have been on my reading lists at school because they were too old for me. But only I knew what was too old for me. I sometimes wonder if I wouldn't know a lot more by now if I had simply stayed in the library during those years and not gone to school at all. It is, after all, an education prescription that George Bernard Shaw recommended for children, and I wish that instead of leaving a large sum of money for work on simplifying the English language, Shaw had left bequests for researchers to test whether kids growing up in libraries rather than in classrooms become smarter and more self-confident than their peers hooked to desks.

"Anyway, as the years went on, I kept making new discoveries in the library. Collections of old newspapers gave me my first sense of the excitement of reading about history as it was turning into history. And magazines—all kinds of magazines, new and old, in all kinds of fields, many of them fascinatingly arcane—I would have known about hardly any of them but for the library.

" I became such a library freak that I could be perfectly content for an hour just going through the card catalog, coming upon the titles of books I simply *had* to read, delighted that they were there, waiting. To this day, I cannot leave a library without spending some browsing time at the card catalog. (Actually, it's not all browsing. I invariably search out the cards for my own books because only their inclusion in a library makes me feel like an authentic author. Seeing them in a bookstore window is not nearly so satisfying.)

". . . Whatever a kid thinks he might want to read, he ought to have a shot at. I remember when I was eleven conniving to take home a huge, scholarly, critical work on Lenin. I don't know why I was interested in Lenin at eleven, but although I couldn't understand most of the book, I felt very proud of getting through as much of it as I did. That journey stretched

my vocabulary; led me later to approach Edmund Wilson's *To the Finland Station* with the supportive sense that I had some background in the subject; and all in all, made me feel like a very competent eleven-year-old boy. That, obviously, is a good way for an eleven-year-old boy to feel." [Nat Hentoff, "The Saturday Library Matinee," *American Libraries,* April, 1976.[1]]

Hentoff's love for books led him into a career as a writer. In various books he has written about racism, the draft, police spying, and educational reform. He has been a columnist for *Village Voice* since 1958 and a staff writer for the *New Yorker* since 1960.

Hentoff began his literary career as a jazz critic. His first novel, *Jazz Country,* was also his most popular teenage novel. It is the story of a white teenager faced with the problems of breaking into a predominantly black jazz scene. "While there was a certain amount of didacticism in my motivation for writing *Jazz Country,* the primary reason was wanting to find out if I could write fiction. And my approach to fiction is one of surprise—self-surprise. Therefore, I did not begin with a list of precepts that had, at all costs, to be imbedded in the text. I did not even have a plot.

(Cover illustration from *This School Is Driving Me Crazy* by Nat Hentoff.)

How can you prove you're innocent when the school says you're guilty?

Does This School Have Capital Punishment?
Nat Hentoff

(Cover illustration from *Does This School Have Capital Punishment?* by Nat Hentoff.)

"I point this out even though I am convinced that readers can tell the difference between a book deliberately shaped to instruct or influence and a book with some of the spontaneity of, let us say, a jazz solo.

"And especially young readers tend to resist the former kind of book—one that was written to perform a community service, however virtuous. The young, after all, are preached at incessantly and I hardly think they would voluntarily pick up a book in order to be preached at yet once more.

"So, as is also true with jazz musicians in their approach to music, I wrote *Jazz Country* to please myself first of all. And while I could provide a considerable ex post facto list of observations about blacks and whites in this country that I could pretend to have *intended* from the start, it did not work that way. Whatever did emerge in this area resulted from the interplay of the characters as I came to know them.

". . . Books are not—or ought not to be—tracts or 'good will' messages. If they are to move the young to a beginning comprehension of the two countries, they must first come from an organic need on the part of the writer to find out who *he* is in relation to those countries. And in the process, he is likely to

uncover ugliness as well as hope, fears as well as desires, confusions as well as discoveries. And all that, of course, ought to be in his book, for the young cannot be conned by a simplistic interracial daydream or an updated Horatio Alger myth.

"Many of the young, in many different ways, are 'up tight' in their worlds. . . . If they are to find reason to read a book ostensibly for them, they require that the writer be 'up tight' too—that he know and be able to tell not only how unsimple it is to stay whole out there, especially when one is young, but that he also be able to communicate his awareness of his own complicity in this distinctly unequal society. I don't mean the writer must be suffused with guilt. I do mean he must show he knows where we are all at and how we got there. And beyond that, compassion is not enough. Attempted empathy isn't enough. There also has to be, I would think, some rage and disgust. We talk so blithely about love, but we are in a time when catharsis through anger and revulsion and basic social change must precede love, or that love will be as fake as all those sermons in all those segregated American churches all these years.

"What I am saying is that if there are to be books specifically for twelve-and-over in the years to come—and I would not be certain this category will long survive—they are going to be much more complex, more shocking to librarians though not to the young, and much more openly—and healthily—erotic than 'books for young readers' have ever been before. (In that last respect, *Jazz Country* was a total failure.)

"That is, they will be more complicatedly honest, in their confusions along with their insights, if they are to be read at all." [Nat Hentoff, "Getting Inside Jazz Country," *Horn Book*, October, 1966.[2]]

One of Hentoff's latest novels for teenagers is *The Day They Came to Arrest the Book.* He has also written numerous books of nonfiction.

HOBBIES AND OTHER INTERESTS: Politics, reading, music, tennis.

FOR MORE INFORMATION SEE: Newsweek, December 21, 1964, September 5, 1966, September 15, 1969; *Negro Digest,* June, 1965, March, 1967; *Times Literary Supplement,* May 19, 1966; *Observer,* August 7, 1966; *Time,* August 12, 1966, October 11, 1968; *New Yorker,* September 17, 1966; *Horn Book,* October, 1966, December, 1972; *Harper's,* November, 1966, April, 1969; *America,* November 12, 1966; *Nation,* November 14, 1966; *Village Voice,* November 24, 1966, July 18, 1968, May 23, 1977; *Punch,* March 29, 1967; *Instructor,* April, 1967, May, 1976; *Spectator,* April 7, 1967; *New York Times,* May 23, 1968, September 11, 1969, March 21, 1980; *New Leader,* August 5, 1968; *Science Books,* September, 1968; *Publishers Weekly,* September 2, 1968; *Negro History Bulletin,* March, 1971; May Hill Arbuthnot and Zena Sutherland, *Children and Books,* 4th edition, Scott, Foresman, 1972; Doris de Montreville and Donna Hill, editors, *Third Book of Junior Authors,* H. W. Wilson, 1972; *Children's Literature Review,* Volume 1, Gale, 1976; *National Observer,* February 28, 1976; *American Libraries,* April, 1976; *Progressive,* December, 1976, July, 1977; *Times Educational Supplement,* January 20, 1978; *Twentieth-Century Children's Authors,* St. Martin's Press, 1978; *Los Angeles Times,* April 13, 1980.

Childhood shows the man as morning does the day.
—John Milton

L. R. HERKIMER

HERKIMER, L(awrence) R(ussell)   1925-

PERSONAL: Born October 25, 1925; married Dorothy J. Brown; children: three. *Education:* Southern Methodist University, B.S., 1948; University of Illinois, M.S., 1949. *Home:* 5902 Westgrove Dr., Dallas, Tex. 75248. *Office:* 9150 Markville Dr., Dallas, Tex. 75243.

CAREER: Southern Methodist University, Dallas, Tex., assistant professor, 1949-51; National Cheerleaders Association (operates clinics for cheerleaders), Dallas, Tex., co-owner, executive secretary, 1951, president, 1982—; Ruse Rouge, Inc. (a manufacturer of cheerleading supplies), Dallas, Tex., co-owner, 1952—; Cheerleader Supply Co. (a distributor of cheerleading supplies), Dallas, Tex., co-owner and president, 1952—. *Member:* Southern Methodist University Alumni Association (life member; president, 1981-82). *Awards, honors:* Honorary letter awarded by Southern Methodist University Lettermen's Association, 1981; Outstanding Business Leader award from Northwood Institute, 1984; Distinguished Alumni Award from Southern Methodist University, 1985.

WRITINGS: Champion Cheers, National Cheerleaders Association, 1959, 3rd edition, revised, 1961; *Pep Rally Skits and Stunts,* National Cheerleaders Association, 1961; *Photographically Illustrated Cheer Routines,* National Cheerleaders Association, 1964; *Champion Cheers and Chants,* National Cheerleaders Association, 1968; *N.C.A. Spirit Manual with Skits and Stunts for Pep Rallies,* National Cheerleaders Association, 1968; (editor with Phyllis Hollander) *The Complete Book of Cheerleading,* Doubleday, 1975.

Illustrator: Betty L. Shepherd, *Go! Fight! Win!* (photographs by Francis Shepherd), Delacorte, 1981.

SIDELIGHTS: As the only national manufacturer in the cheerleading industry, Lawrence Herkimer has amassed a fortune selling everything from pompons to pep rally stunts to saddle shoes. It all began when Herkimer became one of the most popular cheerleaders ever to lead Southern Methodist University (SMU) fans. It was during these college years that he developed the "Herkie jump," a split leap five feet in the air. In 1952, the *New York Times* reports, Herkimer and his wife "borrowed $200 and began making crepe-paper pompons in a garage, . . . convinced that color television would come someday and that, when it did, colored pompons would be more important than chrome twirling batons."

Despite his huge success, Herkimer has not lost interest in the young people involved in cheerleading. About 100,000 cheerleaders perfect their Herkie jumps and other stunts at annual nationwide clinics conducted by the National Cheerleading Association, one of Herkimer's companies, with Herkimer still leading the five-day intensive training sessions held at SMU.

FOR MORE INFORMATION SEE: Sports Illustrated, November 27, 1961; *New York Times,* October 28, 1972; *Seventeen,* September, 1973; *People,* September 4, 1978.

HODGELL, P(atricia) C(hristine)   1951-

PERSONAL: Born March 16, 1951, in Des Moines, Iowa; daughter of Robert Overman (an artist) and Lois (an art professor; maiden name, Partidge) Hodgell. *Education:* Eckerd College, B.A., 1973; University of Minnesota, M.A., 1976, A.B.D., 1981. *Home:* 1237 Liberty St., Oshkosh, Wis. 54901. *Agent:* Adele Leone, 52 Riverside Dr., Apt. 6-A, New York, N. Y. 10024. *Office:* Department of English, University of Wisconsin-Oshkosh, Oshkosh, Wis. 54901.

CAREER: University of Minnesota-Minneapolis, Minneapolis, teaching associate, 1974-81; University of Wisconsin-Oshkosh, Oshkosh, lecturer in English, 1981—. Writer, beginning in 1973. *Member:* Science Fiction Writers of America.

WRITINGS: (With Michael M. Levy) *Modern Science Fiction and Fantasy: A Study Guide,* University of Minnesota Extension, 1981; *God Stalk* (young adult fantasy novel), Atheneum, 1982; *Dark of the Moon,* Atheneum, 1985.

Work represented in anthologies, including *Clarion Science Fiction,* edited by Kate Wilhelm, Berkley Publishing, 1977; *Berkley Showcase,* Volume II, edited by Victoria Schochet and John Silbersack, Berkley Publishing, 1980; *Elsewhere,* Volume III, edited by Terri Windling and Mark A. Arnold, Ace Science Fiction Books, 1984; and *Imaginary Lands,* edited by Robin McKinley, Greenwillow, 1985. Contributor to magazines, including *Empire* and *Riverside Quarterly.*

WORK IN PROGRESS: A short story, "Dark Threshold," for *Last Dangerous Visions,* edited by Harlan Ellison; Ph.D. dissertation, "Images of the Medieval World in the Works of Sir Walter Scott."

SIDELIGHTS: "I never thought of myself as a children's author; consequently, it came as quite a surprise when my first novel sold to a line specializing in young adult literature. I kept expecting my editor to demand major changes—after all, there's a lot of darkness in that book, and more violence than I would have thought appropriate for a young audience—but when the requests came, they were aimed purely at making the novel a better piece of literature.

"That set me thinking. Apparently, I had misjudged the nature of modern juvenile fiction, and possibly of my own work as well. Although I hadn't intended *God Stalk* for the younger reader, the novel had clearly grown out of my own childhood and adolescent dreams (and nightmares), modified by my experiences as an adult. To some extent, it is wish-fulfillment (who wouldn't like to be as active, clever, and well liked as Jame, my heroine?), but it is also concerned with the darker side of this: once you get your wish, what then? Great powers bring great responsibilities. Then too, the novel is deeply concerned with growing up, especially growing up different. Jame is certainly that. She believes herself to be practically an outcast from her society because of it, and yet feels compelled to find a place among her people. Her past is a confused nightmare; her future, a mystery. But eventually things will work out, if only she can keep her personal integrity.

"I didn't write the novel with any such moral in mind. It just evolved along with Jame's character and world. In her case,

there are special problems because she doesn't know yet exactly who or what she is, but then most of us are confused about that at one time or another. I seem to have spent my own life in a state of perpetual confusion. In a sense, Jame has become the focal point for all my own questions and her life a testing ground for possible solutions.

"In this, it's just occurred to me that I'm completing a circle of sorts. As a child, I measured myself against other writer's heroes and heroines. Now, my own fiction helps me to define myself. Someday, perhaps a younger generation will turn to my work as I did to that of my elders. That's quite a responsibility. Answers I can't guarantee, for others any more than for myself, but I can at least try to provide some honest questions.

"For as long as I can remember, I've been making up stories to tell myself. Some children have imaginary friends. I had a host of them, but in a world all their own which I visited only by invitation and rarely in my own person. All of this was largely to compensate for a lonely childhood growing up in an old house with a grandmother after the divorce of my parents. It was (and still is) a wonderful old place, though, full of one hundred years of family history and haunted by the

P. C. HODGELL

P. C. Hodgell's rendering of Jame, the heroine in *God Stalk*.

possessions if not the ghosts of four generations. The house and the stories each provided worlds in which I felt safe and happy, in contrast to the threatening 'real' world outside.

"I was also an avid reader, especially of fantasy and science fiction by such writers as Andre Norton and Edgar Rice Burroughs. This fiction shaped my day-dreams and stirred my ambition someday to become a writer myself. But I was afraid to commit myself.

"Years went by. Through grade school, high school and even college, I spent nearly half my waking time on a secondary level in an imaginary world whose very existence was a secret to all but a few close friends. Despite all this mental activity, however, very little got written down. I was still afraid. Of what? Failure, I suppose, of being just one more would-be, talentless writer. But all this time the pressure was growing . . . and so was the discipline. College taught me that. I had always been a wild fantasizer, groping for control over my material but easily distracted and hardly able to sit still long enough to write a page. Now the studies of literature and foreign languages taught me to concentrate and organize. Ready at last, after college I retreated to my old home with a typewriter and a ream of paper, determined to find out if my wildest day-dream of all—that of becoming a real writer—could be made to come true.

"It would be nice to say that after that long suppression of the writing impulse, the dam burst—but it didn't. Due to lack of practice, I simply didn't know how to put a story down on paper. However, I began to learn. By the next summer, I had several stories done and an invitation to attend the Clarion Writers Workshop. There, for the first time, I found a whole community of people like me—storytellers, wordsmiths, an entire family I never knew I had. Even more wonderful, here suddenly were professionals like Harlan Ellison and Kate Wilhelm telling me that I could indeed write. In fact, Harlan and Kate bought my first two stories. I could hardly believe my luck.

"Then graduate school started and all writing stopped. Try as I would, I couldn't be both creative and academic at the same time, so again the fantasies had to be bottled up although I still lived them as intensely as ever. That lasted until I got my M.A. in English Literature and had safely passed the Ph.D. qualifying exam. Then I took another year's leave, went home, and started writing again. The result was *God Stalk*, a curious blend of Charles Dickens, Fritz Leiber, and *Marvel Comics*. To my great surprise, it sold to Atheneum."

Hodgell has completed a sequel to *God Stalk* entitled *Dark of the Moon*, with plans maturing for at least the third, fourth, and fifth novels in the series. "Actually, I seem to be working on what some people call a hyper-novel, a continuous narrative cut into novel-sized lengths with the trimmings made into short stories. All those years of day-dreaming seem to have generated a lot of material. I may spend the rest of my life writing it all down, sometimes with delight but just as often with exasperation at my stylistic shortcomings. At present, my writing isn't half as good as I hope someday it will be, but that's all right. I may be a chronic dreamer, but I'm also stubborn . . . and I can learn."

FOR MORE INFORMATION SEE: Empire, Autumn, 1980; *Weekend Northwestern,* November 13-14, 1982.

'Tis the good reader that makes the book.
—Ralph Waldo Emerson

HOPPE, Joanne   1932-

PERSONAL: Born January 10, 1932, in Worcester, Mass.; daughter of Albert (a construction superintendent) and Mary (Calvert) San Antonio; married Edward Hoppe (a writer and producer), August 22, 1958; children: Lisa, Lynn, Beth. *Education:* University of Maine, B.A., 1952; University of North Carolina, M.A., 1954. *Politics:* Independent. *Religion:* Catholic. *Home:* 9 Shore Rd., Old Greenwich, Conn. 06870. *Agent:* Curtis Brown Ltd., 575 Madison Ave., New York, N.Y. 10022. *Office:* Greenwich High School, Greenwich, Conn. 06783.

CAREER: "Who Do You Trust?" television quiz show, New York, N.Y., question writer, 1956-59; Greenwich High School, Greenwich, Conn., teacher of English, 1966—. *Member:* National Education Association, Connecticut Education Association, Greenwich Education Association.

WRITINGS: The Lesson Is Murder (novel), Harcourt, 1976; *April Spell* (young adult novel), Warne, 1979; *Mystery at Pretty Penny Farm*, Macmillan, 1986.

FOR MORE INFORATION SEE: New York Times Book Review, June 12, 1977; *Stamford Advocate*, June 18, 1977.

HYDE, Margaret Oldroyd   1917-

PERSONAL: Born February 18, 1917, in Philadelphia, Pa.; daughter of Gerald James and Helen (Lerch) Oldroyd; married Edwin Y. Hyde, Jr., 1941; children: Lawrence Edwin, Bruce Geoffrey. *Education:* Beaver College, A.B., 1938; Columbia University, M.A., 1939; Temple University, postgraduate studies, 1942-43. *Home address:* Box 1861, R.D.4, Shelburne, Vt. 05482.

CAREER: Columbia University, Lincoln School of Teachers College, New York, N.Y., science consultant, 1941-42; Shipley School, Bryn Mawr, Pa., teacher, 1942-48. Temple University, Philadelphia, Pa., lecturer in elementary education, part time and summers, 1942-43. Writer for young people, 1944—. *Member:* Authors Guild, American Association of University Women, National League of American Penwomen. *Awards, honors:* Thomas Alva Edison Foundation National Mass Media Award, 1961, for best children's science book, *Animal Clocks and Compasses;* honorary doctor of letters from Beaver College, 1971.

WRITINGS—All published by McGraw, except as indicated: *Playtime for Nancy*, Grosset, 1941; (with Gerald S. Craig) *New Ideas in Science*, Ginn, 1946; (with F. W. Keene) *Hobby Fun Book*, Seahorse Press, 1952; *Flight Today and Tomorrow* (illustrated by Clifford Geary), 1953, revised edition, 1962; *Driving Today and Tomorrow* (illustrated by C. Geary), 1954, revised edition, 1965; *Atoms Today and Tomorrow* (illustrated by C. Geary), 1955, (with Bruce G. Hyde) 4th edition, 1970; (with husband, Edwin Y. Hyde, Jr.) *Where Speed Is King* (illustrated by C. Geary), 1955, revised edition, 1961; *Medicine in Action: Today and Tomorrow*, 1956, revised edition, 1964; *Exploring Earth and Space*, 1957, 5th edition (illustrated by E. Winson), 1970; *From Submarines to Satellites*, 1958; *Off into Space! Science for Young Space Travelers*, 1959, 3rd edition (illustrated by Bernice Myers), 1969.

Plants Today and Tomorrow (illustrated by P. A. Hutchison), 1960; *Animal Clocks and Compasses* (illustrated by P. A. Hutchison), 1960; *This Crowded Planet* (illustrated by Mildred Waltrip), 1961; *Animals in Science: Savings Lives through Research*, 1962; *Molecules Today and Tomorrow* (illustrated by M. Waltrip), 1963; *Your Brain, Master Computer* (illustrated by P. A. Hutchison), 1964; (with Edward Marks) *Psychology in Action* (illustrated by Carolyn Cather), 1967, 2nd edition, 1976; *Mind Drugs*, 1968, 4th edition, 1981; *The Earth in Action*, 1969; (adapted from Italian) *The Great Deserts*, 1969.

Your Skin, 1970; (with B. G. Hyde) *Know about Drugs* (illustrated by Bill Morrison), 1971, revised edition, 1979; *For Pollution Fighters Only* (illustrated by Don Lynch), 1971; (with others) *Mysteries of the Mind*, 1972; *VD: The Silent Epidemic*, 1973, 2nd edition published as *VD-STD: The Silent Epidemic*, 1983; *The New Genetics: Promises and Perils* (illustrated with diagrams), F. Watts, 1974; *Hotline!*, 1974, 2nd edition, 1976; *Alcohol: Drink or Drug*, 1974; (with Elizabeth Forsyth) *What Have You Been Eating? Do You Really Know*, 1975; (with E. Forsyth) *Know Your Feelings*, F. Watts, 1975; *Speak Out on Rape*, 1976; *Juvenile Justice and Injustice*, F. Watts, 1977, 2nd edition, 1983; *Fears and Phobias*, 1977; *Brainwashing and Other Forms of Mind Control*, 1977; *Know about Alcohol* (foreword by Morris E. Chafetz; illustrated by B. Morrison), 1978; *Addictions: Smoking, Gambling, Cocaine Use and Others*, 1978; (with E. Forsyth) *Suicide: The Hidden Epidemic*, F. Watts, 1978; (with B. G. Hyde) *Everyone's Trash Problem: Nuclear Wastes*, 1979; *My Friend Wants to Run Away*, 1979.

Is the Cat Dreaming Your Dream?, 1980; *Crime and Justice in Our Time*, F. Watts, 1981; *Cry Softly: The Story of Child Abuse*, Westminster, 1981; *My Friend Has Four Parents*, 1981; *Energy: The New Look*, 1981; *Foster Care and Adoption*, F. Watts, 1982; *Computers That Think? The Search for Artificial Intelligence*, Enslow, 1982; *The Rights of the Victim*, F. Watts, 1983; *Know about Smoking* (illustrated by Dennis Kendrick), 1983; *Is This Kid Crazy? Understanding Unusual Behaviour*, Westminster, 1983; (with Lawrence E. Hyde) *Cloning and the New Genetics*, Enslow, 1984; *Sexual Abuse: Let's Talk about It*, Westminster, 1984; (with L. Hyde) *Cancer in the Young: A Sense of Hope*, Westminster, 1985; (with L. Hyde) *Missing*

MARGARET OLDROYD HYDE

Children, F. Watts, 1985. Author of two television scripts, ''How the Mind Begins'' and ''Can Human Nature Be Changed'' for ''Animal Secrets,'' NBC-TV, 1967.

WORK IN PROGRESS: Revisions of *Computers That Think? The Search for Artificial Intelligence, Suicide: The Hidden Epidemic,* and *Cry Softly: The Story of Child Abuse.*

SIDELIGHTS: **February 18, 1917.** Born and reared in Philadelphia, Pennsylvania. ''My father was an engineer and my mother a housewife. I was an only child. I walked every day to Logan Demonstration School, about a mile from our house. Many teachers stood in the back of the classroom, observing teaching methods. School was competitive, and I enjoyed it even though there was a great deal of pressure on us.

''I was an avid reader as a child, much encouraged by my parents. I always received books as presents for holidays, birthdays and was fortunate to live near a public library. I enjoyed the 'Little Orphan Annie' books, the classics, and poetry, especially *A Child's Garden of Verses.* I had absolutely no interest in writing as a child, and never expected to write a book. I even disliked science, because it focused on memorization of classifications. Science teaching has since improved a great deal.''

Attended Beaver College and received an A.B. degree in three years. ''This was followed by graduate work at Columbia University where I received my M.A. the next year. I completed enough credits to qualify for a doctorate but never finished my dissertation because I began writing nonfiction. In graduate school I concentrated on zoology and psychology. I took a pre-medical course because I wanted to become a doctor. My family, however, felt medicine to be an unsuitable profession for a woman and discouraged me from entering the field. It was equally difficult for women to find jobs in the field of genetics which was my major interest. My parents wanted me to teach, and finally, because I wanted a job, I went into teaching. I didn't think I'd like it, but as it turned out, I did. Later I returned to my earlier interest and I have written two books on genetics, *The New Genetics* and *Cloning and the New Genetics.*

''I was married just before [the bombing of] Pearl Harbor. My husband, a reserve officer, was called to active duty three months after we married, and returned four and a half years later. During his absence I lived in New York with a friend whose husband was also overseas.''

Worked as a science consultant at the Lincoln School of Teacher's College at Columbia University. ''In those days, teachers didn't know much about science. I worked as an advisor, helping children with experiments and demonstrating ways to teach science to the different grade levels from kindergarten through sixth grade.

''My advisor at Columbia, Dr. Craig, was an authority in the field of elementary school education. He invited me to assist in his courses at Teacher's College, and in 1944, he asked me to co-author an elementary school science textbook. I laughed at the idea, feeling uncertain over the possibility of writing a book. The only writing experience I'd had was term papers. The textbook, *New Ideas in Science,* my first real writing effort, was one in the series, *Our World of Science.* Years later, the series was published in Japan and used in the Japanese public schools. While I was writing, Dr. Craig, as well as other authors of the series, gave me advice and suggestions about structure and topics. The publishers were very strict in maintaining a vocabulary level appropriate to the sixth-grade reading level, which made it difficult to write.

''When my husband returned from overseas, we started our family. It was during this time that I wrote one book of juvenile fiction, *Playtime for Nancy,* and collaborated on *Hobby Fun Book.* Publishing fiction proved to be highly competitive. I circulated a number of manuscripts that brought only rejection slips and began to feel that my energies might be better spent in the field of nonfiction, where my science background was an advantage. I worked on *Flight Today and Tomorrow* and sent the manuscript to several publishers. McGraw-Hill picked it up and asked me to continue to work for them in this field, so I never had much time to branch out into other forms of writing. They'd assign a new project before I finished a book.

''Nonfiction is a wholly different kind of writing. With fiction, I'd have to learn about plotting, and character, and structure. Nonfiction is much easier for me to write because I can use knowledge that I have as background. The challenge of re-

Very young children learn about alcohol without knowing it. ■ (From *Know about Alcohol* by Margaret O. Hyde. Illustrated by Bill Morrison.)

searching controversial subjects is another factor in my choice of nonfiction."

In her book *Flight Today and Tomorrow,* Hyde included an imaginary trip into space preceding actual space travel. "One of my neighbors laughed and called this a crazy idea, 'That's ridiculous. They'll never be able to get into space or go to the moon.' Years later, I read the chapter again and realized my version wasn't far off the mark.

"During my years at McGraw-Hill, editors would both assign topics and ask for my suggestions. We would mutually decide what to pursue. There was very little turnover in editors at McGraw-Hill. During my many years with them I worked with several wonderful editors whom I came to know quite well. Helene Frye got me started when she had enough faith in me to publish *Flight Today and Tomorrow.* She was a real pioneer who brought science into the McGraw-Hill Junior Book Catalogues. I worked with her until she retired, and then worked with her assistant and successor, Eleanor Nichols.

"I continued teaching science education for a while on the college level at Temple University, but after our children began growing up, I concentrated on writing exclusively. I discontinued teaching and never returned to it again because I didn't have the time. My husband traveled a lot during those years, so it was nice to be able to work at home. I wrote while the boys were napping and in the evenings. That's one of the best things about writing—you can make your own schedule."

Hyde follows a definite procedure in writing each of her books. "After selecting a topic, I check with librarians to see whether there is an existing or future demand for information on the topic. Local librarians are very cooperative and helpful. Then I begin my research. I gather material for as long as several years from many sources and sometimes work on as many as four books at once. I keep a large number of clipping files on any topic I think I might write a book about, as well as collect materials that might be useful to me for revisions. I also keep files on current events in the world of science. I refer to my files for names and addresses of organizations where the researchers in a particular field are working. I don't use information from newspapers or magazines because it may not be accurate enough for my purposes. I go directly to the source. Today one must contact people who are active in research to find out what is happening in the world of science. Such people are most cooperative in talking about their projects and in checking the material I write for accuracy. I often visit researchers, observe their work, collect information, and use their scientific reports.

"Research is usually fun. One time I found myself standing on a stool behind a surgeon who was operating on a human heart. The stool kept spinning and the blood splashed on my hospital gown. Someone reminded me that if I felt faint, it would be wise to fall backward. Space labs, crisis centers, biology laboratories, and astronomy observatories have all been part of my research.

"After my initial research, I write an outline and send it to the publisher. The publisher then makes suggestions, and I begin writing. I continue to gather material and talk to people in the field while I am writing the book, picking up further information. I sometimes conduct taped interviews with authorities in the field, but many times I just take notes and listen to what the experts have to say. They usually give me quantities of scientific paper related to their work. I also talk with a variety of people who might be interested in the subject

MARGARET OLDROYD HYDE

to find out what information prospective readers might want to know.

"I do the actual writing on a word processor now. I have two computers, and they are so helpful, I don't think I could ever go back to the typewriter. The computer makes it easy to revise and make editorial changes. I revise more frequently than I did in the past when I used to give the final draft to a typist. Once the manuscript was typed, I didn't want to make insertions and deletions. Now I make changes up to the very last minute. I believe the possibility of making revisions easily has improved the quality of my writing.

"*Cloning and the New Genetics* was an exercise in making a very complex subject easy to comprehend. We had to rewrite and rewrite and rewrite. Sometimes I'll write a book and it will go right through to print without any major revisions. But with something as scientific as *Cloning,* in which my son and I were trying to describe and explain complex processes in the cells, it was hard. Our editor was a real stickler. She checked and rechecked every detail. She even found a discrepancy in a cloning experiment: two sources said a frog was being cloned and two said a toad. We went back to the original sources, back to authorities in the field, in order to get it right. The material was checked through many times before it went into galleys, and then the galleys were sent off to a professor to be checked again. My latest book on genetics is more technical than the first. So much has changed in the field since 1947 when I wrote *The New Genetics* that I couldn't even refer to it for help on the new genetics book. We started fresh.

"I like the challenge of explaining something complicated. This comes partly from my teaching background. I also think that young people understand a lot more than we give them credit for.''

Hyde has collaborated with her sons on several books. ''I've co-authored books with both of my sons. Bruce worked on *Everyone's Trash Problems: Nuclear Wastes* and Lawrence has collaborated on three books. We split up the writing and the research. We then get together and hash it over. I've co-authored with quite a number of people through the years. I worked on *Psychology in Action* with a psychologist. I've co-authored several books with a psychiatrist friend who also helps me in an advisory capacity. When I finished the book on sexual abuse, she read the manuscript and made suggestions. She also worked as an advisor on *Is This Kid Crazy? Understanding Behavior*. She is co-author of *Suicide: The Hidden Epidemic*, which we are now revising.

''My books are structured chapter by chapter, although I sometimes write by small sections of each chapter. I've done glossaries for the more technical books, and sometimes I do the index, but usually this is done by a professional indexer.

''I began to utilize case histories in my books because people wanted to know about the subject through the real life experience of others. People like to read about true cases. For example, for my book on mental health, friends who are psychiatrists gave me many illustrations of actual cases. I modified these cases slightly, never using true names. The subject matter of some books lends itself to case studies. For example, for books that deal with science such as *Energy: The New Look* I did not include case studies, but case studies fit nicely into books such as *My Friend Wants to Run Away* and *The Rights of the Victim*.

''If I say my recent book, *Sexual Abuse: Let's Talk about It*, is the one I feel closest to, it's because I felt there was a great need for a book that dealt with the subject. I would say the same is true of *Suicide: The Hidden Epidemic*. I have a number of letters from people who said that the book helped prevent them from committing suicide. I get emotionally involved in books such as these. For example, I wrote a book on missing children and was so upset by the subject matter that the publisher advised me to tone it down, to stop being such an 'advocate.' That was very hard to do; it was hard to be objective about a subject like missing children. But for a topic like cloning, I try to present various points of view. In the final chapter of *Cloning and the New Genetics*, we talked about the pros and cons, the problems, the shoulds and shouldn'ts.

''I read constantly . . . the *New York Times, Science News, Science '85*, and many other publications. I read for pleasure and to keep an eye out for information that might be helpful.

''Titles often don't occur to me until the end of a book. Some books, like *Missing Children* are easy to title. Others, like *Is This Kid Crazy?* pose some problems. I didn't like using the word 'kid,' or the word 'crazy' but if I wanted anyone to pick the book off a library shelf, I couldn't very well call it 'Is This Child Mentally Ill?' I might have made a mistake on the title *Is the Cat Dreaming Your Dream?* I don't think people know what that book is about. The title was a bit too facetious.

''Over the years, my personal interest, as well as public interest in mental health has increased. I became concerned about whether people understood mental illness. *Is This Kid Crazy?* was a plea for people to understand rather than to be negatively critical of those who have problems.

''The topic of the criminal justice system was assigned to me by an editor. I had begun a book on runaways when the publisher discovered that there were two authors writing books on the subject for them. When I was asked if I'd do a book on juvenile justice instead, I threw my hands up in despair. I knew nothing about the subject, but the government supplied quantities of resource material, and after reading and researching the subject with experts, I became quite interested. The book was revised not long ago, and just last summer I wrote an article for Grolier's *New Book of Knowledge* concerning juvenile crime.''

Hyde feels that the most pressing social problems today are ''drug abuse, child abuse including sexual abuse, juvenile crime and our lack of ability to deal with them. I wouldn't blame these problems on the government—they are such tremendous problems that nobody has found the answers yet—but there is a real lack of funding for the problems of children.

''In terms of technology, I'm very excited about what's happening in the world of computers. I'm revising a book on artificial intelligence, incorporating that which has happened in the field since I wrote the first edition several years ago. I'm fascinated by what computers will eventually be able to do. I don't think artificial intelligence itself is frightening. We're just at the beginning of the computer revolution. If used wisely, and I feel it will be, artificial intelligence will change our way of living in many exciting and positive ways.

''We just moved to a townhouse and I have one room in which I have a computer, a typewriter and bookcases, as well as a den which I use for leisurely reading. Almost every room houses at least one bookcase. I enjoy writing—I'd feel lost without it—and I don't plan to stop.''

For relaxation, Hyde likes to ''travel, play golf, knit, ride a bicycle, ski, go boating on the lake . . . and with our new video camera, take pictures of our granddaughters.''

FOR MORE INFORMATION SEE: Doris de Montreville and Donna Hill, editors, *The Third Book of Junior Authors*, H. W. Wilson, 1972.

JACOBI, Kathy

BRIEF ENTRY: Born in New York, N.Y. An artist and illustrator of books for children, Jacobi's work has been exhibited in galleries across the United States. Among the books she has illustrated is Paul Fleischman's award-winning *The-Half-a-Moon-Inn* (Harper, 1980), the evocative story of a mute boy who is held captive by an evil proprietoress. *New York Times Book Review* described it as a ''haunting tale . . . [with] dreamlike intensity and compelling inner momentum.'' The same reviewer praised Jacobi's black-line illustrations, calling them ''imaginative . . . and dramatically fitting. . . . The fearsome figures are fearfully large, and their movements are as contorted as their passions.''

The element of fantasy is present in two other children's books illustrated by Jacobi. Patricia MacLachlan's *Tomorrow's Wizard* (Harper, 1982) tells the tale of a grumpy wizard, his apprentice, and a talking horse who travel about the land granting wishes to humans. According to *School Library Journal*, it is a ''collection of six warm, humorous and gentle vignettes'' with ''whimsical and expressive'' drawings. Jacobi provided both illustrations and pochoir stencils for hand coloring in

Grozdana Olujic's *Rose of Mother-of-Pearl* (Toothpaste Press, 1983), a fairy tale translated from the Serbo-Croatian. *Wilson Library Bulletin* took note of the book's design done in Ragston paper and handset Italian Olde Style typeface. "[Jacobi's] line drawings are suitable," added the reviewer, ". . . thin, simple, black-line, with minute suggestions of detail—all unassuming, quiet . . . quaint and charming illustrations. . . ." Jacobi has also contributed illustrations to magazines. *Residence:* California.

JACOBS, Francine 1935-

BRIEF ENTRY: Born May 11, 1935, in New York, N.Y. Author of books for young people. Jacobs graduated from Queens College in 1956 and became an elementary school teacher in Rye, N.Y. that same year. She later taught in Chappaqua, N.Y. and is now a full-time writer. Of her nearly twenty juvenile books, most are about science. Among them is *Supersaurus* (Putnam, 1982), the true story of the discovery, in 1972, of a huge bone from a dinosaur larger than any yet known. *Science Books and Films* commented, ". . . It is refreshing to read a children's book that is scientifically accurate and interesting." She also wrote *Cosmic Countdown: What Astronomers Have Learned about the Life of the Universe* (based on works by Robert Jastrow; M. Evans, 1983). A *Booklist* reviewer remarked, ". . . [Jacobs] not only conveys information concisely but also imparts a sense of scientific excitement."

In a different genre, *Fire Snake: The Railroad That Changed East Africa* (Morrow, 1980) recounts the construction of "the Lunatic Line" during the turn of the century as well as the political and social effects it had on colonial Africa. *New York Times Book Review* stated, ". . . [Jacobs] enlivens the historical narrative with fine details," and added that it was a "compelling story." Likewise, *Horn Book* described it as "a vivid picture of a technological, social, and political achievement." In 1975 Jacobs received an outstanding science book for children award from the National Science Teachers Association and the Children's Book Council for *The Sargasso Sea: An Ocean Desert* (Morrow, 1975). Her other books include: *The Wisher's Handbook* (Funk, 1968), *The King's Ditch* (Coward, 1971), *The Red Sea* (Morrow, 1978), *Coral* (Putnam, 1980), *Bermuda Petrel: The Bird that Would Not Die* (Morrow, 1981), and *Breakthrough: The True Story of Penicillin* (Dodd, 1985). *Home:* 93 Old Farm Rd., Pleasantville, N.Y. 10570.

FOR MORE INFORMATION SEE: Washington Post Book World, January 13, 1980.

We need love's tender lessons taught
  As only weakness can;
God hath His small interpreters;
  The child must teach the man.
          —John Greenleaf Whittier

The greatest poem ever known
Is one all poets have outgrown:
The poetry, innate, untold,
Of being only four years old.
          —Christopher Morley

SUSAN JESCHKE

JESCHKE, Susan

CAREER: Illustrator and writer. *Awards, honors:* Friends of American Writers Award for Ilustration, 1976, for *The Devil Did It.*

WRITINGS—Self-illustrated children's books: *Firerose* (ALA Notable Book), Holt, 1974; *Sidney*, Holt, 1975; *The Devil Did It*, Holt, 1975; *Rima and Zeppo*, Windmill Books, 1976; *Victoria's Adventure*, Holt, 1976; *Mia, Grandma, and the Genie*, Holt, 1977; *Angela and Bear*, Holt, 1979; *Tamar and the Tiger*, Holt, 1980; *Perfect the Pig*, Holt, 1981.

Illustrator: Joan Tate, *Wild Boy*, Harper, 1973; Lucile Clifton, *The Times They Used to Be*, Holt, 1974; Achim Bröger, *Outrageous Kasimir*, translated by Hilda Van Stockum, Morrow, 1976; Johanna Hurwitz, *Busybody Nora*, Morrow, 1976; J. Hurwitz, *Nora and Mrs. Mind Your-Own-Business*, Morrow, 1977; Phyllis R. Eisenberg, *A Mitzvah Is Something Special*, Harper, 1978; J. Hurwitz, *New Neighbors for Nora*, Morrow, 1979; J. Hurwitz, *Superduper Teddy*, Morrow, 1980; Susan Pearson, *Saturday, I Ran Away*, Harper, 1981; Eliner L. Horwitz, *Sometimes It Happens*, Harper, 1981; Marilyn Jeffers Walton, *Bats Aren't Sweet*, Raintree, 1983; M. J. Walton, *Sparky's Valentine Victory*, Raintree, 1983; M. J. Walton, *Possum Crest's Greatest Christmas Show*, Raintree, 1983; M. J. Walton, *Tea and Whoppers*, Raintree, 1983.

SIDELIGHTS: "As a child I read many stories. The words generated a vast array of pictures in my head. I realized that the pictures had the power visually to control a story, to add a thrilling dimension to it. In confronting actual illustration, I became deeply critical, and the criticism was based on whether or not I was indeed thrilled into that higher dimension.

"As an illustrator, I feel it is my obligation to deepen the involvement of the reader's imagination—to enrich and heighten his experience through my illustrations. If I am able to create pictures that remain in the memory of the viewer . . . then I will have succeeded in my goal as an illustrator." [Lee King-

...They both stood facing the east window. As the sun began to fill the small room, everything began to glow.... ■ (From *Mia, Grandma, and the Genie* by Susan Jeschke. Illustrated by the author.)

man and others, compilers, *Illustrators of Children's Books: 1967-1976,* Horn Book, 1978.]

FOR MORE INFORMATION SEE: Lee Kingman and others, compilers, *Illustrators of Children's Books: 1967-1976,* Horn Book, 1978; *Contemporary Authors,* Volumes 77-80, Gale, 1979.

JILER, John   1946-

PERSONAL: Born April 4, 1946, in New York, N.Y.; son of Milton W. (a financial analyst) and Dorothy (Hayes) Jiler. *Education:* Attended University of Pennsylvania, 1964-65; University of Hartford, B.A., 1971. *Home:* 93 Nassau St., #915, New York, N.Y. 10038.

CAREER: Writer and actor. Has been variously employed as an actor both in the United States and abroad, including off and off-off Broadway productions, and in television and motion pictures. *Awards, honors:* Chicago Drama Critics' Award for best supporting actor, 1971.

WRITINGS: Wild Berry Moon (juvenile fiction; illustrated by Susan Y. Harris), Greenwillow, 1982.

Plays: "African Star," first produced at the Eugene O'Neill National Playwrights Conference, 1971; "Ball," first produced at New One-Act Theatre, Hollywood, Calf., 1982; "Early

JOHN JILER

Bird," first produced at Deja Vu Theatre, Hollywood, Calif., 1982. Also author of screenplay, "Pacifica," 1982.

WORK IN PROGRESS: Dogs of Paris, a book for children; "Guava Lagoon," a play.

As if blown by the wind the piglets flew onto her belly with closed eyes and open mouths. ∎
(From *Wild Berry Moon* by John Jiler. Illustrated by Susan Yard Harris.)

SIDELIGHTS: "As I grow older, I find writing more satisfying than acting. It's simply a matter of time. Who has four hours to wait in line for an audition anymore? I could be home writing. And with maturity, my real subject matter begins to coalesce before my eyes. To my delight, my hippie roamings of the late '60s and '70s were not wasted time, as I so often feared. All of it is grist for the mill of the writer. In fact, I still believe that one must take some sort of chance in one's personal life to have anything important to write about. There must always be risk, and the discomfort of growth. The image of the pipe-smoking, gentrified, tweed-elbow-patched, smug writer is a myth, a dangerous illusion, or at least one that must be preserved for the very old."

JONAS, Ann

BRIEF ENTRY: Born in New York. An author and illustrator, Jonas has received praise from reviewers for her innovative illustrative style in five books for preschool and primary-grade readers. *When You Were a Baby* (Greenwillow, 1982) is addressed to preschoolers as a reminder of the days when they were unable to do things like drink from a glass, build with blocks, or make sand castles. *Booklist* observed that "subtle blends of muted and vivid colors attract immediate attention," while *School Library Journal* took note of Jonas's "generous use of secondary colors and her flair for lively perspective." According to *Horn Book*, the illustrations in Jonas's second book for preschoolers, *Two Bear Cubs* (Greenwillow, 1983), are "done in vibrant colors . . . [with] simplified shapes and flat areas . . . [that] create crisp, almost abstract patterns."

In *Round Trip* (Greenwillow, 1983), Jonas creates a picture book that can be read two ways as readers are taken on a trip from the country to the city, and, by turning the book upside-down, back again as the same pictures take on new meanings. "Bold black shapes and vivid white space are juxtaposed," observed *Horn Book*, ". . . [as] the author-artist displays a fine sense of graphic design and balance." Chosen one of *New York Times*'s best illustrated books of 1983, it was described by *Publishers Weekly* as "a visual stunner . . . wonderfully inventive . . . [with] masterful use of contrast." The fourth book written and illustrated by Jonas is entitled *Holes and Peeks* (Greenwillow, 1984), an exploration of the fear of holes held by many preschoolers. In 1984 it was commended by the Notable Children's Books Committee of the Association for Library Service to Children and was selected one of *School Library Journal*'s best books of the year.

Jonas's latest work is *The Quilt* (Greenwillow, 1984), the story of a girl who searches in dreamland for her missing doll, a world created by the different squares of a patchwork quilt. *Publishers Weekly* labeled this tale "a landmark in children's literature" with "intricate illustrations . . . [that] can be described only in superlatives." Jonas is married to children's author Donald Crews and they have two children. *Residence:* Brooklyn, N.Y.

JONES, Hettie   1934-

PERSONAL: Born July 16, 1934, in Brooklyn, N.Y.; daughter of Oscar and Lottie (Lewis) Cohen; married LeRoi Jones (now Amiri Baraka; a writer), October 13, 1958 (divorced 1966); children: Kettie, Lisa. *Education:* University of Virginia, Fredericksburg, B.A., 1955; attended Columbia University, 1955-56. *Agent:* Elaine Markson, New York, N.Y.

CAREER: Columbia University Press, Center for Mass Communication, New York City, staff writer, 1956-57; *Partisan Review,* New York City, managing editor, 1957-61; Mobilization for Youth, New York City, 1967-69, began as staff writer, became director of educational after-school program; free-lance writer, 1970—. Day care worker and substitute teacher. Church of All Nations Day Care Center, community representative and president of board of directors. *Awards, honors: The Trees Stand Shining: Poetry of the North American Indians* was included in the American Institute of Graphic Arts Children's Book Show, 1971-72; *Longhouse Winter: Iroquois Transformation Tales* was included in the American Institute of Graphic Arts Fifty Books of the Year, 1972; *Big Star Fallin' Mama: Five Women in Black Music* was featured by New York Public Library as a young adult best book, 1975.

WRITINGS: (Editor) *Poems Now* (anthology), Kulchur Press, 1966; (compiler) *The Trees Stand Shining: Poetry of the North American Indians* (juvenile; illustrated by Robert A. Parker; ALA Notable Book), Dial, 1971; (adapter) *Longhouse Winter: Iroquois Transformation Tales* (juvenile; illustrated by Nicholas Gaetano), Holt, 1972; (adapter) *Coyote Tales* (juvenile; illustrated by Louis Mofsie), Holt, 1974; *Big Star Fallin' Mama: Five Women in Black Music* (young adult), Viking, 1974; *How to Eat Your ABC's! A Book about Vitamins* (juvenile; illustrated by Judy Glasser), Four Winds Press, 1976; *Mustang Country* (novelization of a screenplay by John Champion), Pocket Books, 1976; *I Hate to Talk about Your Mother* (young adult novel), Delacorte, 1979. Also author of "Action" series, Scholastic Books, 1977; and of *Having Been Her,* 1981.

SIDELIGHTS: "Since 1957 I've been involved with literature and writers one way or another. I owned (with my husband) a small press (Totem), which published Ginsberg, Corso, O'Hara, Dorn, Gary Snyder, etc., and a magazine called *Yugen.* When I have time I like to write short stories for slow readers, textbook stories for kids. I write novelizations to support my children and my writing habit. I have been totally self-employed since 1970, but I'm POOR." Jones also mentioned that she enjoys writing for children because "it's a challenge to simplify and clarify."

HOBBIES AND OTHER INTERESTS: Avant-garde jazz.

FOR MORE INFORMATION SEE: Authors of Books for Young People, supplement to 2nd edition, Scarecrow, 1979.

Come away, O human child!
To the waters and the wild
With a faery, hand in hand,
For the world's more full of weeping than you can
   understand.

—William Butler Yeats

Babies do not want to hear about babies; they like to be told of giants and castles, and of somewhat which can stretch and stimulate their little minds.

—Samuel Johnson

'Tis well to give honor and glory to Age,
   With its lessons of wisdom and truth;
Yet who would not go back to the fanciful page,
   And the fairy tale read but in youth?

—Eliza Cook

(From *The Trees Stand Shining: Poetry of the North American Indians,* selected by Hettie Jones. Illustrated by Robert Andrew Parker.)

KELLER, Holly

BRIEF ENTRY: Author and illustrator of books for children. A native New Yorker, Keller graduated from Sarah Lawrence College and received an M.A. from Columbia University. Her art studies were pursued at Manhattanville College and Parsons School of Design. She is the author and illustrator of seven picture books, all published by Greenwillow and aimed at preschool and primary-grade children. In addition to her cartoon-like animal characters, Keller is noted for her ability to interweave common, everyday childhood experiences into amusing stories that convey a certain therapeutic message to her readers. In *Cromwell's Glasses* (1982), a nearsighted rabbit adjusts to the necessity of wearing glasses after enduring ridicule from his siblings. Another problem between siblings is explored in *Too Big* (1983), namely, the jealousy that oftentimes erupts in an older child with the arrival of a new baby. *Horn Book* observed: "Opossums are the engaging characters in a fresh interpretation of a familiar situation. . . . The humor is gentle rather than condescending, developing naturally from the characters' personalities and actions." *Booklist* added: "The framed, minimally lined drawings, mostly done in shades of baby blue, spice an understanding text with graphic wit."

In *Geraldine's Blanket* (1984), a little piglet refuses (like many children) to give up her beloved baby blanket. Eventually, Geraldine decides to make a piece of clothing out of the frayed material for her new doll. *Booklist* described Keller's artwork as "filled with humorous nuances, many of which are in the expressive faces of the pig family," adding that her answer to the blanket problem "may provide a solution for some families." Keller's other books include *Ten Sleepy Sheep* (1983), *Will It Rain?* (1984), *Henry's Fourth of July* (1985), and *When Francie Was Sick* (1985). She is also the illustrator of Jane Thayer's *Clever Raccoon* (Morrow, 1981), Melvin Berger's *Why I Cough, Sneeze, Shiver, Hiccup, and Yawn* (Crowell, 1983), and Roma Gans's *Rock Collecting* (Crowell, 1984). *Residence:* West Redding, Conn.

Books are the quietest and most constant of friends; they are the most accessible and wisest of counsellors, and the most patient of teachers.

—Charles W. Eliot

KENNEDY, T(eresa) A. 1953-
(Kate Vickery)

PERSONAL: Born June 12, 1953, in Wisconsin; daughter of Charles C. (in the postal business) and Virginia (a psychic; maiden name, Weber) Kennedy. *Education:* Attended University of Wisconsin. *Home:* 235 West End Ave., New York, N.Y. 10023. *Agent:* Beth Bachman, 11 Bank St., New York, N.Y. 10011.

CAREER: Wisconsin Images (magazine), Madison, Wis., writer, 1977; Human Sciences Press, Inc., New York, N.Y., editor, 1978-81; Grosset & Dunlap, Inc., New York City, senior editor of children's book department, beginning 1981. Also worked as assistant literary agent, free-lance editor, and consulting editor for Tempo Books, and New American Library; free-lance editor for individual authors.

WRITINGS: (Editor) *The Illustrated Treasury of Fairy Tales* (juvenile; illustrated by Jessie Willcox Smith, Tasha Tudor, and others), Grosset, 1982; *CAT-A-LOG,* Grosset, 1983; *Summerhouse,* Tempo Books, 1983; (under pseudonym Kate Vickery) *A Question of Time* (young adult novel), Dutton, 1983; (under pseudonym Kate Vickery) *Class Clown* (young adult novel), Dutton, 1983; (under name Teresa Kennedy, with Susan Kosoff) *Cooking with Five Ingredients or Less,* McGraw, 1984; (under name Teresa Kennedy) *American Pie,* Workman Publishing, 1984; (with Pat Parker) *LOGO Fun,* Scholastic, 1985. Contributor of a satire column to *Best Magazine,* and author of short stories for adults.

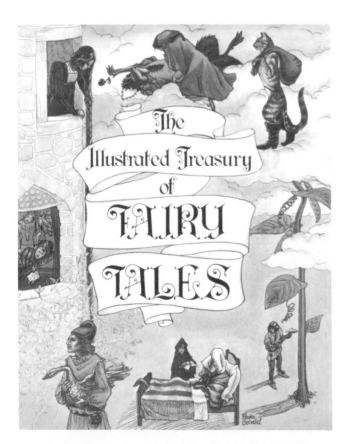

(Jacket illustration by Ponder Goembel from *The Illustrated Treasury of Fairy Tales,* edited by T. A. Kennedy.)

WORK IN PROGRESS: A series on LOGO, a new computer language for children using color graphics.

SIDELIGHTS: "It took me a long time to decide to be a writer, and an even longer time to come to the realization that I probably wouldn't be successful being anything else! After that, things got a whole lot easier.

"Being able to write is, I think, the best way to be talented. You can take it with you wherever you go, comment on whatever you see. You are never at the limits of anyone else's imagination."

KENWARD, Jean 1920-

PERSONAL: Born May 10, 1920, in Pangbourne, Berkshire, England; daughter of Harold and Ruth (Stone) Kenward; married H. David Chesterman (a charity fundraiser), September, 1945; children: Andrew, Clare, Daniel. *Education:* Central School of Speech and Drama, diploma, 1939. *Residence:* Buckinghamshire, England.

CAREER: Harrow School of Art, Harrow, England, part-time lecturer in complementary studies, 1969—. *Member:* Poetry Secretariat, Greater London Arts Association. *Awards, honors:* Recipient of several Premium Prizes from Poetry Society, in the 1940s.

WRITINGS—Juvenile: A Book of Rhymes, Nicholson & Watson, 1947; *The Rag Bag Book,* Autolycus, 1973; (with B. Roe) *Sing for Christmas,* Thames, 1973; *Old Mister Hotch Potch: Twelve Tales for Telling and Sixty Singing Rhymes,* Thornhill Press, 1974; *Songs from the Stable,* Ashdown, 1976; *Ragdolly Anna Stories* (illustrated by Zoe Hall), three volumes, F. Warne, 1979 (contains *Ragdolly Anna, Ragdolly Anna Goes to the Fair,* and *Ragdolly Anna and the River Picnic); Clutterby Hogg: The Story of a Wicked Pig* (illustrated by Gillian Chapman), F. Warne, 1980; *Three Cheers for Ragdolly Anna,* Viking/Kestrel, 1985.

Other: *Rain* (poems; illustrated by Phillip Casse), W. H. Allen, 1946; *A Flight of Words* (poems), Youth Press, 1966; *The Forest: Poems,* Autolycus, 1972; *Theme and Variations: Fifty Poems,* Autolycus, 1981.

Also broadcast writer, including children's scripts for British Broadcasting Corporation (BBC) school programs; drama critic, *Bucks Examiner;* contributor to educational journals and periodicals such as *Country Life, Countryman, Outposts, Poetry Review,* and *Child Education.*

ADAPTATIONS: Twelve-part television series of "Ragdolly Anna" stories, Yorkshire Television, September, 1985.

WORK IN PROGRESS: A new collection of Ragdolly Anna stories.

SIDELIGHTS: "I have been writing since I was eight; poetry for adults, and poetry, rhymes, songs, and stories for children. I'm now writing with my six grandchildren in mind—three boys, and three girls. *Ragdolly Anna Stories* was written for my first granddaughter."

Kenward's poetry for children has been published in a number of anthologies and has been used in the Festival of Arts in

England. Her stories are also frequently broadcast by the BBC. *Ragdolly Anna Stories* and *Three Cheers for Ragdolly Anna* have been adapted into television series, and distribution of the series outside of England is anticipated.

KEYSER, Marcia 1933-

PERSONAL: Born October 17, 1933, in Minneapolis, Minn.; daughter of Maxwell Oliver (a business executive) and Mabel (Hovland) Weiby; married A. Jerry Keyser (an urban economist), December 27, 1964; children: Jeff, Glenn. *Education:* University of Wisconsin-La Crosse, B.S., 1959; University of Wisconsin, graduate study, 1962-63. *Home:* 949 Euclid Ave., Berkeley, Calif. 94708.

CAREER: Racine public schools, Racine, Wis., teacher, 1959-61; San Bernardino, Calif., teacher, 1961-62; Sunnyvale schools, Sunnyvale, Calif., teacher, 1963-64; writer, 1972—.

WRITINGS: Roger on His Own (picture book; illustrated by Diane Dawson), Crown, 1982.

WORK IN PROGRESS: Oscar the Great and Mr. Parsnip (novel or long storybook); *The Yellow Trolley* (novel); *The Gift,* the story of a foster child and his desire for a home; *Priscilla,* a picture book about a little potbellied stove; *El Gato and the Saucer of Milk,* a picture book.

SIDELIGHTS: "Years ago, when I was a student at La Crosse State Teacher's College (now the University of Wisconsin-La Crosse), I had a teacher—a wonderful lady named Mauree Applegate Clack—for a course in creative writing. Some people you tend to forget after a number of years. Not Mrs. Clack! She was a portly lady in her seventies with snapping dark eyes and a warm smile. As a part of the coursework in her class I wrote a short story called 'Old Man Reamy.' Mrs. Clack's comment on the bottom of the manuscript really changed my life. 'Marcia, if you work long enough and hard enough you could become a writer.' I still have that manuscript with that comment. That's how important it was to me.

"The next few years were busy with teaching and graduate school. And then I met my husband—an important event that swept everything else before it!

"Finally, when my two sons were born—in between diapers and making formula—I began to write. Once I began, I found writing to be a trap—a delightful trap!—and I've been writing ever since. It's very exciting seeing characters come alive on a page.

"One summer I wrote a children's story. It became a family project with my husband and sons giving me much help and encouragement. I called the story 'Roger.' Roger's real name was Sally. Sally was a little dog we once had who had gotten lost for three months in the middle of a busy industrial area in Oakland, our neighbor city. She managed all on her own, dodging trains and semitrucks.

"I found an editor at Crown Publishers, Norma Jean Sawicki, who was interested in the story, but it needed to be revised. Three years later the story was accepted for publication; another two years went by before *Roger on His Own* came off the presses. Norma Jean had a lot to do with getting it to that point. That's what a fine editor is all about.

MARCIA KEYSER

"My stories often develop with animals as main characters. When I was growing up we always had an animal: dogs, cats, tropical fish, turtles, hamsters and ducks all shared our quarters over the years. I can't imagine my home without an animal in it.

"My growing up had an important influence on my writing. Living with my mother and father, for my two sisters and brother and myself, was a little like being in the middle of a play. You never knew how the play was going to turn out. Always exciting! They gave me a love for great characters and drama. And they gave me a lot of material for my stories!

"My father never did anything in a small way. He had a wonderful sense of humor and the air crackled when he walked in a room. He believed I could do anything. After all, I was his daughter!

"They grew up in the midwest in the early 1900s. My father sold vegetables door to door at the age of eleven to help support a large family. His father was a blacksmith until a cyclone came through their little Minnesota town and wiped them out. My father remembered afterwards seeing straws imbedded in trees. After that the family ran a hotel. Stories. Stories. I'll never be able to write them all!

"My mother grew up in a little town in North Dakota near the Canadian border. In the winter the wind howled across the prairie and the thermometer dipped to sixty below! My mother was a keen observer of people and kept us in stitches with her imitations of some of the characters from her little town ('Old Man Reamy' was her story). She was an amateur actress and once wanted to be a tightrope walker (at the age of ten)! She

Sam ran into Mr. Brown. Mr. Brown fell. A bag of groceries fell. ■(From *Roger on His Own* by Marcia Keyser. Illustrated by Diane Dawson.)

was also a wonderful storyteller. I hope I've inherited some of her gifts.

"Writing has turned out to be as important to me as breathing. I am literally thinking—or working—on a story nearly every waking moment of the day. As I write I find myself, in a way, saying the same thing over and over, even though the stories themselves are different. I was a very solitary child who read and dreamed a lot. I had a hard time making friends. As a result, my stories often seem to be about friendship and caring for other people.

"Another thing I keep finding myself saying again and again is reach out—stretch—meet life head on (this is the theme of my novel *The Yellow Trolley*)! I was a stutterer as a child. Around the third grade I found out I was 'different' from other children. Some of the children I knew tried to reach out to me but I built a wall around myself and wouldn't let anyone in. Down with the wall, I say!

"Stories happen to me in different ways. Sometimes it's a very laborious affair. I start with an idea and just keep chipping away at it day after day until it starts to take shape. Sometimes

I'm lucky and the words just flow. Other times, many days, even months go by before the right words come to me.

"But then sometimes it seems like the story is just waiting up there in the air, waiting for me to pluck it down!"

KIDD, Ronald 1948-

PERSONAL: Born April 29, 1948, in St. Louis, Mo., son of Paul R. (a producer of religious films) and Ida Sue (a home-maker; maiden name, Smith) Kidd; married Yvonne Leona Martin (a marketing executive), October 1, 1977. *Education:* University of California, Los Angeles, B.A., 1971; California State University, Long Beach, certificate of secondary education, 1972. *Residence:* Altadena, Calif. 91001. *Agent:* Amy Berkower, Writers House Inc., 21 West 26th St., New York, N.Y. 10010.

CAREER: Educational Resource Associates, Los Angeles, Calif., production manager, 1972-75; Family Films, Panorama

City, Calif., writer and producer, 1975-76; Bowmar/Noble Publishers, Inc., Los Angeles, editor, 1976-79; RK Associates, Altadena, Calif., owner, writer and producer of educational films and filmstrips, 1979-85; Walt Disney Music Co., manager of product development, 1985—. *Military service:* California Air National Guard, 1969-75. *Awards, honors:* Grammy Award nomination for best children's recording from the National Academy of Recording Arts and Sciences, 1975, for ''Mr. Popper's Penguins''; Golden Eagle certificate from the Council on International Nontheatrical Events (CINE), 1982, for ''Winnie-the-Pooh Discovers the Seasons.''

WRITINGS—Novels for young adults; all published by Lodestar: *That's What Friends Are For*, 1978; *Dunker*, 1982; *Who Is Felix the Great?*, 1983; *Sizzle and Splat*, 1983; *The Glitch*, 1985.

Picture books; all published by Ideals: *The Littlest Angel Earns His Halo*, 1984; *The Littlest Angel Meets the Newest Angel*, 1985; *The Nutcracker*, 1985.

Other: (With Lisa Eisenberg) *The Official Name Caller's Handbook*, Ace, 1981; (with Verne Bauman) *Power Painting: Computer Graphics on the Macintosh*, Bantam, 1985. Also author of filmscript for pilot to television program ''Welcome to Pooh Corner,'' aired on The Disney Channel, 1983; author of over 100 educational filmscripts.

WORK IN PROGRESS: Sequel to *Sizzle and Splat*.

SIDELIGHTS: ''I guess you could say I became a writer because of the 1971 Los Angeles earthquake. In that quake, a number of library buildings were damaged and the only way

RONALD KIDD

(Jacket illustration by Les Morrill from *Dunker* by Ronald Kidd.)

to continue serving those branches was through the use of a bookmobile. Fate (known to government employees as civil service) decreed that I should be the driver.

''Driving a bookmobile is a wonderful job. You drive to your destination in the morning, you drive back in the afternoon, and in between there's nothing to do but take your pick of five thousand books, most of them for children, and read. Somewhere between *Charlie and the Chocolate Factory* and *Charlotte's Web* I decided I could write one myself.

''These days I no longer make my living driving a bookmobile. Instead, I write and produce educational films and filmstrips. And I write books.

''In *That's What Friends Are For*, I started a story based on my school years but kept getting stuck on one part concerning one of my friends who died of leukemia. My own feelings about death were still surprisingly strong, so I decided to throw out my original idea and concentrate on turning those feelings into a new story.

''*Dunker* was a result of my work producing films and filmstrips. I've dealt with many child actors, and have always looked on those poor souls with a mixture of gratitude, sympathy, and curiosity. Gratitude because their faces have brightened my productions and made me look better; sympathy because something of childhood is inevitably lost in the world of agents, money, and hype; and curiosity because I've often wondered what happens when a young actor gets home from the studio and is faced with the unaccustomed role of 'normal kid.' Some child actors enjoy their strange existence; many

(Jacket illustration by Lydia Rosier from *That's What Friends Are For* by Ronald Kidd.)

don't. In *Dunker*, Bobby Rothman is one who isn't sure, and this book is the story of a year when he is forced to decide between acting and what he sees as real life—translation: basketball.

"My next book, *Who Is Felix the Great?*, reflects my belief that somehow, in spite of the strikes and salary disputes, there's still something magical about baseball. When I go to the ballpark and look down on the clipped grass and the white lines and the players moving in the sunshine, I feel like a boy again. For a moment it seems as if things that used to be perfect still can be, if only I give myself over to the game. This book is the story of a young man and and an old man who together try to do just that.

"*Sizzle and Splat* is about that curious mixture of stuffed shirt and T-shirt known as the youth orchestra. Since I spent six years of my life as a member of one, I decided I'd try writing about it. You'll know how zany those six years were when I say that, except for the central mystery, the characters and events in this book are pretty much typical of the experience I had. Of course, everything in the book is fictional, but the overall picture of life in a youth orchestra is, in this former trumpet player's opinion, accurate.

"My first four novels were written about things I knew and loved: a boyhood friend, basketball, baseball, music. My latest book, *The Glitch*, grew out of an attempt to learn about something new. It's my first novel for kids, ages eight to twelve.

"When I first began reading about computers, I had a terrible time remembering all the different parts. ROM, RAM, CPU, CIA, BVD, MTV—how did people ever keep them straight? So I dreamed up a land, the Computer Kingdom, in which the parts were places and the data were rainbow-colored characters who ran around singing songs and telling dumb jokes and going on glorious quests. Somehow that made the terms easier to remember, and a lot more fun."

KILGORE, Kathleen 1946-
(Kathleen Houton)

PERSONAL: Born July 11, 1946, in Washington, D.C.; daughter of Lowell Berry (a chemist) and Helen (a teacher; maiden name, Ford) Kilgore; married Daniel J. Houton (a program manager), October 7, 1969; children: Hong phung Duong (adopted), Mariah Gifford. *Education:* Oberlin College, A.B., 1968; Fletcher School of Law and Diplomacy, A.B., 1969. *Politics:* Liberal Democrat. *Religion:* Unitarian-Universalist. *Home:* 63 Temple St., Dorchester, Mass. 02126. *Agent:* Llewellyn Howland III, 100 Rockwood St., Jamaica Plain, Mass. 02130.

CAREER: Harbridge House (business consultants), Boston, Mass., editor, 1969-70; *Metro: Boston* (magazine), Boston, contributing editor, 1970-71; *Boston*, Boston, Mass., contributing editor 1972-75; free-lance writer, 1975-78; Word Guild, Cambridge, Mass., subcontractor, 1978-80. Clerk of corporation for Children's Centers, Inc., 1975—. Trustee of First Parish Unitarian Church, 1978-82; member of boards of directors of Benevolent Fraternity of Unitarian Churches, 1979—; secretary of advisory committee of Unitarian-Universalist Legal Ministry in Dorchester, 1982—. *Member:* Irish National Caucus, Massachusetts Bay District Unitarian-Universalist Association (secretary, 1981-83), Lower Miles Civil Association,

KATHLEEN KILGORE

Dorchester Residents for Racial Harmony, Friendly Sons of St. Patrick of Boston.

WRITINGS—Novels for young adults: *The Wolfman of Beacon Hill*, Little, Brown, 1982; *The Ghost-Maker*, Houghton, 1984. Contributor of more than one hundred articles and stories, some written under the name Kathleen Houton, to magazines and newspapers, including *Yankee, Phoenix, New Englander*, and *Boston Herald-American*.

WORK IN PROGRESS: A novel set in Northern Ireland and Boston, entitled *God Made Us Catholic;* biography of former Massachusetts governor John Volpe, entitled *Bright Colors of the Dream.*

SIDELIGHTS: "I grew up in Chevy Chase, Maryland, and spent some of my childhood in Geneva, Switzerland, where my father was a delegate to the General Agreements on Tariff and Trade, and where I served as his translator.

"As a small child, I was alone a great deal. As my only brother was ten years older and there were no other children in the neighborhood, I created my own fantasy world. At fourteen, I won the *Washington Star*'s high school writing contest, but decided to become a foreign service officer after college, as everyone in the family told me that 'one can't live on a writer's income' and 'journalism isn't a respectable career for a lady.'

"I learned Spanish in college, and went to the Fletcher School of Law and Diplomacy to prepare for the foreign service. At Fletcher, I met a Vietnam veteran Naval officer who was studying on the G.I. Bill, and we married.

"I had intended to pursue a career in the U.S. Foreign Service but became involved in Boston politics instead when my husband ran for Congress as a peace candidate in 1970. About this time, while I was looking for a job, I began selling magazine articles. I found there was enough demand for my stories that I didn't really need a regular job, and I preferred part-time work after the birth of my daughter in 1972.

"Some of my writings are a product of my neighborhood, which is a racially-mixed, urban area where I've spent a lot of time involved in politics and organizing. Other stories have come from my travels in Ireland, where my husband's family originates. I also get fiction ideas from my magazine assignments.

"We now live in Dorchester, a working-class neighborhood that seems much farther from Chevy Chase than any foreign service post. I came as an upper middle class WASP into a tight ethnic neighborhood and a large Irish-American family fifteen years ago, and I am still in the process of adjustment.

"My husband's family comes from a fishing village in a remote part of County Donegal, and my husband and I have made extended trips there, including time in occupied Derry and the border areas. We are involved in supporting groups that favor the reunification of Ireland. We see many parallels to the racial situation here in Boston and have organized meetings, committees, marches, and benefit parties around this issue over the past several years.

(Jacket illustration by Bob Zeiring from *The Wolfman of Beacon Hill* by Kathleen Kilgore.)

"Dorchester is an area of racial and ethnic conflict, as the older Irish American community has seen an influx of blacks, South Americans, Haitians, Cape Verdeans, Vietnamese, Laotians, and Cambodians. Two of my short stories, 'The Confrontation' and 'The Night Watch,' dealt directly with this theme, but it has also influenced my work indirectly. My daughter began school in Roxbury at the height of the busing crisis. Then, in 1981, we added to our family's diversity by becoming parents of a fifteen-year-old Vietnamese refugee.

"My first two novels are for young adults, and while I find this an interesting genre, I would like to reach a wider audience. I often find myself torn, in time and energy, between commitments to working on community problems and my profession as a writer. Sometimes the two coincide, and publicizing issues in nonfiction articles generates action. At other times, my community work provides the material for the beginning of a piece of fiction. It is difficult to balance the two."

KNUDSEN, James 1950-

PERSONAL: Surname is pronounced Ka-*newd*-son; born December 7, 1950, in Geneva, Ill.; son of Willard R. (a manager) and Lorraine (a teacher; maiden name, Olson) Knudsen; married Jeanne Cunningham (a teacher and writer), January 6, 1979; children: Seth. *Education:* Attended University of Missouri, 1969-71; University of Iowa, B.A., 1973; University of Massachusetts, Amherst, M.F.A., 1976. *Residence:* New Orleans, La. *Office:* Department of English, University of New Orleans, New Orleans, La. 70148.

CAREER: University of New Orleans, New Orleans, La., instructor in English, 1977—. *Member:* Authors Guild.

WRITINGS: Just Friends (young adult novel), Avon, 1982. Contributor of short stories to *Intro, Kansas Quarterly, Wisconsin Review, Washington Review, Four Quarters, Sonora Review, Puerto del Sol,* and *Denver Quarterly.*

WORK IN PROGRESS: Dzzup Blues, for Avon.

SIDELIGHTS: "I became interested in writing for young adults while attending the Writer's Workshop at the University of Massachusetts. A friend of mine introduced me to the work of M. E. Kerr, and I soon became an avid reader in the field. Adolescence is a dramatic time in the lives of all people and provides a fertile source of fiction's essential element: conflict. Good adolescent fiction is satisfying for both writer and reader because these conflicts are addressed directly and dealt with in a believable manner. Like any great fiction, young adult novels have the capacity to change lives. I hope to continue to contribute to this valuable body of work."

FOR MORE INFORMATION SEE: Library Journal, September 15, 1982.

Ye are better than all the ballads
   That ever were sung or said;
For ye are living poems,
   And all the rest are dead.
                —Henry Wadsworth Longfellow

KRAMER, Anthony

BRIEF ENTRY: Illustrator. Kramer graduated from the Paier School of Art in 1976. Since that time he has illustrated ten books for children, both fiction and nonfiction. His black-and-white line drawings appear in books like Patricia Reilly Giff's *Have You Seen Hyacinth Macaw?* (Delacorte, 1981), James Cross Giblin's *The Skyscraper Book* (Crowell, 1981), the revised edition of Larry Kettelkamp's *The Magic of Sound* (Morrow, 1982), Claudia Zaslavsky's *Tic Tac Toe: And Other Three-in-a-Row Games from Ancient Egypt to the Modern Computer* (Crowell, 1982), and Ruth Goode's *Hands Up!* (Macmillan, 1983). In addition to children's books, Kramer has illustrated four cookbooks. He has also been involved in the designing of children's toys. *Residence:* New York, N.Y.

LAWSON, Carol (Antell)   1946-

PERSONAL: Born February 23, 1946, in Giggleswick, Yorkshire, England; daughter of Charles and Gladys Mary (Antell) Lawson; married Chris McEwan (an illustrator), September 6, 1969. *Education:* Attended Harrogate College of Art, 1962-63; and Brighton College of Art, 1963-67. *Home and office:* The Box Tree, 49 Church Rd., Newick, Lewes, East Sussex BN8 454, England. *Agent:* C.I.A., 36 Wellington St., London WC2E 7BD, England.

CAREER: Illustrator of children's books, 1967—. Lecturer, Brighton College of Art, 1976-81.

Old Trev put his head on her knee. ■ (From *Jenny and the Sheep Thieves* by Griselda Gifford. Illustrated by Carol Lawson.)

ILLUSTRATOR—All for children: Caroline Rush, *The Scarecrow*, St. Martin's Press, 1968; Alan Brownjohn, *Brownjohn's Beasts*, Scribner, 1970; Joan Woodberry, *Little Black Swan*, Macmillan (London), 1970; Griselda Gifford, *Jenny and the Sheep Thieves*, Gollancz, 1975; Deborah Manley, Peta Rée, and Margaret Murphy, *The Piccolo Holiday Book* (nonfiction), Pan Books, 1976; (with Grahame Corbett and Mike Jackson) Tilla Bradings, *Pirates*, Macdonald Educational, 1976; Philip Street, *Colour in Animals*, Kestrel Books, 1977; Ruth Thomson, *Exciting Things to Make With Paper*, Lippincott, 1977; P. Street, *Poison in Animals*, Kestrel Books, 1978. Contributed to Idries Shah, collector, *World Tales*, Penguin, 1979 and Ramsan Wood, reteller, *A Cat May Look at a King*, East-West Publication, 1984.

WORK IN PROGRESS: "I am currently writing children's books—the first will be illustrated by my husband, Chris McEwan, and I hope to write and illustrate my own ideas thereafter."

SIDELIGHTS: "I believe in drawing and design as the basis for a good illustrator, which is what I try to teach my students. This may sound obvious, but unfortunately is too often overlooked, and too many would-be illustrators (i.e., students) attempt a short cut by developing slick techniques which make their work very superficial and impersonal.... I believe that illustration is too important to be ... treated [so lightly], as everyone from the earliest age is exposed to the illustrator's work through books, advertising, etc. We should, therefore, take ourselves and our work seriously, and be constantly working to improve on what has gone before." [Lee Kingman and others, compilers, *Illustrators of Children's Books: 1967-1976*, Horn Book, 1978.]

LEAKEY, Richard E(rskine Frere)   1944-

PERSONAL: Born December 19, 1944, in Nairobi, Kenya; son of Louis Seymour Bazett (a paleontologist) and Mary Douglas (an archaeologist; maiden name, Nicol) Leakey; married Margaret Cropper (divorced, 1970); married Meave Gillian Epps (a zoologist), 1971; children: (first marriage) Anna; (second marriage) Louise, Samira. *Education:* Attended Duke of York School, Nairobi, 1956-59. *Address:* P.O. Box 24926, Nairobi, Kenya. *Office:* National Museums of Kenya, P.O. Box 40658, Nairobi, Kenya.

CAREER: Paleoanthropologist. Conducted safaris in Kenya, 1961-65; leader of expeditions to West Lake Natron, Tanzania, 1963-64, West Lake Baringo, Kenya, 1966, Omo River, Southern Ethiopia, 1967, and East Lake Rudolf (now Lake Turkana), Kenya, 1968-69, Nakali-Suguta Valley, 1978; Leakey Safaris Ltd. (tour company) director, 1965-68; National Museums of Kenya, Nairobi, administrative director, 1968-74, director, 1974—; leader and coordinator of Koobi Fora research project, Lake Turkana, 1969—. Research associate of International Louis Leakey Memorial Institute for Africian Prehistory. Curle lecturer for Royal Anthropological Institute; lecturer at universities in the United States, England, Canada, New Zealand, Kenya, Sweden, and China, 1968—. Trustee of East African Wildlife Society, 1972-77, and vice-chairman, 1980—; trustee of Foundation for Social Rehabilitation and National Fund for the Disabled.

MEMBER: Pan African Association for Prehistoric Studies (secretary), Wildlife Clubs of Kenya (chairman, 1969—), Kenya

RICHARD E. LEAKEY

Exploration Society (chairman, 1969-72), Foundation for Research into Origin of Man (chairman), Explorers Club, Royal Anthropological Institute (fellow), Institute for Cultural Research (fellow), Preparatory Committee on the Environment, Anthropology Museum of the People of New York (chairman, 1980—), Sigma Xi. *Awards, honors:* Franklin L. Burr Prize for Science from National Geographic Society, 1965 and 1973.

WRITINGS—Of interest to young adults: (Contributor) S. L. Washburn and P. C. Jay, editors, *Perspectives on Human Evolution*, Holt, 1968; (contributor and editor) *Fossil Vertebrates of Africa*, Academic Press, 1969; (editor with Y. Coppens and others) *Earliest Man and Environments in the Lake Rudolf Basin: Stratigraphy, Palaeoecology, and Evolution*, Chicago

University Press, 1976; *The Fossil Hominids and an Introduction to Their Context, 1968-1974*, Volume I, Clarendon Press, 1977; (with Roger Lewin) *Origins: What New Discoveries Reveal about the Emergence of Our Species and Its Possible Future*, Dutton, 1977; (editor with wife, Meave G. Leakey) *Koobi Fora Research Project*, Volume I: *The Fossil Hominids and an Introduction to Their Context*, Oxford University Press, 1978; (with R. Lewin) *People of the Lake: Mankind and Its Beginnings*, Doubleday, 1978; (editor with Isaac Glynn) *Human Ancestors: Readings from "Scientific American,"* W. H. Freeman, 1979; (editor and author of introduction) Charles Darwin, *The Illustrated Origin of Species*, Hill & Wang, 1979; *The Making of Mankind*, Dutton, 1981; *Human Origins*, Lodestar Books, 1982; *One Life* (autobiography), Michael Joseph,

1984. Also contributor to *General History of Africa*, Volume I. Contributor to scientific journals, including *Fossil Vertebrates of Africa, Nature, National Geographic*, and *American Journal of Physical Anthropology*.

Television: "Bones of Contention" (documentary), Survival Anglia Ltd., 1975; "Making of Mankind" (seven-part documentary), BBC, 1981.

SIDELIGHTS: Leakey learned to identify fossils almost as soon as he could talk. As a boy he helped his father conduct research work. In one notable experiment, the father and son, using animal bones as their only weapons, attacked a pack of hyenas that had surrounded a dead zebra. They managed to snatch some meat from the carcass before the hyenas closed in, a feat that lent credence to Louis Leakey's theory that early man had survived by scavenging.

Although he grew up surrounded by talk about artifacts and bones, Richard Leakey had not intended to pursue the family profession. He dropped out of high school and established a lucrative business as a safari operator. Soon, however, he grew weary of truckling to tourists, and before long he was back in the digs. After finding the lower jaw of an *Australopithecus* (an ape-man who lived 3.5 to 1.5 million years ago) during an expedition at Lake Natron, Leakey became so enthused about anthropology that he resolved to broaden his scientific background. He traveled to England, where after several months of study he was able to pass his college entrance examinations. But Leakey became impatient—and impoverished—before he could enroll at a university. Determined to gain his education in the field and not in the classroom, he returned to Kenya without a college degree.

Leakey's lack of a college degree was not an insurmountable barrier to his getting established as an anthropologist. In 1967 he participated in an international fossil hunting expedition at the Omo River Valley. This experience deepened his conviction that he was capable of directing his own expedition. On the way home, he flew over Lake Turkana (then known as

Humans have many unusual characteristics, not least of which is our intense curiosity about our relationships with the world around us. ■ (From *The Making of Mankind* by Richard E. Leakey. Photograph from the documentary film adaptation. Presented on BBC-TV, 1981. Courtesy of Time-Life Video.)

(From *Origins* by Richard E. Leakey and Roger Lewin. Illustrated by Richard Bowen.)

Lake Rudolf). Later Leakey recalled his feelings when he first caught sight of the lake's eastern shore: "Looking down at the harsh-sun-baked patchwork of that virtually unknown volcanic terrain, with its eroded sediment layers, I felt certain that I was looking at a great anthropological adventure and a major challenge." Shortly afterwards he returned to Lake Turkana, where a quick search yielded some primitive tools. Accompanied by his father, Leakey went to Washington, D.C., and asked the National Geographic Society for funding to pursue further research at Lake Turkana. Impressed by the chutzpah of the twenty-three-year-old Leakey, the trustees granted his request.

Their decision to finance the expedition was a wise one: Lake Turkana turned out to be a treasure trove for anthropologists. Leakey and his team of Kenyan reseachers, dubbed the "Hominid Gang," made their first major discovery at Lake Turkana in 1969. In a remarkable stroke of luck, they stumbled across the skull of an *Australopithecus*, missing only its teeth and lower jaw.

Anthropology is a popular as well as a controversial topic. In addition to his scientific writing, Leakey has written two books on anthropology for the general reader, *Origins* and *People of the Lake*. The two books, both written in collaboration with Roger Lewin, trace man's evolutionary path and speculate as to how early man behaved.

In *Origins,* Leakey and Lewin repudiated the idea, popularized by Robert Ardrey, that humans are basically belligerent. "The notions of territorial and aggressive instincts and our evolu-

tionary career as killer apes are dangerous myths," Leakey told an interviewer. "In the book we reject the conventional wisdom that violence and war are in our genes. Our long prehistory as food gatherers argues more persuasively that we are a cooperative rather than an aggressive animal." *People of the Lake* elaborated on this idea. Citing as evidence the fossils of early man, the living habits of primates, and the social ties in modern-day primitive societies, Leakey argued that early man was a cooperative, gentle creature rather than a murderous brute. "Sharing, not hunting or gathering as such, is what made us human," Leakey wrote. "We are human because our ancestors learned to share their food and their skills in an honored network of obligation." He went on to say that it was not until farming was invented some 10,000 years ago that man became warlike. Once man had fields and wealth to protect, wars ensued.

Leakey's studies of ancient man have provided him with many other insights into current problems. When he was a schoolboy, Leakey was shunned by the other students for daring to defend blacks and the concept of Kenyan nationalism. As he grew older and learned more about man's origins, he became even more convinced that the color of one's skin is unimportant. "I regard black and white as divisive terms, but I'm sure the ancestors of man were, shall we say, dark skinned," he once commented. "Like it or not, most pale skinned Caucasians can trace their origins to a darker form of humanity in Africa."

An ardent conservationist, Leakey is deeply worried about the problems of overpopulation and pollution. His field work has taught him that any living organism, including man, may become extinct. While he is not a doomsayer, Leakey has said time and time again that the human race must learn to reflect upon its past and upon its future if it wishes to survive. For this reason Leakey is certain that his own fascination with early man will never diminish. "As I grow older my interests continue to broaden," he explained. "I'm interested in Kenyan affairs and international affairs and I would hope that I am able to make contributions in these areas. But, I'm sure I'll always be interested in human evolution. After all, our past, as a species, may help guide us in the future."

FOR MORE INFORMATION SEE: Life, September 12, 1969; *National Geographic,* May, 1970, June, 1973; *Science News,* February 26, 1972, November 18, 1972, March 13, 1976; *New York Times,* November 10, 1972, February 18, 1979; *Newsweek,* November 20, 1972, July 15, 1974, March 22, 1976, September 4, 1978; *Esquire,* October, 1973; *New York Times Magazine,* March 3, 1974; *International Wildlife,* May, 1975; *Psychology Today,* October, 1977, July, 1978; *New York Times Book Review,* October 30, 1977, February 19, 1978, November 19, 1978; *Time,* November 7, 1977, August 14, 1978; *Saturday Review,* November 12, 1977; *Washington Post Book World,* December 25, 1977, August 27, 1978; *Human Behavior,* February, 1978, December, 1978; *Times Educational Supplement,* March 17, 1978; *Times Literary Supplement,* January 20, 1978; *Christian Science Monitor,* September 18, 1978; *Washington Post,* October 3, 1978; *People,* January 8, 1979; *People Weekly,* February 18, 1980; *Maclean's,* March 17, 1980; *Newsweek,* February 16, 1981; *U.S. News and World Report,* February 15, 1982; *Science Digest,* November, 1982; Pamela Weintraub, editor, *The Omni Interviews,* Ticknor & Fields, 1984.

LEESON, Robert (Arthur) 1928-
(R. A. Leeson)

PERSONAL: Born March 31, 1928, in Barnton, Cheshire, England; son of William George (a chemical worker) and Nellie Louisa (a domestic servant; maiden name, Tester) Leeson; married Gunvor Hagen (a teacher, biologist, and geologist), May 25, 1954; children: Frederick Alan, Christine Ann. *Education:* University of London, B.A. (with honors), 1972. *Home:* 18 McKenzie Rd., Broxbourne, Hertfordshire, England.

CAREER: Worked on local newspapers and magazines in England and Europe, 1944-56; *Morning Star,* London, England, reporter, 1956-58, Parliamentary correspondent, 1958-61, feature writer, 1961-69, literary editor, 1961-80, children's editor, 1969-84; free-lance writer and editor, 1969—. Founding member of Other Award Panel, 1975—. Member of British section of the International Board on Books for Young People (treasurer, 1979—). *Military service:* British Army, 1946-48; served in Egypt. *Awards, honors:* Received Eleanor Farjeon Award for services to children's literature, 1985. *Member:* National Union of Journalists, Writers Guild.

WRITINGS—Juvenile; all fiction, except as noted: *Beyond the Dragon Prow* (illustrated by Ian Ribbons), Collins, 1973; *Maroon Boy* (illustrated by Michael Jackson), Collins, 1974; *Bess* (illustrated by Christine Nolan), Collins, 1975; *The Third Class Genie,* Collins, 1975; *The Demon Bike Rider* (illustrated by Jim Russell), Collins, 1976; *The White Horse,* Collins, 1977; *Challenge in the Dark* (illustrated by J. Russell), Collins, 1978;

The Cimaroons (nonfiction), Collins, 1978; *Silver's Revenge,* Collins, 1978, Philomel, 1979; *Grange Hill Rules, O.K.?,* BBC Publications, 1980; *Harold and Bella, Jammy and Me* (short stories), Fontana Books, 1980; *It's My Life,* Collins, 1980; *Grange Hill Goes Wild,* Fontana Books, 1980; *Grange Hill for Sale,* Fontana Books, 1981; *Grange Hill Home and Away,* Fontana Books, 1982; *Candy for King,* Collins, 1983; *Genie on the Loose,* Fontana Books / Hamish Hamilton, 1984.

Other: (Under name R. A. Leeson) *United We Stand: An Illustrated Account of Trade Union Emblems,* Adams & Dart, 1971; (under name R. A. Leeson) *Strike: A Live History, 1887-1971,* Allen & Unwin, 1973; *Children's Books and Class Society: Past and Present,* edited by Children's Rights Workshop, Writers and Readers Publishing Cooperative, 1977; (under name R. A. Leeson) *Travelling Brothers: The Six Centuries Road from Craft Fellowship to Trade Unionism,* Allen & Unwin, 1978. *Reading and Righting, the Past Present, and Future of Fiction for the Young,* Collins, 1985.

WORK IN PROGRESS: Volume of short stories, radio serial and fantasy novel.

SIDELIGHTS: "My main concern in all fields of writing, both for adults and children, is the relative failure of all branches of literature to reflect the vitality, variety, and importance of working class life. Thus, my books for adults deal with so far unexplored aspects of the history of working people, such as travelling craftsmen. My historical novels for children explore such areas as the Puritan side of Elizabethan and Stuart history, or the exploits of groups like the Cimaroons or escaped slaves. My children's books with a contemporary setting center on the lives of those at day school rather than the traditional boarding school of most literature.

ROBERT LEESON

(Cover illustration by Mark Thomas from *The Third Class Genie* by Robert Leeson.)

"Along with concern about the alienation of literature from the potential reader goes a concern with the isolation of the writer. I do a good deal of work in schools, helping children develop their own creative writing style and conducting storytelling sessions for children and adults in libraries, schools, and community centers.

"My method of writing falls into three stages. The first is a long period, perhaps months or years, in which an original idea matures and takes shape. This is followed by a shorter period of perhaps two or three months in which the plot structure is developed. The final writing period is as short as possible, sometimes no more than ten days. The writing begins when the story is so fully formed it *demands* to be told. A good deal of the writing, in fact, has been tried out orally through storytelling before it is set down in its final form."

HOBBIES AND OTHER INTERESTS: Music, walking, gardening.

I never knew so young a body with so old a head.
—William Shakespeare

LENGYEL, Emil   1895-1985

OBITUARY NOTICE—See sketch in *SATA* Volume 3: Born April 26, 1895, in Budapest, Hungary; died after a heart attack, February 12, 1985, in New York, N.Y. Journalist, historian, educator, and author. An authority on World War II and the rise of Nazism, Lengyel had a first-hand view of war and its consequences as a soldier during World War I. He was drafted into the Austro-Hungarian army as a young man and fought in the trenches on the eastern front before being captured by the Russians and sent to Siberia. While imprisoned, the soldier managed to learn a number of languages, including English, and after his release immigrated to the United States, where he worked as a journalist for the *New York Times* and other publications. He subsequently became a professor of social sciences and was associated with New York University for nearly twenty years and with Fairleigh Dickinson University for fifteen years. Lengyel's best-known book, *Siberia*, is a fictionalized account of the author's years of imprisonment. His other works include the juvenile books *Iran* and *The Land and People of Hungary*. Lengyel was also associated with the Foreign Policy Association's "Headline Series" publications and the Oxford Book Company's social studies pamphlets.

FOR MORE INFORMATION SEE: Current Biography Yearbook, H. W. Wilson, 1942; *Who's Who in America,* 40th edition, Marquis, 1978; *Contemporary Authors, New Revision Series,* Volume 3, Gale, 1981; *Directory of American Scholars,* 8th edition, Volume I: History, Bowker, 1982. Obituaries: *New York Times,* February 15, 1985; *Current Biography,* April, 1985.

LEONARD, Constance (Brink)   1923-

PERSONAL: Born April 27, 1923, in Pottsville, Pa.; daughter of Harry William (an educator) and Dorothy (Jessop) Brink; married John D. Leonard (a journalist), June 21, 1949 (divorced, 1969); children: Gillian. *Education:* Wellesley College, B.A., 1944. *Residence:* Francestown, N.H. 03043.

CAREER: Writer.

CONSTANCE LEONARD

WRITINGS: The Great Pumpkin Mystery, Random House, 1971; *The Other Maritha*, Dodd, 1972; *Steps to Nowhere*, Dodd, 1974; *Hostage in Illyria*, Dodd, 1976; *Shadow of a Ghost* (young adult), Dodd, 1978; *The Marina Mystery* (young adult), Dodd, 1981; *Stowaway* (young adult; Junior Literary Guild selection), Dodd, 1983; *Aground* (young adult), Dodd, 1984; *Strange Waters* (young adult), Dodd, 1985.

WORK IN PROGRESS: "Another mystery novel about Tracy James; an adult mystery based on my own wartime experiences."

SIDELIGHTS: "I have 'always' written—stories, verse, anything—but not for publication until the last few years when I've been settled in an old house in a tiny old village in the New Hampshire mountains. As a longtime mystery addict I thought I'd try writing one, and then another, and another.

"*Shadow of a Ghost* was my first young adult mystery and was based on a ghost I heard about in England. The last four, also young adult mysteries, are about a spunky young woman named Tracy James, whose two great loves are sailing and Pete Sturtevant, and who has had to be extremely resourceful to get herself out of the predicaments she has found herself in—in Florida and the Bahamas and Maine and Greece, so far! I did not plan this as a series, but Tracy keeps having exciting adventures, the next of which is now taking shape in my head. And, at the same time, I'm working on another adult mystery, based on my own wartime experiences. Several of my books have been published abroad.

"Aside from writing and reading and friends and good food, travel is my favorite thing, and I've had great fun collecting colorful backgrounds for my novels. At home I'm an enthusiastic—if not exactly expert—potter and tennis player and photographer, and also enjoy cross-country skiing and bridge."

LINDBLOM, Steven (Winther) 1946-

PERSONAL: Born March 29, 1946, in Minneapolis, Minn.; son of Charles Edward (a professor of political science and writer) and Rose Catherine Lindblom; married True A. Kelley (a writer and illustrator); children: Jada Winter. *Education:* Attended St. John's College, Annapolis, Md., 1964-65; Rhode Island School of Design, B.F.A., 1972. *Residence:* Old Denny Hill, Warner, N.H. 03278.

CAREER: Free-lance illustrator and writer. *Awards, honors:* New York Academy of Sciences chose *Messing Around with Water Pumps and Siphons: A Children's Museum Activity Book* one of the best books on science for children, 1982; *The Internal Combustion Engine* was chosen as an Outstanding Science and Trade Book for children, 1982.

WRITINGS—Juvenile: (With wife, True Kelley) *The Mouses' Terrible Christmas* (illustrated by T. Kelley), Lothrop, 1978; *The Fantastic Bicycles Book,* Houghton, 1979; (with T. Kelley) *The Mouses' Terrible Halloween* (illustrated by T. Kelley), Lothrop, 1980; (with T. Kelley) *Let's Give Kitty a Bath* (illustrated by T. Kelley), Addison-Wesley, 1982.

Illustrator: Bernie Zubrowski, *Messing Around with Water Pumps and Siphons: A Children's Museum Activity Book,* Little, Brown, 1981; Ross Olney, *The Internal Combustion Engine,* Lippincott, 1982; Seymour Simon, *Computer Sense, Computer Nonsense,* Lippincott, 1984.

(From *Let's Give Kitty a Bath!* by Steven Lindblom. Illustrated by True Kelley.)

WORK IN PROGRESS: Three juvenile books about croquet, robots, and machine tools.

SIDELIGHTS: "While I have written more fiction than nonfiction at this point, nonfiction writing is my first love.

"I think there are two very negative forces at work on our children today. One is television, which is turning children into drones who are only observers, and who have been convinced that experiences seen on television are somehow as valid as the real thing. (I think a child who neither read nor watched television might be happier and more constructive than one who did both!) The other is that modern technology has become so complex and remote that we begin to see ourselves as its victims rather than its masters and cease accepting any responsibility for the future.

"There are two things good children's nonfiction can do about this: encourage kids to get out and do things for themselves and reduce the world that surrounds them to manageable terms, restoring to them the feeling that they can comprehend it, and therefore control it.

"It's important that kids realize that whenever someone tells them, 'It's too complicated for you to understand,' the person probably is just covering up his own lack of understanding."

HOBBIES AND OTHER INTERESTS: Old bicycles and machinery, designing and building his "solar-gothic" home.

Children's playing are not sports and should be deemed as their most serious actions.
—Michel Eyquem de Montaigne

LIPPINCOTT, Bertram 1898(?)-1985

OBITUARY NOTICE: Born about 1898; died April 28, 1985, in Philadelphia, Pa. Publishing executive, yachtsman, and author. A graduate of Princeton University. Lippincott joined his grandfather's publishing firm, J. B. Lippincott & Company, after serving in World War I. During more than thirty years as an editor, he was responsible for the publication of such popular titles as *The Story of the Trapp Family Singers* and *My Friend Flicka.* One of the editor's hobbies was yacht racing, and he served as the commodore of the Conanicut Yacht Club in Rhode Island. Lippincott also wrote two books of Rhode Island history, *Indians, Privateers, and High Society: A Rhode Island Sampler* and *Jamestown Sampler.*

FOR MORE INFORMATION SEE—Obituaries: *Philadelphia Daily News,* May 1, 1985; *Detroit Free Press,* May 2, 1985; *New York Times,* May 2, 1985; *Chicago Tribune,* May 3, 1985; *Los Angeles Times,* May 5, 1985.

LIVINGSTON, Carole 1941-
(J. Aphrodite)

PERSONAL: Born February 22, 1941, in New York, N.Y.; daughter of Frank and Sally (Rainer) Rose; married Hyman Livingston, June 14, 1959 (divorced, 1972); married Lyle Stuart (a book publisher), February 4, 1982; children: (first marriage)

CAROLE LIVINGSTON

Jennifer Susan. *Education:* Brooklyn College of the City University of New York, B. A., (magna cum laude), 1968. *Residence:* Fort Lee, N.J. *Office:* Lyle Stuart, Inc., 120 Enterprise Ave., Secaucus, N.J. 07094.

CAREER: Lyle Stuart, Inc. (publisher), Secaucus, N.J., 1960—, currently vice president in subsidary rights and publicity. *Member:* Publishers Publicity Association, Confrerie de la Chaine des Rotisseurs, Les Amis du Vin, Wine and Food Society of New York, Women's Party.

WRITINGS—Juvenile: *Why Was I Adopted?,* Lyle Stuart, 1978; (with Claire Ciliotta) *Why Am I Going to the Hospital?,* Lyle Stuart, 1981.

Other: (Under pseudonym J. Aphrodite) *To Turn You On,* Lyle Stuart, 1975; *I'll Never Be Fat Again,* Lyle Stuart, 1980; *How to Lose Five Ugly Pounds Fast,* Lyle Stuart, 1984.

WORK IN PROGRESS: Another book for children.

SIDELIGHTS: "My work brings me in contact with authors, regarding the development of book projects, and with other publishers, both domestic and foreign, regarding the sale of publishing rights.

"My children's books came about after my publisher published *Where Did I Come From?* and *What's Happening to Me?* and many requests from parents of adoptive children came in. *Why Was I Adopted?* was my first title followed by *Why Am I Going to the Hospital?*"

HOBBIES AND OTHER INTERESTS: Food, wine, travel.

MacKINSTRY, Elizabeth 1879-1956

PERSONAL: Born in 1879 in the United States; childhood spent in France; died May 13, 1956, in Pittsfield, Mass.; buried in Lenox, Mass. *Education:* Studied violin under Ysaye, sculpture under Rodin, and woodwork under Ralph Adams Cram. *Residence:* Lenox, Mass.

CAREER: Illustrator, author, sculptor, violinist. When a teenager, MacKinstry established herself as a professional violinist following concerts in France and England. After suffering a severe back injury, she was forced to relinquish all violin playing and turned to drawing and poetry, subsequently becoming an accomplished sculptor as well. She was also employed as a teacher of art at Albright Art School of the Buffalo Fine Arts Academy, in Buffalo, N.Y. from 1911 to 1913. Her career as an illustrator began in 1924.

EXHIBITIONS: Buffalo Society of Artists Exhibition, Buffalo, N.Y., 1922. Work was exhibited in memorial exhibitions at Lenox Library, Lenox, Mass., 1956 and New York Public Library, New York City, 1957. *Member:* Buffalo Guild of Allied Arts.

WRITINGS—For children; all self-illustrated: *Puck in Pasture* (poems), Doubleday, Page, 1925; *The Fairy Alphabet as Used by Merlin,* Viking, 1933.

Illustrator; all for children: Edna Geister, *What Shall We Play?,* Doran, 1924; Rachel Field, *Eliza and the Elves,* Macmillan, 1926; Percy MacKaye, *Tall Tales of the Kentucky Mountains,* Doran, 1926; Hervey White, *Snake Gold,* Macmillan, 1926;

One of the rare existing photographs of Elizabeth MacKinstry.

Kate Douglas Wiggin and Nora Archibald Smith, editors, *Tales of Laughter*, Doubleday, Page, 1926; R. Field, *The Magic Pawnshop: A New Year's Eve Fantasy*, Dutton, 1927; Marie Catherine d'Aulnoy, *The White Cat, and Other Old French Fairy Tales*, edited by R. Field, Macmillan, 1928, reprinted, 1967; George MacDonald, *The Princess and the Goblin*, Doubleday, Doran, 1928; Clement C. Moore, *The Night Before Christmas*, Dutton, 1928; Burges Johnson, compiler, *A Little Book of Necessary Nonsense*, Harper, 1929; Alfred Noyes, *Forty Singing Seamen*, Stokes, 1930; Hans Christian Andersen, *Andersen's Fairy Tales*, introduction by Anne Caroll Moore, Coward-McCann, 1933; K. D. Wiggin and N. A. Smith, editors, *The Fairy Ring*, Doubleday, Doran, 1934, reprinted as *Fairy Stories Every Child Should Know*, 1942; *Aladdin and the Wonderful Lamp*, Macmillan, 1935; Padraic Colum, *The Legend of Saint Columba*, Macmillan, 1935.

Other: Joyce Kilmer, *Trees*, Doran, 1925; Henrik Ibsen, *Peer Gynt*, Doubleday, Doran, 1929.

SIDELIGHTS: MacKinstry's childhood was spent in France, where her early talent for the violin was nurtured. At seven she was sent to Paris to study the violin. "As I didn't go to school on account of the practice,—little violin prodigies work about seven hours a day—I had a governess. We were supposed to be out walking three hours a day, but when it rained, which it does about four days out of seven in winter there, I

played in the Louvre and the Luxembourg. The Louvre is as familiar to me as one's grandmother's house. It was my attic and my play room for years." [Elizabeth MacKinstry, "The Artist's Play Time," *Arts Journal*, Volume VII, number 8, November, 1925.[1]]

Summers were spent in various countries in Europe, where the young girl collected fairy tales and folklore. "It was the old Scottish Ballads that first taught me to love poetry. The loveliest summer of my life was spent with my mother in Scotland. I was about nine years old, and we went to all the places in the old ballads: Banks of Yarrow, Michael Scott's tomb, (he was a grand old wizard, Michael Scott was,) all the places. I wore a plaid, and proud I was of it, and in it I carried a book of Sir Walter Scott's poems. We saw a panorama play of the *Lady of the Lake* at Edemburgh. Alas, I didn't care a rap about the hero and the heroine, but I fell wildly in love with Roderick Dhu, the villain of the piece. I wept so at his death I had to be taken out and shaken, before I could see the rest of it. There were other summers in Ireland, at Barbizon, playing in the forest, and in Thuringia, the forest of Tannhauser. That finished me. What with the violin, there was your romantic started off for life."[1]

MacKinstry loved picture books as well as fairy tales, probably because she loved to draw. "Our piano tuner knew Boutet de Monvel, and told me delightful stories of the artist's dream of painting Jeanne D'Arc when a little gingerbread-eating boy in Rheims. No, I never met Boutet de Monvel outside his own

(From "The Goose Girl," in *The Fairy Ring*, edited by Kate Douglas Wiggin and Nora Archibald Smith. Illustrated by Elizabeth MacKinstry.)

picture books, but I vividly recollect the excitement I felt on seeing his pictures in shop windows for the first time. This feeling of intense excitement over books I saw in shop windows and wanted to own was strong enough to make me save all my pocket money to buy picture books.'' [Anne Carroll Moore, ''The Three Owls Salute Elizabeth MacKinstry,'' *Horn Book,* April, 1957.²]

In her teens, MacKinstry showed exceptional talent with the violin. She studied under the famous violinist, Ysaye, and gained a reputation as a child prodigy. ''When I was about fifteen I went to Brussels to study with Ysaye. Hearing that he required some horribly difficult scales, etc., I studied them with a pupil of his for three weeks. Good thing I did, for when I came to play for Ysaye, what with his wedging me in between a temporary wood stove in his enormous music room, and the piano; his playing the accompaniment himself and vilely, (Romance in F of Beethoven) and my natural timidity; I played about as you would expect.

'' 'I see nothing in her,' said Ysaye. 'It is cold and timid, little tone and talent.'

'' 'Could we try the scales, Master?' said the pupil, who went along.

''We tried the scales, and considering that I had worked eight hours a day, they went well. 'Prodigious industry,' said Ysaye, and took me.

''But the first triumph came later. Waiting at Ysaye's house for the first lesson—as always with Ysaye, one had to wait—I played the Romance in F for myself, very mournful, broken-hearted . . . no talent . . . no good . . . a very woebegone little fiddler. In came Ysaye with his violin, and said, 'Go on.' He played the accompaniment this time on his own instrument, and it was like an orchestra of the gods under one. At the end he kissed my hand and said, 'My child, you have the temperament of an artist, but do you eat enough beefsteak? You must eat twice; once for yourself, and once for the violin. The temperament of the artist is much for a man, too much for a woman.'

''I had drawing lessons in Paris, for I always would draw on Sundays! These were my own days, a concert in the afternoon to hear one of the big orchestras, but the rest of it my own.

''Then came an illness which meant the end of music for me, and presently came also the end, alas, of our little income through not very wise investments. One had the loving debt to a mother who spent so much on music, and the prospect of a living to make—for two.'' ¹

MacKinstry suffered from tuberculosis of the spine, which ended her brief career as a violinist. She turned to art instead, after returning to the United States with her mother. ''I was then recovering from the illness which put out the violin, in an old farm house near Buffalo. I called it, and still call it in memory, 'Lost Orchards.' It was an old farm house kept by three Dunkard sisters. . . . There was snow and cold; much snow, for the windows were out of my room, and the door. My family supplied me with books from the Buffalo Public Library. They came out once a week when the Dunkard sisters went 'to the city' with their farm produce. Great piles of books they were, for I got them on less than twelve cards!!! Any brains I had woke up that winter. There was an open fire and I read and read and read, with the snow powdering across the floor and the books. Afterwards Lost Orchards became a place

It was a Princess. . . But, mercy! how she looked, from the rain and the rough weather! ■ (From ''The True Princess,'' in *Andersen's Fairy Tales* by Hans Christian Andersen. Illustrated by Elizabeth MacKinstry.)

to take the friends to, very happy. But to me the cold sharp touch of the snow means . . . well, something fine for which worlds could well 'grow old' . . . something which cuts away and yet regenerates. That 'Spell of Cold' is straight from life.

"By the way, my first little book of poems, 'Helen's Mirror,' was written in Lost Orchards chiefly, though I saw the volume first in Capri. Alas, it had been proof read by a Presbyterian clergyman in between, so I do not care to dwell on it.

"In the barn at Lost Orchards I relearned modeling. The Misses Roads brought me out clay and wax. I fitted up a sort of studio in the barn and worked . . . like the devil.

"In the meantime I had produced some drafting to do for a cousin who was a civil engineer, and some illustrating of the cheapest sort. Did 'The Manxman' of Hall Caine's for a Buffalo paper that neglected the pay, by the way. Looking back, the drawings were worthy of the publication, but I was immensely serious about them then.'"[1]

MacKinstry was employed as an art teacher in various schools in Buffalo, New York. "'. . . I went up to Buffalo and took a position as teacher at the Albright Art Gallery, or rather the Art School of the Albright Art Gallery.

"It broke my heart to leave the country, as it always does. No work on the violin in past days was comparable to the

(From "Graciosa and Percinet," in *The White Cat, and Other Old French Fairy Tales* by Marie Catherine d'Aulnoy. Illustrated by Elizabeth MacKinstry.)

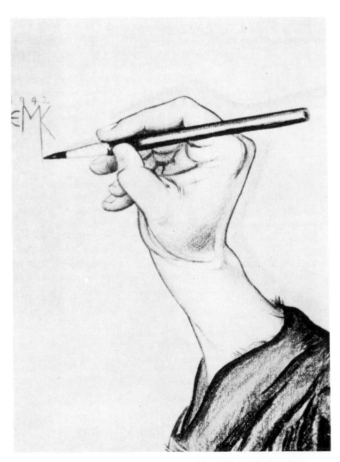

MacKinstry referred to this drawing as a "self-portrait of the artist—the part that counts." ■ (From "The Notebooks of Elizabeth MacKinstry," in *Horn Book,* April, 1957.)

difficulty of holding on to my teaching. The list of the schools I taught in at one time is goodly, and, considering that I had to teach it all to myself, first, and came to it from another trade and training, no wonder I consider it the biggest adventure of my life; the hardest too.

"There lies my real 'work of Art'. . . for teaching certainly wasn't a work of nature with me!

"It made adventures too. One time I had a call to take a death mask of a deceased gentleman, in the country. He wouldn't, er,. . . be there beyond that night . . . funeral tomorrow. I rushed to my ever present help, the Library, as it was then five o'clock and the last train left at six-fifteen. I got a book about the subject, (a wonderful place that library,) and read it on the train. It was ghastly, I never knew anything could be so horrific as that room as I worked into the night. By the grace of the Gods the mask didn't stick, when I pulled it off, but there was some awful moments when I feared it might!

"Another time, dead broke and obliged to have a new evening gown, for artists move in polite society, I tried painting some awful wooden things for trade. The man at the head did not know he was dealing with a teacher at the respected Gallery, and he said they were too poor, but if I kept on, I might do it in a week or so.

"As for the classes, at first, if they had to make an armature I read it up and backed it by European training and utter serenity; they tried it out, poor souls. It was amazing how often it succeeded.

The giant and the conjurer now knew that their wicked course was at an end, and they stood biting their thumbs and shaking with fear. ▪ (From "History of Jack the Giant Killer," in *The Fairy Ring,* edited by Kate Douglas Wiggin and Nora Archibald Smith. Illustrated by Elizabeth MacKinstry.)

So the Emperor went in procession under the rich canopy, and everyone in the streets said, "How incomparable are the Emperor's new clothes! . . ." ■ (From "The Emperor's New Clothes," in *Andersen's Fairy Tales* by Hans Christian Andersen. Illustrated by Elizabeth MacKinstry.)

. . .His eyes saw the falseness of their appearance: those who had mitres on their heads wore them awry, and their croziers were held downwards. . . . ■ (From *The Legend of Saint Columba* by Padraic Colum. Illustrated by Elizabeth MacKinstry.)

"Only an artist could know the technical joys that lay for me under those hard years. I studied sculpture as I taught it. I drew hours daily, and what I wanted to draw. Interested in illuminating, I went into it until I got what I wanted. It is strange how many illuminated manuscripts there are lying around loose. Interested in wood carving, I dug up a wood carver, and carve [sic] on wood.

"It was a rich time for poetry. There were trips to the country, trips abroad, all that lies in such a situation for anyone. To be sure one requires what Ysaye calls 'Prodigious energy,'. . . but it is there, it is all there. If I had a gospel to preach to young artists it would be that of the riches of the provinces, and the obscure job. I'd back it up with Rodin, who worked in Brussels obscurely as a repairer of Gothic ornament, and as a sculptor's assistant for twenty years."[1]

MacKinstry later moved to New York City where she became associated with Ralph Cram Adams, working chiefly in wood and Gothic ornaments and ecclesiastical sculpture. In 1925 her own book, *Puck in Pasture,* which contained her own verses and illustrations, was published. This book launched her career as an illustrator. "When the time came that I dared risk real poverty if need be for myself, my mother was gone, I came away. With too little money in my pocket to tell of, I came to New York to make my mistakes. If *Puck in Pasture* is one of them, I have at least been very happy in making it. And if one asks me how I came to wander so far afield from art as to write poetry, I answer that it takes the place of music to

me. I read it first propped up on my music stand, because one reads while doing scales, and poetry went better than prose. Since then I read it as one would music, write it as one would play, because I like it. It is the music that is left. If art is my job, poetry is my passion.

"Why shouldn't a self-supporting, hard-working artist play the piano, the violin, or the pen in spare times?"[1]

An editor, May Massee, years later recalled MacKinstry's days as an illustrator in New York. "I see her living in a big studio room—a drawing table at which she stood to work, pencils, crayons, paints, inks, artist's tools neatly arranged, books to the ceiling all around, a studio couch, an old chaise lounge with a board back-rest, a chair or two, a big cage with the door open for her pet flying squirrel, a beautiful little golden-brown creature which could be everywhere at once.

"Elizabeth was about five feet four, stoutish and sturdy but quick motioned. A large round head topped by an unruly thatch of darkish gray hair, cut short in tufts—she just chopped it off now and then. Big round eyes, blue or gray or green and piercing, though they could be as bland as a child's. A good-sized nose, not classic, and a generous mobile mouth shaped to speak exquisite French and to make English beautiful too. Her voice was husky but with bright tones now and then. Most of the time she was happy in her painter's smock but she could look very impressive dressed in black silk with a bit of lace and gold about.

''She never lost the grace of the violin player. She always had to wear heavy steel braces for her spine and it was difficult for her to walk but her arms and her head were free and beautifully poised. She held her reed pen like the bow of her violin—she could stand and work for hours and her arms never tired.

''Her flying squirrel liked to sit on the top edge of her drawing board and talk with her as she worked. Even when he scolded and ripped her thumb, he still had an affectionate tone that was only for her.

''He liked Rachel Field, as we all did, for laughter and love always came into the room with Rachel. But when she brought her Scottie as she often did, the squirrel would dart to one of his farthest hiding places and scold until the Scottie barked a reply and then he would pretend to sleep until they left.

''Those were happy days for us all and when *Puck in Pasture* was finally published, it was wonderful to hear that Bruce Rogers said he was glad to see the first book in America that showed a really modern feeling in its deep design.'' [May Massee, ''Elizabeth MacKinstry,'' *Horn Book*, April, 1957.[3]]

MacKinstry felt that her training in music and sculpture influenced her illustrations. She admired the artistic works of Randolph Caldecott, Walter Crane and Lovat Fraser. ''. . . Much of the best popular art of the nineteenth and early twentieth centuries, has gone between the two lids of a book, and notably those intended for children.

''There is a something gay and myth making, a something breaking out into decoration as naturally as a tulip breaks out into color, which is inherent in the human mind, and with this quality art has always concerned itself. Where art itself is a popular thing the people and the greatest artists have, as it were, joined hands, and the artist has rolled out a sort of endless decoration and picture-fable of the beliefs, aspirations, and stories of the heroes of the times, and the layman has read it as easily and delightedly as a child reads a picture book.'' [Elizabeth MacKinstry, ''The Illustration of Children's Books as a Fine Art,'' *Publishers Weekly*, October 16, 1926.[4]]

MacKinstry's later years were spent in retirement in Lenox, Massachusetts. She died on May 13, 1956.

> ''The love of beauty, nothing more or less
>   Has had possession of my soul for years
>   And I have followed after it in tears,
> In failure, every kind of fretfulness
> Of pain and poverty: served in duress
>   To times which had slight use for it. My peers
>   Gave comfort, bless them! Something greater nears,
> And with it healing and forgetfulness. . . .'' [2]

In the spring of 1957 the Central Children's Room of the New York Public Library held a memorial exhibit of MacKinstry's work, which included representative illustrations from her children's books, stage designs and drawings for costumes for the Commedia dell' Arte and Shakespeare, sketches for stained glass windows and tapestries, and a number of studies and illustrations for projected books.

FOR MORE INFORMATION SEE: Elizabeth MacKinstry, ''The Artist's Play Time,'' *Arts Journal*, Volume VII, number 8, November, 1925; Elizabeth MacKinstry, ''The Illustration of Children's Books as a Fine Art,'' *Publishers Weekly*, October 16, 1926; Anice Page Cooper, *Authors and Others*, Doubleday, Page, 1927, reprinted, Books for Libraries, 1970; Bertha E. Mahony and E. Whitney, *Contemporary Illustrators of Children's Books*, Book-Shop for Boys and Girls, 1930, reprinted, Gale, 1978; B. E. Mahony and others, compilers, *Illustrators of Children's Books: 1744-1945*, Horn Book, 1947; *Horn Book*, April, 1957; Muriel Fuller, editor, *More Junior Authors*, Wilson, 1963. Obituaries: *New York Times*, May 14, 1956; *Publishers Weekly*, June 18, 1956.

The Queen of the Fountain

(From ''The Pot of Carnations,'' in *The White Cat, and Other Old French Fairy Tales* by Marie Catherine d'Aulnoy. Illustrated by Elizabeth MacKinstry.)

All Books are either dreams or swords,
You can cut, or you can drug, with words.
—Amy Lowell

MacLACHLAN, Patricia

BRIEF ENTRY: Born in Cheyenne Wyo. Author of children's books. MacLachlan graduated from the University of Connecticut and has been an English teacher, a lecturer, and a teacher of creative writing workshops for both adults and children. The author of ten books, MacLachlan emphasizes the family in much of her work. For example, in *Cassie Binegar* (Harper, 1982), Cassie learns to accept the boisterousness of her casual family instead of longing for a prim family like that of her friend, Margaret Mary. Likewise, in *Arthur, for the Very First Time* (Harper, 1980), ten-year-old Arthur changes his views about life, himself, and others when he spends his summer vacation in the country with relatives. *Booklist* found it to have "fine characterization . . . [and] an intriguing mix of people and problems."

In addition, many of MacLachlan's books combine sensitive stories with wit. In *Unclaimed Treasures* (Harper, 1984), an eleven-year-old-girl longs to find her own true love. *School Library Journal* observed, "MacLachlan's penetration into the dreams of youth merges with her keen sense of humor. . . ." MacLachlan has won awards for two of her books. *Arthur, for the Very First Time* received the Golden Kite Award for fiction from the Society of Children's Book Writers in 1980, and *Unclaimed Treasures* was named an honor book in the fiction category of The Boston Globe-Horn Book Awards in 1984. MacLachlan's other books are: *The Sick Day* (Pantheon, 1979), *Through Grandpa's Eyes* (Harper, 1980), *Moon, Stars, Frogs, and Friends* (Pantheon, 1980), *Mama One, Mama Two* (Harper, 1982), *Tomorrow's Wizard* (Harper, 1982), and *Sarah, Plain and Tall* (Harper, 1985). *Residence:* Massachusetts.

STEPHEN MANES

MANES, Stephen   1949-
(Hans Pemsteen, A. M. Stephensen; joint double pseudonym: Mel Murch and Ward Starr)

PERSONAL: Surname is pronounced *Man*-ess; born January 8, 1949, in Pittsburgh, Pa.; son of Milton (a chemist) and Carol (Freeman) Manes; married Esther Susan Selter (a librarian), December 24, 1969 (divorced, December, 1982). *Education:* Attended University of Chicago, 1965-67; University of Southern California, A.B., 1973. *Residence:* Riverdale, N.Y. *Address:* c/o E. P. Dutton, 2 Park Ave., New York, N.Y. 10016.

CAREER: American Film Institute, Beverly Hills, Calif., assistant librarian, 1969-71; KCET-TV, Los Angeles, Calif., co-producer, "The Curse of Los Feliz," 1971; National Telefilm Associates, Los Angeles, research director, 1972-73; free-lance writer, 1973—; Manhattan Cable Television, New York, N.Y., host of "PCTV," 1983; Hard/Soft Press, New York, N.Y., chairman, 1983—. *Member:* Authors Guild, Writers Guild of America, Poets and Writers. *Awards, honors: Pictures of Motion and Pictures That Move: Eadweard Muybridge and the Photography of Motion* was chosen as an Outstanding Science and Trade Book for Children by the National Association of Science Teachers, 1982.

WRITINGS—Juvenile: *Mule in the Mail* (illustrated by Mary Chalmers), Coward, 1978; *Hooples on the Highway,* Coward, 1978; *The Boy Who Turned into a TV Set* (illustrated by Michael Bass), Coward, 1979; *Slim Down Camp,* Clarion, 1981; *The Hooples' Haunted House* (illustrated by Martha Weston),

Delacorte, 1981; (under pseudonym Hans Pemsteen) *Clash of the Titans Storybook* (illustrated by Mike Eagle), Golden Books, 1981; *Pictures of Motion and Pictures That Move: Eadweard Muybridge and the Photography of Motion,* Coward, 1982; *Socko! Every Riddle Your Feet Will Ever Need* (illustrated by Nurit Karlin), Coward, 1982; *Be a Perfect Person in Just Three Days!* (illustrated by Tom Huffman), Clarion, 1982; (under pseudonym A. M. Stephensen) *Unbirthday,* Avon, 1982; *I'll Live,* Avon, 1982; *That Game from Outer Space: The First Strange Thing That Happened to Oscar Noodleman* (illustrated by Tony Auth), Dutton, 1983; *Video War,* Avon, 1983; *The Oscar J. Noodleman Television Network: The Second Strange Thing That Happened to Oscar Noodleman* (illustrated by Roy Schlemme), Dutton, 1983; (with Esther Manes) *The Bananas Move to the Ceiling* (illustrated by Barbara Samuels), F. Watts, 1983; (with Paul Somerson) *Computer Monsters,* Scholastic, 1984; (with P. Somerson) *Computer Olympics,* Scholastic, 1984; (with P. Somerson) *Computer Craziness,* Scholastic, 1984; (with P. Somerson) *Computer Space Adventures,* Scholastic, 1984; *Life Is No Fair!* (illustrated by Warren Miller), Dutton, 1985; (with Ron Barrett) *Encyclopedia Placematica,* Workman, 1985.

Adult: (With P. Somerson, under joint double pseudonym Ward Starr and Mel Murch) *Underground WordStar,* Hard / Soft Press, 1984.

Screenplays: "The Curse of Los Feliz," first broadcast by KCET-TV, 1971; "First Aid," 1973 (adaptation released as "Mother, Jugs, and Speed," Twentieth Century-Fox, 1976); "We Built the Bomb," 1974; "The Great Thaw," 1975; "The Red Room Riddle" (based on the book by Scott Corbett), ABC-TV, 1983; "The Littles" (based on a series of books by John Peterson), ABC-TV, 1983.

Editor of *Focus!*, 1967-69; contributor to *December* and *Gambit*, 1971; contributing editor, *PC* and *PCjr* magazines, 1983—; monthly column, "Personal Curmudgeon," in *PCjr*, 1984; monthly column, "Parity Check," in *PC*, 1985.

ADAPTATIONS: "How to Be a Perfect Person—In Just Three Days" (film), broadcast by PBS, Highgate Pictures, 1984.

WORK IN PROGRESS: Chicken Trek, third in the Oscar Noodleman series; young adult novel; a novel for adults.

SIDELIGHTS: "Writing has been a part of my life as far back as I can remember. My literary appetite first got whetted in third grade, when I became roving reporter for the *Sunnyside Review,* our school paper. Promotions to feature editor, news editor, and editor-in-chief followed, along with a couple of statewide second prizes for my comic poems. Unfortunately, our junior high had no publications of any kind, and my literary ambitions ended up taking a nap.

"In high school, fired up again by one of those proverbial 'great English teachers,' I spearheaded a drive to start a muckraking magazine to compete with the utterly insipid school paper. Alas, our staff's commitment to what it considered integrity managed to get it in 'Dutch' with the school administration and kept the magazine from ever being published. At the University of Chicago, I founded and co-edited *Focus!*,

All I want you to do is go to the nearest zoo and bring home a fully-grown gorilla. ■ (From *Be a Perfect Person in Just Three Days!* by Stephen Manes. Illustrated by Tom Huffman.)

one of the first American film publications with an auteurist perspective, and almost certainly the only one ever to advance the position that a certain Antonioni film was aesthetically inferior to a strikingly similar one directed by Jerry Lewis.

"While I was living in Los Angeles and working on a variety of unproduced screenplays and television projects, my wife, a children's librarian, kept bringing home kids' books that seemed far more exciting than the contemporary film fare. When one of my scripts was transmogrified into a dungheap called *Mother, Jugs and Speed,* I began to realize that Hollywood and I were constitutionally incompatible and moved back East to try my hand at writing books for kids.

"There's a lot to be said for writing books. Books are among the last commercial products that can still convey an individual's point of view. An editor may make suggestions, an art director may pick the typeface and the illustrator, but, except in the world of 'packaged' books, the words are ultimately the author's. It's a heady experience when it works; when it doesn't you have no one but yourself to blame.

"Writing for kids has its own special pleasures. For kids I can write everything from short picture books to full-fledged novels that happen to be about people who are still in high school. And writing for kids lets me indulge and cultivate a sense of silliness and whimsy too many adults seem to lack.

"As a child of the television era, I'm sure I've been influenced at least as much by such disparate cultural figures as Rootie Kazootie, Ozzie Nelson, Daffy Duck, Max Shulman, Carl Barks, Hank Williams, Jr., and R. Crumb as I have by Winnie-the-Pooh, John R. Tunis and Uncle Remus. The little-known author Shep Steneman, whose best work remains unpublished, remains a kindred spirit and boon companion.

"Ultimately, 'Don't bore me!' is the reader's first commandment to any writer. Much as we authors may hate to admit it, people don't *have* to read fiction. In the struggle to win a portion of people's precious leisure time, books are engaged in a fierce competition with everything from windsurfing to horticulture to video games. Unless writers offer something that's not available elsewhere—honesty, beauty, humor, intelligence, iconoclasm, ideas, personal vision—we can and should expect to find our potential readers hanging ten, hanging plants, or hanging out. But when we get 'em it's wonderful."

MARTIN, René   1891-1977

PERSONAL: Born February 11, 1891 in Paris, France; naturalized American citizen; died August 14, 1977, in Key Largo, Fla.; son of an engraver and artist; married wife, Simone, 1928; children: one son, Luc André. *Education:* Studied art in Switzerland and Italy. *Residence:* Key Largo, Fla.

CAREER: Artist and illustrator of books for children. *Awards, honors:* Received several fine arts grants from the Swiss government.

ILLUSTRATOR: I. Tannehill, *All about the Weather,* Random House, 1953; Frances C. Smith, *The First Book of Conservation,* F. Watts, 1954, revised edition, 1972; Harry Zarchy, *Wheel of Time,* Crowell, 1957; Mae Freeman and Ira Freeman, *Your Wonderful World of Science,* Random House, 1957; Rachel Carson, *The Sea around Us,* adapted for young readers by

Even if your experience has been only with a dead bug, a dead bird, or a dead dog, you know that when an animal dies it can no longer move, feel, see, grow. . . . ▪ (From *Life and Death* by Herbert S. Zim and Sonia Bleeker. Illustrated by René Martin.)

Anne Terry White, Simon & Schuster, 1958; Nancy Larrick, *Color ABC,* Platt, 1959; M. Freeman and I. Freeman, *The Sun, the Moon, and the Stars,* Random House, 1959, revised edition, 1979; M. Freeman and I. Freeman, *The Story of the Atom,* Random House, 1960; Robert S. Lemmon, *Junior Science Book of Trees,* Garrard Press, 1960; M. Freeman and I. Freeman, *The Story of Electricity,* Random House, 1961; N. Larrick, *First ABC,* Platt, 1965; Martha Shapp and Charles Shapp, *Let's Find Out about Fishes,* F. Watts, 1965; Herbert S. Zim, *Corals,* Morrow, 1966; David C. Knight, *Let's Find Out about Weather,* F. Watts, 1967; H. S. Zim, *Waves,* Morrow, 1967; H. S. Zim, *Blood,* Morrow, 1968; M. Shapp and C. Shapp, *Let's Find Out about Snakes,* F. Watts, 1968; H. S. Zim, *Bones,* Morrow, 1969; Marie M. Jenkins, *Moon Jelly Swims through the Sea,* Holiday House, 1969.

D. C. Knight, *Let's Find Out about the Ocean,* F. Watts, 1970; H. S. Zim and Sonia Bleeker, *Life and Death,* Morrow, 1970; H. S. Zim, *Armored Animals,* Morrow, 1971; William M. Stephens, *Life in the Open Sea,* McGraw, 1971; W. M. Stephens and Peggy Stephens, *Sea Turtle Swims the Ocean,* Holiday House, 1971; H. S. Zim, *Your Brain and How It Works,* Morrow, 1972; H. S. Zim, *Your Stomach and Digestive Tract,* Morrow, 1973; (with Gustav Schrotter) H. S. Zim, *The Universe* (Martin was not associated with earlier edition), revised edition, Morrow, 1973; H. S. Zim and Lucretia Krantz, *Crabs,* Morrow, 1974; H. S. Zim and L. Krantz, *Snails,* Morrow, 1975; H. S. Zim and L. Krantz, *Sea Stars and Their Kin,* Morrow, 1976; (with James Gordon Irving) H. S. Zim, *Owls* (Martin was not associated with earlier edition), revised edition, Morrow, 1977.

Painting done by Martin while in Morocco, 1937.

When he was completely armored, a knight had to be lifted with a derrick to mount his horse. ■
(From *Armored Animals* by Herbert S. Zim. Illustrated by René Martin.)

The following *Sidelights* have been contributed by Simone Martin regarding the life of her painter, illustrator husband, René.

SIDELIGHTS: Born **February 11, 1891** in Paris, France. Martin was raised in his parents' native Switzerland. His mother died when he was still a young boy. His father soon remarried. ''René grew up in the town of Morges, midway between Lausanne and Geneva on Leman Lake. His father, an engraver and watercolorist, had a deep admiration for artists and en-

couraged all of his children to pursue fine art, though he felt it was equally important for them to learn a skill with which to support themselves financially. René learned the art of engraving from a printer in Geneva. This skill helped him tremendously in his book illustrations years later.''

Martin attended college in Morges. He was drafted into the Swiss Army during World War I and later discharged when he contracted pneumonia. He then taught art at a Swiss boarding school for girls where he met his future wife. ''Like many

A sudden withdrawal of the sea may be the start of a tsunami.

The Japanese name, tsunami, means a wave seen on shore, but not on the open sea. ■ (From *Waves* by Herbert S. Zim. Illustrated by René Martin.)

René Martin, 1939.

children during World War I, I was sent to Switzerland to take refuge. René gave art lessons at my boarding school, and he fell in love with me.'' The couple married ten years later.

''Rene left Switzerland to study fine art in Italy and then traveled to Morocco. In the summer of 1919, René and his brother built a house on the Leman Lake.''

From the early twenties to the fifties, Martin worked on commissioned portraits and stained glass in Paris. ''At that time, people often donated portraits to the church in memory of a deceased husband or wife. Aside from the portraits and stained glass design, René was commissioned by the Swiss Government to execute frescoes for the Swiss Embassy in Rome.

''In 1928 we married and left for Morocco. I was 22 years old. We always travelled by car. My husband painted constantly, using oil for his landscapes and pastel for portraits.''

Spent winters in Morocco and summers on the Leman Lake. In 1929 their son, Luc André Martin, was born. Always busy with his work, Martin decorated the courthouse in Lausanne, Switzerland with the help of fellow artist Ernest Biéler, exhibited his works in Casablanca, Rabat, Lausanne, and Geneva, and traveled throughout Spain, France, Greece, Italy, and Egypt.

Granted special permission by the French military to paint in the Great Atlas Mountains of North Africa. ''We stayed with French officers as there was no hotel. To give you an idea of our isolation, the nearest grocery store was 150 miles away! Still, we enjoyed our stay. The French General allowed us to go into very deserted areas, where René painted landscapes as well as portraits of the beautiful Berber tribes.

''We had a very unusual lifestyle. We loved to travel and were always together. Our son went everywhere with us and, in

fact, never attended school formally until he was fifteen years old, at which time he entered the L'ecole Internationale in Geneva. He now works for the space shuttle program in Texas and was never interested in becoming a painter. He loved airplanes! René had a studio wherever we lived and if I or any of our friends met a pretty girl, we'd bring her to René and he would paint her portrait, working with pastel on paper. He also worked in charcoal and tempera, as well as combinations of watercolor and pastel.

''Many of his friends were artists from all over the world, and they'd often exchange paintings. Whenever a new painter arrived in Morocco, he was immediately sent to visit René. Young artists also sought René's advice, and he helped them in whatever way he could encourage them, although he felt that artistic talent and inspiration were qualities which could not be taught. He would give lessons, but never on a continuous basis, because we were always moving. In any case, he was busy enough with his own paintings.

''He loved the people of Morocco and the Moroccan ambience. We had an active social life in Morocco, going out frequently to parties and ballroom dances with our many friends. René was polite and amiable. In those years, he was quite urbane, but then, so was Morocco!

''He exhibited in Casablanca, Rabat, and Lausanne every two years. His paintings sold and he was able to make a living. Our son discovered that René created at least 1,600 paintings in his lifetime. At one time, we had wanted to put together a retrospective exhibition, but my son and I have only about fifty paintings left with the rest scattered around the world, and impossible to locate.''

René Martin, about 1969.

Martin was an avid sportsman. "He adored sailing, mountain climbing, skiing and swimming. He loved the house and the land which he and his brother owned on the Leman Lake. Our sailboat was docked in front of our house. We would often take the boat out on the lake for eight or ten days and René would paint landscapes.

"In 1948, we were advised to stay out of Morocco. It was nearing the end of its French protectorate. There were many fanatics, and several of our friends were assassinated. It had also become unsafe to paint Arabs. René decided it would be better not to go back to Morocco. It was a bad time for Europeans."

The Martins moved to the United States in 1948. "My sister was in America and my son wanted to study engineering in the States. René held one exhibition in New York City at the Macdougal Alley Gallery, which was owned by an English painter whom we'd met in Marrakech. René and I traveled throughout the U.S. and Mexico while our son attended the University of Michigan. René was not very inspired by America, but we decided to stay, because our son was living here.

"We met author Dr. Herbert Zim of Western Publishing Co. and soon thereafter René began to illustrate his children's books. During this period René also did illustrations for *Scientific American*. He was extremely interested in nature. He never studied formally, but just observed. When he needed a reference from the museum or the zoo, Dr. Zim would get it for him—shells, rare plant specimens . . . anything! We formed a deep friendship with Dr. Zim and his wife. In fact, I bought a house on the Zims' property in Florida after my husband's death.

"I also helped René with his illustration. When he needed documents, I did the research. We had many reference books at home, including a complete set of the 1911 Larousse Illustrated Encyclopedias."

"René painted every morning and afternoon, He worked all the time and he loved his work. He also enjoyed reading, particularly in French. We always spoke French together and when we didn't want people to understand us, we'd speak Moroccan. René could read and write in Arabic, and spoke many other languages well, including French, German, Spanish, Italian and English."

Died **August 14, 1977** in Key Largo, Florida. "Before René became ill, we had decided to go to Yemen for the winter because we'd heard it was a bit like the Morocco of the old days. He died before we made the trip."

FOR MORE INFORMATION SEE: Illustrators of Books for Young People, Scarecrow, 1975.

MASTERS, Mildred   1932-
(Mildred Heinzen)

PERSONAL: Born July 8, 1932, in Indianapolis, Ind.; daughter of Paul Lewis (a farm manager; in sales) and Mildred (a teacher; maiden name, Carter) Masters; married Bernard Heinzen, December 29, 1956 (divorced, 1975); children: John, Robert, James, William. *Education:* Western College, Oxford, Ohio, B.A., 1954; University of Minnesota, M.A., 1982. *Politics:* Independent. *Residence:* Minneapolis, Minn.

MILDRED MASTERS

CAREER: American Heritage, New York, N.Y., editorial assistant, 1954-56; National Education Association, Washington, D.C., editorial assistant for *NEA Journal,* 1957-58; volunteer library assistant, 1963-77; Minnesota Department of Human Rights, St. Paul, publications assistant and librarian, 1978; Minnesota Department of Education, St. Paul, information officer, 1979-80; University of Minnesota, Minneapolis, librarian at Newman Center, 1981; free-lance writer, 1978—; Hennepin County (Minn.) library system, substitute librarian, 1984—. Member of fee arbitration committee of Hennepin County Bar Association, 1976-84. *Member:* Authors Guild, Authors League of America, Society of Children's Book Writers, National Association of Government Communicators, Special Libraries Association, American Library Association, Minnesota Library Association, Minneapolis Art Institute, Walker Art Center, Minnesota Public Radio, Metropolitan Museum of Art. *Awards, honors:* A guest editor of *Mademoiselle* magazine's college issue, June, 1954; grant from Minnesota State Arts Board, 1979.

WRITINGS: The House on the Hill (juvenile novel), Greenwillow, 1982. Contributor to magazines, often under name Mildred Heinzen.

WORK IN PROGRESS: A novel for children set in Minneapolis; research on the direct and indirect effects of divorce on women and children.

SIDELIGHTS: "My best childhood memories are of sitting on my mother's lap while she read me *The Bears of Blue River* and of sitting on my father's lap while he read me *The Tin Woodsman of Oz.* I had four older sisters and many, many relatives of all ages. Whenever I visited relatives, I found shelves and shelves of books to occupy me. In grade school, I was reprimanded for reading my library books too fast, but I got attention by writing poems and humor which my classmates and teachers liked.

"In high school, I learned a great deal about English by studying Latin for four years, and I studied French too. I edited my high school paper and worked on my college paper and magazine.

"I always wanted to write and work in publishing. I managed to get to New York after college as one of twenty winners of the *Mademoiselle* College Board contest. That got me a month working on the magazine. Then I worked my way up from receptionist to editorial assistant at *American Heritage* magazine. I was hired at the very beginning, six months before the first *American Heritage* was published, and I got to meet and work for some very interesting and talented people. When I married, I moved to Washington, D.C., where I worked as an editorial assistant for the *NEA Journal* of the National Education Association.

"Since 1960, I have lived in Minnesota. I earned a masters degree twenty-eight years after I earned my B.A. For the past few years, I have worked part of the time as a librarian and part of the time as a writer. I love my present work as a substitute librarian because I work with children and adults in twenty-five public libraries.

(Jacket illustration by Jan Palmer from *The House on the Hill* by Mildred Masters.)

"I have written since I could read and have had many nonfiction pieces published, mostly in out-of-the-way places. *The House on the Hill*, a novel for eight-to-eleven-year-olds, is my first published book. This immensely exciting experience was possible only because I received a grant which allowed me to devote all of my time for a brief period to this project. I had been working on it at odd moments for years, while devoting most of my time and energy to family and jobs.

"There is a shortage of novels for children in the middle grades who read well and need books which challenge their minds *and* their emotions as only good fiction can. Nearly all small children enjoy fiction, I think, but too many lose interest in it when they outgrow picture books and easy readers because they are offered too much formula material. It is too bad that many publishers are recruiting writers to produce even more formula material for middle readers and teenagers. This practice will only discourage writing and reading of quality books in the future.

"I've lived on a farm, in a small town, in large eastern cities, in midwestern cities, and in a midwestern suburb. Exploring cities, especially big ones, is one of my favorite things."

FOR MORE INFORMATION SEE: Contemporary Authors, Volume 110, Gale, 1984.

MATH, Irwin   1940-

PERSONAL: Born July 8, 1940, in New York, N.Y.; son of Sol (a real estate owner) and Bess (Sassin) Math; married Ellen Feingold (a public relations director), November 18, 1962; children: Nicole, Robert. *Education:* New York University, B.S.E.E., 1962. *Home:* 5 Melville Lane, Great Neck, N.Y. 11023. *Office:* Math Associates, Inc., 6 Manhasset Ave., Port Washington, N.Y. 11050.

CAREER: Associated with David Sarnoff Research Center, Princeton N.J., 1962-64; Math Associates, Inc. (consulting firm), Great Neck, N.Y., owner and president, 1968-71; Oriel Corporation of America, Stamford, Conn., co-owner, 1971-78; Math Associates, Inc. (supplier of fiber optics components), Port Washington, N.Y., owner, president, and designer of fiber optic data-transmission systems, 1977—. Trustee of Incorporated Village of Saddle Rock, 1971-73. *Member:* Institute of Electrical and Electronic Engineers, American Radio Relay League (life member). *Awards, Honors:* Honorable mention, 1980, from New York Academy of Science, for *Morse, Marconi, and You: Understanding and Building Telegraph, Telephone and Radio Sets.*

WRITINGS—Of interest to young adults: *Morse, Marconi, and You: Understanding and Building Telegraph, Telephone and Radio Sets* (illustrated by Hal Keith), Scribner, 1979; *Wires and Watts: Understanding and Using Electricity* (illustrated by H. Keith), Scribner, 1981; *Bits and Pieces: Understanding and Building Computing Devices* (illustrated by H. Keith), Scribner, 1983. Also author of column "Math's Notes" in *CQ Magazine,* 1970—, and numerous technical articles.

SIDELIGHTS: Throughout his professional career, Math has sought out new challenges both as an entrepreneur and a designing engineer. In its first phase Math Associates was an electronics and engineering consulting firm dealing with anything from medical equipment to moving scenery in Broadway productions. Math then decided to merge the company with

IRWIN MATH

one of its clients, Oriel Optics Corporation, thus forming Oriel Corporation of America. As the new company stabilized, Math became interested in a new area of technology—that of fiber optics.

In 1977, faced with a partner who was reluctant to branch out in the relatively untested field, Math sold his half of the business and again incorporated Math Associates, this time as a supplier of fiber optics components. The new Math Associates began slowly with a staff consisting of Math himself, his wife, and an assistant. After receiving an encouraging reply from an initial request mailing, they managed to compile a catalog which they mailed to about five thousand potential customers.

As Math Associates became firmly established in the field of fiber optics, Math began to turn his attention back to design engineering. Eventually, he relinquished the catalog portion of the business to an associate and currently devotes his time to the design of fiber optic data-transmission systems. He now employs a staff of twenty-five to meet the challenges of his latest venture.

FOR MORE INFORMATION SEE: New York Times, March 2, 1980; *Electronic Engineering Times,* February 1, 1982.

MERRILL, Jane   1946-
(Janie Filstrup, Jane Merrill Filstrup; Phil Merrill, pseudonym)

PERSONAL: Born October 26, 1946, in Oakland, Calif.; daughter of Russell Oswald (a naval officer and mathematics teacher) and Phoebe (Dunn) Merrill; married E. Christian Filstrup (a librarian and writer), August 10, 1968 (divorced, 1984); children: Emma Nilufar and Burton Thomas (twins). *Education:* Wellesley College, B.A., 1968; Harvard University, M.A.T., 1970; Columbia University, M.L.S., 1972, M.A.,

1974. *Residence:* New York, N.Y. *Agent:* F. Joseph Spieler, 410 West 24th St., 3M, New York N.Y. 10011.

CAREER: Iranzamin/Tehran International School, Tehran, Iran, elementary school teacher of English, 1969-71; Cambridge Public Library, Cambridge, Mass., head librarian of North Branch, 1972-73; Atlantic Institute for International Affairs, Paris, France, researcher, 1974-75; U.S. Committee for United Nations Children's Fund (UNICEF), New York, N.Y., assistant director of Information Center on Children's Cultures, 1975-77; free-lance writer, 1978—; *Fifty-Plus* (magazine), New York City, senior editor, 1982. Presently working as a publicist with Hill and Knowlton, New York City. *Member:* American Society of Journalists and Authors.

WRITINGS—All under name Janie Filstrup, except as indicated; nonfiction; of interest to young readers, except as indicated: (With Chris Filstrup) *Beadazzled: The Story of Beads* (illustrated by Loren Bloom), Warne, 1982; (under name Jane Merrill Filstrup; with Dorothy L. Gross) *Monday through Friday: Daycare Alternatives* (adult), Teachers College Press, 1982; (with C. Filstrup) *China: From Emperors to Communes,* edited by Tom Schneider, Dillon, 1983; (under name Jane Merrill; with Wallace E. Lambert) *Bringing Up Baby Bilingual* (adult), Facts on File, 1984; *Tea Time* (adult), Green Tiger, 1985; *Carp Kites on Main Street,* Dodd, 1986. Also contributor to magazines and newspapers, sometimes under pseudonym Phil Merrill, including *New Republic, Harvard, Cosmopolitan, New York, Diversion, Vogue, Christian Science Monitor, Cavalier, Town and Country, Gifted Child Quarterly, Art and Auction, The Connoisseur, Garden,* and *Ford Times.* Contributing editor to *Gallery* and *Baby Talk.*

WORK IN PROGRESS: Finishing Touches, contemporary female *bildungsroman;* a book retelling the last legal duel in France.

JANE MERRILL

The Chinese learned how to make silk thousands of years ago. These young women from a commune in Sichuan Province are gathering the cocoons from which the silk is produced. ■
(From *China: From Emperors to Communes* by Chris and Janie Filstrup.)

SIDELIGHTS: Merrill's first job after college was in Iran where she, who is Persian-speaking, taught elementary school. Before beginning her career as a writer, she also spent a year in France, employed at a research institute. In Paris, she indulged in such activities as the opera, movies, collecting antique earrings, and attending fashion shows. Now the mother of twins, she still makes the time to remove herself from her usual New York environment. As she stated: "Sometimes, for bookish souls, the best preparation for serious writing is an absence of books, a fallow period, distance from familiar ways and even from one's native tongue. . . . Now after working hard for long stretches, I find that I have to construct other times to drop out of my language, and into myself. . . . Travel of the most immersive nature returns me to writing refreshed and a good learner."

Being a generalist is highly important to Merrill. At least for the time being, ghost-writing which she identifies as "my *croissant et beurré,* has a useful allure."

HOBBIES AND OTHER INTERESTS: "Tea drinking, swimming, working with the Open World Theater, a company in New York City dedicated to producing."

FOR MORE INFORMATION SEE: Contemporary Authors, Volume 110, Gale, 1984.

I know well that only the rarest kind of best in anything can be good enough for the young.
—Walter de la Mare

How pleasant is Saturday night,
    When I've tried all the week to be good.
Not spoken a word that is bad,
    And obliged every one that I could.
—Nancy Dennis Sproat

JIM MOORE

MOORE, Jim   1946-

PERSONAL: Born May 9, 1946 in Glendale Calif.; son of James Robert (an executive) and Jeanne (Reineke) Moore; children: Jason A. *Education:* New York University, certificate in film production, 1970; Germain School of Photography, certificate, 1971; also studied mime under Sterling Jensen and Paul Curtis. *Home and office:* One Hudson St., New York, N.Y. 10013.

CAREER: Photographer and mime artist. Hudson Street Studio, Inc., New York, N.Y., founder and teacher of mime, 1975-79; School of Visual Arts, New York City, professor of mime, 1979-80. President, Corporeal Studio Ltd. (non-profit, tax exempt corporation).

ILLUSTRATOR—With photographs; for children: Mark Stolzenberg, *Exploring Mime,* Sterling, 1979; Jeff Sheridan, *Nothing's Impossible: Stunts to Entertain and Amaze,* Lothrop, 1982; Philippe Petit, *On the High Wire,* Random House, 1985.

WORK IN PROGRESS: Comedy In/Sight, "a new project of photographs and interviews with people whose life's work is to make people laugh."

SIDELIGHTS: A former student of Sterling Jensen, protégé of French master Etienne Decroux, and Paul Curtis of the American Mime Theatre, Moore is noted for blending classical mime with vaudeville-style surprises of comedy and "quick-change." His interest in the theater began in 1969 when he became a leader of the popular art of street performing in New York. Moore's unusual knack for relating to a great variety of audiences eventually took him to the streets of other cities across the country and overseas to Holland and France.

In 1976 he was invited to attend the Third Annual Creative Workshop of Mine in Warsaw, Poland, and subsequently performed at Lincoln Center and Town Hall in New York as well as at Kennedy Center for the Performing Arts in Washington, D.C. His one-man show, "Dated Material," has been seen in New York and at colleges and universities throughout the Northeast.

In 1975 Moore founded the Hudson Street Studio, Inc., a non-profit corporation dedicated to developing and encouraging public interest and understanding of mime, clown, and the variety arts. The following year he created The Silent Performer Workshop. It was the first modern school in New York to bring together award-winning performers to teach their special crafts under one roof. Another project of the Hudson Street Studio was "The New York Variety Show," conceived and produced by Moore and featuring a unique mixture of variety arts.

"I perform mime because I found myself doing it in school. I photograph performers because I find I have an affinity with them and can capture their essence on film."

FOR MORE INFORMATION SEE: Dance Magazine, April, 1983; *Stages,* May/June, 1985.

The greatest pleasure in life is that of reading, while we are young.

—William Hazlitt

MORGAN, Tom 1942-

PERSONAL: Born June 20, 1942, in Syracuse, N.Y.; son of George A. (a businessman) and Mary (Cartin) Morgan; married Jean Glasgow (a business manager), July 3, 1965, divorced, 1984; married Erna McReynolds (a broadcasting executive), 1985; children: Pamela Jane, Kathleen Anne, Benjamin Paul. *Education:* Attended Ithaca College, U.S. Navy School of Journalism, and Auckland University. *Residence:* Unadilla, N.Y. *Agent:* Writers House, 21 West 26th St., New York, N.Y. 10010.

CAREER: Commercial writer, syndicated columnist, television and radio host, businessman. Bendix Corp., Sidney, N.Y., technical writer, 1963-64; Charles Haines Ltd., Auckland and Wellington, New Zealand, advertising and public relations writer, 1964-71; Page Seed Company, Greene, N.Y., vice-president and director, 1972-80; host of syndicated television and radio program, "Tom Morgan's Moneytalk," 1980—. Trustee of WSKG-TV and Radio, Binghamton, N.Y. Former board director, Lindsay String Orchestra, Wellington, New

(From *The Building Book* by Tom Morgan. Illustrated by the author.)

Zealand. *Military service:* U.S. Navy, 1960-63; journalist second class. *Member:* Rotary Club.

WRITINGS: *Money, Money, Money,: How to Get It and Keep It* (juvenile nonfiction; Junior Literary Guild selection; illustrated by Joseph Ciardello), Putnam, 1978. Contributor to syndicated child-care column in New Zealand and of editorials and articles to newspapers, including the *New York Times.*

SIDELIGHTS: "I wanted to write as early as the age of eight, and did, with my own school newspaper, a diary, etc. I first learned to write in the U.S. Navy's School of Journalism, and in the fleet, writing news releases and editing newspapers and cruise books.

"I learned more about writing while working with Bendix Corp., and later as an advertising and public-relations writer for agencies in New Zealand. I wrote for such accounts as Mobil, *Reader's Digest,* Coca Cola, Pan American Sunbeam, Ford Motor, and Kodak.

"Back in the United States I immersed myself in business with a national garden-seed company. But I began writing again in 1977. First I wrote an article for the editorial pages of the *New York Times,* then the book *Money, Money, Money,* and lately, a syndicated radio and television program, 'Tom Morgan's Moneytalk.'

"*Money, Money, Money* came to me because Henry Ford II grew weary of the Ford Foundation. In his resignation as a

trustee he suggested, publicly, that some staff and beneficiaries of foundation grants have little understanding or sympathy with the capitalism that made them possible. His remarks inspired me to write for the Op-Ed page of the *New York Times.* I wrote that it was a pity we teach our children so little about the capitalistic system. Regardless of its merits or warts, it is the system by which we live. I suggested that American youth should learn how the participants in the system compete and fail to, how they maneuver, how they coagulate. Putnam's Charles Mercer read the article and asked if I would try a book for the very youth who I felt were in need. Enter *Money, Money, Money.*

"My philosophy about economics: Our economic system influences nearly every facet of our lives, therefore we'd be wise to learn all we can about its nuts and bolts. My philosophy about writing: Forget about 'highly creative' writing until you have truly mastered the craft. In this respect my views are similar to those of the music teacher who says 'no creative jazz until you can play your instrument every which way from Sunday.' My overriding philosophy: No matter how cruel a circumstance, there is some good to be found in it. And discipline, self or otherwise, is a must in order to achieve anything worthwhile."

MUÑOZ, William 1949-

PERSONAL: Surname is pronounced "Moon-yo-s"; born January 12, 1949, in Chicago, Ill.; son of J. John (a research scientist) and Margaret (a teacher; maiden name, Allen) Muñoz; married Sandra Mulberger (a respiratory therapist), November 25, 1976. *Education:* Attended American College, Paris, France, 1967; University of Montana, B.A., 1971, graduate study, 1971-73. *Politics:* None. *Religion:* Baha'i. *Home and office:* Route 1, Box 205, St. Ignatius, Mont. 59865.

CAREER: University of Montana, Missoula, director of technical services, 1974-81; farmer and photographer. *Awards, honors: A Picture Book of Cows* was chosen as an outstanding science and trade book, 1982.

ILLUSTRATOR—With photographs; juvenile; all written by Dorothy Hinshaw Patent: *A Picture Book of Cows,* Holiday House, 1982; *A Picture Book of Ponies,* Holiday House, 1983; *Farm Animals,* Holiday House, 1984; *Where the Bald Eagles Gather,* Houghton, 1984; *Quarter Horses,* Holiday House, 1985; *Sheep Book,* Holiday House, 1985; *Baby Horses,* Dodd, 1986; *Maggie,* Dodd, 1986; *American Bison,* Clarion Books, 1986; *Draft Horses,* Holiday House, 1986.

WORK IN PROGRESS: *Grizzly Bears* for Clarion Books; *Wheat Farms* for Dodd; *Appaloosas* for Holiday House.

SIDELIGHTS: "Photography, for me, is a means of communication. I am able to express my emotions of love and happiness (basic optimistic feelings) through photography. I am happiest when I see someone smile or laugh as a result of one of my photos. This is especially gratifying when it is a child. Children are so much more aware of love, happiness, and joy, so I am especially pleased when I have done something to make them happy. The primary motivating force for me in photography is a deep fascination with and for nature as a manifestation of God's love. To be able to capture any of this expression is my hope.

TOM MORGAN

WILLIAM MUÑOZ

"I have studied French, Hellenistic Greek, and Russian, none in which I am at present terribly competent! I am beginning to study Salish—the language of the Flathead Indians.

"When I graduated from high school, I was able to spend a year in Paris. This was very important, I feel, in that I became much more visually oriented as a result of that year. I have

traveled (and continue to do so as much as I am able) throughout the U.S. I hope to be able to get to Alaska and the Yukon-Northwest Territories of Canada soon.

"Sandy and I live on an eighty acre farm and raise cattle along with horses and chickens. Farming offers the potential for me to observe nature closely, as well as to experience the feeling

Only minutes after it is born, the wet little calf tries to stand up. ■ (From *A Picture Book of Cows* by Dorothy Hinshaw Patent. Photograph by William Muñoz.)

of being a part of nature's ways, able at times to seemingly control her but ultimately knowing that nature will have her way. That above all else is beauty to me!

"The vision underlining direction for me and the motivating force in my life is the Baha'i faith and the teachings of Baha'u'llah, its founder. Baha'u'llah taught, among other things, that there must be unity among mankind—unity through diversity, not sameness."

HOBBIES AND OTHER INTERESTS: Ancient Egyptian history, skiing.

Ah! what would the world be to us
  If the children were no more?
We should dread the desert behind us
  Worse than the dark before.
          —Henry Wadsworth Longfellow

MYRA, Harold L(awrence) 1939-

BRIEF ENTRY: Born July 19, 1939, in Camden, N.J. Publishing executive and author of books for adults and young people. After graduating from East Stroudsburg State College in 1961, Myra joined the staff of *Campus Life* magazine in Wheaton, Ill. He began as an editorial assistant, later assuming the positions of associate editor, managing editor, director of literature, and finally, publisher and vice-president of the literature division. Myra has been the president and publisher of Christianity Today, Inc. since 1975 and has worked as an instructor at Wheaton Graduate School. Among his writings is the juvenile book *Halloween: Is It for Real?* (Thomas Nelson, 1982). In it Myra relates the holiday's origin and its association to paganism and Christianity. He also wrote the juvenile works *The New You: Questions about This Fresh Newborn Way of Life Now That You Believe* (Zondervan, 1972), *Santa, Are You for Real?* (Thomas Nelson, 1977), *Easter Bunny, Are You for Real?* (Thomas Nelson, 1979), and *Today Is Your Super-Terrific Birthday* (Nelson Communications, 1985). *Home:* 1737 Marion Ct., Wheaton, Ill. 60187.

FOR MORE INFORMATION SEE: Who's Who in Religion, 2nd edition, Marquis, 1977; *Contemporary Authors, New Revision Series,* Volume 8, Gale, 1983; *Who's Who in America,* 43rd edition, Marquis, 1984.

NEARING, Penny 1916-
(Anne Maguire)

BRIEF ENTRY: Name originally Meryl Lucile Munn; born April 16, 1916, in Waterport, N.Y. A free-lance writer since 1938 when she graduated from Cornell University, Nearing is the author of seven novels for young adults. All written under the pseudonym Anne Maguire, her works include both romances and mysteries set in the Great Lakes plains and Erie Canal region. Among her titles, all published by Avalon, are *The Folly of Pride* (1974), *Nurse in Las Palmas* (1980), *Run before Midnight* (1981), and *Strings to Love* (1981). Nearing is also a contributor to young adult magazines, including *American Girl* and *Christian Home. Home:* 50 Clearview Dr., Spencerport, N.Y. 14559.

FOR MORE INFORMATION SEE: Contemporary Authors, Volumes 81-84, Gale, 1979; *International Authors and Writers Who's Who,* 9th edition, International Biographical Centre, 1982.

NEWMAN, Gerald 1939-

BRIEF ENTRY: Born May 3, 1939, in New York, N.Y. Educator, writer, editor, and artist. Newman received both his B.A. and M.F.A. from the Brooklyn College of the City University of New York. Since 1962 he has been a teacher of art and creative writing for the New York City Board of Education. He is also the author of several juvenile books, including the introductory work *Eskimoes* (F. Watts, 1978), which was first published in England and then in America as *The Changing Eskimos* (F. Watts, 1979). *Junior Bookshelf* described it as "interesting and informative." Other juvenile books by Newman are: *Elton John* (written with Joe Bivona; New American Library, 1976), *Lebanon* (F. Watts, 1978), *How to Write a Report* (F. Watts, 1981), and *Zaire, Gabon, and the Congo* (F. Watts, 1981). In addition, he is the editor of *The Encyclopedia of Health and the Human Body* (F. Watts, 1977) and the second revised edition of *The Concise Encyclopedia of Sports* (F. Watts, 1979). *Home:* 300 West 23rd St., New York, N.Y. 10011.

FOR MORE INFORMATION SEE: Contemporary Authors, Volume 101, Gale, 1981.

NIXON, Hershell Howard 1923-

PERSONAL: Born August 4, 1923, in Duncan, Okla.; son of James Gilbert (a farmer) and Whirlie (Dickey) Nixon; married Joan Lowery (a writer), August 6, 1949; children: Kathleen Nixon Brush, Maureen Nixon Quinlan, Joseph, Eileen. *Education:* University of Southern California, B.S., 1952. *Home:* 10215 Cedar Creek Dr., Houston, Tex. 77042. *Agent:* Writers House, Inc., 21 West 26th St., New York, N.Y. 10010.

CAREER: Shell Oil Co., Billings, Mont., junior geologist, 1952-56; Getty Oil Co., geologist in Ventura, Los Angeles, and San Francisco, Calif., and Corpus Christi, Houston, and Midland, Tex.; Mitchell Energy Co., Houston, geologist, 1974-77; Strata Energy, Inc., Houston, geologist, 1977-79; Howell Petroleum, Houston, exploration manager, 1980-83; Ridgeway Exploration Company, Houston, vice-president of exploration, 1983—. *Military service:* U.S. Navy, 1942-48; became quartermaster. *Member:* American Association of Petroleum Geologists, American Institute of Professional Geologists, West Texas Geological Society, Houston Geological Society, University of Southern California Alumni Association, Phi Sigma Kappa. *Awards, honors:* Outstanding Science Books for Children certificate from National Science Teachers Association-Children's Book Council Joint Committee, 1979, for *Volcanoes: Nature's Fireworks,* 1980, for *Glaciers: Nature's Frozen Rivers,* and 1981, for *Earthquake: Nature in Motion.*

WRITINGS—All juvenile; all with wife, Joan Lowery Nixon: *Oil and Gas: From Fossils to Fuels* (illustrated by Jean Day Zallinger), Harcourt, 1977; *Volcanoes: Nature's Fireworks,* Dodd, 1978; *Glaciers: Nature's Frozen Rivers,* Dodd, 1980; *Earthquakes: Nature in Motion,* Dodd, 1981; *Land under the Seas: Nature's Secrets,* Dodd, 1985.

SIDELIGHTS: "My wife and I have traveled extensively in the United States and a little in other countries. I was motivated to write books on scientific topics by my children's questions about science. I have the background in science; my wife has the background in writing for young children. I appreciate the blend of the many cultures that make up America, the generosity, the humor of our people, and the way in which Americans face their problems and deal with them."

HERSHELL HOWARD NIXON

Tidal waves caused by the 1964 Alaskan earthquake carried this fishing boat several hundred feet inland . . . . ■ (From *Earthquakes: Nature in Motion* by Hershell H. Nixon and Joan Lowery Nixon. Photograph by R. W. Lemke.)

NOLAN, Dennis 1945-

PERSONAL: Born October 19, 1945, in San Francisco, Calif.; son of Arthur Thomas (an opera singer) and Helen (Fortier) Nolan; married Susan Christine Ericksen, January 28, 1967; children: Andrew William. *Education:* Attended College of San Mateo, 1963-65; San Jose State College (now University), B.A., 1967, M.A., 1968. *Home and office:* 579 Beresford, Redwood City, Calif. 94061.

CAREER: San Mateo County Library, Belmont, Calif., graphic artist, 1970-77; Canada Junior College, Redwood City, Calif., art instructor, 1979—. Art instructor at College of San Mateo,

1982-84, and San Jose State University, 1983-84. Has also been employed as an elementary schoolteacher. Work has been exhibited in six one-man shows and in group shows. *Awards, honors:* John Cotton Dana Public Relations Award, 1973; American Library Association Annual Report award, 1975; Outstanding Science Book award, National Science Teachers Association, 1981, for *The Joy of Chickens.*

WRITINGS—Fiction for children, except as noted; all self-illustrated: *Big Pig,* Prentice-Hall, 1976; *Monster Bubbles: A Counting Book* (Junior Literary Guild Selection), Prentice-Hall, 1976; *Alphabrutes,* Prentice-Hall, 1977; *Wizard McBean and His Flying Machine,* Prentice-Hall, 1977; *Witch Bazooza,*

Witch Bazooza raised her wand, wrinkled up her face, closed her eyes and chanted. ■ (From *Witch Bazooza* by Dennis Nolan. Illustrated by the author.)

Prentice-Hall, 1979; *The Joy of Chickens* (nonfiction for young adults), Prentice-Hall, 1981.

Illustrator: Charles Keller, compiler, *Llama Beans* (fiction for children), Prentice-Hall, 1979; Jim Barrett and others, editors, "*Sunset*" *Homeowner's Guide to Wood Stoves* (adult nonfiction), Lane Publishing, 1979; Bill Nygren, *Gnomes Color and Story Album*, Troubador Press, 1980; Karen Schiller, *Bears Color and Story Album* (fiction for children), Troubador Press, 1982; David E. Clark and others, editors, *Gardeners Answer Book*, Lane Publishing, 1983.

SIDELIGHTS: "My grandparents were artists, as were my parents (my father was an operatic tenor). Art was not only encouraged but always around. Books have always been a large part of my life so the blending of two loves—art and books—seemed natural.

"As an illustrator I approach most of my projects with the visual problems foremost in my mind. The story generally moves along after the pictures have been visualized, at least in my mind if not on paper. Planning the illustrations for the lead-in, the climax, and the ending across a thirty-two page format is also a major concern. Most of my books are humorous, and I plan them in storyboard form somewhat like an animated film. In this way I can control the timing of the punch lines, surprises, and build-ups. I have found that varying my style and technical approach has kept me fresh for each new project."

POLETTE, Nancy (Jane)   1930-

PERSONAL: Second syllable of surname is pronounced "leat"; born May 18, 1930, in Richmond Heights, Mo.; daughter of Willard A. (a lawyer) and Alice (a librarian; maiden name, Colvin) McCaleb; married Paul L. Polette (an engineering planner), December 23, 1950; children: Pamela (deceased), Paula, Keith, Marsha. *Education:* William Woods College, A.A., 1950; Washington University, St. Louis, Mo., B.S.Ed., 1962; Southern Illinois University, M.S.Ed., 1968; University of Missouri, graduate study, 1972-73. *Politics:* Democrat. *Religion:* Disciples of Christ. *Home:* 203 San Jose Court, O'Fallon, Mo. 63366. *Office:* Department of Education, Lindenwood Colleges, St. Charles, Mo. 63301.

CAREER: Elementary school teacher in Jefferson County, Mo., 1950-51, and in Ritenour, Mo., 1954; Pattonville School District, Maryland Heights, Mo., elementary school teacher, 1955-65, coordinator of elementary school materials, 1965-78; Southern Illinois University at Edwardsville, instructor, 1968-78; Lindenwood Colleges, St. Charles, Mo., instructor, 1970—, associate professor of education, 1979—. Editor-in-chief, Book Lures, Inc. Lecturer and workshop leader, 1968—. Educational consultant, ECA, Denver, Colo., 1977-80. Member of board of directors of Leukemia Guild of Missouri, 1959-70. *Member:* American Library Association, American Association of School Librarians, National Council of Teachers of English, Association for Supervision and Curriculum Development, Missouri Library Association, Missouri Association of School Librarians (vice-president, 1973-74), Missouri State Teachers Association, Suburban Library Association, Chicago Children's Reading Round Table.

WRITINGS: Basic Library Skills, Milliken Publishing, 1971; *Library Skills for Primary Grades,* Milliken Publishing, 1973; *Developing Methods of Inquiry,* Scarecrow, 1973; *In Service:*

School Library/Media Workshops and Conferences, Scarecrow, 1973; *The Vodka in the Punch and Other Notes from a Library Supervisor,* Shoe String, 1975; (with Marjorie Hamlin) *Reading Guidance in a Media Age,* Scarecrow, 1975; (editor) Helen Saunders, *The Modern School Library,* 2nd edition (Polette was not associated with earlier edition), Scarecrow, 1975; *E Is for Everybody: A Manual for Bringing Fine Picture Books into the Hands and Hearts of Children,* Scarecrow, 1977, 2nd edition, 1982; *Celebrating with Books,* Scarecrow, 1978; *Katie Penn,* Concordia, 1978; *Exploring Books with Gifted Children,* Libraries Unlimited, 1980; *Picture Books for Gifted Programs,* Scarecrow, 1981; *Three R's for the Gifted,* Libraries Unlimited, 1982; *Tangles* (picture book; illustrated by Jerry Warshaw), Book Lures, 1983; *The Thinker's Mother Goose* (picture book; illustrated by J. Warshaw), Book Lures, 1983; *Books and Real Life,* MacFarland, 1984; *Research Book for Gifted Programs,* Book Lures, 1984.

Author of computer software; all published by Book Lures, 1983: *Who Stole Cinderella's Slipper; Mother Goose for Young Thinkers; The Revenge of Rumpelstiltskin; The Pied Piper Pipes Again.*

Also author of tape and transparencies series for library use and of filmscript, "Anno's Journeys," Weston Woods, 1983. Editor, Miller-Brody Newbery Literary Activities Pack Program, 1974-75. Member of book review staff, *School Library Journal,* 1972-73. Contributor to journals.

NANCY POLETTE

"Just a quiet, sheltered spot with good friends, abundant food and a small dab of tender, loving care. . . ." ■ (From *Tangles* by Nancy Polette. Illustrated by Jerry Warshaw.)

WORK IN PROGRESS: The Research Almanac, for Book Lures.

SIDELIGHTS: "My first, and possibly most thrilling, published work was a poem in a children's magazine at the age of ten. Once bitten by the writing bug it is hard to NOT write. However, until recently most of my writing has been in the children's literature and library field to fill a long overdue need. The lack of materials for elementary library programs in the mid-sixties led to one of my first books in that field called *Developing Methods of Inquiry.* Later books dealt with numerous aspects of library work with children. The emphasis on media in the seventies led me to a good deal of writing for the tape, transparency, activity book, and sound filmstrip areas and to the development of one of the first courses in the country in writing for educational media, a course I still teach at Lindenwood Colleges each summer.

"The library/media field and gifted education make such natural partners that recent years have led to writing in this field. As director of the laboratory school at Lindenwood which features programs for gifted children, I have had a working laboratory in which to integrate literature into gifted programs and to observe the magic which happens with such integration.

"Much of my life today is spent 'on the road' travelling throughout the United States and Canada doing workshops in gifted education for school districts and professional organi-

zations. Perhaps someday those travels will be another book, for few people, I am sure, have ridden across a reservation with an Indian with a shotgun as their guide!

"I'm always seeking new mediums for writing. I am most pleased with being able to do the filmstrip for the Weston Woods production of 'Anno's Journeys,' based on the picture books by Mitsumasa Anno whom I have long admired. In addition, with the computer revolution upon us I experimented with writing for the computer materials which will lead children to books. The response to these programs has been most gratifying."

HOBBIES AND OTHER INTERESTS: Theatre, drama.

POLLOCK, Penny 1935-

BRIEF ENTRY: Born May 24, 1935, in Cleveland, Ohio. Author of books for children and educator. Since 1973 Pollock has worked as head teacher at the Village Nursery School in Brookside, N.J. She also served as lecturer ar Fairleigh Dickinson University in 1980. Pollock combines fantasy with animal lore in several of her books like *Ants Don't Get Sunday Off* (Putnam, 1978), *The Slug Who Thought He Was a Snail*

(Putnam, 1980), a Junior Literary Guild selection, *The Spit Bug Who Couldn't Spit* (Putnam, 1981), and *Stall Buddies* (Putnam, 1984). Another fantasy, *Garlanda: The Ups and Downs of an Uppity Teapot* (Putnam, 1980), is accompanied with pictures by award-winning illustrator Margot Tomes. "What a sweet, old-fashioned story Pollock weaves," observed *School Library Journal*, "authentically recreating Victorian England through the fate of an elegant teapot." In 1983 Pollock received the New Jersey Authors Award for *Keeping It Secret* (Putnam, 1982), her novel about an eleven-year-old girl with a hearing problem who must adjust to a new school. *Horn Book* called it "lively, wryly humorous . . . mainly, a story about human relationships." Pollock's latest works include *Emily's Tiger* (Paulist Press, 1984) and *Water Is Wet* (Putnam, 1985). *Address:* Burnett Rd., Mendham, N.J. 07945.

FOR MORE INFORMATION SEE: Contemporary Authors, Volume 101, Gale, 1981.

PREISS, Byron (Cary)

BRIEF ENTRY: Born in New York, N.Y. Author and editor. Preiss graduated from the University of Pennsylvania and received his M.A. from Stanford University in 1974. Throughout the 1970s, he held positions in both the publications and television fields such as director of graphics at National Periodical Publications, editor and writer for CTW's "Electric Company," head writer at ABC-TV, and independent editor at Harcourt Brace Jovanovich. Preiss's first two books, *The Electric Company Joke Book* and *The Silent "e's" from Outer Space* (both Western Publishing, 1973), were aimed at preschoolers as part of a six book series based on the children's television show. Illustrated by Joe Mathieu, the second title humorously reveals how the addition of an "e" to a word can change its meaning entirely. *New York Times Book Review* described it as "the most imaginative and educational of the six." Among Preiss's other books for preschoolers are *The First Crazy Word Book: Verbs* (F. Watts, 1982) and *The Little Blue Brontosaurus* (Caedmon, 1983). He has also produced works for young adults, including the science fiction novel *Dragonworld* (Bantam, 1979) and the biography *The Beach Boys* (Ballantine, 1979), and adults. *Office:* 128 East 56th St., New York, N.Y. 10022.

FOR MORE INFORMATION SEE: Contemporary Authors, New Revision Series, Volume 14, Gale, 1985.

RICE, Dale R(ichard)   1948-

PERSONAL: Born August 6, 1948, in New Castle, Pa.; son of Paul R. (a shipping and receiving supervisor) and Charlotte (a homemaker; maiden name, Heath) Rice; married: Judy Boyer (a teacher), August 6, 1984; children: (previous marriage) Brandon Dale, Kristin Leigh. *Education:* Pennsylvania State University, B.S., 1970, M.Ed., 1973; Ohio State University, Ph.D., 1977. *Residence:* Mobile, Ala. *Office:* College of Education, University of South Alabama, Mobile, Ala. 36688.

CAREER: Bethel Park School District, Bethel Park, Pa., teacher, 1970-74; Scioto-Darby City Schools, Hilliard, Ohio, teacher, 1977; East Carolina University, Greenville, N.C., assistant professor of science education, 1977-80; University of South Alabama, Mobile, Ala., associate professor of early childhood and elementary education, 1980—. Manuscript reviewer, Charles E. Merrill Publishing Company and *School Science*

and Mathematics; member of the advisory and manuscript review board for *Science and Children;* president and board member, Greenville Jaycees, 1978-79. *Member:* National Association for Research in Science Teaching, National Science Teachers Association, School Science and Mathematics Association, Phi Delta Kappa. *Awards, honors:* Named outstanding instructor by East Carolina University, 1978; nominated for post-doctoral Spencer fellowship, 1982.

WRITINGS—All published by Prentice-Hall, except as indicated: (With Charles R. Coble, Vera Webster, and George S. Fichter) *Prentice-Hall Life Science,* 1980, second edition, 1984; (with C. R. Coble) *Life Science Laboratory Activity Book,* 1980; (with C. R. Coble) *Tests for Prentice-Hall Life Science with Answer Keys,* 1980; (with C. R. Coble) *Prentice-Hall Life Science: Annotated Teacher's Edition,* 1980; (with C. R. Coble and Elaine Murray) *Prentice-Hall Earth Science,* 1981; (with C. R. Coble) *Prentice-Hall Earth Science: Annotated Teacher's Edition,* 1981, second edition, 1984; (with C. R. Coble and Paul Hounshell) *Prentice-Hall Physical Science: Annotated Teacher's Edition,* 1981, second edition, 1984; *A Look Inside: Energy from Fossil Fuels,* (illustrated by Greg King), Raintree, 1983; (with C. R. Coble) *Teaching Science in the Elementary/Middle School,* Wadsworth, in press.

Contributing editor to *Educational Computer,* and contributor of numerous articles to journals including *Science and Children, Educational Research Quarterly,* and *Science Teacher.*

WORK IN PROGRESS: Additional writings for education and science journals; a children's book on childhood fears and anxieties.

RICE, Edward E.   1918-

BRIEF ENTRY: Born in New York, in 1918. A writer and photographer, Rice attended Columbia University and has traveled throughout Asia, Europe, and Latin America. He is the author of over a dozen nonfiction works, many of them of interest to young adults. Through first-hand observations, he records the lifestyle and cultures of the Eastern world in what critics have viewed as an objective yet sensitive and informative approach. An accomplished photographer, Rice's photographs further emphasize the import of his words. As a *New York Times Book Review* critic noted, "He is like a camera with its shutter on 'Time,' ready to record whatever impressions flutter by." For *Mother India's Children: Meeting Today's Generation in India* (Pantheon, 1971), Rice conducted a series of interviews with a sampling of Indian youths. *Library Journal* described the interchanges as "revealing . . . compassionate, knowledgeable analyses."

In *The Ganges: A Personal Encounter* (Four Winds, 1974), Rice delves into the mythical origins and cultural roots of India's sacred river. *Booklist* observed: "This [is] infinitely more than a book about a river; [the author's] vision melds it into a remarkable, arresting portrait of a nation." He has also written a biography on renowned anthropologist Margaret Mead, who was a personal friend, entitled *Margaret Mead: A Portrait* (Harper, 1979). Published by Four Winds, Rice's other young adult books include *The Five Great Religions* (1973), *Marx, Engels and the Workers of the World* (1977), *Ten Religions of the East* (1978), and *Babylon: Next to Nineveh* (1979). *Residence:* New York.

FOR MORE INFORMATION SEE: Contemporary Authors, New Revision Series, Volume 1, Gale, 1981.

(From the Sunday comic strip "Johnny Hazard" by Frank Robbins. Copyright 1944 by King Features Syndicate, Inc.)

ROBBINS, Frank 1917-

PERSONAL: Born September 9, 1917, in Boston, Mass. *Education:* Studied at the Boston Museum of Fine Arts School and the National Academy of Design.

CAREER: Cartoonist and illustrator of books. Author and illustrator of comic strips, Associated Press, 1939-44, King Features Syndicate, 1944—. Writer and contributor of artwork, National Comics. Work represented in exhibitions, including Whitney Museum of American Art, 1956, Corcoran Gallery of Art, 1957, 1958, Toledo Museum of Art, 1957, 1958, National Academy of Design, 1957, 1958, Audubon Artists, 1957, 1958. *Member:* National Cartoonists Society. *Awards, honors:* Rockefeller grant, 1932; National Academy of Design Prize, 1935.

WRITINGS—Comic strips: "Scorchy Smith," Associated Press, 1939-44; "Johnny Hazard," King Features Syndicate, 1944—. Writer for National Comics, including titles such as *Batman, The Flash,* and *The Unknown Soldier.*

Illustrator; juvenile; all written by Howard Liss; all published by Messner: *Football Talk for Beginners,* 1970; *Basketball Talk for Beginners,* 1970; *Hockey Talk for Beginners,* 1973; *Bowling Talk for Beginners,* 1973; *Auto Racing for Beginners,* 1975; *Skiing Talk for Beginners,* 1977. Contributor of artwork for *The Shadow,* National Comics. Also contributor of illustrations to magazines, including *Look, Life, Saturday Evening Post,* and *Cosmopolitan.*

SIDELIGHTS: As a young boy Robbins displayed amazing artistic ability. He won several art scholarships at the age of nine, painted murals for his high school at thirteen, and was awarded a Rockefeller grant by the age of fifteen. Because it was the Depression Era, however, Robbins was unable to continue scholastic training. He moved with his family to New York, looking for work rather than additional schooling. He later recalled: "I can attribute my success today to two scraps of paper. My high school and college diplomas . . . or rather the lack of them! Without them, I went to work at fifteen . . . with them I might have accepted a job as a bank president and gone through life . . . a failure!"

In New York, Robbins worked as an errand boy in an advertising agency until his artistic ability was noticed. He was hired to draw the sketches for the murals of the NBC building, which he undertook until an illness in 1935 forced him to abandon the project.

In 1939, he was asked by Associated Press to take over the "Scorchy Smith" daily comic strip. Under Robbins' hand, the strip flourished so that a Sunday page was added in the 1940s. His popular comic strip was noticed by King Features who asked Robbins to produce an aviation strip for them, and in 1944 "Johnny Hazard" was born.

In the 1960s the "Johnny Hazard" strip met stiff competition, which caused Robbins to work on comic books as well as the strip. He wrote and contributed artwork for such titles as *Batman, The Flash, The Shadow,* and *The Unknown Soldier.*

During the 1970s Robbins branched into another field, illustrating children's books. From 1970 until 1977, he illustrated six sports books written by Howard Liss. He also contributed illustrations to such magazines as *Life, Look* and *Cosmopolitan.*

Besides his comic book work and his illustrations, Robbins has done serious paintings, which have been exhibited at such notable galleries as the Corcoran Gallery in Washington, D.C. and the Whitney and Metropolitan Museums in New York City.

FOR MORE INFORMATION SEE: Pierre Couperie and others, *A History of the Comic Strip,* translated by Eileen B. Hennessy, Crown, 1968; Maurice Horn, editor, *The World Encyclopedia of Comics,* Volume 2, Chelsea House, 1976.

ROSCOE, D(onald) T(homas) 1934-

PERSONAL: Born June 1, 1934, in Manchester, Lancashire, England; son of Thomas (an electrical engineer) and Dorothea Muriel (Jones) Roscoe; married Jean Ann Cambell, August 5, 1961 (divorced, 1975); married Barbara Mary Spark (a university lecturer), August 2, 1975; children: (first marriage) Martin Donald, Brian Douglas. *Education:* Alsager College of Education, teaching certificate, 1958; attending University College of North Wales. *Politics:* Socialist. *Religion:* Agnostic. *Home:* Bwlch y Fron, Gaerwen, Anglesey, Gwynedd LL60 6DT, North Wales, U.K. *Office:* University College of North Wales, Bangor, Gwynedd LL57 2DG, North Wales, U.K.

CAREER: General Post Office, Manchester, England, telephone engineer, 1950-56; schools in Manchester and Stone, teacher of woodworking and physical education, 1958-60; Plas y Brenin, Capel Curig, Gwynedd, North Wales, senior outdoor activity instructor, 1960-64; Loughborough College of Education, Loughborough, Leicestershire, England, 1964-71, and University College of North Wales, Bangor, Gwynedd, 1971-84, lecturer in outdoor pursuits. Fellow of University College of North Wales, 1984. *Military service:* National Service, 1952-54, Royal Electrical and Mechanical Engineers

Barbara and D. T. Roscoe.

(From *Your Book of Camping* by D. T. Roscoe.)

craftsman. *Member:* Climbers Club, Rock and Ice Mountaineering Club, British Canoe Union, Cyclists' Touring Club.

WRITINGS: Llanberis North, edited by C.W.F. Noyce, Climbers Club, 1961, revised and reprinted, edited by John Neill (with photographs by C. Douglas Milner), 1964; *Mountaineering: A Manual for Teachers and Instructors,* Faber, 1976; *Your Book of Camping* (juvenile), Faber, 1980. Also contributor of articles to *Climbers Club Journal* and *Canoeing.*

SIDELIGHTS: "First and foremost I am a mountaineer and do not really see myself as a writer. I have had an interest in mountaineering, particularly rock climbing, since I was about eleven or twelve years old and actually started climbing at the age of fifteen. Since then, I have climbed in many areas of the world and was a founding member of the Rock and Ice Mountaineering Club which was the group of people, headed by Joe Brown, who were instrumental in bringing about a significant leap forward in rock climbing standards and techniques in the British Isles in the 1950s. My work keeps me fit and in touch with the climbing scene and I still climb hard when on form (5b, if that means anything to any one other than British rock climbers).

"My debut into the literary world was almost by chance as I was the only climber around at the time when the guide to Llanberis North (a famous rock climbing area in North Wales) needed a rewriter who had the ability to do most of the climbs and who was prepared to put pen to paper. (A guide book writer's task is a pretty thankless one.) My next book was conceived while working at Plas y Brenin, the national mountaineering course, as there were no textbooks for mountaineering instructors. It seemed that the only solution was for me to write one! This was started as a joint effort, but the co-author failed to produce the goods, hence the long delay before eventual publication under my name. This led on to *Your Book of Camping* as Faber kindly asked me to rewrite it. A children's book was a new and different sort of challenge and one which I really enjoyed. It is my belief that teenagers are capable of much more than most people imagine and with this in mind, I set out to write a book with which they could go and discover camping without adult supervision."

HOBBIES AND OTHER INTERESTS: "Skiing, canoeing, wind surfing, fishing, and my other great love, cycling."

SALZMAN, Yuri

BRIEF ENTRY: Born in the U.S.S.R.; came to the United States in 1976. Salzman began his career in the Soviet Union, where he was an award-winning illustrator, graphic artist, and designer. Among the children's books he has illustrated is Fran Manushkin's *The Tickle Tree,* a story about a squirrel in search of a "Great!" tickle. According to *Publishers Weekly,* ". . . Salzman's sunbright color scenes . . . [increase] the fun." He also illustrated Phyllis Krasilovsky's *The Man Who Entered a Contest,* in which a man enters a cake-baking contest and wins first prize with some most unusual creations. *School Library Journal* stated that Salzman's illustrations "give the tale most of its life and interest," while "lots of detail . . . lends credibility . . . [and] the man's expressive features and movements give him real personality."

Salzman wrote and illustrated the children's book *Hope You're Feeling Better* (Harper, 1979). In the story, a bear named Morry anticipates spending a peaceful summer as a camp counselor but has an accident on a raft trip and winds up in the hospital. During his stay there, Morry worries that everyone will think he is a bad counselor until the campers show their concern with cards and flowers. Salzman is also the reteller and illustrator of *The Three Bears* (Random House, 1980). Other books he has illustrated include: *The Little Hen and the Giant* by Maria Polushkin, *Where Do I Fit In?* by June Noble, *The Fox's Lair* by Ian McMahan, and *The Great Gradepoint Mystery* by Barbara Bartholomew. *Residence:* Hartsdale, N.Y.

SAMPSON, Fay (Elizabeth)   1935-

PERSONAL: Born June 10, 1935, in Plymouth, England; daughter of Edmar Ismail (a member of Royal Marine Staff Band) and Edith Maud (a hotel waitress; maiden name, Cory) Sampson; married Jack Greaves Priestley (a lecturer in religious education), March 30, 1959; children: Mark Alan, Katharine Fay. *Education:* University College of the Southwest, B.A. (with honors), 1956; University of Exeter, certificate in education, 1957. *Politics:* Radical. *Religion:* Christian. *Home:* Christie College, Tedburn St. Mary, Exeter, Devonshire EX6 6AZ, England.

CAREER: Assistant mathematics teacher at high school in Mytholmroyd, England, 1957-58, bilateral school in Nottingham, England, 1959-60, and technical school in Eastwood, England, 1960-61; St. Peter's High School, Exeter, England, part-time assistant mathematics teacher, 1973—, evening class lecturer in writing, 1979—. Volunteer librarian in Zambia, 1962-64; volunteer at work camps in Germany, Greece, France, Jordan, South Africa, and Ireland; organized dramatic readings. Member of international committee of Student Christian Movement, 1956-57; national executive of NALSO (National Association of Labour Student Organizations), 1956-57. *Member:* Social Democratic Party, Methodist Church Council.

WRITINGS—For children: *F.67,* Hamish Hamilton, 1975; *Half a Welcome,* Dobson, 1977; *The Watch on Patterick Fell,* Dobson, 1978, Morrow, 1980; *The Empty House,* Dobson, 1979; *Landfall on Innis Michael* (sequel to *The Watch on Patterick Fell*), Dobson, 1980; *The Hungry Snow,* Dobson, 1980; *The Chains of Sleep,* Dobson, 1981; *Sus,* Dobson, 1982; *Pangur Ban, The White Cat,* Lion, 1983; *Jenny and the Wreckers,* Hamish Hamilton, 1984; *Finnglas of the Horses,* Lion, 1985; *Chris and the Dragon,* Gollancz, 1985; *May Day,* RMEP, 1985.

FAY SAMPSON

WORK IN PROGRESS: A book on Pentecost for a series on festivals; two more volumes in the "Pangur Ban" fantasy series.

SIDELIGHTS: "I was a solitary child, taking pleasure in reading and long walks with a dog on the hills above the fishing village where I lived. I loved writing, but no one ever suggested that I might earn a living by it. That had to wait until I had returned from Zambia and my younger child was starting school. Having made a break in my teaching career, I had to face the question, 'What next?' It was my husband and the late Sidney Robbins, an enthusiast for children's literature in education, who encouraged me to take writing seriously.

"I spent five very enjoyable years writing books that almost, but not quite, got published. I finally struck lucky with *F.67.* At first I wrote out of a deep love of my native west-country, its landscape, history, and legends. But success came when I turned to the present and the near future (I regard *F.67* and *The Watch on Patterick Fell* not as science fiction, but as social fantasy—shaking the kaleidoscope of the present and seeing what new patterns might emerge from the chaos). I still have a strong attachment to the west-country, particularly its Celtic past, and this is reflected in my more recent books. But however old the theme, it must still speak to today.

"Every week of the year I come across a news item or a snippet of history that would make a good book. But nineteen times out of twenty I don't want to write it. It is too rounded, complete. For me the essential motivation in writing is curiosity. 'What would it be like if . . .?' 'What if they *had* . . .?' Or just 'Why?' My books are an exploration of these questions. For instance, *F.67* began with the influx of Ugandan Asian refugees when I visited one of their camps and asked 'What would it be like if my own children were put into this situation?' But if I have done my work well, the books themselves will raise more questions than they answer, so that at the end the reader is just beginning his own adventure of the mind."

HOBBIES AND OTHER INTERESTS: Walking, sailing, travel, Celtic history, mythology, attending plays. "I like to be learning something new all the time."

SAUL, (E.) Wendy 1946-

PERSONAL: Born September 10, 1946, in Paterson, N.J.; daughter of Sylvan A. (a merchant) and Rosalie (a teacher; maiden name, Rappoport) Saul; married Alan R. Newman (a chemist), July 27, 1976; children: Matthew A., Eliza G. *Education:* Knox College, B.A. (with honors), 1968; University of Chicago, M.S.T., 1969; University of Wisconsin—Madison, Ph.D., 1981.

CAREER: Junior High School 22M, New York City, teacher, 1969-1971; Grand Street Settlement House, New York City, director of education, 1971-1973; University of Wisconsin, Madison, Wis., supervisor, instructor, and administrative assistant, 1973-1976; University of Pennsylvania, Philadelphia, Pa., research associate, 1977-1979; Empire State College, State University of New York, Stony Brook, N.Y., assistant professor of English, 1982; University of Maryland, Catonsville, Maryland, teacher of children's literature, adolescent literature, and the reading/language arts sequence, 1985—. Active in anti-nuclear groups, feminist organizations, and local history projects. *Member:* International Research Society for Children's Literature, American Educational Research Association, Children's Literature Association.

WENDY SAUL

WRITINGS: Butcher, Baker, Cabinetmaker: Photographs of Women at Work (photographs by Abigail Heyman), Crowell, 1978; *Science Fare: Books, Toys and Things to Do With Kids,* Harper, 1986. Member of editorial board, *The Advocate,* 1983—. Contributor of articles to numerous periodicals, including *Children's Literature Quarterly* and *School Library Journal.*

WORK IN PROGRESS: Articles for *Children's Literature and Education.*

SIDELIGHTS: "Writing allows me to be paid for what I spend most of my time doing—reading and thinking about my world. My new project, for example, is an effort to actively participate with people who are excited by and committed to science. It's also a way to talk with other parents of young children— I imagine an audience of interested friends. I am similarly motivated in my academic work: *Butcher, Baker, Cabinetmaker: Photographs of Women at Work,* for instance, was an attempt to share a vision of women with children and to frame some excellent photographs with words.

"I write for children, and about children, because I am interested in the way they make sense of things. I am also interested in the ways adults work to turn children into versions of themselves.

"Writing is also frightening to me. Until a project is complete, I doubt that it will ever be finished. I worry that it will not be well-received. I worry that I'll end up disagreeing with my own arguments. I worry that I'll never get another thing published. I worry that I'll run out of excuses for not cleaning my house. To date, my fears have not been realized."

RONALD SEARLE

SEARLE, Ronald (William Fordham) 1920-

PERSONAL: Born March 3, 1920, in Cambridge, England; son of William James and Nellie (Hunt) Searle; married Kaye Webb (divorced, 1967); married Monica Koenig (a theatre designer), 1967; children: (first marriage) Kate, John. *Education:* Attended Cambridge School of Art, 1933-39. *Agents:* Tessa Sayle, 11 Jubilee Pl., London SW3 3TE, England; John Locke, 15 East 76th St., New York, N.Y. 10021.

CAREER: Graphic artist, cartoonist, designer, and animator, beginning in 1935. First work published in *Cambridge Daily News* and *Granta,* 1935-39; creator of cartoon series featuring "St. Trinian's," 1941-53; cartoonist for national publications, 1946—; special features artist for major magazines, including *Life, Holiday,* and occasional cover artist for *New Yorker,* 1955—; film designer, 1957—. Editorial director, Perpetua Books, 1951-62; designer of commemorative medals for the French Mint, 1974—, and British Art Medal Society, 1983—. *Exhibitions:* Work has appeared in numerous one-man shows, including Leicester Galleries, London, England, 1948, 1950, 1954, and 1957; Kraushaar Gallery, New York, N.Y., 1959; Blanchini Gallery, New York, N.Y. 1963; Third Biennale, Tolentino, Italy, 1965; Wolfgang Gurlitt Museum, Linz, Austria, 1966; Galerie La Pochade, Paris, France, 1966-69, and 1971; Art Alliance Gallery, Philadelphia, Pa., 1967; Galerie Gurlitt, Munich, West Germany, 1967-76; Galerie Obere Zaune, Zurich, Switzerland, 1968; Konsthallen, Soedertaelje, Sweden, 1969; Rizzoli Gallery, New York, N.Y., 1969-81; Galerie Rivolta, Lausanne, Switzerland, 1972, 1974, and 1978; Bibliothèque Nationale retrospective, Paris, 1973; Galerie Wuerthle, Vienna, Austria, 1973; Galerie Carmen Casse, Paris,

1975-77; Prussian National Gallery retrospective, Berlin-Dahlem, 1976; Galerie Bartsch and Chariau, Munich, 1981. Work is also represented in the permanent collections of museums, including The Imperial War Museum, London, England, British Museum, London, England, and Victoria and Albert Museum, London, England; Bibliothèque Nationale, Paris; Cooper-Hewitt Museum, New York, N.Y.; Stadt Museum, Munich; Prussian National Gallery, Berlin-Dahlem; and Wilhelm-Busch Museum, Hannover, West Germany. *Military service:* British Army, Royal Engineers, 1939-46; Japanese prisoner of war, 1942-45; Allied Force Headquarters (Department of Psychological Warfare), Port Said Operations, 1956.

MEMBER: Alliance Graphique Internationale, Garrick Club (London). *Awards, honors:* Academy Award nomination, American Academy of Motion Picture Arts and Sciences, 1954, for film "On the Twelfth Day"; eleven awards, including Stratford (Ontario) Festival award, International Film Festival award, and Art Directors Club of Los Angeles medal, for animated film "Energetically Yours," 1958-59; Art Directors Club of Philadelphia Award, 1959; Gold Medal, III Biennale, Tolentino, 1965; Reuben Award from National Cartoonists Society of America, 1966; Prix de la Critique Belge, 1968; Prix d'Humour, Festival d'Avignon, 1971; Médaille de la ville d'Avignon, 1971; Grand Prix de l'Humour Noir "Grandville," 1971; Prix Internationale Charles Huard de dessin de presse, 1972; La Monnaie de Paris Medal, 1974.

WRITINGS: Forty Drawings, foreword by Frank Kendon, Cambridge University Press, 1946, Macmillan, 1947; *Le Nouveau ballet anglaise,* Editions Montbrun, 1947; *Hurrah for St. Trinian's!, and Other Lapses,* foreword by D. B. Wyndham

Lewis, Macdonald & Co., 1948; *The Female Approach, with Masculine Sidelights,* foreword by Max Beerbohm, Macdonald & Co., 1950; *Back to the Slaughterhouse and Other Ugly Moments,* Macdonald & Co., 1951; *Weil noch das Laempchen glueht,* Diogenes, 1952; *Souls in Torment,* preface and short dirge by C. Day Lewis, Perpetua, 1953; *Medisances,* Editions Neuf, 1953; *The Female Approach,* foreword by Malcolm Muggeridge, Knopf, 1954; *The Rakes's Progress,* Perpetua, 1955, new edition published as *The Rake's Progress: Some Immoral Tales,* Dobson, 1968; *Merry England,* Perpetua, 1956, Knopf, 1957.

(Editor and author of introduction) *The Biting Eye of André Francois,* Perpetua, 1960; *The Penguin Ronald Searle,* Penguin, 1960; (editor) Henri Perruchot, *Toulouse-Lautrec: A Definitive Biography,* translated by Humphrey Hare, Perpetua, 1960, World, 1961; (editor) H. Perruchot, *Cézanne: A Definitive Biography,* translated by H. Hare, Perpetua, 1961, World, 1962; *Which Way Did He Go?,* Perpetua, 1961, World, 1962; *From Frozen North to Filthy Lucre,* remarks by Groucho Marx and commentaries by Jane Clapperton, Viking, 1964; *Searle in the Sixties,* Penguin, 1964; *Pardong M'sieur: Paris et autres,* Denoël, 1965; *Searle's Cats,* Dobson, 1967; Greene, 1968;

The Square Egg, Greene, 1968, reprinted, Penguin, 1980; *Take One Toad: A Book of Ancient Remedies,* Dobson, 1968; *Hello—Where Did All the People Go?,* Weidenfeld & Nicholson, 1969, Greene, 1970; *Hommage à Toulouse-Lautrec,* introduction by Roland Topor, Editions Empreinte, 1969, published in England as *The Second Coming of Toulouse-Lautrec,* Weidenfeld & Nicolson, 1970; *Filles de Hambourg,* J.-J. Pauvert, 1969, published in England as *Secret Sketchbook: The Back Streets of Hamburg,* Weidenfeld & Nicholson, 1970.

The Addict: A Terrible Tale, Greene, 1971; *More Cats,* Dobson, 1975, Greene, 1976; *Gilbert and Sullivan: A Selection from Ronald Searle's Original Drawings from the Animated Feature Film "Dick Deadeye,"* Entercom Productions, 1975; *Searle's Zoodiac,* Dobson, 1977, Pantheon, 1978; *Ronald Searle* (monograph), Deutsch, 1978, Mayflower, 1979; *The King of Beasts and Other Creatures,* Lane, 1980, published in the United States as *The Situation Is Hopeless,* Viking, 1981; *Ronald Searle's Big Fat Cat Book,* Little, Brown, 1982; *Winespeak: Ronald Searle's Wicked World of Winetasting,* Souvenir Press, 1983, Harper, 1984; *Ronald Searle in Perspective,* New English Library, 1984, Atlantic Monthly Press, 1985.

Bye Bye Blues. ■ (From *Ronald Searle's Big Fat Cat Book* by Ronald Searle. Illustrated by the author.)

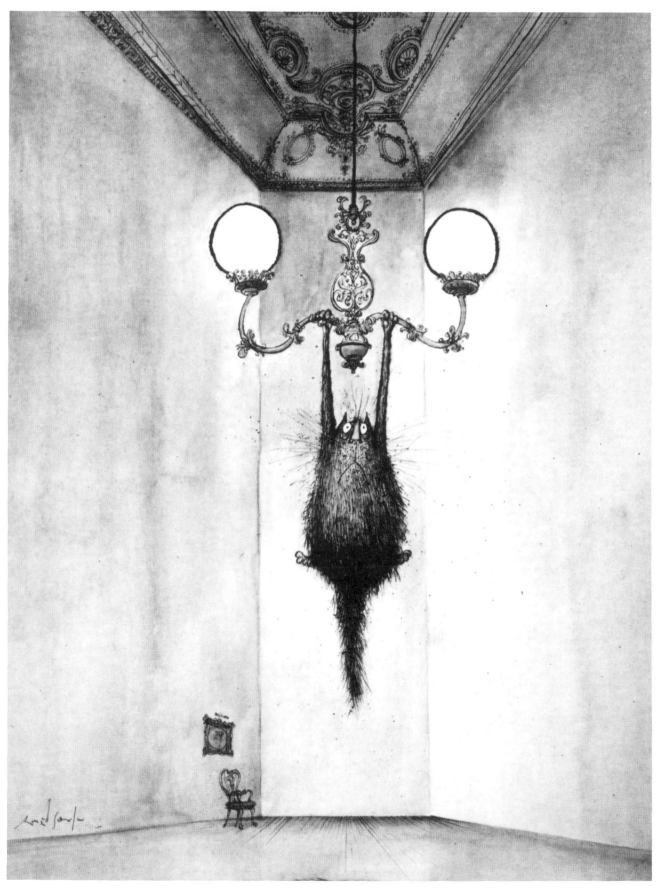

He's very highly strung. . . . ■ (From *Ronald Searle's Big Fat Cat Book* by Ronald Searle. Illustrated by the author.)

(From *Paris! Paris!* by Irwin Shaw. Illustrated by Ronald Searle.)

Co-author: (with Kaye Webb) *Paris Sketchbook,* Saturn Press, 1950, new and revised edition, Perpetua, 1957, Braziller, 1958; (with Timothy Shy [pseudonym of D. B. Wyndham Lewis]) *The Terror of St. Trinian's; or, Angela's Prince Charming,* Parrish, 1952, reprinted, Ian Henry Publications, 1976; (with Geoffrey Willans) *Down with Skool! A Guide to School Life for Tiny Pupils and Their Parents,* Parrish, 1953, Vanguard, 1954, reprinted, May Fair Books, 1968; (with K. Webb) *Looking at London, and People Worth Meeting,* News Chronicle (London), 1953; (with G. Willans) *How to Be Topp: A Guide to Sukcess for Tiny Pupils, Including All There Is to Kno about Space,* Vanguard, 1954, reprinted, Penguin, 1970; (with G. Willans) *Whizz for Atomms: A Guide to Survival in the 20th Century for Fellow Pupils, Their Doting Maters, Pompous Paters, and Any Others Who Are Interested,* Parrish, 1956, published in America as *Molesworth's Guide to the Atomic Age,* Vanguard, 1957.

(With G. Willans) *The Dog's Ear Book, with Four Lugubrious Verses,* Crowell, 1958; (with G. Willans) *The Compleet Molesworth* (includes *Down with Skool!, How to Be Topp, Whizz for Atomms,* and *Back in the Jug Agane),* Parrish, 1958; (with Alex Atkinson) *The Big City; or, The New Mayhew,* Perpetua, 1958, Braziller, 1959; (with A. Atkinson) *USA for Beginners,* Perpetua, 1959, published in America as *By Rocking Chair Across America,* Funk, 1959; (with G. Willans) *Back in the Jug Agane,* Vanguard, 1960; (with A. Atkinson) *Russia for Beginners: By Rocking Chair Across Russia,* World, 1960; (with K. Webb) *Refugees, 1960,* Penguin, 1960; (with

A. Atkinson) *Escape from the Amazon!,* Perpetua, 1964; (with Allen Andrews and William Richardson) *Those Magnificent Men in Their Flying Machines; or, How I Flew from London to Paris in 25 Hours, 11 Minutes,* Norton, 1965; (with Heinz Huber) *Anatomie eines Adlers,* Desch, 1966, translation by Constantine Fitz Gibbon published as *Haven't We Met Before Somewhere? Germany from the Inside and Out,* Viking, 1966; (with Kildare Dobbs) *The Great Fur Opera: Animals of the Hudson's Bay Company, 1670-1970,* Greene, 1970; (with Irwin Shaw) *Paris! Paris!,* Harcourt, 1977.

Illustrator: W. Henry Brown, *Co-operation in a University Town,* Co-operative Printing Society, 1939; Ronald Hastain, *White Coolie,* Hodder & Stoughton, 1947; Douglas Goldring, *Life Interests,* Macdonald & Co., 1948; W. E. Stanton Hope, *Tanker Fleet,* Anglo-Saxon Petroleum Co., 1948; Gillian Olivier, *Turn But a Stone,* Hodder & Stoughton, 1949; Audrey Hilton, *This England 1946-1949,* Turnstile Press, 1949; *Meet Yourself on Sunday* (compiled by staff of Mass-Observation), Naldrett Press, 1949; *Meet Yourself at the Doctor's* (compiled by staff of Mass-Observation), Naldrett Press, 1949; Patrick Campbell, *A Long Drink of Cold Water,* Falcon Press, 1949; Noel Langley, *The Inconstant Moon,* Arthur Barker, 1949; P. Campbell, *An Irishman's Diary,* Cassell, 1950; P. Campbell, *A Short Trot with a Cultured Mind,* Falcon Press, 1950; Oliver Philpott, *Stolen Journey,* Hodder & Stoughton, 1950; Russell Braddon, *The Piddingtons,* Laurie, 1950; P. Campbell, *Life in Thin Slices,* Falcon Press, 1951; Harry Hearson and John C. Trewin, *An Evening at the Larches,* Elek, 1951; R. Braddon, *The Naked Island* (includes drawings made in Singapore and River Kwai prison camps by Searle), Laurie, 1952; Winifred Ellis, *London—So Help Me!,* Macdonald & Co., 1952; Frank Carpenter, *Six Animal Plays,* Methuen, 1953; Denys Parsons, *It Must Be True,* Macdonald & Co., 1953; Richard Haydn, *The Journal of Edwin Carp,* Hamish Hamilton, 1954; P. Campbell, *Patrick Campbell's Omnibus,* Hulton Press, 1954; Geoffrey Gorer, *Modern Types,* Cresset Press, 1955; Reuben Ship, *The Investigator: A Narrative Dialogue,* Sidgwick & Jackson, 1956; K. Webb, compiler, *The St. Trinian's Story: The Whole Ghastly Dossier,* contributions by Siriol Hugh-Jones and others, London House & Maxwell, 1959; Christopher Fry, *A Phoenix Too Frequent: A Comedy,* Oxford University Press, 1959; *Anger of Achilles: Homer's Iliad,* translated by Robert Graves, Doubleday, 1959.

Ted Patrick and Silas Spitzer, *Great Restaurants of America,* Lippincott, 1960; Charles Dickens, *A Christmas Carol,* World, 1961; C. Dickens, *Great Expectations* (juvenile), edited by Doris Dickens, abridged edition, Norton, 1962; C. Dickens, *Oliver Twist* (juvenile), edited by D. Dickens, abridged edition, Norton, 1962; James Thurber, *The Thirteen Clocks [and] The Wonderful O* (juvenile), Penguin, 1962; Lady Isobel Morag Barnett, *Exploring London* (juvenile), Ebury Press in association with G. Rainbird, 1965; Rudolf E. Raspe and others, *The Adventures of Baron Munchausen,* introduction by S. J. Perelman, Pantheon, 1969; Jack Davies, Ken Annakin, and A. Andrews, *Those Daring Young Men in Their Jaunty Jalopies: Monte Carlo or Bust!* (young adult), Putnam, 1969 (published in England as *Monte Carlo or Bust! Those Daring Young Men in Their Jaunty Jalopies,* Dobson, 1969); Leslie Bricusse, adapter, *Scrooge* (juvenile), Cinema Center Films, 1970; *Dick Deadeye,* Harcourt, 1975; George Rainbird, *The Subtle Alchemist,* M. Joseph, 1973; Tom Lehrer, *Too Many Songs,* Pantheon, 1981.

Films designed: "John Gilpin," British Film Institute, 1951; "On the Twelfth Day," Bahamian Films, 1954; "Energetically Yours," Esso, 1957; "Germany," Sueddeutschen Rundfunk Television, 1960; "The King's Breakfast," Montague

Productions, 1963; "Those Magnificent Men in Their Flying Machines" (animated sequences), Twentieth Century-Fox, 1964; "Monte Carlo or Bust" (animated sequences), Paramount, 1968; "Scrooge" (animated sequences), Cinema Center Films, 1970; "Dick Deadeye; or, Duty Done," Intercontinental Releasing, 1975.

Also author of television script, "Toulouse-Lautrec," networked by the British Broadcasting Corp. in 1961.

ADAPTATIONS—Movies; all based on Searle's St. Trinian creation; all produced by Frank Launder and Sidney Gilliat: "The Belles of St. Trinian's," starring Alastair Sim, British Lion Film Production, 1954; "Blue Murder at St. Trinian's," starring Joyce Grenfell, Terry Thomas, and A. Sim, John Harvel Productions, 1957; "The Pure Hell of St. Trinian's" starring Cecil Parker and J. Grenfell, Vale Film Productions, 1960; "The Great St. Trinian's Train Robbery," starring Frankie Howerd and Dora Bryan, Braywild Films, 1966; "Wildcats of St. Trinian's," starring Sheila Hancock and Michael Hordern, Wildcat Film Productions, 1980.

WORK IN PROGRESS: To the Kwai—and Back: War Drawings 1939-1945 for Collins (London), contains 1,950 war and prison drawings and the story behind them.

SIDELIGHTS: **March 3, 1920.** Searle was born in Cambridge, England. "My childhood was unremarkable apart from the fact that I was born and brought up in one of the most beautiful and ancient university towns in England.

"I am left-handed, [and] I drew before I could write legibly.... I swapped comics in the school yard ... copies of 'Comic Cuts,' 'Film Fun' and 'Chips'—the most desirable titles at that time. The more pictures there were to a page and the less text, the happier I was.... My imagination was almost entirely visual and only faintly literary.

"However, my great love was books. I devoured everything in our town library, beginning with the infant shelves and graduating at the age of twelve to the adult library. My thirst was insatiable. I frequently took out five books in a day; making my way through A-B: *British Butterflies in Colour* . . . to

"Send a few bottles up to my room, Miss Wilson, they will do for the old girls' reunion." ■ (From the movie "The Belles of St. Trinian's," based on Searle's characters. Starring Alastair Sim and Joyce Grenfell. Produced by British Lion Film. 1954.)

Out-of-touch unicorn unaware that it is a myth. ■ (From *The Situation Is Hopeless* by Ronald Searle. Illustrated by the author.)

Y-Z: *Zululand, The Journal of My Encounters in*. . . . By the time I was thirteen, I wanted my own library and I began to haunt the secondhand bookstalls. . . . I earned, begged, and scraped together every penny I could and within five years I had accumulated some five hundred volumes for a few penn[ies] apiece. At the outset of my buying, one Saturday, I tumbled onto two or three volumes about caricature. . . . One of these volumes was Spielmann's *History of Punch*. I had already decided I would be either an artist or an archaeologist and with juvenile confidence I now added the intention of being a 'Punch' cartoonist.'' [''Ronald Searle Writes from France,'' *Cartoonist Profiles*, fall, 1969.[1]]

1933. ''That Autumn I enrolled for evening classes in the Cambridge Art School. This had caused some argument between my mother and father for the fee was 7s.6d. a term (about $1.50 then), and we couldn't afford it. But the money was scraped together somehow. I can guess now that my mother probably put a thicker piece of cardboard in her shoe.

''I was obsessed with drawing, and scratched away incessantly. I scrambled through the day at school . . . and then rushed off at six in the evening [to Cambridge Art School] for three hours of art.''[1]

1934. ''[I] graduated from the plaster Discobolos into the life class, and painfully shaded my way through several years of floppy-breasted nudes with blue toes and purple legs. . . . Side by side with my art-school work I scribbled comic drawings.''[1]

1935. "When I was fifteen, the cartoonist of the local paper [the *Cambridge Daily News*] left for London and . . . I stuck a cartoon through [their] letterbox, utterly confident that the editor would take it, and that this would solve an important economic problem for me. He did take the cartoon and asked me for more at (about \$2.00 then) a week. This represented all the drawing materials I needed, a bit for the family and something over for me. I continued with those weekly cartoons . . . until the war, almost without a break. They were dreadful, but they taught me how to draw for reproduction."[1]

1938. "The local council awarded me a full-time art scholarship, and I sweated away for over a year, as a 'real, full-time artist.' [I] completely saturated myself in anatomy, perspective, history of costume, architecture, life drawing, and all the subjects required for passing the Min. of Ed. Drawing Diploma. . . . I carried a sketchbook day and night because I couldn't stop drawing."[1]

1939. "I missed failure by 2%, but achieved the solid Bolshi-Academic Diploma characteristic of Cambridge in the '30's.

"Also in 1939, I found on a secondhand bookstall, a small monograph by Marcel Ray on the work of George Grosz . . . and [it] changed my artistic direction. . . . I had known little about Grosz until I got the Marcel Ray book. I had seen the occasional [Munich] album from the '20's. . . . But now he fitted into place for me. Grosz exposed the rotting military mind; the filth of war and the stench that lingered after it— and, how he could draw! . . . I cannot say that I ever consciously had the desire to copy anybody. But if I have been influenced, it is by Grosz and Rowlandson. . . . Above all I admired 'Roly' Rowlandson with his wit, genius [and] ability to handle line.

"I had already established a pedestal for Picasso as the foremost of my living heroes. . . . Forain I marvelled over . . . and he had joined the line with Gillray, and Cruikshank, as my self-appointed guardian angels. Goya . . . was one of my gods, and I still day-dream that one day the Prado will drop me a note during a period of stocktaking, to say that they wonder whether I might be interested in accepting a couple of drawings of which they have duplicates.

"If any one influenced me in my work it was on the basis of draughtsmanship, rather than painting. I saw in line then, as I still mainly do now."[1]

Searle enlisted in the army and served with the Royal Engineers. "Then the army put me into a camouflage unit." ["The Emasculation of American Humour," *Saturday Review,* November 23, 1957.[2]] "During those years I never stopped drawing. . . . I documented almost every move I made, from my first miserable night in the army to the other side of the world and back."[1]

1942-45. "That was a turning point for me. . . . I was captured [by the Japanese] when Singapore fell, and for four years I stayed a prisoner, drawing like mad. You learn how to feel things in a prison-camp, and I was lucky enough to learn how to draw what I feel."[2]

"This part of my life was perhaps the most formative. At art school I had learned the academic structure of things and in the army I was able—or rather forced—to adapt and apply it. I wanted to draw things I saw about me and to register the impact of a new life. I was a rather *precious* art student who had never left home and who, within a year or so, was slung

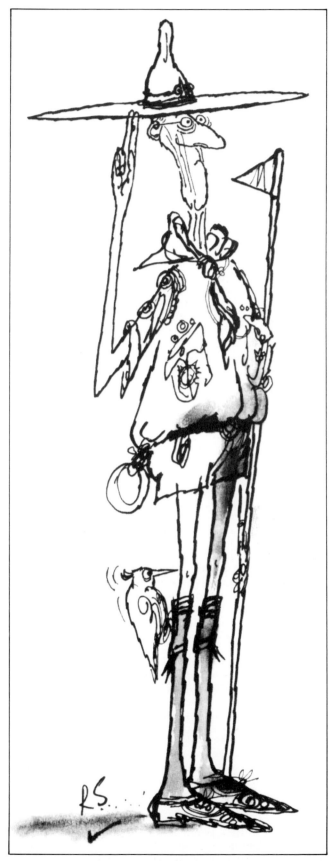

One of the Peewit Patrol's stanchest, and indeed oldest, members. ■ (From *From Frozen North to Filthy Lucre* by Ronald Searle. Illustrated by the author.)

into a Japanese prison. Anyway, it boils down to the fact that by the time I was thrown onto my own resources after the war, I was able to come to grips with most things.'' [Henry C. Pitz, ''Ronald Searle—British Graphic Artist,'' *American Artist,* September, 1955.[3]]

''After four rough years, I had enough experience of humanity to provide me with a measuring-stick for a considerable part of my life. I also had the facility of seven years of practical application with my drawings. . . . I had been isolated from the world . . . but had also developed in that isolation.

''When I came out of . . . prison in 1945, . . . I was faced with earning my living. I had nothing but fantasy in my head, and a small army pension between me and the post-war wolves at the door while I was getting rehabilitated and thinking about long term plans for the future. It seemed to me that the only fast and easy way of keeping myself fed was to sell cartoons. So I sold cartoons. This I rapidly discovered needed no particular ability apart from being able to communicate a personal way of looking at things; and apart from having enough nose to smell out the flavour of what was going on and putting it to use. Coming as I did from an atmosphere of stinking cells, wasted bodies and grim humour, my humour was 'black.' But so was the post-war climate of rationed England, and my work found a ready market there. I cannot say that I ever thought of cartooning as an ultimate career. . . . I wanted to draw, and this was one way of being able to get some of the disgust I felt for human behavior into print.''[1]

1946. Searle published his first book, *Forty Drawings,* a selection from his three hundred war drawings exhibited at the Cambridge School of Art. He married writer and editor, Kaye Webb, with whom he collaborated on several books. He also started contributing to numerous magazines and newspapers, including weekly drawings for ''Punch.'' ''At that point I became a part-time cartoonist. I still am. . . . To sell a sketch was a pleasure because it meant a little less economic worry and more freedom to explore. But if I had not sold, I still would not have stopped [drawing]. . . . It was a compulsion.''[1]

''I cannot tell you how I get cartoon ideas. A lot of artists have attempted to describe it, but the process still remains vague. Mind-Wandering-With-a-Purpose is, I suppose, as close as one can get to it—picking a subject as a starting point, turning it upside down and thumping it like a lump of dough. My cartoons rely more on their pictorial content than on the caption, although of course both are integrated.

''When I have the conception, I start to work the drawing out in detail in pencil on the paper or board on which the final drawing is to be made. When I have brought it to the point where the composition is clearly enough planned, I work quickly and freely over it in pen. Almost invariably . . . I use the same pen with which I write my letters and scribble my notes, consequently I am hardly conscious of the material I am using and I find I am left with an almost effortless [technical] bridge between the idea and the execution. The stain which I use in my pen is not immediately waterproof and allows me to spit on my finger and smudge in my half tone straight from the pen line.

''If I make a mistake I prefer to scrap the drawing rather than patch it and sometimes do as many as three finished drawings before I am satisfied that one is close enough to what I had hoped to achieve.

''. . . I use a sketchbook which I carry around with me—although not as frequently as I did. Once I have sketched a

thing I rarely refer to it again as I can usually retain it in my head. . . . I prefer to work directly into the finished picture whenever possible rather than working from notes.

''I had a very firm academic training which I feel responsible for my feeling of *freedom*. It is worth having to throw away.''[3]

Aside from being a cartoonist, Searle illustrated countless books, either his or others. ''If I am sent a story to illustrate to which I may have committed myself without reading and then find that I do not like it, no matter how many hours I struggle I cannot do my best work. . . . Before I can start drawing I need to picture quite clearly in my head the complete *feeling* of the finished drawing . . . and I usually can tell before I make the first strokes whether it is likely to be successful in the final execution.''[3]

1957. First trip to America. He spent five months in Hollywood working on ''On the Twelfth Day,'' an experimental animated film. ''This was my first trip over to the States, and I must say that I . . . had . . . one of the finest working periods of my life. . . . I detect a sort of marrying between the American and European styles. A great man like Saul Steinberg is an example. This is fine for him; the danger lies in the pseudo-Steinberg, the Steinberg-imitators. Fortunately, I personally am left handed, so a lot of people cannot draw my way. And if too many left-handed cartoonists do appear, so that my way becomes a rat race, I'll start using my feet. . . .''[2]

1958-59. Searle was invited by the United Nations High Commission for Refugees to gather material on refugees' conditions throughout the world. From that experience he created his book, *Refugees.*

1960. Covered the Eichmann trial and the U.S. Presidential election for *Life* magazine. ''Nixon's nose is an absolute treasure. If he becomes President he will be popular with the cartoonists. Kennedy's features are too balanced. All you have to work with is the hair. It took me the better part of a week before I could get the hang of his face.'' [''Seeing the Bright Side of the Campaign,'' *Life,* October 31, 1960.[4]]

''I have been fascinated for years that this huge country should be willing to tolerate such a lack of sharp political cartooning. . . . Part of the reason may lie in the want of graphic tradition. It was in eighteenth century [Europe] that Hogarth, Gillray, and Cruikshank really mastered the art of satirical drawings. . . . These men went beyond what would probably be permissible in England today, but we still remember them and try, to an extent, to come up to their standard of power and wit. The idea of a cartoon, roughly, is to sum up in nine or ten perfectly drawn lines a very complex situation; as all the political situations are, by tearing off the masks and the conventions with which public figures invariably conceal their enterprises. American [cartoonists] seem to shy away from the all-out attack which this sort of comment requires, and so [they] have never built up any traditions of it.''[2]

''. . . An artist with a strong mind and a strong line can be a great national asset. He can make people understand and feel things that they never could expect to understand or feel by reading the full newspaper accounts or the government reports.''

''A caricature must be executed with the dexterity of a surgeon and the intention of a butcher.

''To caricature is the art of making a thrust into the victim's ribs while he or she is still admiring the sword.

Ronald Searle, auto-caricature, 1966.

"To caricature is the art of distorting an image to make it more real." [Gilles Neret, "L'aimable Cruaute," *Connaissance des Arts,* June, 1979.[5]]

1961. Moved to Paris. "Here are the world's best cartoonists: Sine, Copi, Topor, Desclozeaux.... It is in Paris that the art of drawing is alive." ["Nouvelles des arts," *L'oeil,* November, 1974.[6]]

He worked in Paris between trips all over the world from East Berlin to Alaska. During that period, Searle produced large untitled pen and ink drawings which he regarded as a culminating point of his career in graphic work. "I had been seeking a way of 'anatomizing' the character and behaviour of people in our own curious and suspended times. [After] a period of fumbling I feel I am beginning to state a little of what those feelings are. [Those drawings] are meant to be satirical, and in the best sense, rather uncompromising.... The frailty of human character is my mushroom bed, or occasionally my mistletoe bough.... [Those] drawings could be described not so much as 'anatomies' as 'decapitations'.... Their slightly monumental scale enables them to speak louder than some of my other work. But whatever they say—I still like people!" [G. S. Whittet, "Ronald Searle Satirist," *Studio,* March, 1963.[7]]

1966. "In 1966, I set out with three main themes as subjects: *Cats, Birds,* and *People.* Subsidiary themes, such as *Pigs,* and *Snails* crept in soon after.... I do not attempt to force ideas, but rather to let them drift inconsequentially—and frequently into a dead end.

"I work with no fixed market in mind. Some ideas may be expressed in lithography, others as large watercolours, others in pen....

"The only factor I watch is: that whatever I do is thought of as an *international* idea...."[1]

1967. Searle's marriage with Kaye Webb ended in divorce. He then married Monica Koenig, an artist and designer for the ballet.

1973. Searle was the first living foreign artist to have a major exhibition at the Bibliotheque National, Paris, France.

1977. Moved, with his wife, to a mountain village in the South of France.

1978. In his introduction to the book, *Ronald Searle,* Henning Bock pointed out that Searle's view on drawings was changing and that: "Searle [was] no longer interested in mocking individuals."

Searle has been a versatile and prolific artist for many years. He has been working as a cartoonist, graphic artist, illustrator, designer, and animator. He has dredged up ideas from many personal and outside experiences, and always preserved his freedom to explore further.

"To me a line is something which one can explore endlessly, and which keeps me in a constant feeling of excitement and adventure. I know I shall never live long enough to say and do all I want in line. I can only hope to get up each day, bursting to push the exploration a little further.... If satisfaction with one's work creeps in, the time has come to give up and take up prostitution. A sure sign that there is still hope is when one is miserable at not having met one's own demands.

"The hand is feeble and the artist has still to express with exactitude what his brain conjures up. Some day it may be possible."[1]

FOR MORE INFORMATION SEE: American Artist, September, 1955; *Vogue,* November 1, 1957; *Saturday Review,* November 23, 1957; Bertha E. Miller and others, compilers, *Illustrators of Children's Books: 1946-1956,* Horn Book, 1958; *Life,* October 31, 1960; *Studio,* March, 1963; *Graphis,* Volume 19, number 109, 1963; *Idea,* number 78, 1966; *Les Nouvelles Litteraires,* December, 1966; *Les Lettres Francaises,* December 22, 1966, November 15, 1967; *La Quinzaine Litteraire,* December, 1967; *Library Journal,* June 1, 1969; *Cartoonist Profiles,* fall, 1969; *Le Monde,* January 3, 1970, February 2, 1973; *Natural History,* June, 1971; *Opus,* January, 1972; *London Times,* February 12, 1973, May 8, 1973, November 24, 1978; *Times Literary Supplement,* April 6, 1973, June 15, 1973; *International Herald Tribune,* February 17, 1973; *L'oeil,* November, 1974; "A Step in the Jungle" (documentary), BBC-TV, 1975; *New Statesman,* November 17, 1978; *Ronald Searle* (monograph), Deutsch, 1978, Mayflower, 1979; *Connaissance des Arts,* June, 1979; *Graphis 36,* 1980/81; *Quest,* March, 1981; *New York Times Book Review,* March 8, 1981; William Feaver, *Masters of Caricature,* Knopf, 1981; Steven Heller, *Man Bites Man: Two Decades of Satiric Art,* A & W, 1981; *Town and Country,* May, 1983; *Ronald Searle in Perspective,* New English Library, 1984, Atlantic Monthly Press, 1985.

But still I dream that somewhere there must be
The spirit of a child that waits for me.
—Bayard Taylor

When I am grown to man's estate
I shall be very proud and great,
And tell the other girls and boys
Not to meddle with my toys.
—Robert Louis Stevenson

SEIDEN, Art(hur)

BRIEF ENTRY: Born in Brooklyn, N.Y. Painter, and illustrator of children's books. A graduate of Queens College, Seiden also studied art at the Art Students' League and elsewhere. His artwork has been exhibited in one-man and group shows, including those at the National Academy of Design, and is represented in the Kerlan Collection of the University of Minnesota as well as in other public collections. Seiden has also been a guest instructor at New York City Community College. Among his numerous illustrated works for young people is John Randolph's *Fishing Basics. Booklist* found his illustrations for the book "well executed," while *School Library Journal* observed, "Seiden's clear sketches are a useful addition." Similar books he has illustrated include *Bicycling Basics* by Tim Wilhelm and Glenda Wilhelm and *Computer Programming Basics* by Lawrence Stevens. Among Seiden's other illustrated works are: *The Noisy Clock Shop* by Jean Horton Berg, *The Big and Little Book of ABC's* by Ann McFerran, *The Airplane Book* by Bob Ottum, and *One Nose, Ten Toes* by Janet Chenery. *Address:* 380 Howard Ave., Woodmere, N.Y. 11598.

FOR MORE INFORMATION SEE: Who's Who in American Art, 16th edition, Bowker, 1984.

SHEA, George   1940-

BRIEF ENTRY: Born June 12, 1940, in New York, N.Y. A full-time writer since 1976, Shea has worked as an improvisational comedy actor as well as on the stage and radio. He is the author of more than twenty books for young people, including sports stories, mystery novels, and books about animals. In the sports category are three works of fiction of interest to baseball fans. *Strike Two* (Children's Press, 1981) reveals how an ex-convict is set up for a drug bust by a jealous teammate, while in *Big Bad Ernie* (Creative Education, 1978) a youth learns about team work, fair play, and the meaning of a healthy self-image. In *Make the Play-Offs! Blues vs. Sharks* (Wanderer Books, 1983), Shea calls upon his readers to make game decisions that will lead to a win. The same format is applied to football in *Make it to the Superbowl! Panthers vs. Grizzlies* (Wanderer Books, 1983). Shea's other books include *Alligators* (EMC Corp., 1977), *Nightmare Nina* (Creative Education, 1978), *Jody* (Scholastic Book Services, 1980), and *What to Do When You're Bored* (Simon & Schuster, 1982), written with Anique Taylor. He is also the author of television scripts, including the juvenile shows "Who Killed Susie Smith?" and "The Animal Snatchers." *Home:* 96 St. Mark's Place, New York, N.Y. 10009.

FOR MORE INFORMATION SEE: Contemporary Authors, Volume 108, Gale, 1983.

SINGER, Jane Sherrod   1917-1985
(Jane Sherrod)

OBITUARY NOTICE—See sketch in *SATA* Volume 4: Born May 26, 1917, in Wichita Falls, Tex.; died after a long illness, January 26, 1985, in Fullerton, Calif. Educator, publisher, columnist, editor, and author. Singer taught at the University of California, Berkeley, and San Francisco State College (now University) during the 1940s. With her husband, Kurt Singer, she founded B. P. Singer Features, serving as managing editor and president. Under her former name Jane Sherrod, she collaborated with her husband on several books for children, including *Spies for Democracy, Great Adventures of the Sea,* and *Albert Schweitzer, Medical Missionary.* Among her adult writings are *Cooking with the Stars, What You Should Know about Yourself,* and *Positive: Self Analysis.* Singer was also the author of the popular syndicated columns "Pathways to Success" and "Test Yourself."

FOR MORE INFORMATION SEE: Contemporary Authors, Volumes 25-28, revised, Gale, 1977; *Who's Who in the West,* 16th edition, Marquis, 1978. Obituaries: *Editor and Publisher,* March 30, 1985.

SLOANE, Eric   1910(?)-1985

OBITUARY NOTICE: Name originally Everard Jean Hinrichs; name changed about 1930; born February 27, 1910 (some sources say 1905), in New York, N.Y.; died of a heart attack, March 6, 1985, in New York, N.Y. Meteorologist, artist, and author. Noted for his expertise on Americana and for his collection of Early American tools, Sloane was probably best known for his paintings of old barns, covered bridges, and skyscapes. He worked as a sign painter in the 1920s and then worked at an airport painting serial numbers on planes. While working at the airport Sloane became interested in cloud formations and meteorology. He eventually studied the subject at the Massachusetts Institute of Technology and began lecturing on his observations. Among his numerous self-illustrated volumes are *American Barns and Covered Bridges, Our Vanishing Landscape, How You Can Forecast the Weather, Folklore of American Weather,* and the autobiography *I Remember America.* Of special interest to young readers are his *ABC of Early Americana* and *The Sound of Bells.* Sloane also wrote the syndicated column "It Makes You Think" and contributed to periodicals.

FOR MORE INFORMATION SEE: Illustrators of Children's Books: 1957-1966, Horn Book, 1968; *Current Biography Yearbook,* H. W. Wilson, 1973; *Contemporary Authors,* Volume 108, Gale, 1983. Obituaries: *Los Angeles Times,* March 9, 1985; *Newsday,* March 8, 1985; *New York Times,* March 8, 1985; *School Library Journal,* May, 1985.

STEVENSON, James   1929-

PERSONAL: Born July 11, 1929, in New York, N.Y.; son of Harvey and Winifred (Worcester) Stevenson; married; children: nine. *Education:* Yale University, B.A., 1951. *Residence:* 174 Falcon Rd., Guilford, Ct. 06437.

CAREER: Life, New York, N.Y., reporter, 1954-55; *New Yorker,* New York, N.Y., cartoonist and writer, 1955—. Creator of syndicated political comic strip, "Capitol Games." Writer and illustrator of books, beginning in 1962. *Military service:* U.S. Marines, 1951-53.

AWARDS, HONORS: "*Could Be Worse!*" was chosen as a *New York Times Book Review* outstanding children's book of the year, and as one of *School Library Journal's* best books for spring, both 1977; *Monty* was selected as one of *School*

JAMES STEVENSON

Library Journal's best books for spring, 1979; *The Worst Person in the World* was selected as a "Children's Choice" by the International Reading Association, 1979, as were, *That Terrible Halloween Night*, 1980, and *The Night after Christmas*, 1982; *Howard* was one of the *New York Times* best illustrated books of the year, 1980; *The Wish Card Ran Out!* was chosen one of *School Library Journal*'s "Best Books of 1981"; *What's Under My Bed* was chosen one of *School Library Journal*'s "Best Books of 1983"; Christopher Award, 1983, for *We Can't Sleep;* Garden State Children's Book Award from New Jersey Library Association, 1983, for *Clams Can't Sing.*

WRITINGS: *Do Yourself a Favor Kid* (novel), Macmillan, 1962; *The Summer Houses* (novel), Macmillan, 1963; *Sorry, Lady, This Beach Is Private!* (cartoons), Macmillan, 1963; *Sometimes, But Not Always* (novel), Little, Brown, 1967; *Something Marvelous Is About to Happen* (humor), Harper, 1971; *Let's Boogie!* (humor), Dodd, 1978; *Uptown Local, Downtown Express*, Viking, 1983.

For children; all fiction; all self-illustrated; all published by Greenwillow, except as indicated: *Walker, the Witch, and the Striped Flying Saucer*, Little, Brown, 1969; *The Bear Who Had No Place to Go*, Harper, 1972; *Here Comes Herb's Hurricane!*, Harper, 1973; *Cool Jack and the Beanstalk*, Penguin, 1976; *"Could Be Worse!"* (Junior Literary Guild selection), 1977; *Wilfred the Rat*, 1977; (with daughter, Edwina Stevenson) *"Help!" Yelled Maxwell*, 1978; *The Sea View Hotel* (ALA

Notable Book), 1978; *Winston, Newton, Elton, and Ed* (Junior Literary Guild selection), 1978; *The Worst Person in the World* (Junior Literary Guild selection), 1978; *Fast Friends: Two Stories* (ALA Notable Book; Junior Literary Guild selection), 1979; *Monty*, 1979; *Howard* (Junior Literary Guild selection), 1980; *That Terrible Halloween Night* (ALA Notable Book), 1980; *Clams Can't Sing* (Junior Literary Guild selection), 1980; *The Night after Christmas* (*Horn Book* honor list; Junior Literary Guild selection), 1981; *The Wish Card Ran Out!*, 1981; *The Whale Tale*, Random House, 1981; *Oliver, Clarence, and Violet*, 1982; *We Can't Sleep* (Junior Literary Guild selection), 1982; *What's Under My Bed?* (ALA Notable Book; *Horn Book* Honor List; Junior Literary Guild selection), 1983; *The Great Big Especially Beautiful Easter Egg*, 1983; *Barbara's Birthday*, 1983; *Grandpa's Great City Tour: An Alphabet Book*, 1983; *Worse Than Willy!* (Junior Literary Guild selection), 1984; *Yuck!*, 1984; *Emma*, 1985; *Are We Almost There?*, 1985.

Illustrator; all fiction for children, except as indicated: William K. Zinsser, *Weekend Guests: From "We're So Glad You Could Come" to "We're So Sorry You Have to Go," and Vice-Versa* (adult satire), Harper, 1963; James Walker Stevenson, *If I Owned a Candy Factory*, Little, Brown, 1968; Eric Stevenson, *Tony and the Toll Collector*, Little, Brown, 1969; Lavinia Russ, *Alec's Sand Castle*, Harper, 1972; Alan Arkin, *Tony's Hard Work Day*, Harper, 1972; Sara D. Gilbert, *What's a Father For? A Father's Guide to the Pleasures and Problems of Parenthood with Advice from the Experts*, Parents' Magazine Press, 1975; John Donovan, *Good Old James*, Harper,

(From *The Sea View Hotel* by James Stevenson. Illustrated by the author.)

1975; Janet Schulman, *Jack the Bum and the Halloween Handout*, Greenwillow, 1977; J. Schulman, *Jack the Bum and the Haunted House*, Greenwillow, 1977; J. Schulman, *Jack the Bum and the UFO*, Greenwillow, 1978; Charlotte Zolotow, *Say It!* (ALA Notable Book), Greenwillow, 1980; Jack Prelutsky, *The Baby Uggs Are Hatching* (poetry), Greenwillow, 1982; Louis Phillips, *How Do You Get a Horse Out of the Bathtub? Profound Answers to Preposterous Questions*, Viking, 1983; Wilson Gage (pseudonym of Mary Q. Steele), *Cully Cully and the Bear*, Greenwillow, 1983; C. Zolotow, *I Know a Lady*, Greenwillow, 1984; J. Prelutsky, *The New Kid on the Block* (poems), Greenwillow, 1984; Franz Brandenberg, *Otto Is Different*, Greenwillow, 1985. Also author of plays and television sketches. Contributor of articles to *New Yorker*.

ADAPTATIONS: "Fast Friends" (filmstrip with cassette), Educational Enrichment Materials, 1981; "Could Be Worse!" (filmstrip with cassette), Educational Enrichment Materials, 1982; "That Terrible Halloween Night" (filmstrip with cassette), Educational Enrichment Materials, 1982; "New Friends" (16mm film; based on *Howard*), Made-to-Order Library Products, n.d.; "What's Under My Bed" (filmstrip with cassette), Weston Woods, 1984; "We Can't Sleep" (filmstrip with cassette), Random House, 1984.

SIDELIGHTS: Stevenson was born in New York City, and raised in various small towns in New York state. He entered Yale University in 1947, graduating in 1951.

After graduation, he joined the Marine Corps' officer training program. Upon completion of his military duty, Stevenson was a reporter for two years with *Life* magazine before joining the staff of the *New Yorker*. Early in his career at the *New Yorker*, he worked in the art department, where he created cartoon ideas for other artists.

Even though his early career focused on his artistic talents, Stevenson continued to pursue an ambition to become a writer. In 1960, he began to report as well as to illustrate for the *New Yorker*. During his free time, Stevenson wrote fiction, and had three novels and a book of his cartoons published before writing his first children's book.

In the past two decades, Stevenson has written and illustrated numerous picture books, and has become one of the most popular, as well as most prolific, children's authors and illustrators. Besides his own books, he has illustrated books by such notable children's authors as Charlotte Zolotow, Jack Prelutsky, Franz Brandenberg, and a book by daughter, Edwina, entitled *"Help!" Yelled Maxwell*. Many of his books have won awards and have been selected as Junior Literary Guild selections, included on *School Library Journal*'s "Best of the Best" lists, and named as notable books by the American Library Association.

Stevenson began writing and drawing as a child. He has been influenced by movies and comic books rather than by any particular children's book. In several of his books he has used

Last night, when I was asleep, a large bird pulled me out of bed and took me for a long ride . . . . ▪
(From *"Could Be Worse!"* by James Stevenson. Illustrated by the author.)

a comic strip format. Three picture books, *Monty!*, *The Sea View Hotel*, and *Could Be Worse!*, use frames similar to those used in comic books. "I think that my experience and creative mind have been formed much more by movies and comic books. I like the idea of a story board and I like the idea of a movie and all the different angles from which things can be viewed."

Stevenson has nine children and makes his home in Guilford, Connecticut.

FOR MORE INFORMATION SEE: Time, August 4, 1967; "Drawing the Line," *Newsweek,* July 14, 1969; Lee Kingman and others, compilers, *Illustrators of Children's Books: 1967-1976,* Horn Book, 1978.

SUDBERY, Rodie   1943-

PERSONAL: Born April 22, 1943, in Chalmsford, Essex, England; daughter of William (a designer) and Barbara (a writer; maiden name, Jones) Tutton; married Anthony Sudbery (a lecturer in mathematics), July 4, 1964; children: Lucy, Clare. *Education:* Girton College, Cambridge, B.A., 1964. *Home:* 5 Heslington Croft, Fulford, York Y01 4NB, England.

CAREER: Writer of books for children.

WRITINGS—All published by Deutsch, except as noted: *The House in the Wood,* 1968, published as *A Sound of Crying,* McCall Publishing, 1970; *Cowls,* 1969; *Rich and Famous and Bad,* 1970; *The Pigsleg,* 1971; *Warts and All,* 1972, Trans-

RODIE SUDBERY

"So do I," said Lucy, posing in front of the mirror. There wasn't one in her room at home. ▪ (From *Lightning Cliff* by Rodie Sudbery. Illustrated by Sally Long.)

world Carousel, 1973; *A Curious Place,* 1973; *Inside the Walls Walls* (illustrated by Sally Long), 1973; *Ducks and Drakes,* 1975; *Lightning Cliff* (illustrated by S. Long), 1975; *The Silk and the Skin,* 1976; *Long Way Round* (illustrated by S. Long), 1977; *Somewhere Else,* 1978; *A Tunnel with Problems,* 1979; *The Village Secret,* 1980; *Night Music,* Gollancz, 1983; *Grandmother's Footsteps* (illustrated by Vanessa Julian-Ottie), Hamish Hamilton, 1984.

SIDELIGHTS: "I like to write about conflicts and often see my books in terms of power shifts from one character, or group of characters, to another (though readers need not and usually don't). This is particularly true of *Somewhere Else,* in which a boy and girl move in and out of an imaginary world; their relationship in the real world is echoed by that of their counterparts in the other. The girl begins by dominating the boy and ends up at his mercy, and the situation is resolved in the real world when he realizes his power over her and chooses not to use it."

In *Pigsleg,* Sudbery examines a problem involving four families. The children of these families begin daring members of their gang to perform various feats. One girl is dared to remain silent for a year's time, and her attempt to live up to the dare creates much irritation at home. The adults become aware of the gang's activities and finally subdue Cressida, the bossy leader of the gang.

Sudbery's book *A Tunnel with Problems* involves the children of two families in York engaged in typical childhood amusements. A tunnel near the children's homes becomes blocked, and they embark on a search for a buried treasure. The fun comes to a quick halt when one boy gets trapped in the tunnel.

Sudbery has published five books as part of her "Polly Devenish" series. The books follow Polly and the events in her life from age twelve in *The House in the Wood* to her first experiences at York University at age eighteen in *Ducks and Drakes.*

TANNENBAUM, D(onald) Leb   1948-

PERSONAL: Born April 8, 1948, in Orange, N.J.; son of Gustave (a contractor) and Estelle (a secretary; maiden name, Lax) Tannenbaum; married Cheryl Ramette (a quilter), May 15, 1977; children: Nathan, Jonas, Abram. *Education:* Ithaca College, B.A., 1970; Oregon State University, certificate of elementary education, 1974. *Home:* 604 N.E. 61st Ave., Portland, Ore. 97213. *Agents:* Bertha Klausner, 71 Park Ave., New York, N.Y. 10016; and Andrea Carlile, 14964 N.W. Mill Rd., Portland, Ore. 97231. *Office:* The Written Word/C.T. and Associates, 604 N.E. 61st Ave., Portland, Ore. 97213.

CAREER: Catlin Gabel School, Portland, Ore., team teacher of preschool children, 1978—, printer, 1980—; The Written Word/C.T. and Associates, Portland, Ore., owner, 1985—. Director, writer's workshop, 1979—; chairperson, Portland Holiday Project, 1985-86; volunteer, The Hunger Project, 1982—. *Member:* Children, Inc., Society of Children's Book Writers, The Holiday Project, Willamette Writers. *Awards, honors: Getting Ready for Baby* was included in *American Bookseller*'s "Pick of the Lists" selection, 1982.

WRITINGS—For children: *Baby Talk* (illustrated by Maxie Chambliss), Avon, 1981; *A Visit to the Doctor* (illustrated by Dora Leder), Simon & Schuster, 1981; *Getting Ready for Baby* (illustrated by Tony Rao), Simon & Schuster, 1982; *Duck Tales* (illustrated by Greg Andrews), Educational Computer Software, 1985.

Also author and editor of column "Upstarts," in *Young American,* a newspaper supplement for children, 1983—.

WORK IN PROGRESS: A Musician, a picture book about being what you love; *The Sad Blob,* a first self-illustrated book;

Measurements, a combination of rhymes and learning games in a software package.

SIDELIGHTS: "A near trip to Iran in 1977 sparked my writing career. I wrote three manuscripts while waiting in Portland, Oregon to take my hired post as director of a multilingual preschool. My family and I never left the States! One of these three manuscripts, *Baby Talk,* was purchased by Avon/Camelot on a trip I made to New York City the spring after the fall of the Shah's government.

"As a man teaching preschool children for approximately ten years now, it dawned on me one day that many of the books I read daily to children were within the range of writing that seemed no different than the writing I was currently toying with. More simply, I realized that authors were people like myself and that I was capable and qualified. I began to write consistently in late 1979 and sold *Baby Talk* to Avon/Camelot in March, 1980. I felt just like the children I spend so much time with—excited!

"I now consider writing vital to my existence. I love to write and grow from the experience of writing. Writing for children is confronting. It demands the truth. Confronting the truth is not always easy, yet it is rewarding. I lean towards transformation in writing lately. I find that books for children that really move me, move children, have transformational qualities. A great book may transform one's thinking, one's point of view, or, more simply, the moment in the room. I love reading out loud to children and adults as well.

"Paul Hagard's book, *Men, Children and Books* has had a great affect on me. He places children's literature in a historical perspective that is meaningful and enlightening. My summer workshop with Uri Shulevitz in upstate New York has also had a powerful affect on me and my writing. Uri's visual approach to writing is powerful. Uri himself is an excellent teacher as well as skilled craftsperson.

"I have always been fascinated by books. I have poems I wrote and saved from the fourth grade. Books and writing have always been with me. I wrote a strong poem when Pres-

D. LEB TANNENBAUM

Norris kept right on telling Nickel *his* name every day.

(From *Baby Talk* by D. Leb Tannenbaum. Illustrated by Maxie Chambliss.)

ident Kennedy was killed. Another poem followed my first experience of a funeral. I have written my way through experiences of love, hate, joy and sadness for as long as I can remember. In college I wrote for our newspaper. I also wrote music record reviews at Oregon State University. I've been storytelling with children for about ten years. Reading out loud always gives me a lift. At the Catlin Gabel School, a very well-regarded private school in the West, I picked up printing on an offset press. My fascination with the art of putting thoughts on paper led me into this field. The printing process is involved and requires skill. Learning printing techniques has helped me visualize the illustrative side of my writing. I think the printer's name and/or company should be included in the byline of a book's credit. Printers are skilled artists who are an integral part of the creation of a good book. My hat is off to all you skilled printers out there!

"We all have a children's book within us. I am convinced of this. The thrill of self-expression in this form is well worth the effort put out. From Harper & Row to the book made by a caring individual for one special person in his world, the completed project is equally exciting. As Aleksandr Solzhenitsyn said, 'One word of truth outweighs the whole world.' I love it!

"Beginning in 1985, I started a company of writers for hire, myself included!"

FOR MORE INFORMATION SEE: The Oregonian, December 4, 1982.

TERRY, Luther L(eonidas)   1911-1985

OBITUARY NOTICE—See sketch in *SATA* Volume 11: Born September 15, 1911, in Red Level, Ala.; died of heart failure, March 29, 1985, in Philadelphia, Pa. Physician, educator, administrator, and author. A cardiologist, Terry was instrumental in focusing public attention on cigarettes as a health hazard during his term as U.S. surgeon general in the early 1960s. His report to President Kennedy linked smoking to cancer and heart disease and led to the inclusion of a health warning on cigarette packs. Prior to his work as surgeon general Terry practiced medicine at hospitals and other medical institutions throughout the midwestern and southern United States. His many positions included chief of general medicine and experimental therapeutics at the National Heart Institute from 1950 to 1958 and assistant director of the Institute from 1958 to 1961. After his service as surgeon general ended in 1965 Terry became an administrator and professor of medicine at the University of Pennsylvania, where he remained until 1980. Among his notable achievements during this time was his successful campaign to outlaw cigarette advertisements from radio and television. Terry's writings include the young adult book *To Smoke or Not to Smoke,* written with Daniel Horn, and contributions to books such as Lewis Herker's *Crisis in Our Cities* and Seymour Tilson's *Toward Environments Fit for Men.*

FOR MORE INFORMATION SEE: Who's Who in the World, 6th edition, Marquis, 1982; *The International Who's Who,* 48th edition, Europa, 1984. Obituaries: *Los Angeles Times,* March 31, 1985; *New York Times,* March 31, 1985; *Washington Post,* March 31, 1985; *Chicago Tribune,* April 1, 1985.

KATIE THAMER

(From *The Red Shoes* by Hans Christian Andersen. Illustrated by Katie Thamer.)

THAMER, Katie 1955-

PERSONAL: Born March 27, 1955, in Los Angeles, Calif.; daughter of Don Chapman (a lawyer) and Hillary (Fitzpatrick) Thamer. *Education:* Attended University of California at Santa Barbara, 1973-75; University of California at Berkeley, B.A., 1977. *Religion:* Catholic.

CAREER: St. Francis de Sales, New York, N.Y., teacher, 1978-79; painter, 1979—. *Exhibitions:* Atlanta Gallery, Calif., 1977; Galeria Elena, Calif., 1980, 1981; Abraxas Gallery, Calif., 1982; Spiritual Art Show for the June, 1982, Nuclear Disarmament Rally; Chicago Art Expo, 1983, 1984, 1985; New York State University at Albany, 1984.

ILLUSTRATOR: Stephen McClaskey, *The Song of Songs: King James Version,* Green Tiger Press, 1979; Hans Christian Andersen, *The Red Shoes,* Green Tiger Press, 1981; H. C. Andersen, *The Little Mermaid,* Godine, 1984; Marianna Mayer, reteller, *The Black Horse,* Dial, 1984.

SIDLELIGHTS: "Ever since I was a little girl I have loved drawing—and loved illustrated books. The more I paint (I work in oils, watercolours, inks, and acrylics) the more I realize how important the life of the spirit is.

"The artists I have been influenced by are: Kay Nielsen, El Greco, H. Rousseau, Bottecelli, Arthur Rackham, Hugo Vandergoes, Piero della Francesca, Adrienne Segar and Aubrey Beardsley."

FOR MORE INFORMATION SEE: Art Voices, January-February, 1981; *The Collector Investor,* June, 1981; *New York Times Book Review,* November 14, 1982.

Sweet childish days, that were as long
As twenty days are now.

          —William Wordsworth

And he who gives a child a treat
Makes joy-bells ring in Heaven's stree,
And he who gives a child a home,
Builds palaces in Kingdom come.

          —John Masefield

THOMAS, Ianthe 1951-

BRIEF ENTRY: Born in 1951. Author of picture books for children and sculptor. Thomas studied sculpture at the Universidad de Coimbra in Portugal and has exhibited her wrought-iron and mild steel pieces in one-woman shows. In addition to her career as an artist, she has taught nursery school, worked in children's theater, and developed educational curriculum. As an author, Thomas emphasizes the value of caring for others through the depiction of positive and warm personal relationships. In *Hi, Mrs. Mallory!* (Harper, 1979), she creates a friendship between a young black girl named Li'l Bits and an elderly white woman, Mrs. Mallory. Although Li'l Bits is bereft when Mrs. Mallory suddenly dies, she is comforted by the presence of one of Mrs. Mallory's dogs who she keeps as a memory of her friend. *Interracial Books for Children Bulletin* observed, "This is a book about love—a love and caring and sharing which surmount traditional boundaries and extend beyond death. . . ." Thomas is also known for her poetic prose and rhythm. *Children's Book Review Service* noted the "imagery-filled and captivating" text of *My Street's a Morning Cool Street* (Harper, 1976), while *Booklist* found that "warmth and wonder emanate from the melodious verse" of *Walk Home Tired, Billy Jenkins* (Harper, 1974). Other works by Thomas include *Lordy, Aunt Hattie* (Harper, 1973), *Eliza's Daddy* (Harcourt, 1976), and *Willie Blows a Mean Horn* (Harper, 1981). *Residence:* New York, N.Y.

FOR MORE INFORMATION SEE: Children's Literature Review, Volume 8, Gale, 1985.

HANNELORE VALENCAK

VALENCAK, Hannelore 1929-

PERSONAL: Born January 23, 1929, in Donawitz, Austria; daughter of Josef (a foreman) and Auguste (a housewife; maiden name, Gruber) Valencak; married Oskar Kofler, January 3, 1954 (died, February, 1959); married Viktor Mayer (a philosopher), April 28, 1962; children: (first marriage) Robert. *Education:* Graz University, Ph.D., 1955. *Politics:* "Proper and able politics of any ideology." *Religion:* Roman Catholic. *Home:* Schwarzspanierstrasse 15/II/8, 1090 Vienna, Austria.

CAREER: Full-time author, beginning 1975. Has worked as a metal research and patent engineer. *Member:* P.E.N. *Awards, honors:* Staatlicher Förderungspreis für Roman, 1957; Peter Rosegger Literaturpreis des Landes Steiermark, 1966; Kinder- und Jugendbuchpreis der Stadt Wien, 1975, for *Ich bin Barbara,* and 1977, for *Regenzauber;* Österreichischer Staatspreis für Kinder- und Jugendliteratur, 1977, for *Regenzauber.*

WRITINGS—Translated works; novels for young adults: *Ich bin Barbara,* Ueberreuter (Vienna), 1974, translation by Patricia Crampton published as *When Half-Gods Go,* Morrow, 1976; *Regenzauber,* Ueberreuter, 1976, translation by P. Crampton published as *A Tangled Web,* Morrow, 1978. Also author of *Der Blaue Dragoman,* translation by Sandra Celt published as *The Blue Dragoman.* Author of numerous novels, poems, and juvenile books in German.

WORK IN PROGRESS: Stories, poems.

SIDELIGHTS: Valencak writes that "after an extraordinarily happy childhood" she has experienced "an extraordinarily unlucky life, partly due to severe sickness, partly due to circumstances of life." Although she is reluctant to go into great detail, she believes that her "happy childhood amidst good people and a beautiful landscape is the source of my writing." Fortunately, she adds, "In the last years everything has changed to the best again."

FOR MORE INFORMATION SEE: The International Authors and Writers Who's Who, 9th edition, Gale, 1982.

VOJTECH, Anna 1946-

PERSONAL: Surname is pronounced "Voitek"; born February 6, 1946, in Prague, Czechoslovakia; daughter of Leonard (a clerk) and Anna (Jenneova) Vojtech; married Roland Baumgaertel, March 27, 1970; children: Mathis, Lukas. *Education:* Attended University of Fine Arts, Prague, Czechoslovakia, 1965-70, Academy of Fine Arts, Antwerp, Belgium, 1968, and Academy of Fine Arts, Hamburg, West Germany, 1969. *Home:* 3 Bartlett St., Marblehead, Mass. 01945.

CAREER: Academia (publishing house), Prague, Czechoslovakia, assistant editor, 1964-65; Phillips and Deutsche Grammophon Gesellschaft, Hamburg, Germany, illustrator/designer, 1969-70; Verclas and Böltz (advertising agency), Hamburg, Germany, art department, 1969-70; National Film Board of Canada, Montreal, artist and animator, 1971-72; International Cinemedia, Montreal, Canada, artist, 1973-75. Created part of exhibition "Man and His Environment," Biosphere Pavilion, Montreal, 1973; creator of seven filmstrips for Museum of Natural History, Ottawa, Canada, 1973; set design and creator of props for film "Cocology," Aquilon Film, Montreal, Canada, 1977. *Exhibitions:* Montreal (Galerie Laurent Tremblay), Ottawa (Galerie de Vieu marche), Boston

ANNA VOJTECH

(Gallery Passion), 1975-76; Galerie Laurent Tremblay, Montreal, Cowansville, 1981; The Botanical Garden, Montreal, 1981; Centre d'Art, Montreal, 1982; The Boston Athenaeum, 1982; International Exhibition of Botanical Illustration, Pittsburgh, 1983. *Awards, honors:* Chris Bronze Plaque Award, Columbus International Film Festival, 1982, for filmstrip "My Food and Your Food = Our Food"; second prize in printmaking from Marblehead Arts Festival, 1983.

ILLUSTRATOR: Louise Darios, *Tous les oiseaux du monde* (title means "All the Birds of the World"), Beachemim (Montreal), 1974; Madeline Kronby, *A Secret in My Pocket,*

McClelland & Stewart, 1976; Jane Mobley, *The Star Husband,* Doubleday, 1979. Also illustrator of filmstrip "My Food and Your Food = Our Food." Contributor of illustrations to a series of readers by Houghton. Contributor of illustrations to *Magook, Nous, Audubon* and *Horticulture.*

WORK IN PROGRESS: "Series of large canvasses in oils which are partly figurative, partly abstract, using ideas from my floral paintings."

SIDELIGHTS: "I was born in Prague, where I grew up. My childhood with my two older brothers Vojta and Vaclav was

"Oh!" she cried and began weeping. "How lonely I am for my home." ■ (From *The Star Husband* by Jane Mobley. Illustrated by Anna Vojtech.)

rough but beautiful; climbing trees, playing cowboys and Indians, and all kinds of adventures, but I still managed to play secretly with my dolls and all the little girlish things that my brothers considered as stupid. I had my imaginary world of pixies and fairies. I painted and scratched my imaginings on paper, schoolbooks, sidewalks, walls, fences and all suitable and unsuitable surfaces. When I scratched a masterpiece with my hairpin on our fancy furniture, my talents weren't appreciated at all, to say the least.

"At home we always had a lot of fun, music, warmth and noise. My mother was a bottomless well of creative ideas, which she used in our everyday life. Once she made a cake that looked like a piano. It was one piano lesson I mastered and fully enjoyed.

"Now, having my own family, I really understand the wisdom of my mother's 'creativeness' and playfulness. She managed to have an office job, household, three children and still give us and many other people joy, smiles and love.

"Even though I take my profession as an artist very seriously, my aim is to keep the joy and playfulness of my mother's kind of creativity in my work and my life.

"My work in animation, film and experience with storyboards taught me to analyze stories in pictures. The combination of that and my love for detail brought me to book illustration as to the most important part of my profession. I work mostly in watercolor, but also etching, tempera, oil. I also do wood carving, puppets, marionettes, etc.

"I was strongly influenced by the Czech gothic painters, Trebonsky, Brueghel, Bosch, Piero della Francesca, Chagall, and Jiri Trnka, a Czech filmmaker and illustrator."

WARD, John (Stanton)   1917-

PERSONAL: Born October 10, 1917, in Hereford, England; son of Russell Stanton (an antique dealer) and Jessie Elizabeth (Watson) Ward; married Alison Christine Mary Williams, 1950; children: four sons, twin daughters. *Education:* Attended Hereford School of Art, 1932-36; Royal College of Art, 1936-39. *Home:* Bilting Court, Bilting, Ashford, Kent, England.

CAREER: Artist and book illustrator. Artist, *Vogue* magazine, 1948-52; free-lance artist and book illustrator, 1953—. Work exhibited at Agnews, Maas, Trafford, and Arthur Jeffress Galleries. *Military service:* British Army, Royal Engineers, 1939-46. *Member:* Royal Society of Painters in Water Colours, Royal Academy (associate, 1956), Royal Society of Portrait Painters, New English Art Club. *Awards, honors:* A.R.C.A. Royal College Traveling Scholarship, 1947; D. Litt., Kent University, 1980; Commander Order of the British Empire (C.B.E.), 1985.

ILLUSTRATOR—All juvenile, except as indicated: Cynon Beaton-Jones, *The Adventures of So Hi*, J. Barrie, 1951, Vanguard Press, 1956; C. Beaton-Jones, *So Hi and the White Horse of Fu*, J. Barrie, 1952, published as *So Hi and the White Horse,* Vanguard Press, 1967; Laurie Lee, *Cider with Rosie*, Hogarth Press, 1959; Richard Church, *The White Doe*, Heinemann, 1968, John Day, 1969; Mollie Harris, *A Kind of Magic* (adult nonfiction), Chatto & Windus, 1969; (with John Sergeant) M. Harris, *Another Kind of Magic* (adult nonfiction), Chatto & Windus, 1971; Herbert E. Bates, *The Blossoming World* (adult autobiography), M. Joseph, 1971; George

The trust that can exist between even wild animals and man is always a most touching thing. ■ (From *Brown Buck: A Californian Fantasy* by A. L. Rowse. Illustrated by John Ward.)

Ward, *Alphonse*, Chatto & Windus, 1972; Henri Bosco, *The Adventures of Pascalet*, translated from the French by Gerard Hopkins, Oxford University Press, 1976; Alfred Leslie Rowse, *Brown Buck: A Californian Fantasy*, M. Joseph, 1976; Joyce Grenfell, *George, Don't Do That: Six Nursery School Sketches* [*and*] "Writer of Children's Books," Macmillan, 1977; H. Bosco, *Culotte the Donkey*, translated from the French by Mary-Theresa McCarthy, Oxford University Press, 1978; J. Grenfell, "Stately as a Galleon," and Other Songs and Sketches, Macmillan, 1978; Jane Austen, *Pride and Prejudice*, Nottingham Court Press, in press.

HOBBIES AND OTHER INTERESTS: Antiques, architecture, illustrators of the 1960s in England, and the drawings of Pollaivolo, Ingres, and Picasso.

WARD, Lynd (Kendall)   1905-1985

OBITUARY NOTICE—See sketch in *SATA* Volume 36: Born June 26, 1905, in Chicago, Ill.; died of Alzheimer's disease, June 28, 1985, in Reston, Va. Graphic artist and illustrator of books for adults and children. Ward received recognition in the 1930s for his "woodcut novels" in which he used only pictures to examine the social and artistic issues of the Depression. Among the books are *God's Man: A Novel in Woodcuts* and *Prelude to a Million Years*. He later used drawings, mezzotints, and lithographs to embellish thirteen books for the Limited Editions Club, including *Moriae Encomium; or, In Praise of Folly* by Desiderius Erasmus and *The Cloister and the Hearth* by Charles Reade. In 1953 he won the Caldecott Medal for *The Biggest Bear* which he both wrote and illustrated. Ward also illustrated numerous other books, including many for children written by his wife, May McNeer. Books by the husband-and-wife team include: *Prince Bantam, The*

Gold Rush, Martin Luther, America's Abraham Lincoln, The Canadian Story, and *The Wolf of Lambs Lane.* Ward received numerous awards for his work, including a Silver medallion from the University of Southern Mississippi in 1973 for "distinguished service to children's literature."

FOR MORE INFORMATION SEE: Miriam Hoffman and Eva Samuels, *Authors and Illustrators of Children's Books: Writings on Their Lives and Works,* Bowker, 1972; *Contemporary Authors,* Volumes 17-20, revised, Gale, 1976; Doris de Montreville and Elizabeth D. Crawford, editors, *The Fourth Book of Junior Authors and Illustrators,* H. W. Wilson, 1978; John Cech, editor, *Dictionary of Literary Biography,* Volume 22, Gale, 1983. Obituaries: *Publishers Weekly,* July 19, 1985.

WARWICK, Alan R(oss)   1900-1973
(Alan Ross; Frank Sidney, Frank Sydney, joint pseudonyms)

PERSONAL: Born March 25, 1900, in Carshalton, Surrey, England; died December 29, 1973, in Croyden, London, England; son of Sidney (an author) and Sarah (Bennet) Warwick; married Joan Withy Bowers (a civil servant), June 21, 1946; children: John, Sally Warwick Hoult, Jasper. *Education:* Attended secondary school in London, England. *Politics:* Conservative. *Religion:* Church of England.

A huge arch slowly appeared against the clouds. ■
(From *With Whymper in the Alps* by Alan R. Warwick. Illustrated by Harry Toothill.)

CAREER: Civil engineer during the 1920s; member of editorial staff of Odhams Press, about 1935-65; writer through 1973. Also worked as staff writer for Amalgamated Press, as editor of *Sun Bathing Review,* and as a drama critic. *Military service:* British Army, about 1917-22, served with the London Scottish Regiment and with Royal Engineers; British Territorial Army, late 1920s to mid-1930s and about 1945-60, served as member of Artists Rifles and Special Air Service; became captain. *Member:* Norwood Society (founder, 1960; chairman, 1963; vice-president, 1971-73), Critics' Circle, Honorary Society of Masters, Worshipful Company of Upholders (freeman), City Livery Club (London), Savage Club, Constitutional Club, Dulwich and Sydenham Golf Club.

WRITINGS—Nonfiction for children, except as noted: (Editor and contributor) *Fifty-Two School Stories for Boys* (fiction), Hutchinson, 1935; *With Younghusband in Tibet* (illustrated by Harry Toothill), Muller, 1962; *With Whymper in the Alps* (illustrated by H. Toothill), Muller, 1964; *Let's Look at Castles* (illustrated by E. Cumberland Owen), Muller, 1965, Albert Whitman, 1967; *Let's Look at Prehistoric Animals* (illustrated by Norma Ost), Muller, 1966, Albert Whitman, 1967; *A Noise of Music* (adult nonfiction), Queen Ann Press, 1968; *The Phoenix Suburb: A South London Social History* (adult nonfiction), Blue Boar Press, 1972.

Under pseudonym Alan Ross and joint pseudonyms Frank Sidney and Frank Sydney (held jointly with father, Sidney Warwick, and brother, Francis Warwick), author of short stories and serials for boys' periodicals, including *Young Britain, Champion, Scoops,* and *Champion Annual.* Served as picture editor of *John Bull Magazine* during late 1940s; assistant editor of and film critic for *Picturegoer.*

SIDELIGHTS: In 1917, Warwick left school to join the British Army despite the fact that he was underage. A recruiting sergeant of the Artists Rifles Regiment refused Warwick's application but referred him to the London Scottish Regiment where he was able to sign on as a volunteer. His interest in soldiering remained with him throughout his life.

Warwick left the army in the early 1920s and for several years worked as a civil engineer. However, as the son and brother of authors he soon began to pursue a career in journalism, beginning as a drama critic. For many months he accompanied a traveling circus around the British Isles and Europe, gathering information and material for stories and articles.

Warwick worked for Amalgamated Press Ltd. and as a staff member of Fleet Street, publishing numerous boys' stories including those written in collaboration with his father, Sidney, and brother, Frank, under the joint pseudonyms Frank Sidney and Frank Sydney. He also wrote many stories about Markhurst School for *Scout.* Most of the stories included in *Fifty-Two School Stories for Boys* were written by Warwick himself.

As an editor at Odhams Press, Warwick was part of the team which turned the magazine *Woman* into a great success. Upon his retirement, he became interested in historical research which resulted in *A Noise of Music* and *The Phoenix Suburb.*

FOR MORE INFORMATION SEE: W.O.G. Lofts and D. F. Adley, *The Men Behind Boys' Fiction,* Howard Baker, 1970.

What will a child learn sooner than a song?
—Alexander Pope

WATSON, Aldren A(uld)   1917-

PERSONAL: Born May 10, 1917, in Brooklyn, N.Y.; son of Ernest W. (an artist) and Eva (an artist; maiden name, Auld) Watson; married Nancy Dingman (a writer), August 9, 1941 (divorced); children: Wendy Watson Harrah, Peter, Clyde Watson Devlin, Linda Watson Wright, Ann Watson Blagden, Nancy Watson Cameron, Caitlin, Thomas. *Education:* Attended Yale University, 1935, and Art Students' League (New York). *Studio address:* P.O. Box 482, Brattleboro, Vt. 05301.

CAREER: Author, illustrator (books and advertising) and artist (including commissioned murals); has also worked as cartographer. Books have been exhibited in the United States, Canada, and Europe. Textbook designer, D. C. Heath & Co., 1965-66; chief editor of curriculum-oriented material, Silver Burdett Co., 1966-68; official artist, National Aeronautics and Space Administration, 1968. Teacher of bookbinding courses. Field worker, American Friends Service Committee, during World War II. *Member:* Authors Guild, Authors League of America.

WRITINGS— Self-illustrated: *The Village Blacksmith*, Crowell, 1958, new edition, 1977; *My Garden Grows* (juvenile), Viking, 1962; (with father, Ernest William Watson) *The Watson Drawing Book*, Reinhold, 1962; *Hand Bookbinding: A Manual of Instruction*, Reinhold, 1963, 3rd edition, 1975; *The River: A Story Told in Pictures*, Holt, 1963; *Town Mouse, Country Mouse* (juvenile), Holt, 1966; *Very First Words for Writing and Spelling: A Picture Dictionary* (juvenile), Holt, 1966; *A Maple Tree Begins* (juvenile), Viking, 1970; *Country Furniture*, Crowell, 1974; *Where Everyday Things Come From*, Platt, 1974; *Hand Tools: Their Ways and Workings*, Norton, 1982; (with Theodora Poulos) *Furniture Making Plain and Simple*, Norton, 1984.

(From *Gulliver's Travels* by Jonathan Swift. Illustrated by Aldren A. Watson.)

Aldren A. Watson sketching in the woods.

Illustrator: Eileen O'Faoláin, *Little Black Hen: An Irish Fairy Story*, Random House, 1940; Meindert DeJong, *Wheels over the Bridge*, Harper, 1941; *Aesop's Fables*, Peter Pauper, 1941; Le Clair Alger, *The Golden Summer*, Harper, 1942; Elizabeth Goudge, *The Blue Hills*, Coward, 1942; Frances Frost, *Christmas in the Woods*, Harper, 1942, new edition, 1976; May Justus, *Dixie Decides*, Random House, 1942; Dahris Martin, *The Wonder Cat*, Crowell, 1942; Washington Irving, *Rip Van Winkle and the Legend of Sleepy Hollow*, Peter Pauper, 1943; *The Song of Songs Which Is Solomon's*, Peter Pauper, 1944.

Clement Clarke Moore, *A Visit from St. Nicholas*, Peter Pauper, 1945; *One Hundred and Fifty-Four Sonnets of William Shakespeare*, Crowell, 1945; A. E. Houseman, *Shropshire Lad*, Peter Pauper, 1945; *Fairy Tales of the Grimm Brothers*, Peter Pauper, 1945; Henry David Thoreau, *Walden; or, Life in the Woods*, Peter Pauper, 1946; E. O'Faoláin, *Miss Pennyfeather and the Pooka*, Random House, 1946; Robb White, *Three against the Sea*, Harper, 1946; Jonathan Swift, *Gulliver's Travels*, Grosset, 1947; Rudyard Kipling, *Jungle Books*, 2 volumes, Doubleday, 1948; Harold W. Felton, *Pecos Bill: Texas Cowpuncher* (ALA Notable Book), Knopf, 1949.

H. W. Felton, *John Henry and His Hammer*, Knopf, 1950; Giovanni Verga, *Cavalleria Rusticana and Other Narratives*, selected by J. I. Rodale, Rodale Press, 1950; F. B. Jacobs, *Neighbors*, Harper, 1950; H. W. Felton, *Cowboy Jamboree: Western Songs and Lore*, Knopf, 1951; F. Lape, *Barnyard*

(From *The Golden Summer* by Le Claire Alger. Illustrated by Aldren A. Watson.)

Year, Harper, 1951; Meridel LeSueur, *Chanticleer of Wilderness Road: A Story of Davy Crockett,* Knopf, 1951; A. White, *Prehistoric America,* Random House, 1951; Ruth H. Thomas, *Crip, Come Home,* Harper, 1952; Lewis Carroll, *Hunting of the Snark,* Peter Pauper, 1952; Stephen Crane, *The Red Badge of Courage,* Peter Pauper, 1953; Nancy Dingman Watson, *What Is One?* Knopf, 1954; N. D. Watson, *Whose Birthday Is It?* Knopf, 1954; Mabel Louise Robinson, *All the Year Round,* Harper, 1954; M. LeSueur, *River Road: A Story of Abraham Lincoln,* Knopf, 1954.

Kay Avery, *All for a Horse,* Crowell, 1955; H. W. Felton, *Fire-Fightin' Mose,* Knopf, 1955; Humphrey Francis Ellis, *Vexations of A. J. Wentworth,* Little, Brown, 1955; N. D. Watson, *Toby and Doll,* Bobbs-Merrill, 1955; N. D. Watson, *When Is Tomorrow?,* Knopf, 1955; N. D. Watson, *What Does A Begin With?,* Knopf, 1956; K. Avery, *All for a Friend,* Crowell, 1956; N. D. Watson, *The Fairy Tale Picture Book,* Garden City Books, 1957; K. Avery, *All for a Ghost,* Crowell, 1957; N. D. Watson, *Annie's Spending Spree,* Viking, 1957; John Parke, *Moon Ship,* Pantheon, 1958; Elizabeth Jane Coatsworth, *Down Tumbledown Mountain,* Row, Peterson, 1958; Jan Struther, *A Pocketful of Pebbles,* Harcourt, 1958; Ruth L. Holberg, *John Greenleaf Whittier: Fighting Quaker,* Crowell, 1958; Lois Baker Muehl, *My Name is. . . : A Game of Letters and Their Sounds,* Holiday House, 1959; N. D. Watson, adapter, *The Arabian Nights Picture Book,* Garden City Books, 1959.

Lloyd Arnold Brown, *Map Making,* Little, Brown, 1960; William Bixby, *The Impossible Journey of Sir Ernest Shackleton,* Little, Brown, 1960; *Russian Proverbs,* Peter Pauper, 1960; H. W. Felton, *Mike Fink: Best of the Keelboatmen,* Dodd, 1960; Margaret F. Bartlett, *The Clean Brook,* Crowell, 1961; N. D. Watson, *Cat Tales,* Doubleday, 1961; N. D. Watson, *Pig Tales from Old English Nursery Rhymes,* Doubleday, 1961; N. D. Watson, *Pony Tales from Old English Nursery Rhymes,* Doubleday, 1961; N. D. Watson, *Puppy Dog Tales,* Doubleday, 1961; M. F. Bartlett, *Where the Brook Begins,* Crowell, 1961; F. Emerson Andrews, *Numbers, Please,* Little, Brown, 1961; Charles P. Graves, *Mickey-Angelo,* Funk, 1962; Helen Harter, *Carmelo,* Follett, 1962; Alberta W. Constant, *Willie and the Wildcat Well,* Crowell, 1962; R. L. Holberg, *American Bard: The Story of Henry Wadsworth Longfellow,* Crowell, 1963; N. D. Watson, *Sugar on Snow,* Viking, 1964.

Eva K. Evans, *The Snow Book,* Little, Brown, 1965; N. D. Watson, *Katie's Chickens,* Knopf, 1965; Maria Puccinelli, *Catch a Fish,* Bobbs-Merrill, 1965; Regina Kelly, *The Picture Story and Biography of John Adams,* Follett, 1965; Walter R. Brooks, *Henry's Dog, Henry,* Knopf, 1965; Richard O'Connor, *Young Bat Masterson,* McGraw, 1967; Carolyn Horton, *Cleaning and Preserving Bindings,* American Library Association, 1967; Lilian Moore, *Just Right,* Parents Magazine Press, 1968; N. D. Watson, *Carol to a Child* (music by daughter, Clyde Watson), World Publishing, 1969; Bernice Kohn Hunt and G. David Weinick, *A First Look at Psychology,* Hawthorn, 1969; Herbert H. Wong, *Our Terrariums,* Addison-Wesley, 1969.

N. D. Watson, *New under the Stars,* Little, Brown, 1970; William Ivan Martin, *Tatty Mae and Catty Mae,* Holt, 1970; Carleton Coon, *The Hunting Peoples,* Little, Brown, 1971; N. D. Watson, *Tommy's Mommy's Fish,* Viking, 1971; Bernard Middleton, *Restoration of Leather Bindings,* American Library Association, 1972; Murray Hoyt, *30 Miles for Ice Cream,* Stephen Greene, 1974; Winthrop Dolan, *A Choice of Sundials,* Stephen Greene, 1974; Frank Rowesome, *The Bright and Glowing Place,* Stephen Greene, 1975; Howard Roger Garis, *Uncle Wiggily's Happy Days,* Platt, 1976; H. R. Garis, *Uncle*

Wiggily and the Sugar Cookie, Platt, 1977; H. R. Garis, *Uncle Wiggily and the Runaway Cheese,* Platt, 1977; Grant Heilman, *Wheat Country,* Stephen Greene, 1977; J. Rahn, *Weather for Gardeners,* Garden Way Publishing, 1979; *Back to Basics,* Reader's Digest Press, 1981.

Contributor of self-illustrated articles on tools, trades, crafts, and wood-burning to *Country Journal, Vermont Life, Horticulture,* and other periodicals.

WORK IN PROGRESS: A book on the construction of pre-1900 wooden sailing vessels; sequel book on furniture.

SIDELIGHTS: Watson was born on May 10, 1917, in Brooklyn, New York. "I grew up in a family of artists with time divided between the city and the country. In the latter, I helped with the chores, built fences, did carpentry, stone masonry, cabinet work. My father's skill embraced a variety of work over and above the fine arts. The toys he made for us stimulated in me a love of craftsmanship, not only in art, but in life. Educated in a Quaker school, I have been a field worker for the American Friends Service Committee. . . . Out of this background of education and experience come my illustrations: these are the roots." [Bertha E. Mahony and others, compilers, *Illustrators of Children's Books: 1744-1945,* Horn Book, 1947.[1]]

"What is nine?" said Linda. ■ (From *What Is One?* by Nancy Dingman Watson. Illustrated by Aldren A. Watson.)

It's the story of the Deep Cold. ▪ (From "Sunrise in His Pocket," in *Chanticleer of Wilderness Road: A Story of Davy Crockett* by Meridel LeSueur. Illustrated by Aldren A. Watson.)

(From *Uncle Wiggily's Happy Days* by Howard R. Garis. Illustrated by Aldren A. Watson.)

Having parents who were both artists gave Watson daily contact with art. It also made him impatient with the formal educational system. After spending four months at Yale University, he left to attend New York City's Art Students' League, where he could select his instructors and course of study.

As a young artist establishing his career, Watson had many different jobs. "I have earned a living at various trades other than illustration. For example, in Missouri, I picked cotton for some time, and, in partnership with one of my neighbors, contracted to clear a small tract of land. We sold stove wood, fence posts, etc., as by-products of the main task of getting the land ready for the plow. Later on, I worked as a carpenter and cabinetmaker.

"It was during a later period, while cutting timber, that I 'took on' [illustrated] the *Walden* [by Henry David Thoreau]. We got up before dawn, cooked breakfast, fed our hog and chickens, split the day's wood, thawed out the pump, and then set out for a ten-hour day on the saw. It was after supper at night that I hunched up in a small extra room and worked on *Walden* by the 'midnight oil.'

"From the experience with timber I found a great cache of material from which to draw subject matter; and the physical

work itself, in spite of the fatigue, somehow provided the intimate contact and sensing of the subject which I feel is so essential. I did not take on timber cutting for the sake of the *Walden,* although it did point out to me what I had previously believed, that first-hand, detailed knowledge of a subject develops facility with the brush.

"This reflects what I think is an absolute need to enrich one's life in all these various ramifications—not simply to develop one's professional work (though that is certainly very vital), but more than that to dip a bit deeper into life, and, having tasted and digested, to let its nourishment seep out through one's fingers onto paper." [Norman Kent, "Aldren A. Watson: Disciple of Walden," *American Artist,* March, 1946.[2]]

At the end of World War II Watson moved his wife, children's author Nancy Dingman Watson, and his young family to Putney, Vermont. "Living in rural Vermont, coping with snow, bitter cold, routine house maintenance, doing and making things for myself, growing a garden, raising animals for milk and meat, repairing buildings—these have influenced my interest in how-to-do-it with as little effort and time as possible. This led me to find out how people did things a generation or more ago, and why they did them."

Since those early days as a struggling artist, Watson has illustrated over two hundred books for children and adults. He describes his procedure in making brush-drawn illustrations: "I make my very first sketches in an unruled notebook bound in stiff covers, about 9x11. In that way I get the feel of a book. I rule the page dimensions on the notebook pages and work inside them: size and proportion of page influence the design of the illustrations. The first drawings are done in the same color the production man plans for the book, even though the finals have to be rendered in red or black to meet reproduction requirements.

"My drawings are done with #1 and #2 sable brushes—the brushes must point up nicely. The medium is tempera. Opaque color gives a solid line and has a better consistancy for line work. Even for the black I prefer tempera.

"When I have a sketch that seems good enough to develop, I lay tracing paper over it and make refinements—both in composition and drawing. Then I lay another sheet over this and continue to work up details and drawing. Frequently I spend a great deal of time redrawing in this manner—heads, hands, and drapery folds until they seem satisfactory. Sometimes a few drawings from drapery or hands that I pose in a mirror are made before the acceptable stage is reached. As for trees and other subject matter I draw on a file of sketches, made previously outdoors, of stone walls, stumps, trees, woodpiles, landscape, houses and animals. Many types of foliage and trees are pure fabrication, and these require only imagination. Details that are good are checked with pencil and saved for use in the final drawing.

"The finals are made on tracing paper, and immediately mounted on heavy board with rubber cement. Shrinkage does not occur in such a short time. All the heads, and details of illustration are now brought together and redrawn on a single sheet—the final drawing. Even at this stage it is possible to further improve the drawing.

(From *Annie's Spending Spree* by Nancy Dingman Watson. Illustrated by Aldren A. Watson.)

Dry brush is a versatile technique for outdoor sketching. The sketch of the old house . . . illustrates how an experienced artist can more quickly secure line and tonal effects than with either pencil or pen. ■ (From *The Watson Drawing Book* by Ernest W. Watson and Aldren A. Watson.)

''In two-color illustrations, after the first color drawing has been completed and mounted, a sheet of tracing paper is laid over it, and the second color drawn in perfect registry. This too is mounted on board. In this case, registry marks should be made on edges of drawings for the reference of the engraver.

''Drawings are made half again as large as they are to be reproduced. Too much reduction destroys the scale of the line work; and loses the charm of a brush-drawn line.

''Interest can be added to drawings by use of a pattern in clothing or patches of different material. Frequently, too, this

(From *Tommy's Mommy's Fish* by Nancy Dingman Watson. Illustrated by Aldren A. Watson.)

may help delineate form, as on the knee, where the material bends around the joint. In folds, or hanging drapery, a pattern running through the material points up feeling for form and dimension.'' [Aldren A. Watson, ''Aesop's Fables,'' *American Artist*, November, 1941.[3]]

Watson prepared himself in the traditional manner for a career as a professional artist, studying painting and drawing as well as etching, caricature, fashion illustration, and color block printing. But his interests soon broadened and his expertise came to include book illustration, hand bookbinding, type and lettering, and cartography. He designed a new type-face for one of his own books, taught and wrote about bookbinding methods and techniques, and made maps for magazine publication and textbooks.

As an author Watson has produced books for children, a book on bookbinding methods, and books on carpentry and blacksmithing. On his development as a writer, Watson commented: ''Illustrating and writing are separated by a very thin line. Considering my apparent preoccupation with how things get done, it is perhaps logical I got into writing by accident in the interest of further exploring how to convey to others in any and every way possible how it can be done. If you think about it, there isn't much difference between writing and illustrating, or drawing.''

Watson gave the following advice to would-be artists: ''One of the first things to understand is that every one of us is different; hence, there is no one *right way* to draw. If we consider art a language of expression, each person has something personal to say and each must express himself in an individual way. Actually, as psychologists point out, nothing looks the same to any two people. And certainly none of us feels exactly the same as anyone else about anything. That is one of the exciting facts about life and art.

''Some people think and work best in line; others in mass. Some prefer the flexible charms of pencils, others are temperamentally disposed to the vigor and directness of ink, either with the brush or pen. The brush—in wash technique—has its special appeal to other dispositions; and felt brush, a relative newcomer in the drawing field, will most congenially respond to a different personality. So do not expect to be equally proficient in all drawing techniques.

'' . . . Fear is the first enemy to be overcome. You must remember that you are the only person to be pleased with what you do; and if you judge your success principally by the fun you get out of drawing you should get a kick out of your earliest attempts, long before you consider yourself 'proficient.' The very feel of the pencil, the pen, or the crayon as it makes its first strokes on a clean sheet of paper ought to be an esthetic pleasure. And so it is!

''We have much to learn from children. They draw and paint without the fear that often grips the adult beginner, hesitant to put down his first stroke on paper. The expression 'there is nothing to fear but fear itself' made memorable by a former president of the United States, applies to the early efforts of any student. When a layman is urged to 'take up' picturemaking in any form he may exclaim, 'Why I can't even draw a straight line!' not realizing that drawing a straight line is seldom expected of him unless he is thinking of a very mechanical kind of delineation. The saying is merely a symptom of a general fear that he cannot draw anything at all.

''Thus the fear complex is the first stumbling block to be overcome. The conquering of that fear is the initial victory to be won. It can be achieved very quickly by the determination to spoil, intentionally, a great deal of paper. Start with the cheapest paper and the cheapest material. Just splash around with charcoal, ink, or crayon—any material at all. Don't even try to make a decent drawing, merely get acquainted with the feel of your medium and discover something of its nature. For example, with a stick of soft charcoal make rapid sketches of any object in the kitchen or a spray of flowers from the garden. Work on a large scale at first, using arm movement rather than finger movement. The results will be startling from the viewpoint of expression even though lacking accuracy in delineation of form. This is a 'limbering-up' exercise that will give confidence and help to abolish timidity.'' [Ernest W. Watson and Aldren A. Watson, *The Watson Drawing Book,* Reinhold, 1962.[4]]

Two of Watson's daughters are also involved in the field of children's books. Clyde is an author and Wendy, an author and illustrator.

Watson's works are included in the Kerlan Collection at the University of Minnesota.

FOR MORE INFORMATION SEE: American Artist, November, 1941, April, 1945, March, 1946, October, 1965; Ernest W. Watson, *Forty Illustrators and How They Work,* Watson-Guptill, 1946; Bertha E. Mahony and others, compilers, *Illustrators of Children's Books: 1744-1945,* Horn Book, 1947; B. M. Miller and others, compilers, *Illustrators of Children's Books: 1946-1956,* Horn Book, 1958; Ernest W. Watson and

(From *Walden; or, Life in the Woods* by Henry David Thoreau. Illustrated by Aldren A. Watson.)

Aldren A. Watson, *The Watson Drawing Book,* Reinhold, 1962; Lee Kingman and others, compilers, *Illustrators of Children's Books: 1957-1966,* Horn Book, 1968; L. Kingman and others, compilers, *Illustrators of Children's Books: 1967-1976,* Horn Book, 1978; *Contemporary Authors, New Revision Series,* Volume 4, Gale, 1981.

(From *The Jungle Books* by Rudyard Kipling. Illustrated by Aldren A. Watson.)

Youth comes but once in a lifetime.
—Henry Wadsworth Longfellow

Just at the age 'twixt boy and youth,
When thought is speech, and speech is truth.
—Sir Walter Scott

O dearest, dearest boy! my heart
For better lore would seldom yearn,
Could I but teach the hundredth part
Of what from thee I learn.
—William Wordsworth

JOHN L. WEAVER

WEAVER, John L. 1949-

PERSONAL: Born May 5, 1949, in Waco, Tex.; married wife, Terry (a wildlife biologist); children: Anna Mackenzie. *Education:* Utah State University, B.S., 1972, M.S., 1977. *Home address:* Box 8594, Missoula, Mont. 59807.

CAREER: Worked as a consulting wildlife biologist, 1975-78; U.S. Forest Service, Jackson Hole, Wyo., wildlife biologist, 1978-85; National Grizzly Bear Habitat Coordinator, 1985—.

WRITINGS—Nonfiction: *The Wolves of Yellowstone,* U.S. Government Printing Office, 1978; *Grizzly Bears* (juvenile), Dodd, 1982. Also contributor of articles to science journals.

SIDELIGHTS: "To an ecologist, part of the wonder and beauty of the world lies in the intricate relationships between living things and their environment. The poet Robinson Jeffers said it well: 'Integrity is wholeness, the greatest beauty is / Organic wholeness, the wholeness of living things, / The divine beauty of the universe. Love that / Not man apart. . . .'

"An ecologist tries to understand that organic wholeness—to 'see' that beauty. Children have a capacity for responding to

The grizzly bear is a big and potentially dangerous animal. ■ (From *Grizzly Bears* by John L. Weaver. Photograph by Jeff Foott.)

that outer magnificence. In writing for children I hope to point toward a world much larger than the human one—a world that is older and more complete—a world where other living things are not our underlings but our fellow travelers.''

WILLCOX, Isobel 1907-

PERSONAL: Born July 27, 1907, in Long Branch, N.J.; daughter of Oswin William (a science editor) and Margaret (a teacher; maiden name, Kostenbauder) Willcox. *Education:* New Jersey State Teachers College and Normal School (now Trenton State College), B.S., 1933; Columbia University, M.A., 1951. *Home:* 275 Engle St., Apt. J3, Englewood, N.J. 07631. *Agent:* Martha Millard, 357 West 19th St., New York, N.Y. 10011.

CAREER: Teacher at elementary schools in New Jersey, 1928-57; reading specialist in Tenafly, N.J., 1957-66; part-time instructor in sociology at Fairleigh Dickinson University, 1967-68. *Awards, honors:* Acrobats and Ping-Pong: Young China's Games, Sports, and Amusements was selected as one of the children's books of the year, 1982, by the Children's Book Committee of the Child Study Association.

WRITINGS: Reading Aloud with Elementary School Children, Prentice-Hall, 1963; *Acrobats and Ping-Pong: Young China's Games, Sports, and Amusements* (Junior Literary Guild selection), Dodd, 1981. Author of teachers' manuals. Also author of ''Know Your Neighbor,'' 1945-46, and ''Your Child's School,'' 1966-67, columns in the *Hackensack Record*. Contributor of feature articles to the *New York Times*, 1972-73.

WORK IN PROGRESS: A Ticket to People, ''directed to adults who want to make friends and acquaintances in the places

In a Peking park, strollers are pleased when they come upon a chorus of schoolchildren. ■ (From *Acrobats and Ping-Pong: Young China's Games, Sports, and Amusements* by Isobel Willcox. Photograph courtesy of U.S./China People's Friendship Association, Xinhua News Agency.)

ISOBEL WILLCOX

where they travel, it describes effective ways to do that and illustrates them with many examples from my own travel experiences.''

SIDELIGHTS: ''Reading is among my earliest and brightest memories. When I was growing up in Ridgewood, New Jersey, my parents always put good books for me under the Christmas tree. I began to read when I was about four years old, and I've been devouring books ever since. Our diet of books was enriched in the bedtime story hour, when our mother read us such favorites as *David Copperfield*, *Huckleberry Finn*, and Lambs' *Tales from Shakespeare*.

''In vivid flashback from those early days, I see myself stretched out on the living room floor, poring over our tattered atlas. I traced rivers and boundary lines and marveled at how the many pink-colored territories of the British Empire were spread all over the map. A small globe was a treasured gift.

''My father was a science writer. Writing seemed a good thing to do. After my college years, a local club put on the two one-act plays I wrote. A local weekly newspaper paid me ten cents a column inch (this was Depression time) for feeding it items on births, bridal showers, weddings, high school operetta performances, and year-end forecasts by the town's Chamber of Commerce officers. Eventually the *New York Times* paid me for feature articles in its Sunday edition.

''A goodly portion of my earnings began to go for train, steamship, and plane tickets. I sampled the United States from Maine to California, then tasted England and Germany. Soon I discovered Italy and taught myself to read and speak Italian. I've made eleven trips to that country, nine of them to Sicily.

Meanwhile I acquired an M.A. in sociology at Columbia University, the better to understand what I was seeing in my travels. There was time, too, for my first book *Reading Aloud with Elementary School Children*.

''It was thus not at all remarkable that, when I was planning my trip to China, something clicked inside my head. 'Travel—writing—book,' it went. I chose my subject: Chinese children's recreation—and decided to start work on a children's book as soon as I returned. That is the genesis of *Acrobats and Ping-Pong*.''

WILLIAMS, Leslie 1941-

PERSONAL: Born December 15, 1941, in Allentown, Pa.; daughter of Edgar Daniel (an engineer) and Merle (Williamson) Leibensperger; married William Henry Allen Williams (a futurist), June 27, 1964; children: William Henry Allen III, Lavinia Kate. *Education:* University of Pennsylvania, B.A., 1963; National University of Ireland, University College, Dublin, M.A. (with honors), 1971. *Religion:* Society of Friends (Quakers). *Residence:* Phoenix, Ariz. *Agent:* Bolt & Watson Ltd., Cedar House, High Street, Ripley, Surrey GU236AE, England. *Office:* School of Fine Arts, Indiana University, Bloomington, Ind. 47401.

CAREER: Advertising copywriter in Dublin, Ireland, 1968-72; lecturer at secondary school in Kassel, West Germany, 1973-74; Arizona State University Art Museum, Phoenix, Ariz., slide curator, 1976-78; advertising copywriter in Phoenix, 1978-79. *Member:* College Art Association of America, Arizona Women's Caucus for Art (president, 1978-79). *Awards, honors:* Grand prize for television from Cork Film Festival, 1969, for ''Curragh Carpets''; Samuel Kress Fellow, 1985-86.

LESLIE WILLIAMS

The boy took the bear's ankle gently in his hands and said, "This may hurt." ▪ (From *A Bear in the Air* by Leslie Williams. Illustrated by Carme Solé Vendrell.)

WRITINGS: "What Is Work?" (film), Southern Illinois University, 1965; *A Bear in the Air* (illustrated by Carme S. Vendrell), Blackie Group, 1978; *What's Behind That Tree?* (illustrated by C. S. Vendrell), Blackie Group, 1984.

WORK IN PROGRESS: A science fiction novel; a murder mystery; a feminist journal.

SIDELIGHTS: "Six years of living in Ireland, followed by a sudden move to Germany with my (then) five-month-old son, was strong motivation for doing some writing in splendid isolation. With the kindness of children's author Elis Dillon and with the persistence of my agent, I have been published in four countries: England, Belgium, the United States, and Japan. It was made possible by my having enough time at my disposal. Now that I'm working on my Ph.D. in art history while rearing two children, I can only work in snatches at writing. My dissertation topic will be 'Images of Childhood in Victorian Art.'"

WINN, Chris   1952-

PERSONAL: Born March 20, 1952, in Bristol, England; son of Harry (a sales representative) and Joyce (a homemaker; maiden name, Harding) Winn; married Sheridan (a writer and homemaker), July 7, 1979; children: Alexander, Rosalie. *Education:* Attended Brasenose College, Oxford, 1970-72; Bristol Polytechnic, B.A. (first class honors), 1976. *Residence:*

CHRIS WINN

Drayton, Norwich, England. *Agent:* Murray Pollinger, 4 Garrick St., London WC2, England.

CAREER: Free-lance illustrator, 1976—. *Member:* Society of Industrial Artists and Designers. *Awards, honors:* Mother Goose Award runner-up, 1983, for *Outlawed Inventions.*

WRITINGS—All juvenile, except as indicated: (With Jeremy Beadle) *Outlawed Inventions* (self-illustrated), Pepper Press, 1982, published in the United States as *Rodney Rootle's Grown-up Grappler and Other Treasures from the Museum of Outlawed Inventions,* Little, Brown, 1983; *Archie's Acrobats* (self-illustrated), Gollancz, 1983, Schocken, 1984; *Legal Daisy Spacing* (adult; self-illustrated), Random House, 1985.

"Baby Board Books"; published by Walker Books, 1985: *My Day, Holiday, Helping, Playing.*

Illustrator; juvenile: Ritchie Perry, *George H. Ghastly to the Rescue,* Hutchinson, 1983; Elizabeth Russell Taylor, *Turkey in the Middle,* Patrick Hardy, 1983.

Also contributor of illustrations to *Times* (London), *Times Educational Supplement, World Medicine, New Scientist, New Society, Observer,* and of cartoons to *Private Eye* magazine, and others.

WORK IN PROGRESS: (With wife, Sheridan) A second book of inventions for Pepper Press (London).

SIDELIGHTS: "I started drawing as a very young boy and read voraciously as a child. I won several competitions with my drawings as a child and this helped to spur me on.

"I work in a studio in the middle of a lovely garden, and seem to work twelve-hour days as a matter of course. I have dozens of ideas for new books, but there never seems to be enough time to fit them all in.

"I am very involved with my children, Alexander and Rosalie, and find they are a continuous source of inspiration and amusement."

HOBBIES AND OTHER INTERESTS: "I am very fond of walking, reading, cinema, architecture, and cycling."

WISNER, William L.   1914(?)-1983
(Bill Wisner)

PERSONAL: Born about 1914; died of a heart attack, August 3, 1983, in Brightwaters, Long Island, N.Y.; married Dorothy Elizabeth Smith; children: Judy Wisner Devereux. *Education:* Received a degree from Columbia College, 1935.

CAREER: Served as outdoor columnist for *Newsday* and *World Telegram and Sun,* as managing editor of *Sportsmen's Life,* and as editor of *Sportsfishing. Member:* Rod and Gun Editors Association of Metropolitan New York (past president).

WRITINGS—For children: (With Joseph J. Cook) *Your First Book of Salt Water Fishing* (illustrated by John Bunk), Essy Publishing, 1961; (with J. J. Cook) *Killer Whale!,* Dodd, 1963; (with J. J. Cook) *The Phantom World of the Octopus and Squid* (illustrated by Jan Cook), Dodd, 1965; (with J. J. Cook) *Warrior Whale,* Dodd, 1966; (with J. J. Cook) *Blue Whale: Vanishing Leviathan* (illustrated by Jan Cook), Dodd, 1973;

(with J. J. Cook) *Coastal Fishing for Beginners* (illustrated by Jan Cook), Dodd, 1977; *Strange Sea Stories and Legends,* New American Library, 1981.

For adults; all under name Bill Wisner: *How to Catch Salt Water Fish* (illustrated by Jon Gnagy and Glasier Crandall), Essy Publishing, 1955; (with Frank Mundus) *Sportfishing for Sharks,* Macmillan, 1971; *Field & Stream New Guide to Salt Water Fishing,* CBS Publications, 1973; *The Complete Guide to Salt and Freshwater Fishing Equipment,* Dutton, 1976; *Vanished without a Trace,* Berkley Publishing, 1977; *The Fishermen's Sourcebook,* Macmillan, 1983.

Contributor to *Motor Boating and Sailing.*

FOR MORE INFORMATION SEE: (Obituary) *New York Times,* August 6, 1983.

WOODS, Geraldine 1948-

BRIEF ENTRY: Born September 30, 1948, in New York, N.Y. Author of books for young readers. Woods received her B.A. from College of Mt. St. Vincent in 1970. Her teaching background includes the position of remedial reading teacher at St. Jean Baptiste High School in New York City. With her husband, Harold Woods, she has coauthored more than fifteen books for children in the intermediate grade levels. The topics of the Woods's books are diverse, ranging from the hazards of drug abuse to sea monsters to pet care. Among the husband-and-wife team's titles are: *Drug Use and Drug Abuse* (F. Watts, 1979), *Real Scary Sea Monsters* (Shelley Graphics, 1979), *Is James Bond Dead? Great Spy Stories* (Shelley Graphics, 1979), *The Kids' Book of Pet Care* (Waldeman Publishing, 1980), *The Book of the Unknown* (Random House, 1982), and *Pollution* (F. Watts, 1985). They have also written an adaptation of Edgar Rice Burroughs's classic novel *Tarzan of the Apes* (Random House, 1982). *Home:* 307 East 78th St., New York, N.Y. 10021.

FOR MORE INFORMATION SEE: Contemporary Authors, Volumes 97-100, Gale, 1981.

WOODS, Harold 1945-

BRIEF ENTRY: Born September 4, 1945, in New York, N.Y. Author of books for young readers. Woods graduated from Marist College in 1968 and received his M.A. from Manhattan College in 1978. From 1968 to 1970 he was employed as a high school teacher of English in Scotch Plains, N.J. For the next two years he worked as assistant editor of *Catholic Worker* followed by remedial reading teaching positions at high schools in New York City, beginning in 1972. A full-time writer since 1978, Woods has coauthored over fifteen books with his wife, Geraldine Woods. Included among their books are several which serve as overall introductions to various countries or regions of the world such as *Saudi Arabia* (F. Watts, 1978), *The Horn of Africa: Ethiopia, Sudan, Djibouti, and Somalia* (F. Watts, 1978), and *The South Central States* (F. Watts, 1984). They have also written two biographies on public figures viewed as exemplary role models for children: *Bill Cosby: Making America Laugh and Learn* (Dillon, 1983) and *Equal Justice: A Biography of Sandra Day O'Connor* (Dillon, 1985). The Woods are authors of curriculum guides for Prentice-Hall and contributors to magazines like *Babytalk* and *Learning Disabilities Guide. Home:* 307 East 78th St., New York, N.Y. 10021.

FOR MORE INFORMATION SEE: Contemporary Authors, Volumes 97-100, Gale, 1981.

YEATMAN, Linda 1938-

PERSONAL: Born March 24, 1938, in Calcutta, India; daughter of Richard and Nancy (Godwin) Villiers; married Robert Yeatman (a publisher), June 1, 1963; children: Catherine, Lucy, Rosanna. *Education:* St. Andrews University, M.A., 1959. *Politics:* Tory. *Religion:* Church of England. *Home:* 9 Clarendon Rd., Cambridge, England.

CAREER: Author and journalist.

WRITINGS—For children: *The Best Book of Indoor Games* (illustrated by Richard Fowler), Hodder Causton, 1975; *The Best Book of Outdoor Games* (illustrated by R. Fowler), Hodder Causton, 1976; *An Anglo-Saxon Hero* (textbook), W. & R. Chambers, 1976; *The Normans in Europe* (textbook), W. & R. Chambers, 1976; *Let's Have a Party!* (illustrated by Robert Duncan), John Adams Toys Ltd., 1980; (editor) *A Treasury of Bedtime Stories* (illustrated by Hilda Offen), Little Simon, 1981; (editor) *A Treasury of Animal Stories* (illustrated by H. Offen), Little Simon, 1982; *Noah's Ark* (illustrated by

Backwards went the wind, and back went the weathercock, and back went Sam Pig, and back went the pants and the umbrella and all. ■ (From "Sam Pig and the Wind," by Alison Uttley in *A Treasury of Animal Stories,* edited by Linda Yeatman. Illustrated by Hilda Offen.)

Bob Gault), Putnam, 1984; *Buttons, the Dog Who Was More Than a Friend*, Picadilly Press, 1985.

WORK IN PROGRESS: Currently researching ways to coordinate children's book publishing with television and film production.

SIDELIGHTS: "I have always been interested in the world of children, their books and entertainment. This interest has been emphasized by my own family. I believe that rich and varied heritage should be made constantly available to children, as well as the growth of new technology.

"I try to combine work with family life, running a sizeable house in Cambridge with many pets as well as a husband and children. It's tough at times, but never boring!"

YOUNGS, Betty   1934-1985

OBITUARY NOTICE: Born October 1, 1934, in North Staffordshire, England; died January 3, 1985. Pharmacist, author, illustrator, and artist. Youngs is probably best known for her children's picture books which feature appliquéd and embroidered illustrations. She first became interested in needlework as a child, but did not pursue it as a career until after working as a hospital chief pharmacist for many years. In 1969 Youngs began creating pictures out of fabric and thread; some of her artwork appeared as Gallery 5 greeting cards, others she sold privately. Her first book, *Farm Animals*, was published in 1976. She later produced *Humpty Dumpty and Other First Rhymes, One Panda: An Animal Counting Book*, and *Pink Pigs in Mud*, an introduction to color recognition. At the time of her death, Youngs was at work on another picture book, *Two*

by Two, which she adapted from the story of Noah and the ark.

FOR MORE INFORMATION SEE: Illustrators of Children's Books: 1967-1976, Horn Book, 1978. Obituaries: *Junior Bookshelf*, April, 1985.

ZAFFO, George J.   (?)-1984 (Scott Stewart)

PERSONAL: Born in Bridgeport, Conn.; died in 1984; married wife, Sieglinde. *Education:* Attended Pratt Institute; also apprenticed under Norman Rockwell.

CAREER: Author and illustrator of books for children. *Military service:* U.S. Army, World War II, Signal Corps. *Awards, honors: New York Herald Tribune* Spring Book Festival Award picture book honor, 1951, for *The Big Book of Real Building and Wrecking Machines*.

WRITINGS—All picture books for children; all self-illustrated: *The Big Book of Real Trains*, Grosset, 1949, revised edition, with text by Elizabeth Cameron, 1958; *The Big Book of Real Fire Engines*, Grosset, 1950, revised edition, with text by E. Cameron, 1958; *The Big Book of Real Trucks*, Grosset, 1950, revised edition, with text by E. Cameron, 1958; *The Big Book of Real Building and Wrecking Machines*, Grosset, 1951; *The Big Book of Real Locomotives*, Grosset, 1951; (under pseudonym Scott Stewart) *The Big Book of Real Streamliners*, Grosset, 1953; *Your Police: Things to Know about City Police and Their Equipment*, Garden City Books, 1956; *Building Your Super Highways: Things to Know about Road Building and*

The Fire Chief has a red car. ■ (From *Airplanes and Trucks and Trains, Fire Engines, Boats and Ships, and Building and Wrecking Machines* by George Zaffo. Illustrated by the author.)

the Equipment Used, Garden City Books, 1957; *Your Freight Trains: Things to Know about Freight Yard Operations*, Garden City Books, 1958; *The Giant Nursery Book of Things That Go: Fire Engines, Trains, Boats, Trucks, Airplanes*, Garden City Books, 1959; *The Giant Nursery Book of Travel Fun: On a Train, on an Airplane, to a Camp, on a Bus, on a Boat*, Doubleday, 1965; *The Giant Nursery Book of Things That Work*, Doubleday, 1967; *The Giant Nursery Book of How Things Change*, Doubleday, 1968; *Airplanes and Trucks and Trains, Fire Engines, Boats and Ships, and Building and Wrecking Machines*, Grosset, 1968 (contains *The Book of Airplanes, The Big Book of Real Trucks, The Big Book of Real Trains, The Big Book of Real Fire Engines, The Big Book of Real Building and Wrecking Machines*, and *The Big Book of Real Boats and Ships*); *Giant Book of Things in Space*, Doubleday, 1969.

Illustrator; all for children: Charles L. Black, *The Big Book of Real Airplanes*, Grosset, 1951, published as *The Book of Air-planes*, 1966; Benjamin Brewster (joint pseudonym of Mary Elting and Franklin Folsom), *The Big Book of Real Boats and Ships*, Grosset, 1951; Donald Barr, *The How and Why Wonder Book of Atomic Energy*, Merrill, 1961; Harold J. Highland, *The How and Why Wonder Book of Flight*, Grosset, 1961; Martin L. Keen, *The How and Why Wonder Book of Science Experiments*, Wonder Books, 1962; H. J. Highland, *The How and Why Wonder Book of Light and Color*, Grosset, 1963; M. L. Keen, *The How and Why Wonder Book of Magnets and Magnetism*, Wonder Books, 1963; Edwin P. Hoyt, *Heroes of the Skies*, Doubleday, 1963; Robert Scharff, *The How and Why Wonder Book of Railroads*, Wonder Books, 1964; M. L. Keen, *The How and Why Wonder Book of Electronics*, Wonder Books, 1969; M. L. Keen, *The How and Why Wonder Book of Sound*, Grosset, 1970.

HOBBIES AND OTHER INTERESTS: Hunting and model railroads.

CUMULATIVE INDEX TO ILLUSTRATIONS AND AUTHORS

Illustrations Index

(In the following index, the number of the volume in which an illustrator's work appears is given *before* the colon, and the page on which it appears is given *after* the colon. For example, a drawing by Adams, Adrienne appears in Volume 2 on page 6, another drawing by her appears in Volume 3 on page 80, another drawing in Volume 8 on page 1, and another drawing in Volume 15 on page 107.)

YABC

Index citations including this abbreviation refer to listings appearing in *Yesterday's Authors of Books for Children,* also published by the Gale Research Company, which covers authors who died prior to 1960.

Author Index

The following index gives the number of the volume in which an author's biographical sketch, Brief Entry, or Obituary appears.

This index includes references to all entries in the following series, which are also published by Gale Research Company.

YABC—*Yesterday's Authors of Books for Children: Facts and Pictures about Authors and Illustrators of Books for Young People from Early Times to 1960,* Volumes 1-2
CLR—*Children's Literature Review: Excerpts from Reviews, Criticism, and Commentary on Books for Children,* Volumes 1-8
SAAS—*Something about the Author Autobiography Series,* Volume 1

Mazza, Adriana 1928- *19*
McBain, Ed
   See Hunter, Evan
McCaffery, Janet 1936- *38*
McCaffrey, Anne 1926- *8*
McCain, Murray (David, Jr.)
   1926-1981 .... *7*
   Obituary *29*
McCall, Edith S. 1911- *6*
McCall, Virginia Nielsen
   1909- *13*
McCallum, Phyllis 1911- *10*
McCann, Gerald 1916- *41*
McCannon, Dindga Fatima
   1947- *41*
McCarthy, Agnes 1933- *4*
McCarty, Rega Kramer 1904- *10*
McCaslin, Nellie 1914- *12*
McCay, Winsor 1869-1834 ...... *41*
McClintock, Marshall
   1906-1967 .... *3*
McClintock, Mike
   See McClintock, Marshall
McClintock, Theodore
   1902-1971 .... *14*
McClinton, Leon 1933- *11*
McCloskey, (John) Robert
   1914- *39*
   Earlier sketch in SATA 2
   See also CLR 7
McClung, Robert M. 1916- *2*
McClure, Gillian Mary 1948- *31*
McConnell, James Douglas
   (Rutherford) 1915- *40*
McCord, Anne 1942- *41*
McCord, David (Thompson Watson)
   1897- *18*
McCord, Jean 1924- *34*
McCormick, Brooks
   See Adams, William Taylor
McCormick, Dell J.
   1892-1949 .... *19*
McCormick, (George) Donald (King)
   1911- *14*
McCormick, Edith (Joan)
   1934- *30*
McCourt, Edward (Alexander)
   1907-1972
   Obituary *28*
McCoy, Iola Fuller *3*
McCoy, J(oseph) J(erome)
   1917- *8*
McCoy, Lois (Rich) 1941- *38*
McCrady, Lady 1951- *16*
McCrea, James 1920- *3*
McCrea, Ruth 1921- *3*
McCullers, (Lula) Carson
   1917-1967 .... *27*
McCulloch, Derek (Ivor Breashur)
   1897-1967
   Obituary *29*
McCullough, Frances Monson
   1938- *8*
McCully, Emily Arnold 1939- *5*
McCurdy, Michael 1942- *13*
McDearmon, Kay *20*
McDermott, Beverly Brodsky
   1941- *11*
McDermott, Gerald 1941- *16*

McDole, Carol
   See Farley, Carol
McDonald, Gerald D.
   1905-1970 .... *3*
McDonald, Jamie
   See Heide, Florence Parry
McDonald, Jill (Masefield)
   1927-1982 .... *13*
   Obituary *29*
McDonald, Lucile Saunders
   1898- *10*
McDonnell, Christine 1949- *34*
McDonnell, Lois Eddy 1914- *10*
McEntee, Dorothy (Layng)
   1902- *37*
McEwen, Robert (Lindley) 1926-1980
   Obituary *23*
McFall, Christie 1918- *12*
McFarland, Kenton D(ean)
   1920- *11*
McFarlane, Leslie 1902-1977 ..... *31*
McGaw, Jessie Brewer 1913- *10*
McGee, Barbara 1943- *6*
McGiffin, (Lewis) Lee (Shaffer)
   1908- *1*
McGill, Marci
   See Ridlon, Marci
McGinley, Phyllis 1905-1978 ..... *2*
   Obituary *24*
McGough, Elizabeth (Hemmes)
   1934- *33*
McGovern, Ann *8*
McGowen, Thomas E. 1927- *2*
McGowen, Tom
   See McGowen, Thomas
McGrady, Mike 1933- *6*
McGrath, Thomas 1916- *41*
McGraw, Eloise Jarvis 1915- *1*
McGraw, William Corbin
   1916- *3*
McGregor, Craig 1933- *8*
McGregor, Iona 1929- *25*
McGuire, Edna 1899- *13*
McGurk, Slater
   See Roth, Arthur J(oseph)
McHargue, Georgess *4*
   See also CLR 2
McIlwraith, Maureen 1922- *2*
McKay, Robert W. 1921- *15*
McKeever, Marcia
   See Laird, Jean E(louise)
McKenzie, Dorothy Clayton
   1910-1981
   Obituary *28*
McKillip, Patricia A(nne)
   1948- *30*
McKinley, (Jennifer Carolyn) Robin
   Brief Entry *32*
McKown, Robin *6*
McLaurin, Anne 1953- *27*
McLean, Kathryn (Anderson)
   1909-1966 .... *9*
McLeish, Kenneth 1940- *35*
McLenighan, Valjean 1947-
   Brief Entry *40*
McLeod, Emilie Warren
   1926-1982 .... *23*
   Obituary *31*

McLeod, Kirsty
   See Hudson, (Margaret) Kirsty
McLeod, Margaret Vail
   See Holloway, Teresa (Bragunier)
McMeekin, Clark
   See McMeekin, Isabel McLennan
McMeekin, Isabel McLennan
   1895- *3*
McMillan, Bruce 1947- *22*
McMullen, Catherine
   See Cookson, Catherine (McMullen)
McMurtrey, Martin A(loysius)
   1921- *21*
McNair, Kate *3*
McNamara, Margaret C(raig)
   1915-1981
   Obituary *24*
McNaught, Harry *32*
McNaughton, Colin 1951- *39*
McNeely, Jeannette 1918- *25*
McNeer, May *1*
McNeill, Janet 1907- *1*
McNickle, (William) D'Arcy
   1904-1977
   Obituary *22*
McNulty, Faith 1918- *12*
McPhail, David M(ichael) 1940-
   Brief Entry *32*
McPharlin, Paul 1903-1948
   Brief Entry *31*
McPhee, Richard B(yron)
   1934- *41*
McPherson, James M. 1936- *16*
McQueen, Mildred Hark
   1908- *12*
McShean, Gordon 1936- *41*
McSwigan, Marie 1907-1962 ..... *24*
McVicker, Charles (Taggart)
   1930- *39*
McVicker, Chuck
   See McVicker, Charles (Taggart)
McWhirter, Norris (Dewar)
   1925- *37*
McWhirter, (Alan) Ross
   1925-1975 .... *37*
   Obituary *31*
Mead, Margaret 1901-1978
   Obituary *20*
Mead, Russell (M., Jr.) 1935- *10*
Mead, Stella (?)-1981
   Obituary *27*
Meade, Ellen (Roddick) 1936- *5*
Meade, Marion 1934- *23*
Meader, Stephen W(arren)
   1892- *1*
Meadow, Charles T(roub)
   1929- *23*
Meadowcroft, Enid LaMonte
   See Wright, Enid Meadowcroft
Meaker, M. J.
   See Meaker, Marijane
Meaker, Marijane 1927- *20*
Means, Florence Crannell
   1891-1980 .... *1*
   Obituary *25*
Medary, Marjorie 1890- *14*
Meddaugh, Susan 1944- *29*
Medearis, Mary 1915- *5*
Mee, Charles L., Jr. 1938- *8*